THE ENCYCLOPEDIA OF
GUILTY
PLEASURES

THE ENCYCLOPEDIA OF GUILTY PLEASURES

1,001 THINGS YOU HATE TO LOVE

BY SAM STALL, LOU HARRY, AND JULIA SPALDING

QUIRK BOOKS

PHILADELPHIA

Library of Congress Cataloging in
Publication Number: 2004102137

ISBN: 1-931686-54-8

Printed in Singapore

Typeset in Copperplate, Times

Designed by Michael Rogalski
Illustrations by Kevin Sprouls

Distributed in North America by
Chronicle Books
85 Second Street
San Francisco, CA 94105

10 9 8 7 6 5 4 3 2 1

Quirk Books
215 Church Street
Philadelphia, PA 19106
www.quirkbooks.com

DEDICATIONS

To the makers of Zocor,
the cholesterol-busting drug that allows me
to indulge in my favorite artery-clogging guilty pleasures
without keeling over—so far.
—Sam Stall

This one's dedicated to my brother George,
who still believes that E.L.O. rocks.
—Lou Harry

To Mom and Dad for their biggie-size hearts.
They never doubted me—at least not to my face.
—Julia Spalding

What do ABBA, The Franklin Mint, *Gilligan's Island*, Spam, Wayne Newton, White Castle hamburgers, and the song "You Light Up My Life" have in common? Surprisingly, not one but two things. The first, and most obvious, is the fact that discussing them in public inevitably triggers condescending smiles and derisive giggles.

The second is that, in spite of those smiles and giggles, all are (or were) wildly popular.

Of course, these diverse phenomena (and hundreds of others) aren't big with *everyone*. If they were, they wouldn't merit mention in a book called *The Encyclopedia of Guilty Pleasures*. What sorts of foods/people/cultural icons are worthy of mention in these pages? Put simply, anything that causes shame—things people relish in private, but in most cases wouldn't be caught dead eating, visiting, viewing, listening to, touching, or rubbing all over their bodies in public.

This broad definition netted a rich and varied haul—everything from guilt-laden all-stars such as Liberace (page 154) and *Valley of the Dolls* (page 267) to such yeah-come-to-think-about-it-they're-right items as Vienna sausage (page 295) and movies featuring Prince (page 216). In some instances, when the reason for an item's inclusion wasn't readily apparent, as with Tom Clancy (page 56) and Pop-Tarts (page 213), we carefully spelled out what qualified it as a guilty pleasure. In other cases, when the reason was obvious to anyone with the slightest shred of self-awareness (for instance, *Star Trek* on page 258 and pork rinds on page 213), we didn't bother. To paraphrase the Declaration of Independence, we find these guilty pleasures to be self-evident.

This book is extensively cross-referenced—a must, given the amazing amount of interconnectivity among the world's most famous guilty pleasures. For instance, ABC's *Wide World of Sports* popularized both

< 7 >

fishing shows (page 94) and demolition derbies (page 71). Toni Basil, the songstress behind the mind-numbing tune "Mickey" (page 174), worked with Elvis Presley (page 214) in the movie *Viva Las Vegas*, and had her song parodied by Weird Al Yankovic (page 311). Kathie Lee Gifford (page 106) used to sing on a game show (page 103) and also appeared on a spin-off of *Hee Haw* (page 122). And Jerry Lewis (page 154) was one of the fathers of the crank phone call (page 65).

Finally, a few words of clarification: Just because this book names something as a guilty pleasure doesn't necessarily mean we think that you should stop doing it (not that we would ever think you *were* doing it). After all, you're an adult (we assume) who's earned the right to act how you want, when you want. So if that means watching movies about women in prison (page 217) while sitting in your Barcalounger (page 21) drinking Mountain Dew (page 180) and eating jerky (page 137), that's fine by us. Or, more to the point, it's none of our business.

So go ahead and indulge. Just don't talk about it around the water cooler on Monday morning.

< 8 >

ABBA When a band called Björn & Benny, Agnetha & Anni-Frid soldiered out of Sweden in 1974, it looked like just another phonetically challenged novelty act. But thanks in large part to music clips created by fellow Swede Lasse Hallström (who would go on to direct *The Cider House Rules* and *Chocolat*), the popularity of the quartet (sensibly renamed ABBA) endured long after it stopped performing "Waterloo" and "Dancing Queen" in 1982. Credit this to its two-tiered fan base. On one level were the proudly fanatical ABBAnatics; on the other, those who joyously bobbed their heads to "Super Trouper" and "Knowing Me, Knowing You" but wouldn't own up to it in public.

A resurgence began with the 1994 film *Muriel's Wedding*, which appropriated many of the band's greatest hits for its soundtrack. It climaxed with the all-ABBA Broadway smash *Mamma Mia!* (which had all the insight of a *Love, American Style* episode). Nevertheless, it gave the group a longevity and a standing equaling, if not the Beatles, then at least the Bee Gees. See also DISCO (DANCING) and *LOVE, AMERICAN STYLE*.

ABBOTT AND COSTELLO Would anyone give a damn about Bud and Lou today if they hadn't asked the question "Who's on first?" and then repeated the convoluted answer ad infinitum? Not as compulsively silly as the Three Stooges, as transcendent as the Marx Brothers, or as easy to parody as Martin and Lewis, Abbott (the unfunny one) and Costello (the fat one) nevertheless managed to make a string  of semi-amusing films from 1940 (*One Night in the Tropics*) to 1956 (*Dance with Me, Henry*—now there's a money title). Their work, though far from genius, enjoyed a long afterlife as pre-cable Sunday afternoon television fodder. The boys were even horror movie stalwarts, thanks to such flicks as *Abbott and Costello Meet Frankenstein* and *Abbott and Costello Meet the Invisible Man*. See also LEWIS, JERRY and THREE STOOGES, THE.

ABC AFTERSCHOOL SPECIALS A more appropriate title for this series of kid-oriented one-hour diatribes might have been the *ABC Afterschool Lectures*. Shown sporadically from 1972 to 1997, they endeavored to improve the moral fiber of the nation's youth by regaling

< 9 >

them about the dangers of . . . well, pretty much everything. The very first was a cartoon called "Last of the Curlews," a cautionary tale about a bird species slowly dying out. But the most memorable specials were the live-action tales loaded with whack-you-over-the-head agendas and sporting nothing-left-to-the-imagination names such as "The Boy Who Drank Too Much"; "Just a Regular Kid: An AIDS Story"; and the Scott Baio classic, "Stoned" (in which Baio plays an over-the-top pothead straight out of *Reefer Madness*). Other than in live-action Disney movies, this is the best place to see big stars as insecure adolescents. Helen Hunt appeared in one (in which she jumped out of a school window while high on drugs), as did Ben Affleck, Rob Lowe, Rosanna Arquette, and Jodie Foster (who did three). See also DISNEY FILMS FEATURING DEAN JONES AND/OR KURT RUSSELL and TV MOVIES.

ABC's WIDE WORLD OF SPORTS (THE GUY ON THE SKI JUMP WIPING OUT DURING THE OPENING CREDITS OF) The man who symbolized the Agony of Defeat—and who compelled us to watch that agony week after week—is former Yugoslavian ski jumper Vinko Bogataj. He took his famous tumble during his third (and, for obvious reasons, final) jump at the International Ski Flying Championship in 1970. Sustaining only a minor concussion, he recovered and now lives in Slovenia with his wife and two daughters. He even does some coaching. Lesson One: Don't ski off the side of the damn ramp. See also DEMOLITION DERBY; FISHING SHOWS; KNIEVEL, EVEL; MORONS (ENTERTAINING, UNTIMELY DEATHS OF); and STUNTS (INSANE, TELEVISED).

ADVICE COLUMNISTS Think of a major personal problem that can be condensed into four newspaper column inches. Now imagine an answer to that problem that could fit in the same space. Absurd? Of course. And yet we have a track record of seeing Dear Abby, sis Ann Landers, and dozens of regional rip-offs as life-changers. Rarely have we paused to ask how serious we really are about fixing a problem if we're willing to send it to a columnist who may take months to reply—if she replies at all. But that argument misses a fundamental point. It's not about the letter writer, it's about the reader. We turn to these columns rather than to news and editorials because we're attracted to a world where problems can actually be solved, whether it's by Miss Manners or the Playboy Advisor. See also *PLAYBOY*.

AEROBICS PROGRAMS Hirsute men perform power lunges in tiny nylon

< 10 >

running shorts. Disturbingly fit octogenarians sweat to the oldies in full Olivia Newton-John attire. Orderly rows of spandex-clad hotties step and kick to a soft porn beat. Back in the '80s, when it was estimated that 20 percent of Americans participated in aerobics, this was the preferred way to stay toned. But these days, if the appalling statistics for U.S. obesity are accurate, most viewers of *Denise Austin: Fit and Lite* and *Aerobics Oz Style* have already lost the battle of the bulge. Instead of a fun way to get in shape, such tapes become nothing more than a mocking indictment of our own sloth—or a great place to watch hot, sweaty bodies when there's nothing good on Cinemax. See also CINEMAX and SIMMONS, RICHARD.

AIRBRUSH ART Like graffiti? Want to wear some on your shirt? Then head to your nearest airbrush artist. This technique, which reached its heyday in the '80s but is still available at tourist traps worldwide, produces roughly the same effect on cloth that spray paint does on bricks. And it looks almost as good. But whereas paint in cans is ejected via a blast of hydrocarbon propellants, the airbrush gets its umph from an air compressor. The artist wields a penlike instrument out of which issues a thin patina of pigment. Ironically, though airbrush work can be completed in no time flat,

the technique is fairly tough to master. Make one false move and that "Camaro Power" T-shirt is ruined forever.

AIRPLANE! See MOVIES THAT PARODY OTHER MOVIES.

ALBUM COVER ART The generation that was raised on CDs will never know that fabled time when some people considered album covers an art form. Rockers loved to debate the symbolism of Led Zeppelin's *Houses of the Holy* children-on-the-rocks imagery (inspired by Arthur C. Clarke's sci-fi novel *Childhood's End*); Pink Floyd's *Dark Side of the Moon* pyramid prism; and *The Velvet Underground & Nico* with its Andy Warhol banana. Of course, yesterday's designers admittedly had more space to play with. In a CD world, the *White Album* would have been merely the *White Drink Coaster*.

ALF Okay, so it was *Mork & Mindy* with a puppet. And even for an alien-stranded-on-Earth story, credibility was stretched pretty far. (If your home planet was blown up, would you be *that* quick with wisecracks?) Still, none of this kept audiences from giving *ALF* (which stood for Alien Life

< 11 >

Form) a four-season run between 1986 and 1990. The tons of *ALF* plush dolls, toothbrushes, bed linens, and other merchandise that was sold only reinforced the inexplicable fact that audiences loved this E.T. with an attitude. His appeal was so strong that, years after his show was canceled, the *ALF* puppet was hired to do TV spots for a long-distance phone service.

ALLEN, IRWIN Had he only given us *The Towering Inferno* and *The Poseidon Adventure*—two flicks where the primary pleasure was guessing who among the star-studded casts would die—film producer Irwin Allen would have earned a place of honor in this book. But the Academy Award winner (for a 1953 oceanic documentary, not for *The Swarm*) just couldn't stop giving. Seemingly determined to destroy every conceivable human edifice in every conceivable way, the "Master of Disaster" went on to helm such TV movies as *Flood!* and *Fire!* and *Cave-In!* In a (slightly) less destructive vein, Allen also was the man behind a trifecta of classic guilty pleasure TV shows: *Lost in Space, Land of the Giants,* and *Voyage to the Bottom of the Sea.* See also GIMMICKS, MOVIE; HESTON, CHARLTON; and RAMPAGING ANIMALS (MOVIES ABOUT).

AMBROSIA In Greek mythology, ambrosia was a magical food that preserved the immortality of Zeus, Apollo, and the rest of the Mount Olympus crew. In real life, it's an unlikely combo of marshmallows, coconut, chilled fruit, and, sometimes, gelatin. Emerging from the American South in the early 20th century, this dish earns bonus guilty pleasure points if served before your entrée as a fruit salad. See also JELL-O.

AMERICA (THE BAND) It's tough deciding which America is more absurd: the band that birthed such lyrics as "I've been through the desert on a horse with no name," "'Cause I understand/You've been runnin' from the man/That goes by the name of the Sandman," and "Muskrat Susie/Muskrat Sam/Do the jitterbug out in muskrat land"—or the America (as in "United States of") that made the group's 1975 greatest hits album a record collection staple. See also GREATEST HITS ALBUMS.

AMERICAN BANDSTAND It's hard to believe that this program was once so revolutionary (nay, *subversive*) that it was denounced by mainstream America. But that's just what happened when *Bob Horn's Bandstand* debuted in 1952 as a local Philadelphia show. It was taken over by radio deejay Dick Clark in 1956, when original host Horn was indicted on charges of statutory rape and drunk driving.

< 12 >

Taken national by ABC and Clark in '57, *American Bandstand* introduced armies of teenage fans to everyone from Jerry Lee Lewis to Fabian. Now kids could shake their moneymakers *right in their parents' living rooms*.

As the years went on, Clark got older (though it never seemed to show) and the show's format (a bunch of kids sitting in bleachers, watching artists lip-sync their latest tunes) got lamer and lamer. Especially the "Rate-a-Record" segment, where random goofballs were hauled out of the stands to pass judgment on new tunes. This is where the phrase "It's got a nice beat and you can dance to it" came from. And yet, a tremendous nostalgia factor surrounds old *AB* episodes—which is why NBC scored a semi-hit with the *Bandstand*-set show *American Dreams,* and why VH1 rebroadcast the '80s editions a few years back. It was kind of fun watching the likes of Prince and Madonna, at the dawn of their careers, actually seeming excited about the prospect of talking to Dick Clark. See also *DICK CLARK'S NEW YEAR'S ROCKIN' EVE* and *SOUL TRAIN*.

AMERICAN GLADIATORS Was this ultra-low-budget program truly a game show? Maybe, but instead of answering lame-brain questions from an emcee, contestants tried to overpower a pack of muscle-bound, spandex-clad "gladia-tors" with bad stripper names like Zap, Nitro, and Laser. Hapless participants, most of them half the size of their opponents, would do everything from run obstacle courses to play a particularly violent-looking game of half-field football called Powerball. The show ran from 1989 to 1997 and ushered in a whole new type of "game show"—the trial by ordeal, as perfected by the likes of *Fear Factor* and *Survivor*. See also GAME SHOWS and REALITY SHOWS.

AMERICAN PIE See GUYS LOSING THEIR VIRGINITY (MOVIES ABOUT).

AMERICA'S FUNNIEST HOME VIDEOS Vin Di Bona, creator of this insanely popular landmark series (actually, he adapted it from the Japanese program *Fun with Ken and Kato Chan*), understood something essential about the American character: We like to watch people fall down. But until his series came along, we had to rely on (A) bogus stunts à la Chevy Chase; (B) deliberately causing other people to fall down à la lunchroom bullies; or (C) serendipitously catching sight of someone falling on his or her ass.

Suddenly, thanks to Di Bona—and to that ubiquitous 1990s toy, the camcorder—we got to see brides and grooms falling literally head over heels; baseball bats that seemed magnetically attracted

< 13 >

to parental crotches; and pre-*Jackass* jackasses getting their comeuppance via backyard extreme sports. According to one scholar, "significant is the series' premise that the typical consumers of television may become its producers— that the modes of television reception and production are more dialogic than unidirectional." We couldn't have said it better. But while some people weren't afraid to admit that they watched the show, no one admitted to enjoying the narration of original host Bob Saget. See also *JACKASS* and KICKED IN THE NUTS (WATCHING SOMEONE GET).

ANDERSON, LONI See REYNOLDS, BURT and *WKRP IN CINCINNATI.*

ANDERSON, PAMELA In 2003 Anderson started voicing a grown-up cartoon called *Stripperella,* about an exotic dancer who fights crime, or something. The job was perfect, because the woman was already a caricature of sorts. Famous for her larger-than-life attributes (you know which ones), this native of Canada gained fame by starring on the international phenomenon *Baywatch* as C.J.—a lifeguard in a tiny red bathing suit who excelled at running up and down the beach in slow motion. If you tell someone you're a Pamela Anderson fan, please don't invite snickers by saying you think she's a great actress. Just

admit you watched the porno tape of her and then-husband Tommy Lee so many times your VCR finally ate it. See also *BAYWATCH;* MASTURBATION; MOVIES, PORNOGRAPHIC; and NAKED CELEBRITIES (PHOTOGRAPHS OF).

ANDERSON, RICHARD DEAN See *MACGYVER.*

ANDREWS, V. C. All you need to know about this author, who gained fame by penning a long-running series of incest-in-the-attic books (starting with 1979's *Flowers in the Attic*) is that she *died in 1986.* And yet, roughly twice a year, new volumes bearing her name appear. Does her editor have a Ouija board in the office?

ANDY GRIFFITH SHOW, THE Everyone wants to escape to a simpler life, but life on *The Andy Griffith Show* seemed downright elemental. The program, which ran from 1960 to 1968 (then transitioned to *Mayberry R.F.D.* through 1971), chronicled the adventures of Sheriff Andy Taylor (Andy Griffith) and the residents of the mythical North Carolina town of Mayberry. It was a very peculiar Southern hamlet, with no crime, no rednecks (unless you count the

< 14 >

Darling family), and scarcely any black people. Sad to say, back in the '60s this probably sounded like a little slice of heaven to much of Middle America. The show was a hit from its first episode and camped in the No. 1 slot until it left the airwaves. Rabid fans have kept the show in reruns ever since. Some guilty pleasure postscripts: Don Knotts, who played Deputy Barney Fife, became the replacement landlord on *Three's Company,* and George Lindsey (Goober) recorded an album, *Goober Sings,* and became a regular on *Hee Haw.* He still shows up at personal appearances in his Jughead-style hat. See also *HEE HAW* and *THREE'S COMPANY.*

ANGELS (AS PLOT DEVICES) See *HIGHWAY TO HEAVEN*; *IT'S A WONDERFUL LIFE*; and *TOUCHED BY AN ANGEL.*

ANGELS (DECORATIVE USE OF) Okay, so maybe angels aren't on the aesthetic radar at *Metropolitan Home* or *Architectural Digest.* One thing's for sure: If Botticelli were painting naked little babies with wings during the 21st century instead of the 15th, he wouldn't have died in obscurity. From the purveyors of estate-style statuary to the guy selling gilded-frame prints out of his hatchback on the side of the road, today's cherub merchants offer a celestial spirit to fill every corner of the home and garden.

Consider the 3-D angel crystal, the angel shower curtain, or (*finally,* the perfect addition to your collection of souvenir spoons and decorative thimbles) the angel ashtray.

ANIMAL HOUSE Raise a 21-beer salute to the movie that made it cool to screw up in college. Filmed in 1977 with a budget of $2.7 million and a cast composed mostly of nobodies (director John Landis, who got his job after nearly every director under the sun turned it down, wanted Chevy Chase to play Otter, Dan Aykroyd to play D-Day, and *Jack Webb* to play Dean Wormer), *Animal House* became the second-biggest movie of 1978 (after *Grease*). It holds the distinction of being the best movie starring a *Saturday Night Live* alumnus (John Belushi) ever made; forms an indispensable link in the Six Degrees of Kevin Bacon game (yes, he was in there, as were Donald Sutherland and Tim Matheson); and inspired a short-lived TV series called *Delta House,* which introduced a very young Michelle Pfeiffer to the world. See also MOVIES TURNED INTO TV SHOWS and *NATIONAL LAMPOON.*

ANTIQUES ROADSHOW A PBS staple for roughly a decade, *Antiques Roadshow* (based on a British series by the same name) draws viewers by playing on

< 15 >

wishful thinking. To wit: What if that old doll/old book/old plate collecting dust in the attic is really a fancy antique that's worth a fortune? *Roadshow* answers such questions by hauling a troupe of appraisers out to the sticks (say, Indianapolis or Cleveland), waiting for the locals (around 5,000 on each visit) to bring in their garage sale leftovers, and then telling them if they've got something. The most entertaining part is watching people's expressions when they find out that, say, Uncle Festus's ear-wax crock is worth six figures. (That's not an exaggeration—among their all-time most valuable discoveries was an old Navajo blanket worth $350,000 to $500,000.)

AQUA NET What do you get when you take 14 ounces of dimethyl ether, SD alcohol 40-B, and aminomethylpropanol, doll it up with a throat-coating fragrance, then pour it into a purple aerosol can spiked with enough propellants to inflate one hundred party balloons? That would be the fixative of choice for little old ladies, New Jersey coquettes, and anyone else seeking a hairstyle so high and rigid that it poses a hazard to air traffic. Sure, people make fun of the goofy can and the product's "distinctive" bouquet. But if you want to do something to your tresses that your tresses don't espe-cially want to do, a blast of Aqua Net will settle the issue faster than you can say "ozone hole."

ARCHIE COMICS This comic line has survived, nay, thrived, for more than 60 years, even though getting caught with a copy is a gold-embossed invitation to (at best) a savage razzing. The extremely nerdy, white-bread adventures of teen-aged Archie, Betty, Veronica, Jughead, and the rest of the denizens of Riverdale began in 1941, when MLJ Magazines (soon to be renamed Archie Comics) developed a teen book to capitalize on the then-popular Andy Hardy movies. The result was a cultural phenomenon that spawned a radio show, numerous Saturday morning cartoons, and even a No. 1 pop single (1969's "Sugar, Sugar," performed by a studio band and released under the name The Archies). More recently, side character Sabrina (the Teenage Witch) got a long-running TV series, while Josie and the Pussycats landed a big-screen flick—impressive achievements for a group of kids who haven't managed to graduate from high school in 60 years.

ARMY-NAVY SURPLUS STORES These little shops of wonders caught on big after World War II, when there was, to put it mildly, a lot of surplus Army and Navy stuff lying around. Loaded with

< 16 >

everything from mess kits to fatigues to gas masks, they were the perfect places to gear up for camping, fishing, or hunting expeditions. They were big in the '70s with stoners, who loved to wear Army-issue jackets with lots of hidden pockets for storing . . . well, you know. And in the '90s, militia guys purchased everything they needed to look the very model of modern major fruitcakes. But throughout the decades, fashionistas of every political stripe prowled the olive-green sales racks, seeking to get that smart-looking military look without having to march around in the hot sun, and maybe even take a bullet, to earn it. See also MARIJUANA and RED DAWN.

AS SEEN ON TV PRODUCTS People who purchase Flowbee haircutting systems, Ginsu Knives, Nads, or anything sold by Ron Popeil seldom brag about it. Yet a secret segment of society must love such products. Otherwise infomercials (just like some of the products they hawk) wouldn't work. Existing as long as television, but fueled by the Reagan administration's deregulation of the broadcast industry (which paved the way for program-length pitches), infomercials are now as ubiquitous a part of the television landscape as Saturday morning cartoons and Tony Danza sitcoms. So we keep watching, we keep buying, and we keep putting these products on high shelves in the garage when we realize we have no use for them. See also K-TEL RECORDS and RONCO PRODUCTS.

A-TEAM, THE See MR. T.

ATLANTIC CITY Admitting that Atlantic City is a favorite resort destination is akin to admitting that *Jaws 2* is your favorite shark flick. Shouldn't A.C., with its beach, have it over Las Vegas, with its trackless desert? In theory, yes. But the Vegas strip issued its first gambling license in 1931. Atlantic City didn't start rolling the dice until 1978. Even worse, it plunked casino gambling on top of a dying resort town. Vegas started with a clean (albeit hot and dusty) slate.

While an occasional big-name entertainer still comes to town, the Atlantic City nightlife is nothing like it was when Dean and Jerry were working out their act at the 500 Club. As Atlantic City strove to be the gambling Mecca for East Coasters, it also found state and city governments around the country embracing gaming as a revenue generator. Nowadays, half the states in our country offer some form of casino betting. But that hasn't kept Atlantic City gamblers from ignoring the sunshine outside (and the annual Miss America hubbub) and staying true to their slot machines. See also CASINOS; LAS VEGAS; LEWIS, JERRY; and SLOT MACHINES.

< 17 >

AUSTRALIAN RULES FOOTBALL What sports nut, checking ESPN at 2 A.M., hasn't at one time or another happened upon this horrific—and horrifically entertaining—sport? Developed in the 1850s as Down Under's answer to rugby (which, apparently, just wasn't studly enough for the Aussies), Australian rules football (also known by the hugely inappropriate nickname "footy") is chock full of all the quirky touches we'd expect from the land of *Mad Max*. The field is oval instead of rectangular; each team puts a staggering 18 players in action at once; and participants are allowed to catch the ball *by standing on teammates' shoulders.* Of course, all of this is done while wearing shorts, a rugby shirt, and no protection more elaborate than a cup. Footy is Australia's No. 1 spectator sport—and American armchair quarterbacks' No. 1 late-night indulgence. See also STUNTS (INSANE, TELEVISED).

AUTOGRAPHS Big-time celebrity signatures can be worth plenty. Recently a President Nixon–autographed yo-yo sold for more than $16,000, and one of Lou Gehrig's canceled checks brought in over $10,000. But while the John Hancock of, say, John Hancock is worth having, those of most second-string luminaries will never be worth more than the paper they're scrawled on. So what accounts for the hundreds of other-wise-normal people who line up for signed photos of, say, the guy who wears the R2-D2 costume? Pure delusion. Snagging a celeb's signature may seem, for a moment, to bring you closer to the white-hot center of cool, but it really sends you to a very different place—a place named Grovelville. Here's a reality check: Willie Mays doesn't remember signing your baseball. David Lee Roth doesn't recall scribbling his name on your concert T-shirt. And that porn star has absolutely no memory of signing your, well, you get the idea.

AUTOPSIES (TELEVISION) We've come a long way since *Quincy, M.E.*, a TV coroner who never waved a bloody scalpel—let alone a bloody appendage or severed limb. These days gory morgue scenes have become television set pieces, with every police procedural worth its salt showing streetwise detectives loitering near the Big Metal Table while the coroner (usually in midslice) nonchalantly says, "See these cuts on the forearms? They're what's called 'defense wounds.' She didn't die easy."

The path to today's graphic autopsies was pioneered by *The X-Files*. Toward the end of that program's run, no episode seemed complete without Scully cracking open the chest of at least one desiccated/mutilated/flame-broiled corpse. Later, the bone saw was passed to the

< 18 >

CBS series *CSI*, where on-camera dissection was raised to an art form. You wanted to look away but . . . okay, maybe you didn't want to look away. After all, *CSI* was the highest-rated show in the country. See also *QUINCY, M.E.*

AVON What woman circa 1975 didn't have Avon's Dutch Maid decanter displayed on a nice lace doily somewhere in her house? What man didn't splash on aftershave from a bottle shaped like a stagecoach? What little girl wouldn't have *sold her soul* for that miniature pink ice cream cone with a waxy shaft of strawberry lip gloss hidden under its plastic soft-serve cap? Sadly, that golden era of naive toiletries is gone. Like the elderly woman who Clairols her hair in a painfully obvious effort to look younger, the cosmetics company that hit its stride during the June Cleaver era has updated its roster of beauty aids to include newfangled potions such as Cellu-Sculpt anti-cellulite cream and the Shake It Up bronzing brush.

Still, Avon (founded in 1886 as the California Perfume Company, but renamed in 1939 after Shakespeare's hometown) reminds us of a gentler era of consumerism, when an immaculately coifed Avon Lady showed up on your doorstep every two weeks with her case of pinkie-sized lipstick samples and then floated into your living room on a cloud

of Sweet Honesty. See also DRUGSTORE PERFUMES.

AWARD SHOWS See GOLDEN GLOBES; MTV VIDEO MUSIC AWARDS, THE; and PEOPLE'S CHOICE AWARDS, THE.

B

THE BABY-SITTERS CLUB Wouldn't it be cool to run a business with all your best friends? One where you could share all the responsibilities and help each other with personal problems? *Of course it wouldn't!* Yet millions of preteen girls buy into this severely flawed business model courtesy of author Ann M. Martin's world of The Baby-Sitters Club, a seemingly endless series of novels about a group of girls who run a baby-sitting business and, of course, care, share, and grow as people. Preteen females eat this up, but once puberty sets in, their copies of book 75 (*Jessi's Horrible Prank*) and book 116 (*Abby and the Best Kid Ever*) get shoved to the backs of their lockers. Soon it's time to ditch this club altogether and move on to Judy Blume. See also BLUME, JUDY.

BAC~OS The idea of putting a pork product into a sprinkle can sounds like the ultimate guilty pleasure. Alas, it isn't. There's no *bacon* in Bac~Os. This General Mills staple is made of flavored soy. Vegetarians love it. It's even kosher. Somehow, we feel betrayed. See also PORK RINDS.

BAD RONALD This 1974 made-for-TV horror flick tells the story of Ronald Wood (Scott Jacoby), a sheltered mama's boy who accidentally kills a taunting classmate. To conceal him from the cops, his mom walls off an entire room of their house to use as his hideout. But mom dies suddenly, the house changes hands, and a new family moves in, even though Ronald never moved out. What follows is a small masterpiece of paranoia, as the ever-more-deranged teen spies on the new owners—especially their three teenage daughters. Incredibly, almost everyone who watched this film wound up sympathizing with poor, confused Ronald. It made such an impression that a popular, MTV-quality band recently took Bad Ronald as its moniker. See also TV MOVIES.

BAER, MAX See *BEVERLY HILLBILLIES, THE* and *MACON COUNTY LINE*.

BAIO, SCOTT See *ABC AFTERSCHOOL SPECIALS* and *HAPPY DAYS*.

BAKKER, JIM See TELEVANGELISTS.

BAKSHI, RALPH Let us begin by saying that the work of animator Ralph Bakshi is first-rate and, in many cases, ground-breaking. The man who began his career working on such mediocrities as *Deputy Dawg* went on to create visual extrava-

< 20 >

ganzas such as *Fritz the Cat* (the first X-rated animation feature), *Wizards*, and *The Lord of the Rings* (the 132-minute 1978 adaptation, not the 9-hour trilogy of recent years). Watching Bakshi's work is always fun, but watching it while *stoned* is a double-barreled blast. Which explains why midnight showings near college campuses always sold out—and why the concession stand inevitably ran out of popcorn. See also *LORD OF THE RINGS, THE* and MARIJUANA.

BANANA SPLITS, THE Almost no one knew what the hell Bingo, Fleegle, Drooper, and Snorky, the Muppet-like stars of the 1968–1970 Saturday morning series *The Banana Splits Adventure Hour*, were supposed to be. But whatever they were, they must have been a guilty pleasure of some sort. What was the plot of this program? There wasn't any stinking plot. The four costumed freaks simply cavorted around the set, providing the glue between several short, serialized adventures. The best-known was a live-action cliffhanger called *Danger Island* (starring Jan-Michael Vincent). Watching *The Banana Splits* was bizarrely compelling for Vietnam-era teens and preteens, in much the same way that the *Teletubbies* would mesmerize infants 30 years later. Side note: Daws Butler, who voiced Bingo, also did the honors for Cap'n Crunch,

Elroy Jetson, and Yogi Bear. Now *that's* a résumé. See also CAP'N CRUNCH; KROFFT, SID AND MARTY; *LAND OF THE LOST*; *MUPPET SHOW, THE*; and *TELETUBBIES*.

BARBEAU, ADRIENNE Apparently this woman was an actress of some sort. She was on the sitcom *Maude* and in movies such as *The Fog* and *Escape from New York* (both directed by her then-husband, John Carpenter). We have no idea what roles she played, what she said, or whether she was any good. Because, sadly, we couldn't stop staring at her *awesome and majestic breasts.*

Is that fair? Of course not. But this is the burden that fate, and lavish nature, destined Barbeau to bear. In every generation, it seems, a woman appears with cleavage that stands at the pinnacle of aesthetic perfection. In the 1970s (and into the '80s, before Pamela Anderson took up the mantle) this was Barbeau. Not looking at her chest (revealed in all its shirtless glory in 1982's *Swamp Thing*) was like visiting Wyoming and not looking at the Grand Tetons. Sadly, those headlights blazed and then dimmed, as is the way of all flesh. But we'll always have the mammaries . . . or rather, memories. See also ANDERSON, PAMELA and *HALLOWEEN* (THE MOVIE SERIES).

BARCALOUNGERS Today's trendy male may trick out his home in IKEA and

< 21 >

Stickley furnishings, but what he really wants is his own big, fat Barcalounger, plopped down dead-center in front of a blaring TV, just like dear old Dad. Stylish it isn't, but something about those overstuffed, leg-elevating monstrosities, indented with one's own distinct butt print, says comfort like nothing else. Back in 1940, when Edward Joel Barcolo started building his "scientifically articulated" motion chairs (which were patented by Dr. Anton Lorenz), he forever changed the landscape of

 American living rooms—to the chagrin of many a wife faced with decorating around a piece of furniture only slightly smaller than a life raft. Though today's Barcaloungers come in everything from wing chairs to swivel gliders, with more than 600 choices of fabric and leather coverings, nothing beats the traditional behemoth rocker covered in butt-swaddling, sweat-absorbing corduroy.

BARDOT, BRIGITTE The idea of a model trying to make it in the acting world is nothing new. Take, for example, yesteryear bombshell Brigitte Bardot (born in Paris with the just-as-sexy but less alliterative name Camille Javal). After appearing in the pages of *Elle* magazine at age 15, she jumped to the screen a few years later in the French film *Le Trou Normand*. Her sex kitten persona was defined by 1956's *And God Created Woman*, about a free spirit, the two men who love her, and the town that lusts after her. At 18 she married the film's director, Roger Vadim (who would go on to marry Jane Fonda and Marie-Christine Barrault, a hottie Triple Crown that has yet to be equaled in the horndog record books). Never much of an actress, Bardot bailed on the business in 1973 to devote herself to animal rights activities. If only Kathy Ireland had been so smart. See also FONDA, JANE.

BARKER, BOB See *PRICE IS RIGHT, THE*.

BARRIS, CHUCK See DATING SHOWS and *GONG SHOW, THE*.

BAT BOY See *WEEKLY WORLD NEWS, THE*.

BATH STORES There's so much promise stacked on the vanilla-scented shelves of a store with "Bath," "Body," or "Beauty" in its name. Choose a physical imperfection (be it as small as a blackhead or as large as a cellulite-dimpled backside), and you'll find a remedial goo among the orderly rows of bottles and tubes. A pioneer in the business of self-serve beauty, the Body Shop sold its first product in 1976, before anyone even knew

< 22 >

that tea trees had oil or that avocados could make body butter. The Body Shop now sells a product every 0.4 second, while its gingham-themed competitor, Bath & Body Works, is busy coming up with clever new scents like Water Blossom Ivy and Tangerine Spice to peddle at more than 1,600 U.S. stores. Of course the people who buy these potions and then pile them up in medicine cabinets from Manhattan to Malibu may be seeking something else besides shower gel/body lotion combos. When they drop $100 on cosmetics at Aveda, they're bringing home not just a bagful of plant-based tonics, but a whole new lifestyle attractively packaged to suit a wood nymph's mood. And when that mood changes, there are plenty of other testers to sniff at Sephora, Origins, and all the other modern apothecaries that have saturated the market—or at least made it smell like calendula.

BATMAN (THE TV SHOW) How do you treat a show that was *designed* to be a guilty pleasure? From the moment this series premiered in 1966, absolutely no one thought the tilted sets, the Bam!s and Boom!s that appeared during fight scenes, or even Adam West's codpiece were to be taken seriously (except, perhaps, for West himself). Still, even after all these years, it's fun to watch the likes of Victor Buono (King Tut), Eartha Kitt and Julie Newmar (both as Catwoman), and Otto Preminger (Mr. Freeze) act all menacing and stuff. See also SUPERHEROES.

BATTLE OF THE NETWORK STARS Caring about what TV celebrities do when they aren't in front of the cameras is, of course, silly. Caring about the results of amateur athletic events is, of course, silly as well. But caring about the results of amateur athletic events *involving TV celebrities* is more than that—it's the very definition of guilty pleasure. Long before *Celebrity Fear Factor*, the one place to savor this bizarre delicacy was *Battle of the Network Stars*, launched in 1976 and hosted by Howard Cosell. That season featured Gabe Kaplan, Robert Conrad, and Telly Savalas captaining teams that included Loretta Swit, Gary Burghoff, and Jimmie "J.J." Walker. In 1984, Scott Baio and Debby Boone joined Cosell in his effort to add play-by-play excitement to "battles" between Michael J. Fox, C. Thomas Howell, Charlene Tilton, and Richard Dean Anderson. Does anyone remember which network's stars dominated the competition? No. But there are lots of then-teen boys who remember what *Maude's* Adrienne Barbeau looked like while running. See also BARBEAU, ADRIENNE; GAME SHOWS; and "YOU LIGHT UP MY LIFE."

< 23 >

BATTLESHIP (THE BOARD GAME) Some kids' games—Cootie, for instance—are only fun for kids. There are a few, however, that even seasoned adults would like to take one more crack at. Take Battleship, in which each player positions an aircraft carrier battle group on a grid his opponent can't see. Then they take turns calling out Bingo-like coordinates (B-7, I-10, etc.), seeing who can "hit" the other's fleet. Nowhere outside of a Tom Clancy novel can one take so much satisfaction in sinking a submarine. Note: The nerds who still play Battleship consider the people who play Electronic Battleship to be nerds. See also CLANCY, TOM.

BATTLESTAR GALACTICA What was lamer than being a *Star Wars* nerd? Being a fan of this short-lived ABC series. Offered in 1978 to cash in on the success of Luke, Han, and the rest of the gang, it featured a massive budget (for TV), elaborate sets, a filling-loosening orchestral score, and state-of-the-art special effects. Everything but a reasonable premise and decent scripts. It told the story of a bunch of guys in spaceships trying to elude a pursuing band of Cylons, robots that boasted more chrome on their chassis than you'd find on a Cadillac's grille. Referred to by incensed critics as *Battlestar Galaxative*, the show folded after only 24 episodes.

Reruns can be unintentionally entertaining because, though *Galactica* was set in some distant corner of the galaxy, everything about it was oh so '70s. All the women had Farrah-style feathered 'dos, and off-duty astronauts relaxed in an outer space disco. See also CADILLACS; DISCO (DANCING); DISCO (FASHIONS); and *STAR WARS*.

BAYWATCH Arguably the most unlikely international sensation since Zamfir, Master of the Pan Flute, this show began life as a quickly canceled 1989 NBC series starring post–*Knight Rider* David Hasselhoff and post–*Hardy Boys* Parker Stevenson. After NBC bowed out, the program's creators, perceiving a huge pent-up demand for a show about California lifeguards who perform rescues and deal with their complicated personal lives while running around mostly naked, took the project into syndication. Budgets were cut, Parker Stevenson was handed his walking papers, and expensive action sequences were dropped in favor of music-video-like montages of the actors (especially the female actors) running in slow motion. The changes created a media juggernaut seen in some 140 countries worldwide. It also made David Hasselhoff, for some reason, a huge international star, and ignited the careers of Pamela Anderson and Carmen Electra.

< 24 >

Ironically, 65 percent of the show's fans were female. See also ANDERSON, PAMELA and HASSELHOFF, DAVID.

BEACH VOLLEYBALL (WATCHING) Rare is the sport that can be enjoyed by spectators who don't even know the rules. Boxing is a magnificent spectacle of endurance that needs no explanation. The purpose of a marathon is also self-evident. As for beach volleyball, a firm grasp of the game is not needed to appreciate hardbodied men and women wearing skintight outfits and bouncing up and down in pursuit of a ball. Who cares about the rules? If you're watching on TV, you don't even need to turn up the sound.

BEACHES See CHICK FLICKS (IN WHICH SOMEONE DIES).

***BEAUTY AND THE BEAST* (THE TV SHOW)** Fans of this late-'80s television program, which updated the fairy tale to contemporary New York, gush over its inspired storyline. But anyone who watched the CBS drama about Catherine Chandler (Linda Hamilton) and her very special relationship with the sexy man-beast Vincent (Ron Perlman) knows its cult following was mostly interested in the duo's slow dance around the topic of Getting It On. When Hamilton left the production after the second season to have a baby, attempts to write her out of the show didn't fly with viewers. A dozen episodes into season 3, the writers tied up some loose ends and closed shop. As a result, Perlman (who endured five  hours in a makeup chair every day to play Vincent) went from being a top TV sex symbol to playing big, scary guys in such sci-fi flicks as *The Island of Dr. Moreau*, *Alien: Resurrection*, and (under a prosthetic skull) an alien guy in *Star Trek: Nemesis*. See also *STAR TREK*.

BEAUTY PAGEANTS Credit the Greeks. Or, at least, the mythological Greeks. It was Zeus, after all, who ordered Paris (the guy, not the city) to judge whether Hera, Athena, or Aphrodite was the most beautiful of goddesses. Aphrodite won. (History leaves no record of the first runner-up, who would have filled in for the winner had she been unable to complete her duties.) That contest led, indirectly, to the Trojan War.

These days, beauty pageant fallout is limited to couch potato arguments over the merits of Miss New Hampshire vs. Miss Texas and an occasional "whoops-I-forgot-to-mention-the-nude-photo-shoot" scandal. Still, not all such events are created equal. Some, such as Miss

< 25 >

America, shun the term "beauty pageant," require contestants to display some sort of learned skill beyond their God-given physical assets, make them sweat through an interview, and stress that the bathing suit competition is really about "fitness." That sort of denial is a sign that it's not just the folks at home who feel a tinge of guilt about their participation in such an antiquated, yet fun, form of ogling. See also HART, MARY.

BEAVIS AND BUTT-HEAD A pair of music-video–critiquing teens next to whom even the *Wayne's World* guys seem intellectual, this duo made their first limited-animation appearance in 1992 as part of the MTV series *Liquid Television*. Their own show followed a year later, and a movie, *Beavis and Butt-head Do America*, hit the cineplexes in 1996. Mocking both teen losers and pretentious critics (B & B's standard line of criticism: "This blows."), the show faced frequent attacks for the boys' dubious behavior. One season 2 episode came complete with the disclaimer, "Breathing paint thinner will damage your brain . . . look what it's done to Beavis and Butt-head." Another: "WARNING: If you're not a cartoon, swallowing a rubber full of drugs can kill you." See also CHICKEN SOUP FOR THE SOUL; HUMPERDINCK, ENGELBERT; and MTV.

BEE GEES, THE While John Travolta's hoofing in *Saturday Night Fever* got most of the attention, the soul of that film belongs to the Bee Gees, the British trio whose name is short (kinda) for the Brothers Gibb.

Of course Maurice, Robin, and Barry had a career prior to the movie and its blockbuster soundtrack (including the 1975 hit "Nights on Broadway") and they stayed on the charts afterward (remember "Too Much Heaven"?). However, it's the *SNF* disc and the Beatles defilement known as the movie *Sgt. Pepper's Lonely Hearts Club Band* that are the trio's cultural touchstones. Each is in its own lovable way a guilty pleasure—the first for reminding us that disco was vapid but fun (even without the de rigueur nose full of cocaine); the latter for being the worst film ever made (but as disturbingly watchable as the pictures in a textbook of medical anomalies). See also DISCO (DANCING); DISCO (FASHIONS); *SATURDAY NIGHT FEVER*; *SATURDAY NIGHT FEVER* (SOUNDTRACK); and *SGT. PEPPER'S LONELY HEARTS CLUB BAND* (THE MOVIE).

BEFORE AND AFTER PHOTOS There's something disturbing yet fascinating about seeing a hideous "before" picture juxtaposed next to a look-how-much-weight-I-dropped; a look-how-good-I-look-when-fashionistas-get-hold-of-me;

< 26 >

or a don't-I-look-svelte-without-my-conjoined-parasitic-twin? "after" shot. That's why everyone from the *Ricki Lake* show to ads for diet supplements in *Us* magazine love showing them. Never mind that the subject is grim in shot No. 1 and hap-hap-happy in shot No. 2. Never mind that the first pic looks like it was developed in mud, while the second was handled by Francesco Scavullo. Just mitigate your jealousy of the second figure with the rationale that you would *never* let yourself go like Mr. or Ms. Before.

BENNY HILL SHOW, THE Even though silent comedy supposedly died with the advent of sound films, no one seemed to have told Benny Hill. Think of the British comic (real name Alfred Hawthorn Hill) whose antics aired from 1969 to 1989 on British TV and were syndicated to  America in 1979, and the likely image is of Hill and his cohorts chasing women to the sounds of Boots Randolph's "Yakety Sax." While sophisticated lovers of English comedy might claim to appreciate the subtleties of Wilde, Shaw, and even the Monty Python troupe, it's the naughty Mr. Hill who tickled the common man. His secret?

Never underestimate the humor potential of pairing fat men with buxom women. That short bald guy was pretty funny, too.

BENTON, BARBI Yes, she appeared on *Hee Haw* and on a boatload of *Love Boat* episodes, but the former Barbara Klein is best known for being Hugh Hefner's girlfriend and a four-time *Playboy* cover girl (though she was never Playmate of the Year). In addition to the standard guilt associated with lusting after an unattainable sex symbol, this one carried an even deeper shame. You were messing with Hef's woman—even if only in your mind. See also *HEE HAW*; *LOVE BOAT, THE*; and *PLAYBOY*.

BERENSTAIN BEARS, THE Ever since *The Big Honey Hunt* was published in 1962, Stan and Jan Berenstain's bruins have been a mainstay in the libraries of parents who don't know what else to get their kids. In such books as *The Berenstain Bears Get the Gimmies*, *The Berenstain Bears Think of Those in Need*, and *The Berenstain Bears Don't Pollute (Anymore)*, Papa, Mama, Sister, and Brother Bear moralize like TV preachers in grizzly suits, leaving little doubt as to why these ponderous tomes are garage sale staples. Still, even smart parents sometimes pull the books from the shelf when some important lesson—some extremely *obvious* lesson—must be

< 27 >

taught. But they won't brag about it at the next playgroup meeting.

BEVERLY HILLBILLIES, THE If mainstream America was so straitlaced in the mid '60s, what accounts for that era's proliferation of bizarre sitcoms? This was the heyday of such well-nigh unclassifiable hits as *Bewitched*, *Green Acres*, *Gilligan's Island*, and *I Dream of Jeannie*. But when it came to sheer density of weirdness per episode, nothing could touch *The Beverly Hillbillies*. Originally titled *The Hillbillies of Beverly Hills*, it followed a pack of poor mountain folk who got rich and moved to "Californy." Of course there's no need to explain how this happened: The theme song (which is undoubtedly playing in your head right now) tells everything.

America ate it up. *The Beverly Hillbillies* spent nine years in the CBS lineup, from 1962 to 1971, and enjoyed two seasons at No. 1 in the Nielsen ratings. Even today it sustains a fan base that includes Stephen King, Dan Aykroyd, and Billy Bob Thornton. (Okay, maybe Billy Bob isn't that big of a surprise.) A movie redo did good business but was quickly—and mercifully—forgotten. See also KING, STEPHEN and VARNEY, JIM.

BEVERLY HILLS 90210 High school kids played by way-too-old-for-high-school actors is a grand American thes-pian tradition. It stretches from *The Many Loves of Dobie Gillis* (with 24-year-old Dwayne Hickman as the title teen and 24-year-old Bob Denver as his beatnik buddy), through *Grease* (with 34-year-old Stockard Channing as Rizzo, the Pink Ladies probably had no problem scoring beer).

BH90210 more than upheld that ancient policy. When it first aired in 1990, it told the story of twins adjusting to life at their new, tony school. To populate this cauldron of teen angst, executive producer Aaron Spelling rounded up 24-year-old Luke Perry (who looked like he already had crow's-feet); 26-year-old Ian Ziering, and the grandma of the group, 29-year-old Gabrielle Carteris. Plus there was Aaron's 17-year-old daughter Tori, a guilty pleasure in and of herself. But at least she was age appropriate. See also SPELLING, AARON and SPELLING, TORI.

BIBLICAL EPICS There's something really twisted about the pleasure we get from big-budget Hollywood movies based on the Testaments, Old and New. Cecil B. DeMille and other, lesser directors realized early on that straight-up fire and brimstone didn't sell tickets. The trick was to lure audiences with sin and then deliver salvation. Thus the presence of hot-as-hell Anne Baxter in *The Ten Commandments* and exotic Anouk Aimée in *Sodom and Gomorrah*, along

< 28 >

with a retinue of pinup-quality high priestesses. The violent action in these films is also a little icky, but in a good way. What do you remember more clearly about *Ben-Hur*, the religious message or the butt-kicking chariot race?

BIG MAC Two all-beef patties special sauce lettuce cheese pickles onions on a sesame seed bun. Or so litanized the famed

 McDonald's commercial. What wasn't mentioned? The 33 grams of fat. The 85 milligrams of cholesterol. The 1,050 milligrams of sodium. Okay, it does have 3 grams of dietary fiber. That's *something*, isn't it? See also MCRIB and NUGGETS, CHICKEN.

BIG MOUTH BILLY BASS This mounted, singing fish was to interior décor what Jeff Foxworthy is to comedy. It was all the rage in the early days of the 21st century, indicating to one and all that being a redneck and being whimsical were not mutually exclusive. Bill Clinton even gave one to Al Gore, which pretty much said it all.

It took just a couple of months of massive overexposure for the snob factor to kick in. Soon it was the rare consumer who would admit to cracking a smile the first time they heard BMBB croon "Take Me to the River." Created by Texas-based Gemmy Industries and based (in look, not voice) on a bass acquired from an East Texas taxidermist, Billy started out as a big fish in a relatively small pond. But after an overwhelmingly successful market test at Cracker Barrel and Bass Pro Shops, Billymania exploded. Soon came not just spin-offs, but so many rip-offs that Billy was on the verge of being pushed off the shelves by singing pike, trout, turkeys, and pretty much every other imaginable game species.

But though the talking bass craze has passed, the genre survives. The infamous dancing hamster series (including the famous, now-retired Kung Fu Hamster) is also a product of Gemmy. See also FOXWORTHY, JEFF.

BIG RED (THE SOFT DRINK) What, exactly, is the attraction of a beverage that seems to consist of nothing but a toe-curling blast of sugar, a not-to-be-trifled-with 38 milligrams of caffeine, and enough FD&C red 40 food color to turn it as crimson as the sun on Judgment Day? Perhaps it's the mystery. Big Red, invented in 1937 in Waco, Texas, (and originally called Sun Tang Red Cream Soda), doesn't claim to have a particular flavor. It's just a color. Some describe it as tasting like liquid bubble gum, while others compare its cloying bouquet to cot-

< 29 >

ton candy—way too much cotton candy. None of which has stopped it from becoming a pop culture icon in its Texas homeland, as well as a key ingredient in recipes ranging from barbecue sauce to cake. See also COTTON CANDY; FRESCA; MOUNTAIN DEW; RED BULL; and SOFT DRINKS (GIANT PLASTIC CUPS FILLED WITH).

BILLY JACK The pitch meeting for this 1971 cinematic counterculture mainstay must have been a classic. "Here's the idea: a film about a pacifist. A pacifist *who kicks the shit out of people.*" Such was the plot of the sleeper hit *Billy Jack* (as well as that of its lesser-known sequels, 1974's *The Trial of Billy Jack* and 1977's *Billy Jack Goes to Washington*). In each installment, Tom Laughlin played the title character, a half–Native American, half-white ex-Green Beret who tries and tries to keep his anger in check. But finally, after endless on-screen discussions about the importance of nonviolence, someone (usually a whole bunch of someones) ticks him off so much that he just has to open up a 64-ounce, jumbo-sized can of whoop-ass. Suggested movie slogan: Go for the moralizing, stay for the beatings! See also *DEATH WISH*; RAMBO MOVIES; SCHWARZENEGGER, ARNOLD; and *WALKING TALL*.

BILLY MADISON See SANDLER, ADAM.

BINACA Before Altoids mania hit the United States, there was something vaguely cool about toting around a bottle of this aerosol breath freshener. It seemed to say, "I am so hot that I could be called on to suck face at any moment. Therefore, I must be prepared." John Travolta even used it on *Welcome Back, Kotter*. Of course, all it really meant was that you needed to brush your teeth—which made taking a public "blast" seem about as cool as smearing on deodorant.

BIONIC WOMAN, THE See *SIX MILLION DOLLAR MAN, THE*.

BIORÉ STRIPS Early commercials for these revolutionary sebum-grabbing patches featured a demure young woman who, having supposedly just used Bioré's patented C-Bond adhesive to purge her nose pores of trapped oils, makeup, and dead skin cells, could barely stand to look at the evidence— a tiny grove of black-  heads stuck to a little white strip. It didn't take long for the product's handlers to realize that this "Dance of the Seven Veils" routine negated Bioré's biggest selling point, which is that people actually *like* to see how much gunk they can tug out of their pores. Accordingly, the company released a new batch

< 30 >

of ads showing giggly teenage girls pulling the starchy white strips off of their noses and then comparing the results. In no time at all, the Bioré ritual—wet skin, apply patch, wait 15 minutes, peel off patch—became a Girls' Night In favorite. Never before had a beauty routine been so immediate, so *tangible*, and so strangely addictive. Which makes Bioré's package warning, "Do not use more often than once every three days," seem almost cruel. See also CLINIQUE PORE MINIMIZER MAKEUP.

BLAIR, LINDA The pea-soup spewing little girl in *The Exorcist* has put together possibly the most hilariously misguided film career of all time. Blair appeared not just in bad films, but in projects that marked the low points of their genres. Most famously, she starred in what some call the worst sequel of all time, *Exorcist II: The Heretic*. She also did history's most over-the-top teen TV drama, *Sarah T: Portrait of a Teenage Alcoholic*, as well as the unforgettable (but not in a good way) TV movie *Born Innocent*, which spotlighted the problem of young girls who are sent to reform school and then raped with a broom handle by their fellow inmates (which Blair's character was, right in the middle of prime time). She went on to star in the definitive '70s schlock music pic *Roller Boogie* and in the babes-in-prison movie *Chained Heat*. These days she's deeply involved in animal rights—but not so deeply that she can't add such efforts as *Gang Boys* and *Double Blast* to her bizarre résumé. See also COREYS, THE (FELDMAN AND HAIM); DEMONIC CHILDREN (MOVIES ABOUT); and PRISON MOVIES FEATURING WOMEN.

BLAXPLOITATION FILMS At its best, this '70s genre was all about African Americans making movies for other African Americans. It all began in 1971 when Melvin Van Peebles wrote, starred in, and produced (indeed, he did pretty much everything but run the catering truck) *Sweet Sweetback's Baad-asssss Song*. A long line of ghetto fabulous hits followed, including (but by no means confined to) *Shaft*, *Blacula*, and *Foxy Brown*. Unfortunately, the movies soon began to exploit the community they were supposed to elevate, emphasizing violence and the thug life over reality. Which in no way changes the fact that they're fun to watch, if for nothing else than the Ohio Players–era clothes. But for white viewers, the creepy tinge of guilt comes when characters start talking about The Man—and you realize they mean *you*. See also GRIER, PAM.

BLAZING SADDLES See MOVIES THAT PARODY OTHER MOVIES.

< 31 >

BLOOD PRESSURE MACHINES (AT THE DRUGSTORE) You could browse the candy aisle while waiting for your prescription to be filled, or perhaps check out the magazine rack. Or you could pretend that you care about your health by taking a seat at the complimentary, self-serve blood pressure monitor. Like a video game with unresponsive controls, the device doesn't take very well to attempts to control it. And psyching yourself into a mellow state as you shoot for the magic 120 over 80 isn't easy — especially if you're shopping with kids. Not worried about your blood pressure? Then play the "How much can I move my arm without getting the 'I'm sorry, we could not retrieve your information' message" game.

BLOOMIN' ONION To find the surface area of any object, add up the square inches (or feet, as the case may be) on each exposed surface. Naturally you can increase the amount of surface area by cutting said object into pieces, creating more exposed spaces. Such was the high-powered geometry used by Outback Steakhouse (founded by three Americans) to create their elaboration on the onion ring, the Bloomin' Onion (which is reported to have its roots in a Japanese food decoration cookbook). Rather than cut their tearjerkers into conventional circles of breaded pleasure, Outback sliced and fanned an entire onion, increasing the amount of surface area that could be coated with batter and then deep fried. In the process the chain provided local news stations with plenty of fodder for their annual sweeps week "You Won't Believe How Much Fat There Is in Restaurant Food" reports. See also HOOTERS.

BLOOPERS There was a time when TV shows buried their flubbed scenes, perhaps only airing them at wrap parties. But these days those screwups aren't only shown, they're milked for all they're worth. Thanks in part to the '80s hit *TV's Bloopers & Practical Jokes*, the networks offer up an endless stream of shows featuring on-air flubs, from game show hosts falling off their podiums to soap stars slamming face-first into unopened doors. It's easy to understand why viewers enjoy this. Who doesn't want to see beautiful, overpaid actors make asses of themselves? It's also no mystery why the networks provide them. Just take a bunch of blown takes from *Everybody Loves Raymond*, mix in some muffed scenes from a couple of underperforming one-hour dramas, and you've got an hour's worth of low-cost summer replacement programming.

BLUME, JUDY Other authors might rank higher on the literary scale, but Judy

< 32 >

Blume elevated the genre of rebellious reading to a fine art. From our first snicker over seeing the word "bra" on the pages of *Are You There God? It's Me, Margaret* to our final white Zinfandel–fueled binge reading (hurry, before the kids get home) of the indulgent adult novel *Wifey*, we turned to Blume whenever our literary habits needed a little corrupting. The award-winning writer didn't disappoint, teaching us—with perfect slumber party technique—that kids can be cruel (*Blubber*); that we must, we must, we must increase our bust (*Are You There God? It's Me, Margaret*); that "Once you have sex you can't go back to holding hands" (*Forever*); and that adultery happens (*Wifey*). It could be argued by people who have a little too much time on their hands that what Shakespeare did for romantic love in *Romeo and Juliet*, Blume did for puberty in titles such as *Then Again, Maybe I Won't* and *Starring Sally J. Freedman as Herself*. But that kind of frankness came with a price. One of the most banned authors in the history of school libraries, Blume also serves as a spokesperson for the National Coalition Against Censorship.

BOB'S BIG BOY He's got the hair of Ace Ventura, the pants of an Italian eatery tablecloth, and the smile of a psychopath. And he lures diners who don't want to admit that they take comfort in his standard-issue selection of breakfasts, burgers, and melts.

When an anonymous but rotund kid wandered into Bob's Pantry, a Glendale, California, eatery (which founder Bob C. Wian opened in 1936), history was made. Now, more than 450 Big Boy restaurants dot the landscape, and Big Boy banks, dolls, and other memorabilia show up in kitsch collectable shops around the country. Frankly, it makes a lot of sense. If you want a truly representative fast-food mascot, which is more accurate—a clown or a tubby kid?

BOLOGNA Lord Byron claimed that the city of Bologna was "celebrated for producing popes, painters, and sausage." We don't know about the popes and painters, but we certainly thank the Bolognapolitans, or whatever, for the sausage. Actually, the spicy concoction created in this Italian city has little in common with the mild, pinkish slices Americans stuff between pieces of Wonder Bread. Ranked only slightly above Spam in the hierarchy of embarrassing meat products, bologna's continuing popularity is proof that people love it, even if they won't admit it. Also, it's great fried, between pieces of white toast. Not that we've ever had it that way. Note: Anyone who pronounces it bah-LOH-nyah is a weenie. See also

< 33 >

SPAM; VIENNA SAUSAGE; and WONDER BREAD.

BOLTON, MICHAEL Imagine there was a singer/songwriter who had co-written music with Bob Dylan and Babyface, performed with B. B. King and Ray Charles, and written songs for Kiss and Patti LaBelle. Pretty cool, huh? Not necessarily. Those credits are just part of the résumé of pop superstar Michael Bolton, one of the most-mocked musicians of the last 50 years. Sample joke: You are in a room with Michael Bolton, Hitler, Stalin, and Saddam Hussein. You have a gun with two bullets. What do you do? Answer: Shoot Bolton twice.

Why the hostility? Perhaps it was Bolton's Fabio-like looks (at least until he cut off his mane in the late '90s, thank the Lord). Or maybe it was his habit of recording pandering pop-ified cover versions of great soul songs. Or maybe it was because Bolton  snagged a 1991 Best Male Pop Vocal Performance Grammy for his cover of "When a Man Loves a Woman" but failed to thank the man who made the tune famous, Percy Sledge. Whatever the reason, it's still best, when you buy a Michael Bolton disc down at Sam Goody, to say it's for your cousin. Or

better yet, order online. See also FABIO and KISS.

BOMBS (BIG-BUDGET MOVIES THAT TURN OUT TO BE) Hollywood cranks out lousy movies by the bushel, but only a select few are worthy of being called Bombs. Gaining that dread title requires three things: a bloated budget; a woefully inept script; and an out-of-control, ego-tripping director, producer, or star (or perhaps all three). That's how such career-maiming, Hiroshima-like conflagrations as *The Adventures of Pluto Nash*, *Hudson Hawk*, *Cutthroat Island*, and *Ishtar* made their way into (and quickly out of) cineplexes. Watching them (or, more likely, fast-forwarding through DVDs of them) offers several different kinds of fun. In the case of straight-up abominations such as *Nash* and *Hawk*, it comes from wondering if anyone involved in the project understood the magnitude of the travesty being perpetrated. With such earnest efforts as *Ishtar* (a rambling, occasionally interesting Dustin Hoffman/Warren Beatty "buddy" movie), one can ruminate about what might have been achieved had there been just one grown-up on the set, watching the clock and tracking expenses. Or (as in the dreadful *Heaven's Gate*, for which an entire 19th century town was constructed from scratch in a remote corner of Montana)

< 34 >

seeing the goofy ways money can be wasted. Occasionally, such morbid interest in a potential Bomb can work to its advantage. For instance, intense audience fascination with the soggy Kevin Costner vehicle *Waterworld* actually helped it to break even. The same could not be said of Costner's follow-up stinker, *The Postman*, which cost between $80 and $100 million but didn't even make $20 million in domestic release. But just try to find a video store that doesn't stock it. See also PRINCE (MOVIES OF); SGT. PEPPER'S LONELY HEARTS CLUB BAND (THE MOVIE); and XANADU.

BOND FILMS FEATURING ROGER MOORE When it comes to flicks about the world's most famous spy, the Moore isn't the merrier. In fact, Roger Moore's tenure from 1973's *Live and Let Die* through 1985's *A View to a Kill* is widely acknowledged to be the low point of the James Bond franchise (ignoring George Lazenby, who parlayed his single Bond appearance into gigs in a series of soft-core *Emmanuelle* flicks). Take this simple test: Tell a group of friends you want to have a get-together to watch *Goldfinger*. Now, watch their reactions when you tell those same friends you've changed your mind and plan to screen *Moonraker* instead. Moore actually made a handful of decent non-Bond movies, but his spy work

remains an embarrassment—not that we don't still watch when they turn up on TV. See also BOND GIRLS (SUGGESTIVELY NAMED) and EMMANUELLE (MOVIES FEATURING THE CHARACTER OF).

BOND GIRLS (SUGGESTIVELY NAMED) Fans of James Bond movies like their women sexy, submissive, and saddled with nasty-sounding names. For hardcore acolytes, the unveiling of each installment's sophomoric, sexually charged moniker is as highly anticipated as Q's latest gadgets. Admittedly, making up new ones gets harder as the years go by and all the obvious (and not-so-obvious) wordplays are taken. Who could top such "triumphs" as Honey Ryder (Ursula Andress in *Dr. No*), Holly Goodhead (Lois Chiles in *Moonraker*), and the never-to-be-improved-upon Pussy Galore (Honor Blackman in *Goldfinger*)? The addition of Pierce Brosnan as Bond in 1995's *Goldeneye* spawned an attempt to bring the franchise's views on women into the '90s (or, at least, the late '70s). But that didn't stop the writers from offering up a female assassin named Xenia Onatop. See also BOND FILMS FEATURING ROGER MOORE.

BOOKS ON TAPE (IN LIEU OF READING) "Sure, I read that book," you say smugly. But what you really did was lis-

< 35 >

ten to it in 20-minute installments during your daily commute. You got into the whole books-on-tape scene by convincing yourself that you would catch up on all the classics (Homer, Dickens, Woolf). But that lasted for half a tape. Who knew it was so hard to fathom Nietzsche while negotiating freeway traffic? So now you've quickly regressed to the same stuff you used to read when you used to read (Clancy, King, the Collins sisters). See also CLANCY, TOM; COLLINS, JACKIE; COLLINS, JOAN; and KING, STEPHEN.

BOONE'S FARM STRAWBERRY HILL The motto of this, the official high school party beverage of the '70s, should have been, "Fly now, pay later." Strawberry Hill, not unlike its bastard redneck cousin, Country Kwencher, was sweeter than a stack of Mary-Kate and Ashley Olsen movies and cheap as a six-pack of domestic beer. But inexperienced drinkers (and almost everyone who touched this stuff was inexperienced, because grownups had the cash and smarts to get something better) often found themselves weathering morning-after headaches and retching bouts that they would remember for the rest of their lives. And it's no wonder. These "wines" came from the darkest, most low-rent corner of the vineyards of Ernest and Julio Gallo, the same folks who proudly market such illustrious brands as Ripple and Thunderbird. See also OLSEN TWINS, THE.

"BORN TO BE WILD" Once the anthem of every chopper rider in America, "Born to be Wild" was popularized in 1969's damn-near-unwatchable hit *Easy Rider*. The song had been released a year earlier as part of the band Steppenwolf's self-titled debut album (a disc completed in four days on a $9,000 budget). Unfortunately this tune isn't nearly as cool as it once was. It's now the theme song of millions of balding, desperate, middle-aged men who still want to think they're bad. Rare is the fortysomething baby boomer who hasn't sung the lines "lookin' for adventure/and whatever comes our way" while merging onto the highway in his SUV. See also SUVs.

BOWERY BOYS, THE *Dead End* and *Angels with Dirty Faces* were classics of late '30s tough guy cinema. While Humphrey Bogart appeared in both, their real unifying element was a gang of young troublemakers led by actors Leo Gorcey and Huntz Hall.

Thanks to the title of their first flick, the crew was initially called The Dead End Kids. In later films they evolved, with some changes in the supporting players, into the East Side Kids and, finally (and most famously), into the Bowery Boys. Not as violent as the

< 36 >

Three Stooges, not as anarchic or as musically talented as the Marx Brothers, and not as easy to pigeonhole as Abbott and Costello, the Bowery Boys hold a visceral appeal for New Yorkers. Who but a Gotham resident would admit to sitting through, more than once, such Bowery Boys stinkers as *Spooks Run Wild* and *Hard Boiled Mahoney*? See also ABBOTT AND COSTELLO and THREE STOOGES, THE.

BOWLING Archaeologists have uncovered pieces for a bowling-like game in the graves of ancient Egyptians. The modern version is enjoyed by some 95 million people the world over. Why is it so popular? Perhaps because it's the only sport in the world that can be played while drinking a beer and eating nachos. See also BUDWEISER and NACHOS.

BOY BANDS Requiring at least three guys, stylish clothes, and a target audience of screaming female fans, boy bands encompass a range of musicians from the Four Freshmen through Frankie Valli and the Four Seasons to, if you want to get technical, the Beatles. But the term most commonly refers to quartets and quintets who rise to teen-magazine-cover success on the wings of bubblegum pop (think the Osmonds, New Kids on the Block, New Edition, and the Backstreet Boys). Fortunately most disappear as soon as their fan base grows old enough to know better.

BOY IN THE PLASTIC BUBBLE, THE Exactly one year before he became the Man in the White Polyester Suit, John Travolta starred in this 1976 TV movie about a teen with no immune system who lives in a germ-free environment that he can't leave and no one else can enter. Goofy? You bet. But many a strong man misted up during the final scene, when Travolta finally emerged from his cocoon and went horseback riding with his girlfriend. See also *SATURDAY NIGHT FEVER*; TEARJERKER MOVIES (FOR MEN); and TV MOVIES.

BRADY BUNCH, THE A widower with three boys and a widow with three girls all move into the same house. Hijinks ensue. Sound like the plot for a controversial, groundbreaking HBO series? Of course it does— unless it's the '70s and the family in question is named Brady. From 1969 until 1974 this odd composite  clan moralized and philosophized, without once dealing with the nitty-gritty questions that intrigued fans. For instance, how did Greg rub up against Marcia every morning in that tiny bath-

< 37 >

room they shared without getting, ahem, *ideas*?

Despite the psychosexual chasm that separates the Bunch from any real-life family we've ever met, TV lovers nevertheless hang on every detail of their idyllic suburban lives, passing down Brady lore (via reruns) from generation to generation. Even as the episodes' references become ever more dated and bizarre (Davy Jones as the dream prom date? Card-house building as a problem solver?), they remain our national injoke. It's no surprise that when the inevitable big-screen flick appeared (*The Brady Bunch Movie*, 1995), it played the family for camp laughs. Still, it wasn't nearly as funny as *The Brady Bunch Hour*, a legendary (as in legendarily bad) variety show produced by Sid and Marty Krofft. See also GILLIGAN'S ISLAND; KROFFT, SID AND MARTY; and VARIETY SHOWS.

BRANSON The founders of this Ozark Mountain city set out to create a lumber-producing industrial center. Well, a funny thing happened on the way to the sawmill. In the mid-1970s, a four-lane bypass helped spark development, and over the following years, country music halls bred like (Eddie) rabbits, turning Branson into a music and tourism Mecca. Fans swarmed in because Branson was less about the music industry (à la Nash-

ville) and more about putting on a show. Hundreds of shows. Sparked by early pioneers such as Boxcar Willie and Roy Clark, other acts like Mickey Gilley, Moe Bandy, and, inexplicably, Yakov Smirnoff saw the value of having their own venues. These days, there are more theater seats in Branson than there are on Broadway. And those seats are filled with visitors experiencing the guilty pleasure of catching a show by a "name" entertainer such as Jim Stafford or Mel Tillis—even though that "name" hasn't been on the general public's lips in decades.

BREAKFAST CLUB, THE *Long Day's Journey into Night* is to Eugene O'Neill what *The Breakfast Club* is to John Hughes—the artistic summary of everything its creator is about. Of course, John Hughes was all about teen angst, making a name for himself (and for Molly Ringwald) with *Sixteen Candles*, *Pretty in Pink*, and this, the apex of his career. Although it's a teen flick—one that traffics in stereotypes, then pats itself on the back for breaking them—many an adult has secretly seen themselves in Emilio Estevez's misunderstood jock, Molly Ringwald's misunderstood priss, Anthony Michael Hall's misunderstood smarty-pants, Judd Nelson's misunderstood hood, and Ally Sheedy's misunderstood freak. See also *WEIRD SCIENCE*.

< 38 >

BREASTS (ARTIFICIAL AUGMENTATION OF) See FREDERICK'S OF HOLLYWOOD and WONDERBRA, THE.

BREASTS (OGLING) See ANDERSON, PAMELA; BARBEAU, ADRIENNE; BARDOT, BRIGITTE; *BAYWATCH*; FARRAH FAWCETT POSTER, THE; PARTON, DOLLY; TUBE TOPS; VICTORIA'S SECRET CATALOG, THE; and WONDERBRA, THE.

BRIAN'S SONG See TEARJERKER MOVIES (FOR MEN).

BRIDAL MAGAZINES Regardless of what is said over Cosmos during Girls' Night Out, no wife-to-be is 100 percent immune to bride mag fever. The symptoms are mild at first: a harmless perusing of *Modern Bride* and *Elegant Bride* on the magazine rack at Borders; a few sudden, unexplained references to fondant icing; an updo or two. Then comes an obsessive-compulsive hoarding of Vera Wang ads, the ever-present copy of *Martha Stewart Weddings*, and finally an uncontrollable urge to register. With a multibillion-dollar bridal industry pushing everything from bridesmaid dresses to personalized wedding logos, it's hard for a woman not to fantasize about how she and her betrothed would look in some of those happy white-on-white photo shoots. Especially if they've already had their second date. See also *LUCKY* MAGAZINE and STEWART, MARTHA.

BRIDGES OF MADISON COUNTY, THE Just before the inevitable backlash began—and before its author put out a second novel that nobody wanted—Robert James Waller's tale of a photographer's romantic entanglement with an unhappy housewife was the talk of not-very-well-read short-attention-spanners everywhere. Socked into a slim, handsomely designed volume, *The Bridges of Madison County* even spawned a film that, thanks to stars Clint Eastwood and Meryl Streep, was much more watchable than it deserved to be. Soon, however, the novel became such a cliché that trying to find someone who admitted to liking it was tougher than locating someone who would admit to being genuinely moved by *Jonathan Livingston Seagull*. See also *JONATHAN LIVINGSTON SEAGULL*.

BRITISH ROYAL FAMILY, THE What is it about the House of Windsor that stirs so many inquiring minds? Is it the way their freakishly large ears pink up so nicely when they tromp around Balmoral in giant rubber boots? Is it the fairytale accoutrements of castles and horse drawn carriages? Perhaps. But more likely it's all the juicy revelations suggesting that the Queen and her kin are just as human as the rest of us. Rumors of infidelity, same-sex liaisons, addic-

< 39 >

tion, topless sunbathing, and other royal screwups make for fascinating tabloid reading—the grainier the accompanying photo, the better. Even ancient scandals have an undeniable allure, whether they involve Queen Victoria's possible love affair with her Scottish manservant John Brown or the sensational antics of King Edward VIII, who would have made a terrific guest on a special Jerry Springer "Hey, Mom! Take this crown and shove it!" episode. See also DIANAMANIA; QUEEN OF ENGLAND, THE; and SPRINGER, JERRY.

BRONSON, CHARLES See *DEATH WISH*.

BUBBLE YUM All forms of bubble gum are guilty pleasures. But when you make a variety that's chunky, soft, comes in bizarre colors, and even has a silly name, you've got a chew that no self-respecting adult will admit to buying, let alone masticating. Yet Bubble Yum has been making jaws ache since 1975. Roughly 1.3 billion chunks are sold each year— enough since the brand's inception to circle the equator seven times. Not that you'd want to do that. It's tough enough getting just *one* piece off your shoe. See also CHARMS BLOW POPS and CHICLETS.

BUDWEISER Drinking snobs consider the self-anointed "King of Beers" to be the Wonder Bread of the brewing world—a well nigh tasteless beverage that's perfect for college kids, blue-collar workers intent on getting plastered, and little else. And yet, maddeningly, "Bud" is America's best-selling beer. Introduced in 1876, it is made from only five ingredients: barley malt, hops, yeast, water, and, of all things, *rice*  (which apparently helps improve the clarity of the finished product). But the truly creepy thing is that every batch, whether brewed near the Anheuser-Busch headquarters in St. Louis or in Japan, tastes almost exactly the same as every other batch. This is both a technical achievement of the highest order and a source of horror to aficionados, who think each vat of fermented grain should be as distinctive as a fingerprint. Which is fine if you're at a tasting party. But sometimes, all you really need is something cheap and inoffensive to fill up the beer bong. See also WONDER BREAD.

BUFFETS Sure, it isn't haute cuisine. Sure, it's a guaranteed diet buster. And sure, it's unhealthy. But there's something about those steam trays full of shrimp, that vat of banana pudding at the dessert bar, and all those tubs of buttered corn that sets our mouths watering. Of course, this being America, a gut-

< 40 >

busting, belt-loosening buffet is never farther than the nearest cruise ship, strip mall, or casino. Be careful, however. Nutritionists warn that someone who eats with abandon at a buffet may download as many as 7,000 calories in one sitting. But then, if you worried about things like that, you wouldn't *be* at the buffet, would you?

BUILDING IMPLOSIONS On a popular *SCTV* recurring sketch, "The Farm Film Report," a pair of yokels praised movies where stuff "blowed up real good." The series poked fun at these guys, but the show struck home because we all know that there's something primal—and pleasurable—about watching things explode on-screen. And there's fun, too, in watching things deliberately imploded in real life. Since 1773, when 150 pounds of gunpowder were used to bring down Waterford, Ireland's Holy Trinity Cathedral (more of an explosion than an implosion, but still an industry landmark), the curious have lined up to watch as firepower, math, and luck have their way with supposedly immovable objects.

BUMPER STICKERS (HUMOROUS) Go ahead and sing the praises of Longfellow, Keats, and Byron. We venture to say that none of the "great" poets' words, well-chosen as they were, have been seen by as many people as "Ass,

gas, or grass: nobody rides for free." The lowly bumper sticker, the most underappreciated form of mass media, can offer sentiments as delicately as a haiku, mostly because its anonymous message crafters must wedge everything necessary to make you chuckle into a space that fits on a car bumper. And, admit it, you *did* chuckle the first time you saw "Hung like Einstein and smart as a horse," "Honk if you're Jesus," or "My other bumper sticker is funny."

BUSCAGLIA, LEO The cuddliest of the self-help gurus—assuming you're into cuddling self-help gurus—Buscaglia often out–Stuart Smalleyed Stuart Smalley with his gospel of hugs and love. "Starting each day, I shall try to learn something new about me and about you and about the world I live in," he wrote in his seminal tome, *A Start*. Similar thoughts emerged again and again, like herpes cankers, in such books as *Loving Each Other: The Challenge of Human Relationships*; *Living, Loving and Learning*; *Born for Love: Reflections on Loving*; and the inevitable *Love*. See also INSPIRATIONAL BOOKS.

< 41 >

C

CADDYSHACK At the time of its theatrical release, this raunchy farce set at a fancy country club was considered a bomb—little more than a poor man's *Animal House*. Well, a funny thing happened on the way to the video store. Out of nowhere, fans started reciting "immortal" dialogue from cast members Bill Murray ("It's in the hole!"), Rodney Dangerfield ("So let's dance!"), and Chevy Chase ("Do you take drugs, Danny?"). Like a lowbrow *Citizen Kane*, the movie—considered in some circles the best flick about golf ever made—took on a life of its own. In the pantheon of films that men watch when there are no women present, it rates just behind porn (any porn) on the desirability scale. Conversely, the sequel, *Caddyshack II*, is in some circles considered to be the *worst* flick about golf ever made. See also *ANIMAL HOUSE*.

CADILLACS There was a time, back in the early '40s, when Cadillac was the soul of luxury. Now, thanks to some extremely odd design decisions in the '50s, '60s, and '70s, it's got a reputation for styling excess that its maker, General Motors, has yet to shake. The saga began in 1948, when Cadillac rolled out its first tail-finned model. In short order Cadillac "owned" the fin look, slapping versions on its cars that would have done honor to a 20-foot-long great white. But though the fin trend died in 1964, ostentation didn't. Caddies grew larger and larger, sporting every "luxurious" gewgaw short of chandeliers. The party ended in 1973 with the Arab oil embargo, which highlighted the impracticality of rumbling around in a vehicle with the turn radius (and gas mileage) of an ocean liner. But perhaps a comeback is on the horizon. Americans still love their big cars; they just want them tall (SUVs) instead of long. Which explains why Cadillac now makes its own SUV—the Escalade ESV. Just 161 pounds shy of three tons, it is reportedly the largest Cadillac ever produced. See also SUVs.

CAFFEINE (EXCESSIVE USE IN BEVERAGES) See MOUNTAIN DEW and RED BULL.

CAMAROS See MUSCLE CARS.

CAMPBELL, GLEN Country music mavens will tell you that Glen Campbell is actually a respected guitarist and song stylist, responsible for such hits as "Wichita Lineman," "Gentle on My Mind," and "Galveston." He even

< 42 >

played rhythm guitar on Frank Sinatra's "Strangers in the Night." But Campbell teetered into the realm of guilty pleasure when he hit a kitsch trifecta—offering a terrible performance opposite John Wayne in the otherwise terrific 1969 cowboy flick *True Grit*, hosting his own TV variety series, *The Glen Campbell Goodtime Hour* (even Steve Martin, who was one of the show's writers, couldn't make Campbell funny), and, most importantly, transitioning from country to Vegas country with his '70s hits "Rhinestone Cowboy" and "Southern Nights." Note: Go to www.glencampbell.com and you'll find a New York car dealership.

CANDID CAMERA The granddad of all hidden camera shows was truly a classic back in the days when it was filmed in black and white and Allen Funt was host. But once son Peter Funt took over and lots of low-budget copycats took to the airwaves, the show became a pure guilty pleasure. Peter Funt, you see, is to public embarrassment what Frank Sinatra Jr. is to crooning. Yet the stunts—such as the store clerk who takes his "no change" sign literally and refuses to give change—remain compelling. And is there a soul so dead that he has not wondered what he would do if someday someone stepped up to him and said, "Smile, you're on *Candid Camera*"?

CANDLE STORES The story of candle addiction isn't a pretty one. The first step is often just a few harmless apple-cinnamon votives to chase the stink out of a dorm room. But that soon turns into a pillar-a-week habit. Then it's on to the hard stuff: scented gel candles that burn for 225 hours, three-wickers the size of fire hydrants, imported candle pots, floating candles shaped like exotic flowers . . . you name it, and the candle stores have it. Candles are a lucrative market niche because you can never have just one—as illustrated by the fact that Americans buy roughly $2 billion worth each year. Not surprisingly, this flame-happy craze raises eyebrows at the National Fire Protection Association. It would like to remind the world's romantics that in one year, 1997, candle fires caused more than $170 million in property damage, almost 1,200 injuries, and 156 *deaths*. Ouch.

CAN'T STOP THE MUSIC See VILLAGE PEOPLE, THE.

CAP'N CRUNCH Commercials always showed a tiny bowl of this orange-colored confection sitting amidst toast and fruit, as "part of a complete breakfast." What a crock. The best way to

< 43 >

enjoy this cereal (introduced in 1963) is to pour half a box into a bowl big enough to mix cake batter, then add a half gallon of milk and hope you finish before the abrasive kernels damage the roof of your mouth. Despite its unusual taste, the Cap'n has inspired more spin-offs than *Happy Days*. Cap'n Crunch's Crunch Berries debuted in 1967, followed by Cap'n Crunch's Peanut Butter Crunch in 1969, and, in what may be a sign of the apocalypse, Cap'n Crunch's Choco Donuts in 2002. Balanced breakfast? Not unless you mean balancing the bowl on your stomach while you watch TV.

CAR CHASES (TELEVISED) Police pursuits have supplied us with vicarious thrills since the days of the Keystone Kops. O. J. Simpson only raised the ante during his famous June 17, 1994, outing in a white Ford Bronco—an event that 95 million viewers watched live. That day, news directors around the world learned a valuable lesson: Car chases sell. They responded with helicopter-mounted cameras delivering ever-more-frequent "live from the 405" bulletins, complete with unintentionally amusing copspeak by the stations' commentators. To hear a usually staid newsman shrill, "Looks like the perp's gonna try to bail in that cul-de-sac!" is well worth spending an hour in front of the boob tube, watching an aerial view of a pickup truck.

The genre is now so popular that it has its own "greatest hits." Remember the flaming lumber truck barreling through Dallas? Or the time the New Zealand cops got so mad they threw their nightsticks at a fleeing vehicle? But all those episodes pale in comparison to the doings in the car chase capital of the world, Los Angeles. It led the nation in police chases in 2002, with more than 700 incidents—many of them, if they lasted long enough, beamed straight into L.A. living rooms. Critics wonder if such dangerous trivia might be bad for us, or if criminals might actually get off on having their 15 minutes of fame broadcast live. But questionable ethics aside, we believe car chases provide a valuable public service: They teach us the topography of our cities. See also *COPS*.

CARNATION INSTANT BREAKFAST The popularity of Tang might be waning, but this powdered breakfast drink is still going strong. Indeed, you could do a lot worse than downing a glass of this foamy, lumpy beverage. The first *Men's Health* Nutrition Awards, in 2002, included a nod to Carnation Instant Breakfast, a serving of which furnishes 25 percent of the adult daily requirement for protein, along with half the required calcium. Of course, the label doesn't mention that the drink is also recommended by Carnation to doctors whose

< 44 >

patients want to gain weight. See also TANG.

CARPENTERS, THE No '70s-era critique of pop music was complete without a scathing indictment of this brother-and-sister act's schmaltzy-sounding tunes. Not that Karen (who started out as a drummer) and Richard Carpenter helped their case much. Seemingly existing, like *The Boy in the Plastic Bubble*, inside some sort of rarified place that no thundering guitar solo could ever reach, they crafted such ultra easy listening hits as "(They Long to Be) Close to You," "Rainy Days and Mondays," and "We've Only Just Begun" (originally a jingle for a bank commercial). It was only after Karen's death from complications of anorexia in 1983 that critics reconsidered. Fact is, the tunes (one of which is undoubtedly going through your head right now) were quite catchy. So catchy, in fact, that in 1994 a tribute album called *If I Were a Carpenter* was released. With cutting-edge (for 1994) bands such as the Cranberries and Sonic Youth covering Karen and Richard's songs, the two were on top of the world again. See also *BOY IN THE PLASTIC BUBBLE, THE*.

CARREY, JIM It's sad to see this rubber-faced gross-out artist try to move, à la Tom Hanks, into more serious cinematic roles. Admit it: The whole time you watched him smile and play nice in *The Majestic*, you were expecting, at any moment, to see him lean over and try to make his butt talk. This makes Mr. Carrey a double guilty pleasure. You feel like a dork when you watch him do fart jokes as a Rhode Island state trooper in *Me, Myself & Irene*. Then you feel like an even bigger dork when you sit through his more highbrow offerings, *wishing* he would do a fart joke. See also *DUMB & DUMBER*.

CARRIE See KING, STEPHEN.

CARS WITH HUMAN QUALITIES See HASSELHOFF, DAVID and KING, STEPHEN.

CARTLAND, BARBARA The women in Barbara Cartland's novels are typically wide-eyed, demure virgins with names ending in "a." The men are invariably dark, square-jawed, and fully clothed (preferably in a uniform). By the time they finally hook up, somewhere around page 118, it is with such breathlessly anticipated passion that when he "kisses her until she [is] no longer herself but his" you can practically taste the salt on his lips. But wait . . . *gasp, gasp . . . we mustn't*! Cartland, the flamboyant British author who published a record-setting 723 books before she died in 2000, never wrote beyond a PG-13

< 45 >

rating. The Queen of Romance was many things, including Dame of the Order of the British Empire; mother of Princess Diana's stepmother; champion of vitamins, the elderly, gypsies, and pink chiffon; and the person with the most lines in *Who's Who*. However, a smut monger she was not. On the subject of her notoriously chaste sex scenes, Cartland pointed out that "You can't get more naked than naked, can you? And then where do you go from there?"

CARTOONS (ADULT INTEREST IN) It's okay for adults to watch *The Simpsons* or an animated Disney release, but most folks still think cartoons are just for kids. To them, getting busted enjoying, say, *The Powerpuff Girls* or *Ren and Stimpy* is tantamount to being caught playing Candyland. Grownup cartoon heads challenged by unsympathetic friends/roommates/spouses shouldn't make things worse by defensively asserting that while the slapstick action is geared to the kindergarten crowd, the plots and dialogue are meant for adults. Instead, they should just smile sheepishly, switch the channel, wait for their persecutor to leave—and then switch back. See also BAKSHI, RALPH; *FLINTSTONES, THE*; HANNA-BARBERA CARTOONS; SATURDAY MORNING CARTOONS; and SCOOBY-DOO.

CASINOS Since the days of ancient Greece, the wealthy have worked gambling into their vacations. However, the word *casino* only dates back to 1600s Italy, where places offering games of chance were called *casini*, or "little houses." These days, the descendants of the "little houses" have gone big time. And they're not just luring in the wealthy. With flashing lights ("Pay attention to ME!"), noisy pay-off areas ("Listen to all these people WINNING!"), no clocks ("Who cares what time it is? ENJOY!"), no windows ("Outside world? What outside world?"), free drinks ("We like you. KEEP PLAYING!"), and entertainers you wouldn't look at twice anywhere else ("Sorry you lost. Have some WAYNE NEWTON tickets!"), modern gambling dens are designed to satisfy the fantasies of players of all classes. The only one they won't satisfy is the wish to go home a winner. See also ATLANTIC CITY; CLAY, ANDREW DICE; LAS VEGAS; LIBERACE; NEWLEY, ANTHONY; NEWTON, WAYNE; and SLOT MACHINES.

CASSIDY, DAVID If you're a female between the ages of 40 and 55, chances are you've drooled over Shirley Jones's stepson. Well, don't feel too bad about it, because back in the early '70s he was the hottest thing in tight, fringed pants. The star of the sitcom *The Partridge Family*

< 46 >

from 1970 to 1974, he parlayed his role as the front man for a pretend rock band into a real career as a pop idol. At age 21 he was the world's highest-paid performer, selling out venues worldwide and scoring eight straight gold and platinum records. Of course once he reached the summit of fame, there was nothing to do but take the inevitable donkey ride down to Has-been Valley. Today he knocks around Vegas, headlining casino shows and, perhaps inevitably, singing old Rat Pack standards. See also CASSIDY, SHAUN and *PARTRIDGE FAMILY, THE.*

CASSIDY, SHAUN The star of that '70s phenomenon *The Hardy Boys/Nancy Drew Mysteries* is living proof that eye candy has the shelf life of sushi. While his older half-brother, David, cornered the high school market, angelic-looking Shaun nabbed the 10-to-13 crowd. He did it with a cover of the 1963 hit "Da Doo Ron Ron" and a platinum-selling No. 1 album, *Shaun Cassidy.* But though he was white hot in '77, he was toast by '79. A "serious" rock album called *Wasp* bombed in 1980, and his 1979 turn as a retarded man in the TV movie *Like Normal People* failed to open doors. These days he's "taking his career in new directions," which is celebrityspeak for messing around in regional theater and producing a handful of short-lived

TV shows (*American Gothic, Roar, The Agency*). See also CASSIDY, DAVID; HARDY BOYS, THE; MENTALLY IMPAIRED (MOVIES WHOSE STARS PRETEND TO BE); and *PARTRIDGE FAMILY, THE.*

CATS It's the most-mocked musical since . . . actually, we can't think of any others. But though critics have skinned this cat in almost every conceivable way, that didn't stop it from running nearly 18 years on Broadway, with road companies breeding like, well, you know. Admitting that you witnessed the antics of these felines as  they try to make it to the "Heaviside layer" is embarrassing even to people who thought Andrew Lloyd Webber's *Evita* was deep and his *Phantom of the Opera* was actually opera. See also WEBBER, ANDREW LLOYD.

"CAT'S IN THE CRADLE" Getting emotional the first time you hear a song is okay. (Perhaps, for example, you really weren't expecting there to be 100 yellow ribbons 'round the old oak tree.) But when a song—and the song we're talking about is Harry Chapin's weepy 1974 hit—climbs the charts on the backs of people who listen to it over and over, even though they *know* that the dad who

< 47 >

doesn't pay attention to his son is destined to wind up a lonely old man, we're not talking about guilty pleasure anymore. We're talking about masochism. See also DEATH SONGS and ORLANDO, TONY (AND DAWN).

CELEBRITIES (EXCESSIVE INTEREST IN THE LIVES OF) See CELEBRITY IMPERSONATORS; CELEBRITY ROASTS; CELEBRITY TRIALS; "CONFIDENTIAL" AND "BABYLON" (BOOK TITLES THAT INCLUDE THE WORDS); DIANAMANIA; *E! TRUE HOLLYWOOD STORY*; *ENTERTAINMENT TONIGHT*; FEMALE IMPERSONATORS (PROFESSIONAL); HART, MARY; HOLLYWOOD WALK OF FAME; *INSTYLE* MAGAZINE; KING, LARRY; NAKED CELEBRITIES (PHOTOGRAPHS OF); *NATIONAL ENQUIRER, THE*; *OSBOURNES, THE*; OSCAR ACCEPTANCE SPEECHES (EMBARRASSING); *PEOPLE*; PEOPLE'S CHOICE AWARDS, THE; STARS' HOMES; SUSANN, JACQUELINE; UNAUTHORIZED BIOGRAPHIES; *US WEEKLY*; *VH1*'S *BEHIND THE MUSIC*; WHERE ARE THEY NOW?; and WORST-DRESSED LISTS.

CELEBRITY IMPERSONATORS Technically, the casts of *Saturday Night Live* and *Mad TV* are celebrity impersonators. But the term is more often used to describe nightclub entertainers such as Frank Gorshin, Louise DuArt, and Rich Little, all of whom are best-known for "doing" other performers (and we don't mean in the

Pamela Anderson sense). A staple for years on TV variety shows, impersonators amazed audiences with their ability to voice and, in many cases, morph into celebrities and heads of state. They were also occasionally tapped for behind-the-scenes work in the entertainment world. When David Niven's vocal cords couldn't handle retakes on his last film, *Curse of the Pink Panther*, Rich Little was called in to dub his scenes. And when Stacy Keach was in prison, Little did voiceovers for the *Mickey Spillane's Mike Hammer* TV series. Yet as dexterous and fun as the better impersonators may be, there's still that nagging knowledge that you, as an audience member, are accepting the Molly McButter of entertainment. After all, saying that you saw Frank Sinatra is a lot different than saying you saw Rich Little *as* Frank Sinatra. See also ANDERSON, PAMELA.

CELEBRITY ROASTS There's a good reason why this hoary old concept—as seen in vintage tapes of the Dean Martin Celebrity Roasts that originally aired on NBC between 1973 and 1984; the occasionally aired (with heavy bleeping) insult fests at the famed Friars Club; and the more recent roasts created for Comedy Central—remains popular. While the good-natured ones can be funny (Milton Berle saying at a Frank

< 48 >

Sinatra roast: "What a crowd. I would say 'mob,' but you know how sensitive Frank is."), the real guilty pleasure comes when the fangs get bared (Laraine Newman on fellow Not Ready for Prime Time Player Chevy Chase: "Chevy announced he was leaving *Saturday Night Live* to pursue a dream he had since he was a little boy: to make shitty movies and the worst talk show in history. We knew he could do it."). Stars being mean to each other? What could be more fun? See also RICKLES, DON.

CELEBRITY TRIALS Nothing arouses prurient interest quite like the sight of a movie star or sports hero on the witness stand. You can practically *smell* the dirty laundry. Of course, spectacular celebrity trials have been with us for decades. Errol Flynn faced statutory rape charges in 1942, only to be acquitted by an all-female jury. But it took television to turn them into public spectacles. These days the entire nation can watch as big names try to beat the rap for everything from shoplifting (Winona Ryder) to murder (O. J., Robert Blake). Not that celebrity careers are necessarily ruined by even the most terrible indiscretion. Author Norman Mailer, after stabbing his wife in a domestic dispute in 1960, got off with third-degree assault and went on to win two Pulitzer Prizes. As for O. J., sitting through a double murder trial

doesn't seem to have hurt his golf game. See also CAR CHASES (TELEVISED) and COURT TV.

CELEBRITY-OWNED RESTAURANTS See THEME RESTAURANTS.

CENTERFOLDS See BENTON, BARBIE; *HUSTLER*; *PENTHOUSE FORUM*; *PLAYBOY*; *PLAYGIRL*; and SMITH, ANNA NICOLE.

CHAN, JACKIE See KUNG FU MOVIES.

CHAP STICK (FLAVORED) Anyone can appreciate the fresh-as-a-first-kiss taste of cherry-flavored Chap Stick and its strawberry cousin. Their waxy crimson heads conjure up images of ripe berries—a far cry from the original menthol-and-camphor Chap Stick developed in the early 1880s by Lynchburg, Virginia, physician C. D. Fleet. His foil-wrapped wickless candles were the perfect remedy for people who couldn't be bothered to lick their own lips, but after failing to turn a decent profit on his soothing unguent, the doctor sold his recipe to fellow Lynchburgian John Morton in 1912—for $5. The formula changed hands a few more times before Chap Stick's current maker, the Wyeth pharmaceutical company, took over, advertising that "There's a Chap Stick for every pair of lips." Considering the little containers' universal tendency to

< 49 >

turn up missing (and be replaced again and again by fresh tubes purchased impulsively at the checkout counter), the slogan might as well be "There's a Chap Stick for every purse, medicine chest, junk drawer, glove box, dryer vent, public restroom floor, and space between the sofa cushions." See also LUDEN'S WILD CHERRY THROAT DROPS.

CHARLIE (THE PERFUME) See DRUGSTORE PERFUMES.

CHARLIE'S ANGELS "Jill, you're going undercover in a massage parlor. Kelly, I want you to crack a safe while wearing a bikini. Sabrina, you'll put on a white lab coat and impersonate a chemical engineer until further notice." You never knew what boundaries of practical gumshoeing would be broken when the  three employees of the Charles Townsend Detective Agency gathered around Bosley's speakerphone to receive a new assignment. All you knew was that millions of Americans would gather around their TVs to find out. Seemingly from the moment Aaron Spelling first introduced "three little girls who went to the police academy" in 1976, the team of Farrah Fawcett-Majors, Jaclyn Smith, and Kate Jackson became a national obsession.

The ABC series, which almost took the title *The Alley Cats*, lasted until 1981, creating a "jiggle TV" phenomenon that topped ratings in spite of its paper-thin plots and Menudo-like cast changes. Viewers, it seemed, expected little more from the Angels than a strict no-bra dress code and a good skateboard chase every now and then. In 2000, Columbia Pictures took the *Charlie's Angels* franchise to a new level by releasing a wildly successful (and sequel-friendly) movie version starring Drew Barrymore, Lucy Liu, Cameron Diaz, and (inexplicably) Crispin Glover. This new generation of heavenly crime fighters could dive from airplanes onto speedboats, race moto-cross bikes, infiltrate highly secure data systems, scale high-rise buildings, and of course kick butt, all without smearing their lip gloss. As the enigmatic Charlie would say, "Good work, Angels." See also FARRAH FAWCETT POSTER, THE and SPELLING, AARON.

CHARMS BLOW POPS Most lollipops eventually conclude with a final lick (or, more likely, bite). Even a Tootsie Pop's chocolate center has a finite life span. But the Charms Blow Pop goes on indefinitely, provided the eater doesn't mind the substandard chewing gum at the core of the candy shell. See also BUBBLE YUM and TOOTSIE POPS.

< 50 >

CHASE, CHEVY   See *CADDYSHACK* and CELEBRITY ROASTS.

CHAT ROOMS   Imagine a singles bar where everyone is hot, sexy—and blind. That, in a nutshell, is the attraction of Internet chat rooms. Participants can ditch real-world names such as Maury and Helen in favor of monikers like 2coolguy and sexxxyladi. And they can change their age, their sex, and pretty much any other detail of their personality and physicality as well, with no one the wiser. This takes lying to an entirely new level, in a venue where you can never be held accountable for your actions. How could it *not* be a guilty pleasure?

CHEECH AND CHONG   The bitter truth, man, is that these guys are only funny if you're stoned. During the '70s (when else?), the comedy "stylings" of Richard "Cheech" Marin and Tommy Chong not only led to a series of albums (the most famous, *Big Bambu*, featured a cover based on rolling paper packaging), but also to a string of plotless-but-profitable movies beginning with 1978's *Up in Smoke*. Ah, but even the sweetest highs must end. By the time they took a shot at more conventional comedy in *Cheech & Chong's The Corsican Brothers* in 1984, it was the audience's turn to snort. The magic was over, and the two went their separate ways. Marin built a diverse

résumé, playing opposite Don Johnson in the cop series *Nash Bridges* and providing the animated voice of a hyena in *The Lion King*. Chong stayed closer to his roots (or, rather, his leaves and stems) by appearing in the stoner flick *Spirit of '76*, the stoner flick *Far Out Man*, and the stoner flick *Half Baked*. Oh, and he landed a recurring role on *That '70s Show* as a down-on-his-luck Vietnam vet trying to get his life together. Just kidding! He played a stoner. See also MARIJUANA.

CHEERLEADERS   In 1898, the University of Minnesota introduced something new to sport: cheerleaders. These gleeful, spirited folk supported the players on the field and kept the crowd motivated. Of course there were a few differences between that squad and today's hotties. For one, they wore slacks and sweaters. For another, they were all boys. It wasn't until 1927 that Marquette added women to the mix. The NFL didn't catch on until 1961, when the Pittsburgh Steelers started try-outs for the league's first cheerleading squad (applicants were required to take a written test on gridiron knowledge). Lusting after cheerleaders quickly became an American pastime—perhaps because these spirited individuals possess innocence, enthusiasm, athletic skills, and the ability to lift their legs over their heads.

< 51 >

CHEESE See FONDUE; HICKORY FARMS; KRAFT MACARONI AND CHEESE; NACHOS; and VELVEETA.

CHEF BOYARDEE The real Chef Hector Boiardi was born in Italy in 1898 and made a name for himself at the Ritz-Carlton and other restaurants in New York City and beyond. He even catered President Woodrow Wilson's wedding. Now his Americanized name is synonymous with canned pasta that carries upward of 1,190 mg of sodium per serving. It's hard to imagine a more text-book example of entropy. Still, his ravioli is pretty good with a side of white bread and butter. See also SPAGHETTIOS and WONDER BREAD.

CHER (WITH SONNY) Cher (born Cherilyn Sarkisian) was 16 when she met record producer Sonny Bono (born Salvatore Phillip Bono). Soon the duo (for a while known as Caesar and Cleo) were in nightclubs singing "I Got You Babe" and joking between acts (she got the punch lines, he played straight man). They made a bizarre pair, like a counter-culture fusion of Steve & Eydie and Burns & Allen. But the act struck a cord, due in part to their hippie-dippy chemistry and obvious affection for each other. Soon they were hosting their own variety series which, for one season, included then-unknown Steve Martin as a regular. The show ran from 1971 through 1974, when the couple divorced. An attempt to revive the show in 1976 failed to recapture the magic, although it did give work to mimes-of-the-moment Shields and Yarnell. See also CHER (WITHOUT SONNY) and VARIETY SHOWS.

CHER (WITHOUT SONNY) A singer of earnest novelty songs ("Gypsys, Tramps, and Thieves," "Half-Breed"), an Academy-Award-winning actress (*Moonstruck*), a dance-music diva ("Believe"), an infomercial shill (Lori Davis hair care products), and a popular drag show archetype, Cher has proven that her hit-making time with Sonny was just an opening act. Her appeal springs from our fascination with seeing how many comebacks one entertainer can possibly make. See also AS SEEN ON TV PRODUCTS and CHER (WITH SONNY).

CHICK FLICKS (CINDERELLA FANTASIES) Feminist sensibilities melt like butter-flavored topping under the heat of a good old-fashioned Cinderella story, one in which the geeky girl takes off her glasses and gets the boy; the ugly girl has a makeover and gets the boy; the low-income girl inherits a fortune and gets the boy; or the gawky girl learns to

< 52 >

dance and gets the boy. The myth that launched a million Women's Studies theses is the same yarn that has kept tissue makers in business for centuries, beginning with the ancient Chinese tale of "Yeh-Shen" and continuing—by way of the Native American "Rough-Face Girl" fable—into the *Pretty Woman* era. Leading ladies from Audrey Hepburn (*Sabrina*) to Sandra Bullock (*Miss Congeniality*) to repeat offender Renée Zellweger (*Jerry Maguire, Bridget Jones's Diary, Nurse Betty*) have endlessly reprised the Ugly Duckling role, upgrading their existences by landing a great big Richard Gere/Harrison Ford/Tom Cruise trophy hunk. And women couldn't be happier for them. We get so swept up in these movies that when Toula finally hooked up with Ian in *My Big Fat Greek Wedding*, it was as much our victory as hers. Likewise for Jennifer Grey in *Dirty Dancing* and Debra Winger in *An Officer and a Gentleman*. It's not something women like to talk about outside the anonymous rows of the multiplex, but deep down we'd give anything to be Sandy in the final funhouse scene of *Grease*. See also DIRTY DANCING.

CHICK FLICKS (FEMALE BONDING)

No man in the history of moviegoing has ever "gotten" such gender-specific film moments as, say, the naming ceremony in *Divine Secrets of the Ya-Ya Sisterhood*, or Kathy Bates's car-bashing episode in *Fried Green Tomatoes*. And frankly, that's not a problem. There's no shortage of female fans waiting to savor such high-five-worthy Girl Power scenes, the kind that cause grown women to wave their fists in the air and leave the theater shouting a new battle cry such as *"Ya-Ya!"* or *"Towanda!"* Even when the setting is as unfamiliar as *Girl Interrupted's* psych ward or the monster waves of *Blue Crush*, as long as there are strong female characters watching each other's backs, a few token cardboard males with balls to bust, some sort of conflict to overcome (together), and a soundtrack featuring at least one Melissa Etheridge tune, women are on familiar ground.

Writer/director Callie Khouri might not have invented the idea of female bonding, but she is credited with making it a Hollywood commodity. Khouri won a Best Original Screenplay Oscar for *Thelma & Louise* in 1991. In its wake came an entire convoy of girl buddy flicks, including *A League of Their Own*, *Foxfire, Muriel's Wedding, Waiting to Exhale, Romy and Michele's High School Reunion, Bring It On*—and on and on and on. Clearly, these are movies about women, for women, and by women. But a trend toward sexy action-oriented chick flicks from the *Lara Croft/Charlie's Angels* school of theatri-

< 53 >

cal ass-kicking is threatening a testosterone crossover—a hybrid, if you will, meant to draw in the male youth audience. What that means, Governor Schwarzenegger, is that the sisters are sneaking up on you and your target demographic. So be afraid. Be very afraid. See also *CHARLIE'S ANGELS*; CHICK FLICKS (IN WHICH SOMEONE DIES); CROFT, LARA; MOVIE SOUNDTRACKS; *ROMY AND MICHELE'S HIGH SCHOOL REUNION*; and SCHWARZENEGGER, ARNOLD.

CHICK FLICKS (IN WHICH SOMEONE DIES) If the movie poster features a large, rambling house with a wraparound porch, if the characters have Southern accents, and if the reviews contain such phrases as "hold the popcorn, and pass the Kleenex," it can mean only one thing. One of the major characters is headed for life's cutting room floor. Death, one of cinema's favorite money shots, can strike quickly, catching us unprepared (*Beaches*). Or it can ride into town on a slow train that we can see coming for the entire 118 minutes (*Dying Young*, *My Life*, *Steel Magnolias*). Either way is fine. As any woman who snotted up with Debra Winger in *Terms of Endearment* will tell you, a movie-induced crying jag is a delicious form of masochistic escapism. Through the magic of marked souls such as Mary-Louise Parker (who expired so beautifully in *Fried Green Tomatoes*, then did an encore slow dance with death in *Boys on the Side*), it is possible to feel all the wrenching, cathartic drama of tragedy without having to experience actual loss. Bring us ailing mothers, lost loves, and children gone too soon. When the house lights come up, we will look around at the sea of mascara-smeared faces and know that something wonderful just happened. See also CHICK FLICKS (FEMALE BONDING) and *LOVE STORY*.

CHICKEN SOUP FOR THE SOUL Consisting of short, inspirational essays easily read between crying jags, *Chicken Soup for the Soul: 101 Stories to Open the Heart and Rekindle the Spirit* rocked the publishing world when it was released in 1993. Who would have thought that the equivalent of a book full of *Reader's Digest* columns would spark sales of more than 65 million? That figure, to be fair, incorporates not just the original collection of inspirational essays, but also its dozens of spin-offs, including *Chicken Soup for the Canadian Soul*, *Chicken Soup for the Christian Teenage Soul*, and *Chicken Soup for the NASCAR Soul*. Of course the men who came up with all this, Jack Canfield and Mark Victor Hansen, don't see a dime from the army of inevitable parodies, including *Chicken Shit for the Soul* and *Beavis and*

< 54 >

Butt-head's Chicken Soup for the Butt. See also *BEAVIS AND BUTT-HEAD* and INSPIRATIONAL BOOKS.

CHICLETS Sporting an old-timey logo that makes it look like the brand goes back to Arthurian England (actually, it dates only to the early 1900s), Chiclets packaged the chew of gum and the crunch of a candy coating in one impossibly thin box. Thus it became a household name—even though today's kids would rather go for Bubble Yum. Maybe it's because Chiclets are so high maintenance, requiring a good three or four pieces just to develop a decent wad. Still, has there ever been a vending machine cooler than the chrome-and-glass Chiclets gum machine? See also BUBBLE YUM and GUM BALL MACHINES.

CHILI, WENDY'S People who take their chili seriously argue the merits of vegetarian vs. meat, of pinto vs. kidney beans, of chili powder vs. real chili peppers. The rest of us excuse ourselves from the debate and sneak off to Wendy's for a bowl of the house specialty (washed down with a Frosty).

CHIP DIP There's one thing better than eating a bag of chips all by yourself— eating a bag one chip at a time and scooping each one into a bowl of onion dip (made with real sour cream).

CHRISTMAS DECORATIONS (EXCESSIVE, TASTELESS USE OF) What is it about the birth of Christ that makes people lose all sense of aesthetic perspective? According to the *2002 Christmas & Seasonal Decorations Report* by Unity Marketing, Americans spent some $6.4 billion on lights, trees, and other decorations in 2001 alone. Decking the halls can be fun, but placing too many options in the hands of aesthetically challenged individuals can produce horrifying results. Who hasn't, while on some mission of holiday cheer, slowed down to snicker at a lawn featuring a life-sized nativity scene or blithely stared at a living room filled with motion-activated, snoring, and/or dancing Santas, miniature Christmas villages, and a nutcracker army big enough to pacify Afghanistan? Let such wretched excess be a lesson: When it comes to boughs of holly, a little goes a long way.

CIGARETTES Cigarettes once were a guilty pleasure because your parents didn't want you to smoke them. Then they became an even bigger guilty pleasure because you knew they were bad for you. The thrill was further compounded when prices for coffin nails skyrocketed, leaving you to ruminate about the other things you could have spent your smoking money on. Then came reports on the dangers of second-

< 55 >

hand smoke and stories of the shameful practices of the tobacco companies. Then everything from offices to sports arenas to military barracks were made smoke-free environments. Of course smoking is still a guilty pleasure— maybe the guiltiest of all, considering the repercussions. But things sure were easier, albeit unhealthier, back when it wasn't *quite* so guilty.

CINEMAX This also-ran cable channel doesn't offer the sort of groundbreaking original programming that's made its big brother, HBO, such a powerhouse. Why should it? It has something people desire even more: soft-core porn. Want *Six Feet Under* or *The Sopranos*? Look elsewhere. Want *Marilyn Chambers' Naked Fairy Tales*, *Deviant Obsession*, and/or *The Erotic House of Wax*? Then Skinemax—we mean, Cinemax—is the place. See also MOVIES (PORNOGRAPHIC) and SPECTRAVISION.

CINNABON Even in the world of pastries, the Cinnabon chain, which seems to operate a kiosk in every airport and shopping mall food court in the world, stands out for its sinfulness. Perhaps that's why you never see two people dining there together—just lone mall shoppers furtively pounding down a week's worth of calories, or commuters at the airport slamming a half-pound roll cov-

ered with icing before catching the 8:30 A.M. to Amarillo. It's probably best to keep this particular addiction under your hat. The original Cinnabon reportedly clocks in at 670 calories with 34 grams of fat, while the Caramel Pecanbon (a cin-

namon roll with caramel and pecans) contains a staggering 900 calories and 41 grams of fat. See also FOOD COURTS.

CLANCY, TOM Clancy, a former Maryland insurance salesman, has been the patron saint of war groupies ever since his first novel, *The Hunt for Red October*, became an international bestseller in 1984. His follow-up tomes, each of them around two inches thick and filled with enough technical jargon to befuddle a four-star general, likewise sold millions. But Clancy's chief attraction isn't his terrorist-, war-, and intrigue-infested plots; it's the fact that he's living the life that millions of closet battle nerds (the kind of guys who have 10 or more books about World War II in their rec rooms) fantasize about. The U.S. military loves him, which means he can hitch a ride on pretty much any piece of cool hardware that catches his eye, be it a tank, jet fighter, or nuclear-powered attack submarine. Let Norman Mailer try *that*.

< 56 >

CLASSICS ILLUSTRATED Finally, the perfect study aid for those who find Cliffs Notes too taxing and cumbersome—comic books based on great works of literature. First published in 1941 under the name Classic Comics (the first "classic" was *The Three Musketeers*), the series, renamed Classics Illustrated in the late '40s, had a remarkable run that included titles ranging from Goethe's *Faust* to Fleming's *Dr. No*. Though new titles stopped appearing in the U.S. after 1962, the books have been reissued numerous times over the decades, and several companies have attempted to revive the format. But for some reason, teenagers just don't seem interested in a cartoon version of *Tom Brown's School Days*. See also CLIFFS NOTES.

CLAY, ANDREW DICE In every East Coast neighborhood there's at least one blowhard tough guy whose asinine diatribes are only tolerated because (A) he could pound and/or humiliate anyone who objected, and (B) every once in a while he says something that, against your better judgment, you find kind of funny.

Between dirty nursery rhymes ("Hickory Dickory Dock/Some chick was sucking...") and in-your-face rudeness (album title: *Face Down, Ass Up*), Andrew Dice Clay (a.k.a. Andrew Silverstein, a.k.a. The Diceman) turned that persona into a gold mine, entertaining men who felt that the *Penthouse* joke page simply wasn't raunchy enough.

He first grazed the consciousness of America with brief—and, admittedly, kind of charming—appearances in the movies *Pretty in Pink* and *Casual Sex?* but found serious success as an album and cable special comic. Stumbling in an effort to achieve mainstream success, he tanked in the flick *The Adventures of Ford Fairlaine*, then tried to soften his image by starring in the family sitcom *Bless This House* (as Andrew Clay).

America didn't buy it. So Clay read the writing on the bathroom wall and returned to his raunchy roots, becoming one of Las Vegas's most popular acts. His fan base now consists of conventioneers drunk enough to believe they are seeing the successor to Lenny Bruce and Richard Pryor. See also COMEDY ALBUMS.

CLIFFS NOTES Has anyone actually read *Moby-Dick? Don Quixote? Tristram Shandy?* Well, they certainly don't have to. Credit this series of guidebooks, available since 1958, for allowing generations of college students to party all weekend but still get a C on their

< 57 >

English Lit final. The most popular pamphlet, year in and year out, is for *The Scarlet Letter*. Which means that *The Scarlet Letter* could well be the world's most-loathed book. See also CLASSICS ILLUSTRATED.

CLINIQUE PORE MINIMIZER MAKEUP We'll never know how many smooth-skinned beauties owe their complexions to this miracle spackle. Even if your mug is pocked with pores the size of sink-holes, this Clinique product can provide a complexion smooth as satin. Whether worn alone or beneath foundation, Clinique's Pore Minimizer compounds— from the Instant Perfector to the T-Zone Shine Control and Refining Lotion— provide a natural-looking matte finish not too dissimilar to pristine drywall in a newly built home. Though few women would admit to owning such a high-maintenance product (or that their pores, of all things, have begun to fail them), you can bet that most of them do.

CLINTON, BILL It's a little sad that a former leader of the free world should be a guilty pleasure. Yet no matter which side of the aisle you're on, you must admit that there has never been a public figure who garnered so much support from so many people who were so embarrassed about supporting him. The man seems to have spent eight years in office trying to test the limits of American tolerance. First, he put his wife in charge of a major policy initiative (health care). Then he held up air traffic while getting a $200 haircut on Air Force One. Then he rewarded political donors with an unprecedented number of sleepovers at the White House. Then he had sexual relations with "that woman, Miss Lewinsky." Then he quibbled about the definition of "sexual relations," and on and on. Yet like a jar of mayo at the back of the refrigerator, Clinton has stayed around well past his political expiration date, continuing to steal headlines from other Democrats, piss off Republicans, and provide an inexhaustible gold mine of jokes for late-night talk show hosts. See also LEWINSKY, MONICA.

COCKTAIL During that brief, shining moment when Tom Cruise was a star but wasn't yet an actor (post–*Top Gun*, pre–*Rain Man*), he headlined this fluffy flick about a superstar bartender—yes, a superstar bartender. Saddled with perhaps the worst ad line in the history of the movies ("When he pours, he reigns"), *Cocktail* featured endless scenes of Cruise tossing bottles in the air while women looked on admiringly. Female moviegoers were equally admiring, while guys yearned to sign up for a drink-mixing course. In addition to a

< 58 >

lame story and lamer dialogue, the film also featured a hard-to-avoid-in-the-summer-of-'88 soundtrack that unleashed both the Beach Boys' "Kokomo" and Bobby McFerrin's "Don't Worry Be Happy" on an unsuspecting world. See also TOP GUN.

COFFEE-MATE This used to be the generic white powder one sprinkled in Styrofoam cups of office coffee in order to cut the metallic taste. Now, however, Coffee-mate comes in an assortment of flavors ranging from Amaretto to French Vanilla to Hazelnut—the better to sprinkle in Styrofoam cups of office coffee in order to cut the metallic taste. By the way, they aren't kidding about this being a "non-dairy" creamer. The top two ingredients are sugar and vegetable oil. See also FLAVORED COFFEES.

COLLINS, JACKIE The 1980s are alive and well in the coke-snorting, free-loving, zebra print–adorned world of Jackie Collins, the naughty British novelist who brought us *Hollywood Wives*, *Hollywood Husbands*, *Hollywood Wives: The New Generation*, and a whole stack of tomes that rankle the sensibilities of comparative literature students far and wide. The younger sister of actress Joan Collins carved out her niche in beach chair literature by writing about love, lust, and power in Hollywood. She re-

fuses to name names (wink, wink), but if you do your *National Enquirer* homework, you might notice some parallels between a few select celebrities and Collins's vaguely familiar "character composites." Collins's books have sold some 400 million copies in more than 40 countries. Of course, not everyone's a fan of her raunchy prose. The late romance writer Barbara Cartland (no Tolstoy herself) described Collins's first book, *The World Is Full of Married Men*, as "a nasty book, filthy and disgusting." As if those were bad things. See also CARTLAND, BARBARA; COLLINS, JOAN; and *NATIONAL ENQUIRER, THE*.

COLLINS, JOAN Most actors trained at London's Royal Academy of Dramatic Art would shy away from projects with titles such as *The Stud* and *The Bitch*. Not Joan Collins. The High Priestess of Bitchcraft has a knack for turning seemingly bad career moves into strokes of PR genius. As the conniving, one-dimensional Alexis Carrington on Aaron Spelling's prime-time soap opera *Dynasty*, Collins delivered eight years of corny lines with so much glamorous, mouth-twitching venom that some are moved to call her the original Shannen Doherty. In addition to tackling scores of movie and television roles, Collins penned a short stack of trashy novels, though her literary success never

< 59 >

matched that of younger sister Jackie Collins. In fact, the elder Collins's purple prose was the subject of a high-profile lawsuit filed by her publisher, Random House, which asked for return of a $1.3 million advance on a two-book deal. When the jury vindicated the raven-haired beauty, you could almost see her flash an Alexis Carrington–like victory sneer, proving once and for all that it's okay to flop, as long as you make enough of an attention-grabbing thud. See also COLLINS, JACKIE; *DYNASTY*; and SPELLING, AARON.

COMEDY ALBUMS Laugh and the world laughs with you. Laugh alone and you're probably listening to a comedy album. But in the early '60s, discs such as *The Button-Down Mind of Bob Newhart* and *The First Family* were chart toppers that were discussed amongst friends. Credit this to the fact that it was impossible to see club comics do their thing anywhere besides the best nightclubs—or in small doses on TV. These days, with Comedy Central, HBO, videos, DVDs, and comedy clubs in every market, full-length stand-up comedy isn't the rarity it once was. That makes it more embarrassing to admit you spent an evening at home listening to a comedy disc. While still produced (often by traveling stand-ups to sell after their gigs), it's unlikely that such recordings will ever again become huge hits. That's a shame, at least for everyone who has well-worn copies of Bill Cosby, George Carlin, and Richard Pryor vinyl in their collection. See also FOXWORTHY, JEFF.

COMMERCIAL CATCHPHRASES (QUOTING OF) There's a brief window of time in which it's acceptable to repeat an expression you heard in an ad. After that, as much as you want to say "Can you hear me now?" or "Where's the beef?" or "I can't believe I ate the whole thing," and as much as a situation may call for it, sorry, the parade has passed. This golden moment can range from days (for local ads) to seconds (for, say, Super Bowl pitches). See also SUPER BOWL COMMERCIALS and VARNEY, JIM.

COMMERCIALS (HALLMARK) See COMMERCIALS (TEAR-JERKING) and *HALLMARK HALL OF FAME, THE*.

COMMERCIALS (TEAR-JERKING) You know what's going to happen the minute you see the "I just called to say, 'I love you, Mom,'" commercial. Why is it that we can often watch a two-hour tragedy and not so much as blink an eye, yet a 30-second spot for a long-distance service, or a Kodak hired hand singing about how time has slipped away, can make us bawl like babies?

< 60 >

CONCERT T-SHIRTS You know beyond all doubt that the black T-shirt hawked by the vendor outside the concert venue isn't worth $25. You could probably get a better-quality one at the nearest Spencer Gifts for half the price. But you plunk down the money anyway because the music's hot and you've just *got* to prove to the world that you—and 30,000 other iconoclasts—were there. See also SPENCER GIFTS.

"CONFIDENTIAL" AND "BABYLON" (BOOK TITLES THAT INCLUDE THE WORDS) Find either of these two words on the spine of a book and you are almost guaranteed a fun, trashy read that you'll hate yourself for in the morning. The genre's touchstone is Kenneth Anger's 1975 tome *Hollywood Babylon*, which read like an entire season of *E! True Hollywood Story* with all the commercial breaks removed. Dragging to the surface scandals ranging from Fatty Arbuckle's wild parties to the Sharon Tate murder, it paved the way for a parade of volumes reminding us that screen idols are all too human. It also spawned a series of imitators including *Nashville Babylon*, *Hollywood Confidential*, and the more recent best seller *Kitchen Confidential*. See also *E! TRUE HOLLYWOOD STORY* and *NATIONAL ENQUIRER, THE*.

CONSERVATIVE RADIO TALK SHOWS Empowering for listeners to the right of center, radio commentators such as

Rush Limbaugh, G. Gordon Liddy, Laura Ingraham, and Sean Hannity also provide compelling listening for those of other political persuasions. Specifically, they offer liberals the chance to get really, really angry in the confines of their very own gas-guzzling SUVs. See also SUVs.

CONSPIRACY THEORIES The truth is that astronauts really did land on the moon in 1969, and Princess Diana died in a meaningless automobile accident. Of course that truth isn't nearly as interesting as the tens of thousands of convoluted conspiracy theories that have sprung up to "explain" those two (and dozens of other) high-profile events. This Web-fueled cottage industry would have us believe that almost every tragedy during the last half century was caused by shadowy plots more complicated than a New York City subway schedule. Why are so many people willing to listen? Perhaps, experts theorize, because buying into off-the-wall conspiracies is less frightening than facing the simple truth: Life is a crap shoot, and the fate of nations and individuals can

< 61 >

COOKING SHOWS While legions of TV viewers like to watch these programs, most never get around to preparing any of the recipes they see. But that's okay, because shows such as *Iron Chef* and *Emeril Live* aren't for home cooks; they're for food voyeurs. That's probably why the very first program of this kind, which premiered in 1946, was called not *I Love to Cook* but *I Love to Eat*. Featuring appearances by legendary chef James Beard, it paved the way for the Madonna of TV epicureans, Julia Child, who debuted her first and most famous program, *The French Chef*, in 1963. Today's food groupies can partake of a never-ending video smorgasbord on the Food Network. For a true guilty pleasure, try watching these shows while dining on a fast-food hamburger or a bag of microwave popcorn. See also *IRON CHEF* and MICROWAVE POPCORN (AS A MEAL SUBSTITUTE).

COOL WHIP Introduced in 1966 as the first nondairy whipped topping, Cool Whip hit its stride during the 1970s when Mrs. Sarah Tucker, a fictional commercial character, started using it in the fancy desserts at her quaint country inn. "If Mrs. Tucker can serve it to her guests," a willing nation said, "why can't I plop it on my Jell-O?" Although Sarah Tucker hasn't been heard from in years, her real-life counterpart, actress Marge Redmond, best known as one of the earthbound sisters on *The Flying Nun*, still gets an occasional movie gig. More important to food lovers, Cool Whip continues to expand its line (one recent addition is French Vanilla), offering even more options for potluck dinner invitees who draw the "dessert" card. See also JELL-O.

COPPERFIELD, DAVID See HENNING, DOUG and MAGICIANS.

COPS Nothing's more fun than examining (from a safe distance) the seamy side of life, which is why *COPS* has been both a cultural phenomenon and a maker of cultural phenomena since its 1989 debut. The premise (cameramen follow real-life beat cops on their appointed rounds) has inspired parodies on everything from *Saturday Night Live* to the movie *There's Something About Mary*. It also introduced mainstream America to the wife beater T-shirt (as seen on an endless parade of usually drunk, always disorderly rednecks) and hepped us to the fact that winos can't seem to keep their pants up. Given what the uniformed "stars" of the series have to contend with, it's a wonder police

(continued from previous) hinge on random fortune—or the actions of a random loon. See also DIANAMANIA and URBAN LEGENDS.

< 62 >

officers don't shoot more people just on general principle. See also REALITY SHOWS.

COREYS, THE (FELDMAN AND HAIM) During the '80s, Corey Feldman and Corey Haim each enjoyed a brief, brief moment of respectability. For Feldman, the ugly one, it was *Stand by Me*. For Haim, the other one, it was *Murphy's Romance* and parts of *Lucas*. But then the two pushed each other's self-destruct buttons by appearing together in the alleged comedies *License to Drive* and *Dream a Little Dream*. (They also reunited for a sequel to the latter. Yes, there was a sequel to *Dream a Little Dream*. No, we don't understand Hollywood either.) Part of the kick of watching the Coreys' "career arc" is savoring the sheer volume of schlock work they've done. Even if you've seen, say, *Meatballs 4* (Feldman), *Demolition High* (Haim), *She's Too Tall* (Feldman), and *Snowboard Academy* (Haim), you still might have missed *The Stepmonster* (Feldman), *Prayer of the Rollerboys* (Haim), or *My Life as a Troll* (Feldman).

CORMAN, ROGER No one feels particularly proud watching films with titles such as *A Bucket of Blood*, *Teenage Caveman*, or *Slumber Party Massacre III*. But at least the mastermind behind those flicks (and dozens of other lurid, straight-to-the-drive-in-or-video-store projects) delivers what he promises. Producer/director Roger Corman got his start in the 1950s, when he began a lifetime's obsession with retaining creative control of his projects—even if that meant filming them on a shoestring, recycling sets from other, bigger productions, and filling everything from the lead roles to the director's chair with no-names who worked cheap. Fortunately for Corman, those no-names included Francis Ford Coppola, Jack Nicholson, Robert De Niro, Peter Bogdanovich, and Dennis Hopper. The result was a handful of genuinely innovative films (a groundbreaking drug flick called *The Trip*, several well-received adaptations of Edgar Allan Poe stories, and the original, nonmusical *Little Shop of Horrors*) to go with the kitsch. Corman's eye for young talent also explains why he gets grateful cameos in such big-budget blowouts as *Apollo 13* and *The Silence of the Lambs*. See also *DEATH RACE 2000*.

CORVETTES America's most pretentious sports car began life in 1953 as a nimble, surprisingly cool-looking roadster. Over the decades the Corvette got bigger, faster, and more bizarre looking (the high-water mark was its 1963–67 "Sting Ray" phase). However, a few things haven't changed: the 'vette's cramped passenger compartment, tiny storage

< 63 >

area, and its undying appeal to men in the throes of midlife crises.

Cosmo Quiz, The Chances are you can't remember one article you read in *Cosmopolitan* magazine in the last two years. Yet you can probably recall at least one *Cosmo* quiz you've taken. Thanks to the great minds at *Cosmo*, you can answer the questions "Are you a ball buster?" (our verdict, according to *Cosmo*: Balanced Babe), "Do you give off a sexy vibe?"(*Cosmo* says we're a subtle seductress), and "What's your *Sex and the City* personality?" (Miranda). As popular in sorority houses as they are in newlywed bedrooms and beauty salons, these multiple-choice space-fillers-mas-querading-as-articles promise to offer insight into one's personality but really reveal something else: Our ability to select the answers that will guide us toward the judgment we want. Warning: Don't fill out the *Cosmo* quiz and then loan the magazine to your mother.

Costumed Mascots It went something like this: First, humans painted animals on cave walls to bring luck. Then they took it a step further and started dressing up like animals. Then humans started playing sports. Then they started dressing up like animals so that people in the crowd would have something to watch when either nothing was happen-ing (in other words, if it was a baseball game) of if the home team was getting slaughtered (in other words, if it was a Red Sox game). Yet in a world where players are traded, free agents skip town for other franchises, and every year brings another crop of unknown merce-naries, it's sometimes difficult to drum up hometown loyalty. In that context, sports mascots fulfill a very important role: offering an on-field, comforting constant in an ever-changing world.

Cotton Candy If you want a sweet treat with no redeeming nutritional qual-ities whatsoever, this is it. Cotton candy (originally called fairy floss) is nothing but raw sugar that's melted, spun into gossamer filaments, and then collected on a paper cone. Ironically, one of the four men who developed the process in the early 20th century was a dentist named Josef Delarose Lascaux. We're guessing business at his practice picked up after he introduced the confection.

Cotton Panties (Enormous) The lingerie industry has invented a number of euphemistic product names for under-pants that could double as pillowcases. Bali calls its version the Cotton Craze Hi Cut, while Olga prefers Secret Hug Cotton Brief, and Jockey sells a Comfies Cotton Brief. Most commonly known as granny pants, these reliable unmention-

< 64 >

 ables work because they don't expect much from the poor, put-upon derriere. In fact, while other styles push, pull, and ride up, enormous cotton panties do nothing but give, give, give. You'd be hard-pressed to find a woman who doesn't have at least one pair at the bottom of her drawer. Bottom line: if your tush needs a soft place to land and plenty of room for liftoff, you can't beat a cotton seat. See also THONG UNDERWEAR.

COUNTRY MUSIC See BRANSON; CAMPBELL, GLEN; *HEE HAW*; and PARTON, DOLLY.

COURT TV Go ahead and pretend that you watch this cable channel to gain insight on American jurisprudence. What you're really doing is watching living, breathing soap operas. Launched in 1991, Court TV has evolved from its original fly-on-the-courtroom-wall programming into a lineup that includes original series, made-for-Court–TV movies, and reruns of network detective shows. Still, it's the trials that supply the guilty pleasure, especially high-profile cases such as those of O. J. Simpson or the Menendez brothers. Unlike fictional dramas, Court TV reveals a Perry Mason–less world that remains compelling despite the complete impossibility of a surprise witness or of the guilty parties making on-the-stand confessions. See also *PEOPLE'S COURT, THE.*

CRACKER JACK The song "Take Me Out to the Ballgame" not only legitimized the consumption of this boxed popcorn-peanuts-and-molasses treat, it almost made it a patriotic duty. But that doesn't reduce the guilty kick you get from digging to the bottom of the box in search of the prize. Tin toys, whistles, and metal rings (like the one Holly Golightly had engraved in *Breakfast at Tiffany's*) are things of the past, but each box still contains, say, tattoos, quiz cards, miniature books, fortune tellers, or state capital punch cards. These gimmes have been part of the mix since 1912 (Cracker Jack itself dates back to 1893). Collectors, of course, take it all very seriously. The rest of us, even though we know it's destined for the trash, still gamely open the little paper prize packet to see what bounty Sailor Jack and his dog brought us. See also MICROWAVE POPCORN (AS A MEAL SUBSTITUTE).

CRANK PHONE CALLS What was once the domain of bored teenagers calling drugstores to see if they had Prince Albert in a can ("Well, you better let him out before he suffocates!") has in recent

< 65 >

years become a cottage industry. Not only do morning radio deejays thrive on making crank calls, but the dubious hobby has been spotlighted on TV shows such as *Crank Yankers* and by acts such as the Jerky Boys. A well-done phone prank is like *Candid Camera* without the camera. Alas, caller ID means that crankers can call, but they can no longer hide. See also CANDID CAMERA and LEWIS, JERRY.

CREAM OF MUSHROOM SOUP (RECIPES INCLUDING) It is possible to serve Campbell's Cream of Mushroom soup as an actual soup. However, as anyone who grew up with a busy, hard-pressed mom already knows, no one ever does. Cream of mushroom soup serves not as a free-standing appetizer, but as a foundation for the main course. Poured over everything from chicken and rice to meatballs to green bean casserole, it's the gray, salty mortar that's pulled together millions of on-the-go meals. See also GREEN BEAN CASSEROLE.

CRICHTON, MICHAEL Though he's penned plenty of other books (including *The Andromeda Strain*, *Terminal Man*, *Congo*, and the original screenplay for the TV series *ER*), Crichton is best known for creating a series of movies and novels besmirching the theme park industry. It all began in 1973 when he wrote and directed *Westworld*, in which robots in a futuristic entertainment center go berserk and kill the guests. He followed it up in the early '90s with the blockbuster novel *Jurassic Park*, in which dinosaurs in a futuristic park go berserk and kill the guests. His most recent installment is *Timeline*, in which the denizens of a theme park based on time travel go berserk and . . . well, let's just say they don't serve the visitors tea and biscuits. It's mindless fun, but one has to wonder if Mr. Crichton is working through a traumatic childhood Disneyland experience. See also PRE–*STAR WARS* '70S SCI-FI FILMS and THEME PARKS (NOT OWNED BY DISNEY).

CROCODILE HUNTER Back in the days of *Mutual of Omaha's Wild Kingdom*, viewers wondered why the host, Marlin Perkins, was never out there in the danger zone, putting his life on the line. Nobody ever expressed such curiosity about Steve Irwin, a.k.a. the Crocodile Hunter. The brave-bordering-on-suicidal Aussie specializes in capturing crocs all by his lonesome. What makes him so telegenic is his obsession with doing it his way, using ropes, sticks, and his own two hands. Much more fun before the show became a phenomenon, *Crocodile Hunter* has been on the air since 1996 and even spawned a dud film in 2002. See also *MUTUAL OF OMAHA'S WILD KINGDOM*.

< 66 >

CROFT, LARA She's hot, she's sexy, and she comes with a set of controls so you can make her do whatever you want. That, in a nutshell, is the guilty appeal of Lara Croft, the cybervixen star of the Tomb Raider video games. A media darling even before her official debut in 1996 (she's appeared on nongaming magazine covers and even does product endorsements), Croft is famous for racing around in form-fitting outfits, armed with a pair of 44s—and a gun, too. What more could a man want? Especially if that man is a PlayStation freak living in his parents' basement. Thankfully, a film series starring the startlingly Croft-like Angelina Jolie has given fans something—or, rather, someone—slightly more realistic to fixate upon. See also VIDEO GAMES.

CRUISES At one time cruising was all about uncompromising luxury: fine dining, elegant dress, and of course, only enough lifeboats for the first-class passengers. But the era of leisurely oceanic crossings vanished with the arrival of the passenger jet. Today cruising (at least as practiced by such industry leaders as Carnival Cruise Line and Royal Caribbean) is a distinctly more proletarian affair. Instead of crossing the Atlantic, ships bum around the Caribbean or Mexico's Pacific shores, or dodge icebergs off the coast of Alaska. Instead of formal dinners and fancy balls, passengers (about 8 million U.S. citizens per year) tackle all-you-can-eat buffets, floating shopping malls, casinos, and rock-climbing walls. Still, this sort of vacation has its advantages, particularly for the traditional "ugly American" tourist. Closet xenophobes who book passage on one of these floating hotels (most are double or even triple the size of the 40,000-ton *Titanic*) can visit a rustic foreign land, then retreat to the ship's air-conditioning and indoor plumbing if things get *too* rustic and foreign. See also GILLIGAN'S ISLAND and LOVE BOAT, THE.

CUJO See KING, STEPHEN and RAMPAGING ANIMALS (MOVIES ABOUT).

CURRY, TIM See ROCKY HORROR PICTURE SHOW, THE.

< 67 >

D

DAIRY QUEEN The local ice cream shop (or shoppe) is an American icon, a place of sweet treats, innocent flirting, and highly desirable summer jobs. Unfortunately, that place only exists in fantasy land. For the rest of us, there's Dairy Queen. The DQ system began in 1938 when a father and son in Green River, Illinois, developed a "soft frozen dairy product" and talked a friend with an ice cream shop into giving customers a taste. Soon, the "product" (described in company literature as a "delicious and nutritious reduced-fat ice cream") rated its own store, with many more to follow. Growing from 100 locations in 1947 to 1,446 in 1950, Dairy Queen became a household name and an early success in the world of franchising. Now that number has ballooned to nearly 6,000 outlets (useless fact: about 10 percent of them are in Texas) ready to service our cravings for Dilly Bars, Blizzard Treats, Misty Slushes, and impossibly tall soft serve dipped in chocolate.

DALLAS Who will J.R. screw next, either literally or figuratively? Will Sue Ellen stay on the wagon? Who will get the snot kicked out of him at the Cattleman's Ball? Such were the questions that ate at fans of this granddaddy of all prime-time soap operas, which ran from 1978 to 1991.  Though it wasn't the first evening soap (ABC's *Peyton Place* holds the title), it was the first to become a monster hit, ushering daytime TV's outlandish plot twists and endless backstabbing into prime time, without demanding a five-days-a-week commitment. Three hundred million worldwide viewers—many of whom wouldn't have been caught dead in the vicinity of General Hospital—tuned in, shaking up network programming assumptions as thoroughly as a longhorn steer at a Southfork lawn party. See also DYNASTY; PEYTON PLACE; and SOAP OPERAS, NIGHTTIME.

"DANCING QUEEN" See ABBA.

DARK SHADOWS Today, talking dolls, ghosts, and possession are standard daytime soap opera plot devices. Not so when *Dark Shadows*, possibly the strangest suds fest of all time, debuted in 1966. Originally it was merely a Gothic-themed program, until low ratings prompted producer Dan Curtis to add a new character—a 200-year-old vampire named Barnabas Collins. Business

< 68 >

picked up, and werewolves, ghosts, witches, and even a Frankenstein-like monster followed. The show folded in 1971, disappointing millions of grade schoolers who each day ran breathlessly home from the bus stop to catch new episodes. Two feature films and a '90s television redo (starring *Chariots of Fire*'s Ben Cross) did little to turn this freak of TV history into a franchise. See also SOAP OPERAS, DAYTIME.

DATING SHOWS Dating is one of life's most awkward, stressful experiences. That's why dating shows make great, addictive television. In the olden days, *The Dating Game* gave us a God's-eye view of a matchup in the making. Later, *Love Connection* brought fixed-up couples back to the studio for a recap of their adventures. Now, thanks to shows such as *Blind Date*, *Elimidate*, *Star Dates*, and *Taildaters*, fans see everything— from arguments over where to eat all the way to that first dip in the hot tub. Shows like *The Bachelor* and *Married by America* even attempt to take things to their logical conclusion by guiding contestants to the altar. That may be overreaching, but we still can't resist tuning in. Maybe it's because the urge to find true love is as universal as our joy at watching others fall on their faces pursuing it. See also *NEWLYWED GAME, THE* and REALITY SHOWS.

DAY, DORIS The former Doris Kappelhoff was never billed as one of cinema's finest actors, which is okay by us. If we want to gunk up the movie-watching experience with sophisticated plots and well-developed characters, we'll rent *Citizen Kane*. When we're in the mood for a happy sing-along (*Lullaby of Broadway*), a formulaic romance (*Pillow Talk*), or a cute flick about a small-town girl who brings out the good in people (*It's a Great Feeling*, *My Dream Is Yours*, *Young at Heart*), then it's off to the Technicolor Classics aisle we go, twirling our dirndl skirt all the way. From 1948 to 1968, Day served as Hollywood's girl next door, flashing her Colgate smile at leading men ranging from Rock Hudson to Ronald Reagan. Then she *que sera sera*-ed her way into TV Land by starring in 128 episodes of the CBS sitcom *The Doris Day Show*. Fans might be surprised to know, however, that the star of *The Pajama Game* wasn't all peaches and cream. In her early days she melted microphones as one of the most sultry swing band vocalists on the circuit, prompting Oscar Levant to famously note, "I knew Doris Day before she was a virgin."

DAYS OF OUR LIVES The fictitious Midwestern town of Salem has grown significantly since its creators dreamed it

< 69 >

up in 1965. Residents of the once-sleepy burg now enjoy the comfort and convenience of an advanced teaching hospital and international airport as they go about their daily business of switching babies, exorcising evil spirits, getting lobotomies, and undergoing extensive plastic surgeries that somehow turn them into completely different people. In spite of all the changes, one thing remains the same. The dulcet voice of the late Macdonald Carey (Salem's fatherly Dr. Tom Horton) still opens the show with the often-imitated "Like sands through the hourglass . . . so are the days of our lives." It sends a sentimental chill down our spines every time. See also GENERAL HOSPITAL; SOAP OPERA DIGEST; SOAP OPERAS, DAYTIME; and SOAP OPERAS, NIGHTTIME.

DAYTIME TALK SHOWS See DR. PHIL; OPRAH; and SPRINGER, JERRY.

DEATH RACE 2000 This 1975 drive-in classic is one of cut-rate movie producer Roger Corman's greatest triumphs—if you can call a film about a cross-country race in which the participants get points for running over pedestrians (40 for teens; 70 for children under 12; and 100 for oldsters over 75) a triumph. Still, there are reasons why this flick remains a video store staple. There are plenty of car wrecks, plenty of breasts, plenty of campy humor, and, perhaps best of all, a very young Sylvester Stallone chewing up the scenery (and running down bystanders) as car driver Machine Gun Joe Viterbo. It was followed by a sequel called *Deathsport*, which sucked, and a video game called Death Race, which ruled. See also CORMAN, ROGER and STALLONE, SYLVESTER.

DEATH SONGS The first time you hear "Billy, Don't Be a Hero," you are justified in listening to the bitter end to find out if that darn fool *does* go out and try to be a hero, losing his life in the process. (Spoiler: He does.) The same morbid curiosity can lead you, once, through "Leader of the Pack" (protagonist killed in motorcycle accident); "Teen Angel" (train-car accident); "Ebony Eyes" (plane crash); "Tell Laura I Love Her" (racing mishap); "Patches" (suicide, with another foreshadowed at song's end); "Tom Dooley" (murder and, soon, execution); and "Seasons in the Sun" (dying singer). But when you listen *repeatedly* to such tunes, knowing how things turn out, it might be time for counseling. Especially if you groove on the ballad "Timothy" (young man murdered and *eaten by his work associates*). See also "ESCAPE (THE PIÑA COLADA SONG)."

DEATH WISH When three punks (one played by a very young, very miscast

< 70 >

Jeff Goldblum) assault the wife and daughter of a businessman (Charles Bronson), you pretty much know, based on watching a thousand other vigilante films, what will happen next. Except that when this movie was released in 1974, the idea of taking the law into one's own hands was still taboo. Hard as it is to believe, many viewers were shocked and unnerved when Bronson switched into Payback mode, whipped out a gun, and started capping people. These days *Death Wish* is still shocking, but in a guilty way. The icky feeling comes from realizing that absolutely *nothing* about Bronson's behavior seems strange anymore. Now it's just standard action movie fare. See also RAMBO MOVIES and SCHWARZENEGGER, ARNOLD.

DEMOLITION DERBY In the real world we spend a great deal of time keeping our cars in top shape and avoiding accidents. So it's no wonder we take perverse pleasure in a "sport" built around the idea of smashing those sacrosanct vehicles into scrap. Basing the concept on another guilty pleasure (namely, that people go to legit auto races just to see crashes), stock car driver Larry Mendelsohn is credited with staging the first demolition derby, at Long Island's Islip Raceway in 1958. It became a national sensation after ABC's *Wide World of Sports* started broadcasting competitions in 1962 and has been a cornerstone of state fairs ever since, reaching an even wider audience when it became a key component in *Happy Days'* fourth season three-part "Fonzie Loves Pinky" episodes. In it, the Fonz famously competed against the notorious Mallachi brothers (hence the "Mallachi Crunch" in wheel-to-wheel action). See also ABC's *WIDE WORLD OF SPORTS* and *HAPPY DAYS*.

DEMONIC CHILDREN (MOVIES ABOUT) Kids can be devils. The little hellions ruin restaurant outings, annoy us at the movies, and turn visits to carnivals into the Bataan death march. Yet not since W. C. Fields was in his prime could we publicly admit that we'd like to see the Garanimals-wearing miscreants get theirs—big time. Which is where this guilty pleasure comes in. As long as we know, for example, that young Damien in *The Omen* is truly the son of Satan (who else would knock Lee Remick off that balcony ladder), then it's okay to cheer for those who want to clean his clock. It's also okay to scream for blood in *It's Alive* and *The Bad Seed*. But you might want to curb your enthusiasm during *Home Alone*. See also BLAIR, LINDA.

DENNY'S GRAND SLAM BREAKFAST A more truthful name for this morning tradition might be the Heart Stopper or the Gut Expander. Still, even though the

< 71 >

Original Grand Slam (two pancakes, two eggs, two bacon strips, two sausage links) weighs in at 665 calories and 49 grams of fat, there's no denying that it makes a first-rate morning pig-  out—arteries be damned. Plus, there are worse things to eat. For instance, the Farmer's Slam, loaded with 1,200 calories and a near-inconceivable 80 grams of fat.

DENVER, JOHN Is it possible for someone to be *too* nice? Perhaps, if that person is singer/songwriter John Denver. Born Henry John Deutschendorf Jr., in Roswell, New Mexico, he was an Air Force brat who spent his youth shuttling from base to base. His first early '70s hit, "Take Me Home, Country Roads," set the template for every tune to follow. It was a simplistic, naive song that was nevertheless as relaxing as a Valium with a white wine chaser. In an age that questioned authority and mocked convention, Denver was a looking-on-the-bright-side kind of guy who preferred to sing about highs rather than lows (a proclivity that spilled into his film and TV work, which included the hit flick *Oh, God!* plus TV appearances with the Muppets). Apparently lots of people saw

things the same way. *John Denver's Greatest Hits* has sold more than 10 million copies and can be found (no doubt carefully hidden) in the collections of many a highbrow Music Nazi. See also CARPENTERS, THE and *MUPPET SHOW, THE*.

DEYOUNG, DENNIS See STYX.

DIAMOND, NEIL Often lumped in with Tom Jones, Engelbert Humperdinck, and other sideburned soloists of the '60s and '70s, Neil Diamond stands out as both a songwriter and an entertainer. His early hits, such as "Solitary Man," "Cracklin' Rosie," and especially "Sweet Caroline," can still spark spontaneous sing-alongs. Just try the latter at any karaoke bar and listen to the crowd join in on the "bohm, bohm, bohms." He's also earned respectability with the roots rock crowd (yes, that's him in the legendary rock film *The Last Waltz*, about the farewell concert of The Band). The Vegas crew loves him, too, in part for his willingness to don sequined duds. And fans of light rock appreciate his string of late '70s hits, including his "You Don't Bring Me Flowers" duet with Barbra Streisand. Of course, if you say you actually liked 1980's *The Jazz Singer* (Diamond's attempt to cross over into acting), then you've taken idolatry a little too far. See also HUMPERDINCK, ENGELBERT; JON-

< 72 >

ATHAN LIVINGSTON SEAGULL; JONES, TOM; KARAOKE; and STREISAND, BARBRA (AS SINGER).

DIANAMANIA Media analysts have called it morbid, exploitive, and an out-of-control, merchandise-driven myth machine. But the truth of the matter is that *everybody* remembers what they were doing when they heard about Princess Diana's fatal 1997 encounter with pillar 13 of the Pont de l'Alma underpass in Paris. A 2002 History Channel poll revealed that Brits considered Di's death to be their nation's most historic 20th-century moment, edging out World War II. The sentiment is almost as strong on this side of the pond, where the princess's face launched thousands of magazine covers and fans of the royal towhead fill their bookshelves with sappy requiems such as *Diana: The People's Princess* and *Diana: The Lonely Princess*—as well as a few juicy tell-alls, such as Windsor insider Lady Colin Campbell's *The Real Diana*. We can't seem to get enough of this story, with its tragic heroine and an entire cast of bad guys—the paparazzi, the icy mother-in-law, and the cheating husband. Years from now, long after we've put away our "Shy Di" commemorative plates and Dodi Fayed is but a line on a Trivial Pursuit game card, we'll probably still get a little misty during the piano interludes of "Candle in the Wind." See also BRITISH ROYAL FAMILY, THE; and QUEEN OF ENGLAND, THE.

DICK CLARK'S NEW YEAR'S ROCKIN' EVE The turning of the year is traditionally a time for celebration. So why, for going on four decades, have millions of Americans celebrated it with a creepy little ex-deejay? Back in the early '70s, when Dick Clark went up against Guy Lombardo and his big band for the hearts and minds of homebound New Year's Eve revelers, he was already being compared to Oscar Wilde's fictional character Dorian Gray, a guy who never aged. Gray had a cursed portrait in a closet that got old for him. Clark's got, well, maybe it's his multimillion-dollar TV/restaurant/blooper empire that keeps him young. Each year the ball drops on Times Square and each year Clark, looking ever more incongruous, presents the likes of Busta Rhymes, Pink, Kiss, and whomever else his company can round up and keep sober until midnight. Admitting you watched all this is tantamount to admitting you aren't the party person you once were. See also *AMERICAN BANDSTAND* and BLOOPERS.

DIETS, FAD In our heart of hearts, we know that permanent weight loss can only be accomplished by eating sensibly and exercising wisely. But we also know,

< 73 >

in our heart of hearts, that if that sort of thing held any appeal we wouldn't be wearing size 44 Dockers right now. So we try fads. One year it's the grapefruit diet. The next it's the Hollywood diet. Then Jared tries to convince us to eat Subway sandwiches for lunch and dinner. Of course most people embark on these programs with the best of nonguilty-pleasure intentions. The guilt comes later, when we realize we've spent a month eating nothing but (fill in the blank), only to lose perhaps five pounds—pounds we regained, with interest, when we ordered a double-cheese pizza to celebrate the end of the diet.

DILLY BARS   See DAIRY QUEEN.

DINNER THEATERS   Somehow, an amateur production of *Hello, Dolly!* goes down better with overcooked roast beef and a basket of dinner rolls. But for God's sake, don't take someone here on a first date.

DIRTY DANCING   Set in 1963, this chick flick extraordinaire unfolds as 17-year-old Baby (Jennifer Grey, pre-rhino-plasty) vacations with her family at a hokey Catskills resort. Bright, innocent, and bored with the organized activities, Baby finds her way into the staff quarters, where she witnesses some pre-

Lambada bump-and-grind dancing and gains a whole new appreciation for the resort's amenities—especially its hunky dance instructor, Johnny (Patrick Swayze). He teaches her some new dance moves (including the horizontal mambo), but mis-understandings ensue when Baby's father (pre–*Law & Order* Jerry Orbach) accuses Johnny of knocking up his

dance partner. Of course Baby and her beau inevitably merengue their way out of trouble. Seeing this 1987 box-office hit on the big screen is understandable; watching it on home video during every dateless Friday night is a sign that you need help. See also CHICK FLICKS (CIN-DERELLA FANTASIES) and LAMBADA, THE.

DISASTERS (MOVIES ABOUT)   See ALLEN, IRWIN.

DISEASE AS A PLOT DEVICE   See CHICK FLICKS (IN WHICH SOMEONE DIES); *LOVE STORY*; and TV MOVIES.

DISCO (DANCING)   There's one at every wedding reception. Somewhere on the crowded dance floor, he straightens the collar of his silk shirt, pops a polyester hip, and raises an index finger to the strobe-lit heavens in homage to that

< 74 >

single Travolta moment that defined an entire era. And while you're watching in judgment, you're also feeling the urge to get out on the floor yourself, even if you've long since retired your Brothers Gibb outfit.

Before the Macarena, before hip-hop, before video killed the radio star, there was disco and its delicate tango of foot swivels, cross-steps, and Tony Manero bravado. Not that *Saturday Night Fever* started it all. Far from it. Before that 1977 blockbuster came along, the Bee Gees were harmonizing "More Than a Woman," Shirley & Company was scolding "Shame, Shame, Shame," Van McCoy was doing "The Hustle," and Diana Ross was suffering from a "Love Hangover." *SNF* didn't start a trend. It just told the folks in Omaha that one was going on.

The craze began to fade around 1981. Yet decades later, clubbers still pull out a few of the signature moves when they're feeling retro—proof that the dance craze that bankrolled ABBA *and* the gold lamé industry has survived. And why wouldn't it? Did you think it would crumble? Did you think it would lay down and die? See also ABBA; DISCO (FASHIONS); *SATURDAY NIGHT FEVER*; and *SATURDAY NIGHT FEVER* (SOUNDTRACK).

DISCO (FASHIONS) Back in the day—when a man's worth was measured by the width of his collar—the dance floor dress code tipped quite clearly toward ostentation. Six-inch heels, glittery blouses, and plunging necklines were de rigueur—and then there were the *women's* fashions. On any bare-shouldered diva who ever kissed Deney Terrio at the end of *Dance Fever*, a strappy Gucci pump with inlaid rhinestones was no mere shoe but an extension of her body. Is it any wonder that a new generation of Gloria Gaynors has adopted the sequined halter as the standard issue for dancing 'til dawn (followed by the mortifying Sunday morning "walk of shame")? Or that every year around Halloween, resale shops see a huge run on pimp daddy wide-brimmed hats? No denying it: A white polyester suit over a patterned "burn baby burn" rayon shirt is a surefire conversation starter. Does it matter if the conversation is behind your back? See also ABBA; DISCO (DANCING); HALLOWEEN (ADULT CELEBRATION OF); *SATURDAY NIGHT FEVER*; and *SATURDAY NIGHT FEVER* (SOUNDTRACK).

DISNEY FILMS FEATURING DEAN JONES AND/OR KURT RUSSELL The folks at Walt Disney Studios are justly celebrated for the brilliance of their animated works. But not every flick that comes out of the Mouse House features an adorable rodent, sea creature, or jungle dweller. Many feature actual human beings,

< 75 >

and two of those actual human beings are Dean Jones and Kurt Russell. Jones's distinguished Disney career includes appearances in *Blackbeard's Ghost*, *The Ugly Dachshund*, *That Darn Cat!* and (his crowning achievement) *The Love Bug*. Russell, on the other hand, launched his career playing scrappy guys in *The One and Only*, *Genuine, Original Family Band* and *Now You See Him, Now You Don't*, before going on to semi-macho star status and fame as Goldie Hawn's arm piece.

True connoisseurs of live-action Disney, though, understand that Russell's *The Barefoot Executive* is not only a great movie, but a media satire that rivals *Network*. Just don't say that in your film studies class. Note: Jones and Russell appeared together in *The Horse in the Gray Flannel Suit*. See also *ABC AFTERSCHOOL SPECIALS*.

DOCTOR WHO Everyone makes fun of *Star Trek* geeks, but Trekkies save their furtive looks and sarcastic snickers for fans of *Doctor Who*, a British science-fiction series that's appeared in various forms on the BBC (and around the world in syndication) since 1963. Basically the story of a time-traveling alien whose ship resembles a police call station, its plots are sadistically hard to follow, with nonexistent action and special effects that look like something George Lucas did in his backyard at age 10. The series petered out in 1990, though in 1996 Fox tried to Americanize the franchise with an unsuccessful *Doctor Who* TV movie. None of this has stopped *Who* fans from forming clubs and holding conventions, far from the sneers and snide comments of the Trekkies. They think they're so *cool*. See also *STAR TREK*.

DODGE BALL The most Darwinian, and politically incorrect, of all gym-class activities was only considered a guilty pleasure by those with strong throwing arms. Participants divided into teams and hurled balls (sometimes soccer balls and occasionally even softballs) at their opponents. Get hit and you had to quit. The action continued until one side was entirely knocked out—or until some unlucky player was so entirely knocked out that he had to be carried to the nurse's office.

In recent years schools across the nation have banned the game—also known, tellingly, as murder ball. Not that this has dampened its popularity among certain segments of adult society. In the western Chicago suburb of Schaumburg, Illinois, the National Amateur Dodge Ball Association (NADA) holds summer and winter tournaments. Ex-gym-class bullies, mark your calendars. See also *LAWN DARTS*.

< 76 >

DOG POOP (FAKE) Cousin to fake vomit, artificial dog poop is offered in nearly as many varieties as the real thing, including a pretzel-like twist, a comma-shaped log, and a moist, splatty mess. A mainstay in gag shops for generations, it's even available in a gift box—in case you want to test whether your hope-to-be fiancée will put up with your nonsense till death do you part. But just because you get someone to fall for this trick doesn't mean that you're the next Allen Funt. Or that he or she isn't going to get you back, when you least expect it, with some fake vomit. See also *CANDID CAMERA* and VOMIT (FAKE).

DOG SHOWS What could be more pointless and absurd than a beauty pageant? How about a beauty pageant for dogs? That, essentially, is the nature of dog shows. Staged since the mid-19th century and including such internationally renowned events as New York's Westminster Dog Show, they celebrate not the intelligence, fortitude, and loyalty of canines, but rather how closely they adhere to a long list of technical parameters dreamed up for each particular breed. It's as if Miss America contestants were all herded onstage, weighed, measured, felt up, made to run in circles, and then judged. At least the dogs in these competitions (unlike the majority of the Miss America contest-ants) haven't the vaguest idea what's going on. As far as they're concerned, they're just being led around in circles by humorless women with thick ankles.

DOLLAR STORES The old saw "You get what you pay for" doesn't resonate with the hordes of happy shoppers who, like guys at strip clubs, understand the value of an old-fashioned dollar bill. These are the folks who keep off-brand dollar stores—including Family Dollar and 99 Cents Only, to name just two—not only alive but thriving. Whether it's a sub-sub-Barbie doll or a box of Cheerios with Arabic on the back, the aisles of these stores are packed with bargains. Provided your definition of "bargain" is a very relaxed one. Shopping here can be productive and even fun, in a wow-I-would-have-paid-$1.59-at-the-super-market-for-that-giant-bag-of-Twizzlers kind of way. But you'd best leave your pride in the parking lot.

DOLPHIN SHOWS See SEAWORLD.

DONNY AND MARIE She's a little bit country. He's a little bit rock and roll. We're a little bit nauseous. Yet for some reason we kept watching. The *Donny and Marie* show (1976 to 1979) was developed out of a co-hosting gig the magnificent Mormons did on *The Mike Douglas Show*. ABC chief Fred Silver-

< 77 >

man caught their act and offered it to producers Sid and Marty Krofft, who were at the time known only for oddball kiddy shows such as *H. R. Pufnstuf* and *Land of the Lost*. The duo  applied more than a little of that off-kilter sensibility to the Osmond siblings, creating some of the strangest moments in the history of the variety show, and rivaling anything seen on that *other* Krofft project, *The Brady Bunch Hour*. There were ice-skating segments. There was Marie punching Donny in the stomach. There were musical perform-ances by Andy Gibb, Tina Turner, and Kate Smith. There was Donny being thrown into a 96-gallon cream pie. There was a musical spoof of *Star Wars* featuring Kris Kristofferson (as Han Solo) and Redd Fox (as Obi Wan) with Chewbacca and the actual movie droids joining in the fun. And there was Marie punching Donny in the stomach. What's not to love? See also *BRADY BUNCH, THE*; KROFFT, SID AND MARTY; *LAND OF THE LOST*; and VARIETY SHOWS.

DOOM Where once video games were merely mindless fun, Doom ushered in the era of mindless mayhem. The point of this most popular of all "first-person shooter" games isn't to negotiate mazes or run races or gather tokens. It's to kill things. Lots of things. And not just with a gun, but with rocket launchers, laser cannons, even a chainsaw. When is it over? When everything else is dead and you aren't. Not surprisingly, one doesn't see Doom consoles at video arcades. Like watching pornography, this isn't the sort of activity you want to do in public. Still, the game, released in 1993 and developed by id Software, does have a certain sick appeal. After a hard day of kissing ass at the office, there's some-thing cathartic about firing up the PC and blowing away a few dozen (or a few hundred) computerized adversaries. Who knows? Maybe Doom has actually kept someone, somewhere, from climb-ing a water tower. See also VIDEO GAMES.

DOUGHNUTS See DUNKIN' DONUTS and KRISPY KREME DOUGHNUTS.

DR. DEMENTO As a teenager, boasting that you listen to the Dr. Demento radio show is tantamount to bragging about being a D&D dungeon master or presi-dent of your local chapter of the *Saved by the Bell* Appreciation Society. You might as well write "geek" on your fore-head—or just wait for someone at school to do it for you. After all, listening to Dr. Demento (real name, Barret Hansen),

< 78 >

who has spun novelty song after novelty song since 1970, implies that you've suffered through multiple listenings of "Fish Heads," and that you actually care when the next Weird Al Yankovic album will be released. See also DUNGEONS AND DRAGONS; *SAVED BY THE BELL*; and YANKOVIC, WEIRD AL.

DR. LAURA Ever since she started syndicating her radio show and reaching a national audience in 1994, huge audiences have been attracted to Dr. Laura Schlessinger's particular brand of tough love, whether she's telling a career woman to go home and take care of her kids, scolding a couple for shacking up, or writing about the *Stupid Things Parents Do to Mess Up Their Kids*. It's understandable why dysfunctional folks listen to her show and purchase her books, but why is she so compelling to those who *don't* buy into her conservative, anti-gay-rights, anti-day-care, anti-premarital-sex agenda? Could it be that we listen out of an honest desire to have our convictions tested? Or, more likely, is tuning in to Dr. Laura a sign of a masochistic need for a good (verbal) whipping for our transgressions? See also CONSERVATIVE RADIO TALK SHOWS.

DR. PHIL We've got problems. But rather than work them out ourselves or pay for a face-to-face encounter with a licensed psychologist or psychiatrist, we do what most other Americans do: turn to the media for guidance. And as the new millennium began, no electronic counselor was more sought after than Dr. Phil. A human spin-off from *The Oprah Winfrey Show*, Dr. Phillip C. McGraw proved that Americans were so in need of help that they would gladly turn to a bald know-it-all initially known for running a litigation consulting firm called Courtroom Sciences, Inc. Winfrey "discovered" him when she needed help lining up just the right jurists after Texas cattlemen sued her for bad-mouthing the meat industry. Since then, Dr. Phil has topped the best-seller lists, scored big with his own daytime show, and caused many a lame comic to note his similarity to *The Larry Sanders Show* sidekick Hank Kingsley. All of which ignores the fact that when Dr. Phil talks, we listen. See also DR. LAURA and OPRAH.

DRAGNET He was a nerdy-looking guy with a buzz cut and a monotone voice. But you didn't want to mess with Joe Friday—or miss his show, for that matter. A radio staple from 1949 to 1957 and a TV fixture from 1952 to 1959 and again from 1967 to 1970, *Dragnet* (and Jack Webb, as the LAPD gumshoe) set the template for the never-crack-a-smile police procedural—a tradition carried on

< 79 >

today by the *Law & Order* franchise, the creator of which also revived *Dragnet* in 2003. The show, just as its voice-of-God announcer claimed each week, was based on true cases. Interestingly, though Webb's famous tag line became "Just the facts, ma'am," he never really said this on the air (his actual phrase was "All we want are the facts, ma'am"). True fans never speak of the 1987 big-screen *Dragnet* parody starring Dan Aykroyd and Tom Hanks.

DREW, NANCY The gimmick of a "girl detective" may now seem passé, but it was fresh as a still-warm corpse when the first Nancy Drew mystery novel debuted in 1930. Authored by a series of ghostwriters, the books (almost 200 to date) maintained their audience even as the concept became ever more shop-worn. Over the years there have been Nancy Drew movies, two Nancy Drew TV shows, even *The Nancy Drew Cookbook: Clues to Good Cooking*. And of course, the novels (which seem to make inordinate use of such props as secret panels and spooky houses) just keep coming. See also HARDY BOYS, THE.

DRUDGE REPORT, THE The big winner in the Bill Clinton/Monica Lewinsky debacle was Matt Drudge, a CBS gift shop manager who, in 1994, decided it would be neat to relay gossip via the Internet. Featuring little more than a handful of Drudge-reported stories, a few headlines from other Web sites, and a long list of links to editorial writers and columnists, the *Drudge Report* now attracts more than a billion hits each year from short-attention-span newshounds and scandal seekers too cool to be seen buying a *National Enquirer*. See also NATIONAL ENQUIRER, THE.

DRUGSTORE PERFUMES You can find them parked together on one neglected stretch of shelf, like some sort of olfactory scrapbook: Tabu, Charlie, Emeraude, Jean Naté, Love's Baby Soft, Wind Song, Skin Musk, and Jōvan Musk. Reeking of SD Alcohol 40 and citrus, some smell more like furniture polish than perfumes. Others remain as cloyingly sweet and floral as when your big sister fogged her bedroom with them to mask the equally fragrant bouquet of her best high school buddy, Mary J. Uana. But though cheap  and cheap-smelling, they nevertheless retain a pungent place in the toiletries section of our hearts. Perhaps one of them was the first grown-up Christmas present you bought your mom or the gift set you purchased for your fourth-grade teacher. Or maybe they remind you of the time you and your friends went nuts

< 80 >

with the tester bottles, exiting the store smelling like French whores and as flammable as Molotov cocktails. Chances are that, whatever the memory, the scent that stirred it is still on sale for less than $15 a bottle. See also IMPOSTOR PERFUMES and MARIJUANA.

DUMB & DUMBER Jokes about bowel movements are funny. Jokes at the expense of the handicapped are funny. And jokes about being stupid are the funniest of all. That's the mind-set behind this 1994 Jim Carrey vehicle, often hailed (though rarely in public) as the greatest movie ever made about idiots on a cross-country journey (a surprisingly large category, if you stop and think about it). It's also, arguably, the pinnacle of Carrey's career—not the Jim Carrey who wants to be a serious actor, but the Jim Carrey who wants to swing from street lamps and use his butt as a ventriloquist's dummy. See also CARREY, JIM; JOKES, DIRTY; and JOKES, SICK.

DUNGEONS AND DRAGONS Developed in 1973, this mother of all role-playing games is basically a complex computer simulation that doesn't use a computer. Players become fantasy characters such as wizards and dwarves, equipped with varying degrees of intellect, strength, and skill based on values assigned them by rolls of dice. The players then go on "adventures" that exist only in the mind's eye, guided by a "dungeon master"—an all-powerful, all-knowing player who serves as the game's controller. For a while during the '80s D&D was so popular that parents, fearing the game was an occult plot, formed groups to combat it. A very young Tom Hanks even starred in a TV movie warning of its dangers. Those concerned parents needn't have been so worried, because D&D was a threat to nothing but one's social standing. Getting good required endless hours spent studying manuals and boning up on the latest strategies—as opposed to, say, hanging out with friends, meeting members of the opposite sex, or even walking around in the fresh air. For obvious reasons, the advent of computer gaming put a huge dent in D&D. Why waste your life hunched over a bunch of dice when you can waste it as God intended: Hunched over a computer screen? See also *LORD OF THE RINGS, THE* and VIDEO GAMES.

DUNKIN' DONUTS You can keep your fancy scones, lattes, and bagels with schmear. Sometimes our breakfast jones can only be satisfied by visiting Dunkin' Donuts, the store that's been cranking out doughy gut bombs nonstop since founder William Rosenberg opened the first one near Boston in 1950. Sure, you can order things like breakfast sand-

< 81 >

wiches and frozen coffee drinks, but the mainstay is still big cups of steaming, fresh-brewed joe—the better to go with Cinnamon Cake Sticks (450 calories each) and Apple Crumb Donuts (230 calories). This is definitely your father's donut shop—especially if your father is a cop. See also KRISPY KREME DOUGHNUTS.

DURAN DURAN See EIGHTIES NOSTALGIA RADIO STATIONS.

DYNASTY For nine seasons spanning the 1980s, television viewers from as far afield as Serbia followed Aaron Spelling's decadent nighttime soap opera about a dysfunctional Colorado oil family that put the "filthy" in "filthy rich." Bribery, extortion, seduction, cat fights, and diamond-studded functions were regular occurrences in the Carrington household. Though the cast chewed the scenery so voraciously that some episodes bordered on comedy, the series nevertheless won a Golden Globe Award in 1984 and a People's Choice Award in 1985. It also managed to secure guest appearances by Gerald Ford, Henry Kissinger, and a list of actors who should have known better, including Ali MacGraw, Charlton Heston, and the late Rock Hudson, whose on-screen kiss with *Dynasty* principal Linda Evans caused a tabloid stir in the early days of AIDS awareness. In too deep to turn back, we followed the story line through every ridiculous plot twist until the writing team's literary cop-outs (UFO abduction! Miracle recovery! Plastic surgery! *More* plastic surgery!) collapsed under their own weight at episode 218. It has been suggested that the gimme-gimme economic climate of the '80s made *Dynasty's* fantasy world particularly appealing to the 250 million average Joans who watched each Wednesday-night episode. If so, bless the Carringtons for bringing us all together, if only to show us that having money out the wazoo does have its downside. See also, COLLINS, JOAN; GOLDEN GLOBES; HESTON, CHARLTON; PEOPLE'S CHOICE AWARDS, THE; and SOAP OPERAS, NIGHTTIME.

< 82 >

E

ages get, say, a few bucks off the Salisbury steak and the opportunity to get home by 7:00 . . . just in time for reruns of *Matlock* or *The Golden Girls*.

E! TRUE HOLLYWOOD STORY Like its music business mirror image, VH1's *Behind the Music*, the *E! True Hollywood Story* combines vintage clips, current interviews, and brilliantly written "stay tuned" teasers to get you past the commercials to the next segment's revelations. Sometimes the show looks at major stars (Elvis, Steve McQueen); other times at actors on the fringe (Traci Lords, Hervé Villechaize). Increasingly, it broadens its format by treating television shows and movies as subjects (*The Young and the Restless*, *Billy Jack*). Compellingly constructed, these documentaries should win special Emmy Awards just for their ability to get us to care about the career ups and downs of Gallagher, Brigitte Nielsen, and the cast of *Growing Pains*. See also *BILLY JACK*; *FANTASY ISLAND*; GALLAGHER; PRESLEY, ELVIS; and VH1'S *BEHIND THE MUSIC*.

EARLY-BIRD SPECIALS Jokingly written off as the meal plan for geriatrics who can barely see over their steering wheels, early-bird specials were designed by savvy restaurateurs to generate pre-6 P.M. business. Rather than catching the worm, early birds of all

EBAY This online auction service calls itself a "grand experiment in Internet commerce." Others (particularly those who spend hours placing bids for things like Smurf Pez dispensers and *Land of the Giants* lunch boxes) think of it as a grand experiment in testing the limits of obsession. It begins innocently enough. Newbies sign on and explore the site. Then they give themselves a cute user ID such as AuctionPowers or Bidder-Woman. Then they put together a "watch list" of items they covet, win a few bids, lose a few bids, develop a strategy, and then another strategy. Pretty soon they can't even walk by their computers without typing in a quick search for "vintage Levis" or "Fisher Price Little People." Within days, the world slips away, and all that matters is their keyboard, their mouse, and their PayPal account. Founded in 1995 by former software developer (and current billionaire) Pierre Omidyar, the San Jose, California-based company has reeled in more than 50 million such cyber scavengers, all clicking away at an array of items broken down into thousands of categories. To understand eBay's iron grip on e-commerce, consider that more than 100 Barbie dolls

< 83 >

are sold on the site *every hour*. It's no exaggeration to say that you can buy anything on eBay. Some of us have tried. See also LUNCH BOXES and PEZ.

EIGHTIES NOSTALGIA RADIO STATIONS Remember how you razzed your parents for listening to music that was decades out of date? Well, the wheel has turned. MTV's first generation has spun the dial and discovered, just as Mom and Dad did, that there's nothing good on the radio anymore. That is, if you define "good" as songs that conjure up sweet memories of one's fading youth. Programmers were quick to cater to these New Fogies by dusting off the Duran Duran, Mötley Crüe, and Big Country, and giving them their own radio stations—stations where Reagan is still president, leg warmers are still cool, and Live Aid is the greatest concert ever.

ELECTRA, CARMEN See *BAYWATCH*.

ELECTRIC SLIDE Born after the release of reggae legend Marcia Griffiths' 1982 song "Electric Boogie," the Electric Slide dance craze served a deep cultural need: It got everyone, talented or not, drunk

or sober, onto the dance floor. Unlike the showboating moves of disco and swing dancing, the Slide, like its let's-all-do-the-same-thing brethren (the chicken dance, the Achy-Breaky, et al.), can be handled with roughly the same degree of expertise by children, senior citizens, and everyone in between. The magic of the Electric Slide is that even if you are dragged onto the dance floor, you truly believe for a moment—after the fourth or fifth flub-free turn—that you can actually dance. *That's* when you bowl over your cousin. See also LINE DANCING.

ELVIRA, MISTRESS OF THE DARK In the pre-infomercial days, stations aired just about anything during low-ratings time periods. That's why horror movies became a staple of weekend daytime and late-night television, with some programmers sweetening the cauldron by adding local hosts or hostesses. The leader of the pack was Cassandra Peterson, who, in 1981, started wearing big hair and low necklines to become Elvira, Mistress of the Dark, on L.A.'s KHJ-TV. Her series, *Movie Macabre*, was soon syndicated nationally and Peterson became a cult star—appearing, among other places, on MTV Halloween specials, in beer commercials, in her own self-titled flick, and on a pinball machine. Perhaps her most enduring legacy is the annual rush on black dresses and

< 84 >

fright wigs come Halloween. See also HALLOWEEN (ADULT CELEBRATION OF).

ELVIS See PRESLEY, ELVIS.

ELVIS IMPERSONATORS They come in all shapes, sizes, and personalities. But they all have one thing in common: They aren't Elvis. They aren't even close. Such acts are a joke in the entertainment industry, but judging from their popularity there's still a large audience pining for an evening with a man (and, occasionally, woman) who would be King. But the truly creepy, kitschy part is that lots of impersonators don't just want to make money. They want to bring people closer to the spirit of Elvis by (they keenly hope) channeling some of his Burning Love. How many impersonators are there? Let's just say that on the August 16 anniversary of Elvis's death, Graceland is always surrounded by jumpsuited, sequined, sideburned acolytes. See also PRESLEY, ELVIS.

EMMANUELLE (MOVIES FEATURING THE CHARACTER OF) Many an early cable TV aficionado was introduced to the world of soft-core porn courtesy of the Emmanuelle movies—a long-running series of French films concerning a liberated woman who roams the world spouting fuzzy free love philosophy while freely loving pretty much every-

one she encounters. The scripts are peculiar, the sex scenes brief, and the sequels so numerous, and with so many different actresses, that it's a wonder they haven't done an *Abbott and Costello Meet Emmanuelle* (which, by the way, we would gladly pay to see). Frankly, the only reason so many people are familiar with these films is because the pay cable services showed them relentlessly back in the '80s. The best of the bunch star minor-league sex goddess Sylvia Kristel, who also appeared in the classic boy-losing-his-virginity flick *Private Lessons* (1981). See also ABBOTT AND COSTELLO; GUYS LOSING THEIR VIRGINITY (MOVIES ABOUT); and MOVIES (PORNOGRAPHIC).

END-OF-THE-WORLD MOVIES If everyone in the world was annihilated except for you and a handful of other folks, there would be a fair amount of tears, ennui by the bucketful, and a stink to end all stinks. But in the movies, where the last people on Earth might be played by Harry Belafonte (*The World, the Flesh, and the Devil*), Charlton Heston (*The Omega Man*), or Ray Milland (*Panic in the Year Zero*), being around for the endgame can be a thrilling adventure. A subgenre of science fiction, end-of-the-world flicks tap our desire to be left alone and take it to its ultimate extreme. Plus, such movies save money by eliminating walk-ons and extras. But if you're

< 85 >

a director, there's always the danger of being handed a page of script that reads, "Times Square at noon. Absolutely no one is on the streets." See also HESTON, CHARLTON.

ENTERTAINMENT TONIGHT There's a blurry line these days between "news" and "entertainment news." Much of the credit/blame goes to *Entertainment Tonight*. Its 1981 launch (original host: Army Archerd) changed the course of television history by using the evening news format—complete with field reporters, exclusives, and breaking events—to serve up celebrity pap. It treated fan magazine fluff as serious journalism and made an art out of lobbing softball questions at everyone from Morgan Fairchild to Madonna. The cultural downside? Not only did the show launch the blighted careers of Leeza Gibbons and John Tesh, its popularity also convinced news producers nationwide that what America really wanted wasn't politics and world events, but a behind-the-scenes chat with Ted Danson from TV's *Becker*. And as ratings prove every day, they were correct. See also HART, MARY and TESH, JOHN.

ENYA Connoisseurs of New Age music will point out the sonic incorrectness of listening to just *one* Enya song (namely her 1989 hit "Orinoco Flow," played ad nauseam at dentists' offices) instead of pulling up a butterfly chair and enjoying a nice, leisurely repast of the Gaelic warbler's entire album from start to finish. Maybe we'll try that some time, even if it does sound a bit like crunching through the whole Oreo cookie when all you want is the cream filling. For now, we just really like that "sail away, sail away, sail away" part, which goes to show that there's a lot we don't know about Eithne Ni Bhraonain—including what she's saying in most of her songs. Then again, does it really matter? Aren't you supposed to shut down your cerebellum and let your mind take a happy elevator ride when you slide *Watermark* or *A Day Without Rain* into the CD player? Sail away, sail away, sail away. It's Muzak to our ears.

"ESCAPE (THE PIÑA COLADA SONG)" Girl writes lonely hearts letter. Guy answers letter without realizing that the two of them already know each other. This timeworn plot was the subject of such movies as *The Shop Around the Corner*, *In the Good Old Summertime*, *I Sent a Letter to My Love*, and *You've Got Mail*—along with the Broadway musical *She Loves Me*, and sitcom episodes too numerous to mention. It also underpinned this one-hit wonder from Rupert Holmes. Annoying but very, very catchy, "Escape" is one of those tunes where

< 86 >

everyone knows the chorus but not the verses. And no matter how much you like piña coladas, you still have to wonder: Is anyone really "into" champagne? (Incidentally, Holmes also co-wrote the fabled death song "Timothy," which was aimed squarely at folks who were "into" cannibalism.) See also DEATH SONGS.

EUCHRE For a while there ("there" being the late 1800s and early 1900s) euchre was the most popular card game in America. While its roots are disputed— some trace it to the Pennsylvania Dutch, others to the French, still others to the Spanish—its stubborn popularity is not. Especially in the "Euchre Belt" states surrounding the Great Lakes. Variations exist, but this "poor man's bridge" is most often played by two opposing teams using a 32-card deck. It's helped many a Midwesterner make it through the winter months without going nuts. It's also strangely popular on college campuses, where euchre fads sweep the dorms every few years, helping students fill the downtime between visits to Internet porn sites.

< 87 >

F

F TROOP These days, watching any western that doesn't deify Native Americans is a guilty pleasure. Watching a television show with wacky, money-grubbing "Injuns"—played by a bunch of white guys, no less—takes those guilty feelings to a different level. This 1965–67 series (one season filmed in black and white, the next in color) focuses on Fort Courage, a frontier outpost whose military contingent includes the bumbling Corporal Agarn (Larry Storch), the equally bumbling Captain Parmenter (Ken Berry), and the frustrated-by-their-bumbling Sergeant O'Rourke (Forrest Tucker).

Before you feel too guilty, though, consider this. Years ago *Spy* magazine documented startling similarities between the *F Troop* premise and that of the ultimate revisionist western *Dances With Wolves*. Both involve accidental Civil War heroes (Costner, intending to kill himself, instead leads a victorious cavalry charge; Captain Parmenter pulls off a similar feat while in the throes of an asthma attack) who find themselves stationed at forgotten frontier forts. See also *BEVERLY HILLBILLIES, THE* and *GILLIGAN'S ISLAND*.

FABIO Sporting long, blond hair, super-model looks and low-cut shirts that show off his pec cleavage, Italy's Fabio Lanzoni (you can call him Fabio) has made a fortune serving up Grade A beef-cake to the ladies. He started out as a cover model for romance novels, branched out into TV and an occasional movie, and has even written his own books (with a coauthor, of course). The best part about Fabio is watching women squirm when you ask what they like about him. Is it his personality or sense of humor? Truth is, most ladies have never so much as  heard the man speak—which is probably a good thing. Fabio works best as a tabula rasa for free-form feminine fantasy. The less known about the actual person, the better. See also BOLTON, MICHAEL and HARLEQUIN ROMANCES.

FACIAL HAIR (INAPPROPRIATE, HUMOROUS) See SIDEBURNS.

FACTS OF LIFE, THE You take the good, you take the bad, you take 'em both and there you have . . . a TV show that lasted from 1979 to 1988 with almost no one in the sitcom-viewing world admitting that they watched it. Yet somehow, the adventures of boarding school denizens Tootie

< 88 >

(the spunky one), Jo (the tomboy), Blair (the snob), and Natalie (the less said the better) lodged in TV watchers' subconsciouses like a caraway seed under an upper plate. True guilt lies in remembering that Cloris Leachman took over during the final seasons for Charlotte Rae as the dispenser of life lessons. And that pre–John Hughes Molly Ringwald and pre-*ER* George Clooney were once regulars—although it's unlikely to appear on the résumé of either.

FAME "Remember my name" was both the tagline and an oft-repeated lyric from this 1980 film. And although few actually remember the names of stars Lee Curreri, Irene Cara, Maureen Teefy, Paul McCrane, and Gene Anthony Ray (okay, maybe you recall Irene Cara and recognize McCrane's face from *ER*), few from that era can forget the movie or its hit soundtrack. Set at New York's High School for the Performing Arts—and expecting audiences to believe that students do traffic-stopping dances in the streets and impromptu instrumental numbers in the lunchroom—*Fame* followed the intertwined lives of a group of students trying to make it in a pre–*American Idol* world. By turns gritty and sappy, it captured the hearts and eardrums of a generation that wanted to live forever, learn how to fly, and make it to heaven.

FAMILY CIRCUS, THE Self-taught artist Bil Keane has been warming the hearts of newspaper readers since 1960 with the single-panel exploits of Billy, Dolly, Jeffy and, of course, P. J. Considered by many as the only serious rival to *Prince Valiant* for the title of Un-Hippest Comic of All Time, *The Family Circus*'s observations on home life are as dated as an episode of *The Brady Bunch*. By the way, Keane himself is aware that his strip isn't exactly a gut buster in the humor department—and that's just fine with him. "I would rather have the readers react with a warm smile, a tug at the heart or a lump in the throat," he reportedly said. See also *BRADY BUNCH, THE* and *ZIGGY*.

FAMILY FEUD Public humiliation is part of the raison d'être of just about every television game show ever made. But *Family Feud* took the concept a step further by allowing entire families to humiliate themselves. Spun off by creator Mark Goodson from his popular *Match Game* show—and bringing with it frequent celebrity gamer Richard Dawson as host (followed by Ray Combs, then Louie Anderson, then Richard Karn)—the Feud premiered in 1976 and quickly became television's top daytime quiz fest. That's pretty impressive, considering that was also the year of *The Gong Show*'s debut. Respon-

< 89 >

sible for burning the phrase "Survey says" into the national consciousness, the program—whether hosted by Dawson, Combs, Anderson, or Karn—never required knowledge of "facts." All one needed was the ability to guess how others might respond to such mind-taxing probes as: "Name a yellow fruit." See also GAME SHOWS; *GONG SHOW, THE*; and *HOGAN'S HEROES*.

FAMILY MATTERS A spin-off of the oddball buddy show *Perfect Strangers*, *Family Matters* started off as a sitcom about the Winslows, a middle-class suburban Chicago clan. But like *Happy Days*, it was taken  over by an ancillary character. And what a character it was. Not since Jimmie "J.J." Walker in *Good Times* has one man embarrassed a generation of African-American males as effectively as Jaleel White did while playing Steven Quincy Urkel on this 1989–98 series. Yet he turned *Family Matters* into, if not a breakaway hit, at least one of those "I didn't realize that was still on" shows that seemed to keep going and going. Equipped with every nerd accessory, including hiked-up pants, annoying voice, and, of course, glasses, Urkel found himself with more and more screen time as the series went

on. Eventually, in a plot device as far-fetched as anything in *Dallas*'s "It was all a dream" season, Urkel's parents moved to Russia and he moved in with the Winslows. Whatever works. See also *HAPPY DAYS*.

FANNIE MAY CANDIES Eat enough candies, and you'll get a wide behind. How ironic, then, that two of the leading retail chocolate chains had first names that are a euphemism for the posterior. Both Fannie May and Fanny Farmer began around 1920, with May expanding out of Chicago and Farmer emerging from Boston. The two companies joined forces in 1992 when May's parent company, Archibald Candy Corporation, bought out Farmer's owner. Known to court impulse shoppers and gift givers who are too cool for Wal-Mart candy and too poor for Godiva, the two chains went out of business in early 2004—yet another casualty of the vanishing middle class. See also WAL-MART.

FANNY FARMER CANDIES See FANNIE MAY CANDIES.

FANTASY ISLAND Real-life resorts brag about being all-inclusive. Yet no resort this side of Westworld was ever as inclusive as the one presided over by Ricardo Montalban in this 1978–84 ABC series. Guests arrived on the island ready to act

< 90 >

out a fantasy—whether it was Bert Convy as an escape artist seeking to make the ultimate prison break, or a waitress (Adrienne Barbeau) who wanted to be treated like a queen. Sure it was cheesy, but viewers made it a hit in large part because they couldn't help wondering what *they* would ask for. But while Montalban was suave, the show's real casting coup was landing former James Bond–villain sidekick Hervé Villechaize as the "Zee Plane! Zee Plane!"–shouting sidekick Tattoo. When he ditched the show in its last season (in a Charlotte Rae–like overestimation of his personal star power), the producers hired a pre–*Mr. Belvedere* Christopher Hewett (also noted for his gig as Roger De Bris, the drag queen director in Mel Brooks's 1968 film version of *The Producers*) to fill his tiny shoes. It didn't work and the show disappeared—except for an ill-fated, one-season remake starring Malcolm McDowell. See also BARBEAU, ADRIENNE; BOND FILMS FEATURING ROGER MOORE; MIDGETS; and SPELLING, AARON.

FANTASY LEAGUE SPORTS What was once a way for sports stats geeks to play armchair manager has become a multi-million-dollar business that may supplant poker as the great nonathletic bonding ritual of American men. The premise is simple. Players in a fantasy league draft an imaginary team from the ranks of real-life players. A fantasy team's record depends on how those real-life players perform in their real-life games. Okay, so maybe it isn't so simple. Yet more than 10 million people participate in such leagues, spending untold hours studying upcoming drafts, making trades, and otherwise taking time away from their families. It's a far cry from the game that started as a lark invented by some Oakland sportswriters and a Raiders limited partner in a hotel room in 1962. These days, for a fee, Web sites such as ESPN.com and NFL.com take care of the math, leaving the "managers" free to fret over their decisions, make side bets, and learn to cope with the fact that they don't *really* control the careers of Deion Sanders and Emmitt Smith.

FARRAH FAWCETT POSTER, THE In 1977 the bedrooms of pretty much every male teenager in America were equipped

with this legendary pinup, some 8 million copies of which were printed by its creator, Pro Arts. But why did this image become one of the most widely used (and abused) masturbatory aids of all time? Just one (or, technically, two) reason: nipples. Sure, Farrah was leggy, tanned, and crowned with a mane

< 91 >

of sun-kissed tresses. But you could also see her hi-how-do-you-dos poking against the swimsuit fabric. Schwing! See also *CHARLIE'S ANGELS* and MASTURBATION.

FARTING From the squeaker at the church service to the silent-but-deadly shot in the elevator to the taco-fueled eyeburner in the car during a long, winter drive, breaking wind has always been a source of both discomfort and laughs. It wasn't until 1974, though, that we collectively acknowledged its importance as an object of humor. That's when *Blazing Saddles* hit movie screens. Thanks to Mel Brooks's groundbreaking (and pants-tearing) bean-eating-around-the-campfire scene—and Brooks's refusal to cut it when studio execs put on the pressure—we as a people could finally acknowledge the beauty of expressively expelled human gas. There's no scientific proof, but perhaps that film and its endless imitators (it seems that no Disney movie these days is complete without some sort of fart joke) have made us all feel a little less guilty about letting one rip. See also WHOOPEE CUSHIONS.

FASHION EMERGENCY We all have friends who don't know how to dress. Most of us also have friends who think *we* don't know how to dress. Which made this E! series, in which ordinary people are given extraordinary wardrobe and hair renovations, compelling viewing—at least until it was eclipsed by ABC's *Extreme Makeover* and Bravo's *Queer Eye for the Straight Guy*.

FAST FOOD SEE BIG MAC; BOB'S BIG BOY; CHICKEN NUGGETS; CHILI, WENDY'S; DAIRY QUEEN; FOOD COURTS; FRIES, FRENCH; HOT DOGS (CONVENIENCE STORE); LONG JOHN SILVER'S; MCRIB; NACHOS; ORANGE JULIUS; SOFT DRINKS (GIANT PLASTIC CUPS FILLED WITH); and WHITE CASTLE.

FEMALE IMPERSONATORS (PROFESSIONAL) As anyone who saw *Shakespeare in Love* knows, the stage didn't always allow for actresses. In the Bard's time, men played every role, regardless of gender. These days you can still see the same thing, except that the guys *want* to play girls—if the girls are Judy Garland, Marilyn Monroe, Barbra Streisand, Cher, and other gay icons. A kitschy step removed from mere celebrity impersonators, entertainers such as Garland specialist Jim Bailey, Dame Edna's alter ego Barry Humphries, and Craig Russell, who specialized in Mae West and Carol Channing, pursued an odd kind of excellence. They took audiences into a gender-bending world where fabulousness was everything and where we are reminded that, under the skin, we are all . . . well, kind of creepy. See also

< 92 >

CELEBRITY IMPERSONATORS; CHER (WITHOUT SONNY); GARLAND, JUDY; and STREISAND, BARBRA.

FERRETS   Cats and dogs are without doubt America's favorite four-legged pets. But look a bit farther down the companion animal depth chart (past fish and birds and rabbits) and you'll find a distant No. 6—ferrets. Not as elegantly beautiful as felines, as obedient as canines, nor, arguably, as smart as either (a healthy percentage of ferrets never learn to use a litter box), these domesticated relatives of polecats, skunks, and weasels nevertheless number between 6 and 14 million in the United States alone. Without doubt, ferrets give off (along with a rather pungent smell) a certain lowbrow aura that makes them a poor topic for discussion at, say, a gallery opening or symphony recital. Still, they have their place. Sure they're not that cute, not that cuddly, and not all that bright, but you could say the same for a lot of men, and most of *them* manage to find homes.

FIREWORKS, BACKYARD   There's a certain segment of the population for which no Independence Day celebration is complete without risking life and, if not limb, at least a finger or two. We're talking about the backyard fireworks display, an illegal-in-most-states practice in which dads (it's always dads) light off a series of bottle rockets, Roman candles, and M-80s. What these amateur pyrotechnomanics may not realize is that they're part of a grand tradition of accidents going back generations. In the late 1800s, a Philadelphia diary noted that "As a general rule 30 to 40 houses are set afire every Fourth of July."

FISH STICKS   Eating these requires a wanton disregard for the nature of the fish itself—kind of like eating meat on a stick without knowing if it's cow, lamb, or dog, for that matter. A fixture at elementary school cafeterias and in lower-to-middle-class freezers, this cousin of the British staple fish  and chips rose to prominence thanks in large part to the efforts of Gorton's and Mrs. Paul's—the latter a brand that dove into the seafood biz in the mid–1940s with deviled crab cakes, but waited until 1952 to introduce its first fish stick. The dish actually enjoyed brief notoriety in 1988, when it was used as a plot device in the film *Rain Man*. See also MEAT ON A STICK and MENTALLY IMPAIRED (MOVIES WHOSE STARS PRETEND TO BE).

FISHER, AMY   Proof positive that you don't have to be from the South to be

< 93 >

white trash, "The Long Island Lolita" became a media darling after shooting the wife of her lover (Joey Buttafuoco, a story in himself) in the face. Whereas the proper response to such an idiotic occurrence would be revulsion, much of America reacted with fascination—and a desire to hear all the details. The squalid incident went on to inspire endless editorial debate along with three TV movies, in which Fisher was played by Drew Barrymore, Alyssa Milano, and some actress we've never heard of. After a jail stint, Fisher went on to write an advice column (seriously) for the *Long Island Press*. See also TV MOVIES.

FISHING SHOWS Given the peculiar popularity of this genre, it's only a matter of time before someone, somewhere decides to offer an all-fishing channel. If they do, they'll owe a debt of gratitude to ABC's *Wide World of Sports*, which popularized the format. It all began when the show aired film of noted sportscaster Curt Gowdy's fishing expeditions. Soon this riveting concept was spun off into its own Sunday afternoon series, *The American Sportsman*, which lulled audiences into a torpor from 1965 to 1984. The revived version, 2003's *New American Sportsman*, takes sports and Hollywood celebs along for the ride with host Deion Sanders. Not that there aren't plenty of other options, including everything from highbrow fly-fishing broadcasts on ESPN to good ol' boys chasing bass. But whatever the quarry, it's perfect viewing for people who think televised golf is just too fast paced.

FLAMBÉ See FLAMING FOODS.

FLAMING FOODS No matter how much you're in the mood for bananas Foster, Greek saganaki, or baked Alaska, it's difficult not to be embarrassed when pyrotechnics are involved in the serving of your meal.

FLATLEY, MICHAEL See *RIVERDANCE*.

FLAVORED COFFEES If you think taking a shot of vanilla or cinnamon in your coffee is sophisticated, think again. It's pretty much the same thing as putting ketchup on steak. The practice began in the mid-'70s, when skyrocketing coffee prices forced low-quality beans onto the market—beans so unpalatable they had to be augmented with chocolate hazelnut and Irish creme. Nowadays, most purists beieve that if you need flavorings in your joe, you're either drinking crappy coffee, or you're a wimp. See also COFFEE-MATE.

FLA-VOR-ICE Traditionally the cheapest item in the ice cream man's ice chest, Fla-Vor-Ice is the cool-down choice of

< 94 >

cheapskates everywhere. The manufacturer, Jel Sert, also markets former rival Otter Pops, a nearly identical tear-off-the-top-and-push-the-colored-ice-up-the-tube treat. The only difference is that Otter Pops gave names and personalities to each of the flavors (which all happen to be, for some reason, otters). Thus you don't just suck down an orange-ish tasting chunk of ice—you build a relationship with Little Orphan Orange. Whether charactered or characterless, the treat provides one of the great pleasures of adulthood. You can buy a box of them the size of a file cabinet at Wal-Mart, then have as many as you want on sweltering days. See also WAL-MART.

FLEA MARKETS Saks Fifth Avenue shoppers wouldn't be caught dead at the local swap and shop. Or, at least, they wouldn't admit it. Yet the thrill of the hunt attracts folks from across the economic spectrum to empty parking lots, abandoned drive-ins, off-season fairgrounds, and disenfranchised Kmarts in search of bargains, baseball cards, and Beanie Babies that missed the boat.

FLINTSTONES, THE An animated knock-off of *The Honeymooners*? Perhaps. A satire of contemporary consumer culture? You could make that argument. An endless series of stone, rock, and slate puns? Absolutely. Not particularly funny? God, yes. And yet generations of TV addicts can quote *The Flintstones* (original title: *The Flagstones*) chapter and verse, citing the birth of Pebbles, the appearance of the Great Gazoo, and the disappearance of Barney's saber-toothed tiger as if those events changed the face of television. One thing is certain, however: Fred and Barney definitely married up. For guys, choosing between Betty and Wilma is as popular a bar game as deciding between Mary Ann and Ginger. See also FLINTSTONES CHEWABLE VITAMINS and *GILLIGAN'S ISLAND*.

FLINTSTONES CHEWABLE VITAMINS There's something vaguely wrong about making a nutritional supplement this tasty—so tasty that parents must keep the tiny tablets way out of reach of children. Manufactured by Miles Laboratories (one of the original sponsors of *The Flintstones* TV show), each bottle includes vitamins shaped like the various Flintstones characters—except for Betty Rubble, who wasn't added to the mix until the mid–1990s. Urban legend holds that vitamins shaped like Barney's wasp-waisted wife snapped in half in the bottle. However, the true reason for her long absence was that she simply didn't seem that popular with kids. When enough people wrote nasty letters, she finally joined her co-stars in the bottle. See also *FLINTSTONES, THE*.

< 95 >

Flowers in the Attic See ANDREWS, V.C.

FLYNT, LARRY See *HUSTLER*.

FOGELBERG, DAN Coming across as James Taylor's less talented, less charismatic brother (a role already taken by one-hit wonder Livingston "I Will Be in Love with You" Taylor), Dan Fogelberg built a career out of such mellow, soundalike hits as "Leader of the Band" and "Same Old Lang Syne." His 1981 recording of his song "Run for the Roses" made a bid to usurp Michael Murphey's 1975 "Wildfire" as the all-time cheesiest pop hit about a horse.

FONDA, JANE The Vietcong's favorite pinup girl has sparked guilty pleasure with nearly every one of her career changes. Early on she starred in *Barbarella*, a film packed with powerful images that can still make viewers blush even though it was made in 1968  (i.e., dolls with razor-filled mouths attacking a nude Jane, and a mad scientist trying to kill her with sexual pleasure). Later, during her "Hanoi Jane" period, when many thought her antiwar activism (particularly her supremely ill-advised trip to North Vietnam) crossed into the traitor zone, liking a Fonda film made audiences risk feeling unpatriotic. In the '80s she became a fitness guru, spreading guilty inferiority among the doughy millions who bought her tapes, used them twice, and then set them out at the next garage sale. Fonda in recent years has denounced her Vietnam-era antics (regarding a famous photo of her astride an antiaircraft gun, she said, "It was the most horrible thing I could possibly have done"), which, retroactively, makes activists feel guilty for listening to her in the first place. See also AEROBICS PROGRAMS.

FONDUE Originally pioneered by the Swiss as a way to get rid of old, dried-up cheese (namely, melt it and dip stuff in it), fondue came into its own in the 1950s, when the method was applied to cooking meats in hot oil (and, shortly thereafter, dipping fruit and cake in melted chocolate). The technique goes in and out of style, but if you're in the right frame of mind, cooking your dinner one bite at a time can be quite entertaining. But the guilt—nay, the horror—comes at the end of the repast, when you look at the fondue pot and realize the oil level has dropped by several inches.

FONZIE See *HAPPY DAYS*.

FOOD COURTS These days no shopping

< 96 >

mall worth its Bath and Body Shop can be without a food court—basically a bunch of tables and chairs surrounded by food stands selling everything from pizza slices to kung pao chicken. Food courts are a glutton's dream, because they generally serve big portions and don't cost much. They also are a godsend to parents when little Becky wants a burrito while Sammy begs for chicken fingers. Getting the most out of the experience requires only two things: a high tolerance for background noise (particularly, the sound of screaming children) and the ability to use a spork. Advanced food court aficionados can create impromptu banquets by purchasing individual meal components from places with names like Hoagies Heroes, Wok Your World, You Wanna Pizza Me, and Flan-tastic. Put it all together and you've got a veritable United Nations on your plate—followed shortly thereafter by World War III in your stomach.

FOOSBALL While soccer is still a fringe sport in America, foosball (a.k.a. table soccer) is a rec room obsession. Some say the game was developed in Germany—a logical conclusion, since foosball is the German word for soccer. Others credit the French. Whatever the case, Belgian foosball leagues formed in the 1950s and the European Table Soccer Union was founded in 1976. Today the game is a staple in American taverns, as well as in trying-to-be-cool offices. By the way, official foosball rules (not that anyone uses them) call for no spinning of the rods.

FOXWORTHY, JEFF Unless you're living in a trailer park, it's unlikely, when the subject turns to favorite comedians, that you'll cite Jeff Foxworthy. Yet the appeal of the "You might be a redneck if . . . " guy reaches far beyond the double-wides. How else can one explain his status as the top-selling album comic in history? Or the fact that his book *No Shirt, No Shoes, No Problem* landed on the *New York Times* best-seller list, his calendars take in more than $1 million each year, and he's even developed a successful line of greeting cards? Still, Foxworthy seems as reticent about trumpeting his ubiquity as his non-snuff-dipping fans. After all, when your popularity is based on jokes about cars up on blocks and brothers-in-law sleeping on your couch, it doesn't pay to let the world know you're the master of a media empire. See also COMEDY ALBUMS.

FRAMPTON COMES ALIVE! The mania for this biggest-selling live album of all time (more than 12 million copies since its 1976 release) is still somewhat of a mystery—kind of like that totally

< 97 >

wrong-for-you girl or guy who was nevertheless fun to have around (for a while). Filled with Frampton's famous "talking guitar" effect ("Wah . . . wah-wah-wah-wah-wah"), *Frampton Comes Alive!* was undeni-

ably a blast to listen to, but the after-glow didn't glow for long. He scored one more hit album, *I'm in You*, then went out like John Wayne in *The Alamo* by playing Billy Shears in the so-bad-it's-funny *Sgt. Pepper's Lonely Hearts Club Band*. See also SGT. PEPPER'S LONELY HEARTS CLUB BAND (THE MOVIE) and WAYNE, JOHN.

FRANCIS THE TALKING MULE See TALKING ANIMALS (MOVIES ABOUT).

FRANKLIN MINT, THE Launched in 1964 by Joseph Segel (also the founder of the QVC shopping network), the Franklin Mint has been mocked ruthlessly for offering junk "collectibles" to the lowbrow masses. Yet almost everyone has been enticed, at one time or another, by an ad offering an Irish Princess Ring or the near-legendary *Star Trek* chess set. These days, however, the company's lineup has swollen to include a long list of over-the-top items that look like they were developed during the

Cross Promotional Meeting from Hell. How else to explain such you-have-to-see-them-to-believe-them items as Kristy: The Ultimate Harley-Davidson Bride Doll; the *Gone With the Wind* Miniature Egg Collection Display; or the John Wayne "Little Duke" Porcelain Collector Doll? See also KENNEDY FAMILY, THE; MUSEUM GIFT SHOPS; NASCAR; QVC; *STAR TREK*; and WAYNE, JOHN.

FREDERICK'S OF HOLLYWOOD If Hugh Hefner was the father of the sexual revolution, then naughty underwear magnate Frederick Mellinger was its chief engineer. A Hungarian-American from Lower Manhattan, he opened his first lingerie store in New York City right after World War II. In 1946 he relocated to the West Coast, reopening his boutique as Frederick's of Hollywood. In the years that followed, Mellinger (assisted at one point by industrial designers from the Army Corps of Engineers) invented pretty much every piece of naughty underwear in the modern repertoire. In 1947 Frederick's unveiled the first padded bra, followed in 1948 by the push-up bra, and then (over the next couple of decades) the padded girdle, push-up bikini, and the thong panty (introduced to the U.S. in 1981). Today the company is mostly famous for peddling crotchless drawers and stiletto pumps to the trailer park

< 98 >

crowd, but it's worth remembering that without Mellinger (who died in 1990), today's women might still be wearing cone-shaped bras and enormous cotton panties. See also COTTON PANTIES (ENORMOUS); *PLAYBOY*; THONG UNDERWEAR; and VICTORIA'S SECRET CATALOGS.

FREE GIFT WITH PURCHASE It makes sense that the same generation of consumers who pulled prizes from their cereal boxes would grow up to covet complimentary travel mugs, tote bags, and other logo-festooned incentives offered by companies trying to lure business. The strategy works, too. Every time Starbucks doles out a free half-pound of coffee with a $20 gift card purchase, or Victoria's Secret delivers gratis thongs to members of its Angel Club, the word of such "deals" goes out on *Sports Illustrated* Sneaker Phones across the country. But no one plays the Free Gift with Purchase card more effectively than department store cosmetic counters. Witness the occasional free-for-alls at Clinique, where shoppers purchase $26 eye creams and subject themselves to humiliating skin analyses, all in the name of (yet another) gratis Honey Blush mini compact and a dab of Turnaround Lotion. See also BATH STORES; CRACKER JACK; MAKEOVERS, MAKEUP COUNTER and VICTORIA'S SECRET CATALOGS.

FRENCH'S FRENCH FRIED ONIONS Traditionally only making an appearance when an idea-strapped relative brings a green bean casserole to a Thanksgiving feast, these crunchies date back to 1933, when a company called Olney & Carpenter introduced them to a not-very-excited world. It wasn't until 1955, when they were featured as a topping in that now famous casserole recipe, that they truly caught on. Their popularity led to the company's eventual incorporation into Durkee, a 100-year-old spice company founded by a door-to-door salesman. The product, and the company, were later renamed French's. Now the onion bits are featured in hundreds of recipes, including Oniony Corn Muffins, Oniony Bacon 'n' Egg Salad, and Oniony BBQ Meat Loaf. We know, though, that only one recipe really matters—the one with green beans. See also GREEN BEAN CASSEROLE.

FRESCA Introduced in 1966 and reformulated in 1985 to incorporate the calorie-free deliciousness of aspartame, this grapefruit-flavored soda in the green can isn't exactly the pride of the soda pop aisle, especially since for years it was the diet drink of choice for chunky moms nationwide. But that hasn't stopped the Coca-Cola Company's citrus underdog from garnering a cult following among such Fresca devotees as Lyndon B.

< 99 >

Johnson (who kept a special stash on tap outside the Oval Office).

FRIES, FRENCH Linguists argue over which came first, the French or the frenching. Specifically, some say that even though they originated in Paris (as *pommes frites*), French fries get their name not from the country, but from the fact that they are cut in long strips, or "frenched." Others contend that the term frenching arose in response to French fries. Whatever the case, they arrived in the States as French fried potatoes and were shortened in the 1930s to their current moniker. Today they're eaten by the handful by fast-food customers who couldn't imagine a hamburger without them. The preferred condiment here is ketchup. In England, it's malt vinegar.

In a rare case of one guilty pleasure spawning another, potato chips were created when a Saratoga Springs, New York, restaurant customer sent a plate of fries back to the kitchen because he thought they were too thick. The cook's wiseass response (slicing them razor thin and frying them to a crisp) made junk food history.

FRITZ THE CAT See BAKSHI, RALPH.

FROZEN CANDY BARS What's worse for your teeth than a candy bar? How about a candy bar as solid as a brick?

FROZEN COOKIE DOUGH This convenience food has been around for decades, most famously as a sliceable roll. According to the commercials, it's a wonderful time-saver when you want to whip up some cookies for your smiling, adoring kids. But if you don't have any smiling, adoring kids—or if the kids you *do* have hate you, or if your husband is a jerk, or you *don't* have a husband or even a boyfriend—then frozen cookie dough is best when eaten unbaked, straight from the wrapper like a giant candy bar. Throw in a box of tissues and a Lifetime TV movie, and you have all the makings of a very guilty Girls' Night In. See also LIFETIME.

FRUIT ROLL-UPS Who knew that the secret to getting kids to eat fruit at lunchtime was to flatten it? Launched in 1982, the Fruit Roll-Up (and its brethren, such as Fruit by the Foot) is not much more sophisticated than the fruit leather (dried fruit puree) enjoyed by previous generations. The only difference is that the pioneer version didn't have dinosaurs stamped on it.

FULGHUM, ROBERT According to this best-selling author of sermons-disguised-as-essays, everything we needed to know we learned in kindergarten. This theory doesn't exactly explain air travel, the Salk vaccine, or international bank-

< 100 >

ing, but it does give some indication as to why so many book buyers took pleasure in Fulghum's slim best sellers (including *Uh-Oh* and *It Was on Fire When I Lay Down on It*). They sent the comforting, though highly debatable, message that everyday life already held the answers to all our problems and that fulfillment could be yours if only you were smart enough to take a nap.

FUZZY SLIPPERS Footwear fashionistas might consider UGG's Australian shearling boots, Hush Puppies' snuggly terrycloth scuffs, or Isotoner's classic satin ballerina slippers to be the height of house shoe style. But rare is the woman who can deny her deep-seated love of fuzzy footgear—even though they're trailer-park tacky and impractical (unless worn as mobile dust mops), and no amount of machine washing can faze their lint-collecting, dust-mite-harboring propensities. Plus, wear them more than a few times and they morph into mangy-looking mounds of matted faux fur. And yet, there's not a microfiber moccasin on the market that elicits so many warm childhood memories—especially the pastel (particularly pink or baby blue) models. So Orvis, L.L. Bean, and Daniel Green can keep their stylish designs. Women know they can always find the fluffy footwear of their dreams at Kmart, Wal-Mart, or, let's face it, in the front of their own bedroom closets. See also COTTON PANTIES (ENORMOUS); SWEATPANTS; and WAL-MART.

< 101 >

G

G, KENNY Why feel guilty about liking the best-selling instrumental artist in history? Because, at least to critics and music purists, this performer's smooth jazz stylings are so languid they don't even qualify as jazz. Maybe as Muzak, but certainly not jazz. And such questionable career moves as G's "virtual" duet with the late Louis Armstrong border on sacrilege. Even those who don't hold the man in abject contempt understand that getting caught listening to his music won't win them any style points—unless you're a guy trying to show a not-very-hip woman your sensitive side. See also TESH, JOHN and YANNI.

GABOR SISTERS, THE Eva was the one on *Green Acres* and *Petticoat Junction* and the voice of the mom in *The Aristocats*. Zsa Zsa was the one whose film career ranged from *Queen of Outer Space* to Orson Welles's classic *Touch of Evil*. However, she was better-known as a *Merv Griffin Show* guest and tabloid headline generator (for slapping a Beverly Hills cop and marrying nine times). Magda is the one you never heard of. See also *MERV GRIFFIN SHOW, THE* and TWISTER.

GAG GIFTS By definition, gag gifts are those that get a laugh—okay, maybe just a smile—when opened. From that point on they're pretty much useless. In other words, if the person whose name you drew in the office gift exchange actually *displays* his Big Mouth Billy Bass, then you've both got problems. So why do we keep giving them? Maybe it's to avoid the risk of buying something sincere but unappreciated, or of missing the mark in some truly embarrassing way. Or maybe, just maybe, all we want to do is give someone (even if it's just us) a moment of silly pleasure. See also BIG MOUTH BILLY BASS and SPENCER GIFTS.

GALLAGHER Stand-up comics don't respect him. Hollywood never gave him a sitcom. But vast TV audiences gave up channel surfing the first time they saw this Larry Fine–haired comic position a watermelon center stage and prepare to swing his "Sledge-o-Matic." The man born Leo Anthony Gallagher got a taste of show biz as road manager for novelty singer Jim ("My Girl Bill") Stafford before conquering mid-'80s TV with a series of produce-smashing  specials (audience members in the front rows were covered with tarps). More recently, in one of the oddest moments

< 102 >

in pop culture history, Gallagher took his kid brother, Ron, to court for copying his act and performing as Gallagher 2. You can bet *that* never happened to Seinfeld.

GAME SHOWS A TV contest can be either so difficult it makes you feel like a moron (*Jeopardy!*), or so simple it makes you feel like the participants are morons (*Wheel of Fortune*). But one thing they all have in common is their power to grab the attention of even the most highbrow viewer and, in short order, have him screaming "The Continental Divide, dumbass! *Continental Divide!*" at the TV screen. Entertainment execs figured this out back in the golden age of radio, when programs such as *Professor Quiz* and *Information, Please* pioneered the format. Real success came in the 1950s with television, when such shows as *The $64,000 Question* and *Twenty-One* ruled the airwaves. Trouble was (as a congressional investigation revealed), many were rigged. After the scandal the surviving shows reduced the size of their prizes and also their ambitions, confining the likes of *Match Game*, *The Hollywood Squares*, *The Dating Game*, and *The Joker's Wild* to other-than-prime-time slots. There they stayed until the late 1990s, when game shows returned to the evening lineup. Of course there were a few 21st-century twists: they were pricier (*Who Wants to Be a Millionaire?*); meaner (*Weakest Link*); and scarier (*Fear Factor*). But the ratings prove that millions of people at home still watch, some of them no doubt screaming "Eat the roach, dumbass! *Eat the roach!*" at the TV screen. See also AMERICAN GLADIATORS; HOLLYWOOD SQUARES, THE; MATCH GAME; NEWLYWED GAME, THE; PRICE IS RIGHT, THE; and TIC TAC DOUGH.

GAMES, DRINKING Most students don't need an excuse to get drunk, but they can sometimes use an excuse to get drunker quicker. That's where drinking games come in. The fact that the loser is usually the one who has to toss back a round doesn't quite make sense, considering that getting liquored up is the raison d'être for such gatherings. But no matter. Drinking games not only kick the inebriation factor to a higher level, they also provide a convenient cure for party awkwardness. Immerse yourself in a game of, say, Quarters, and you can stare at your opponents' open legs with impunity. See also GAMES, MAKE-OUT.

GAMES, MAKE-OUT Seven Minutes in Heaven, Spin the Bottle, and other such party games allow for lip-locked pairings without the bother of actually selecting and talking to a potential partner. Don't you wish adult hook-ups were this easy? See also GAMES, DRINKING and TWISTER.

< 103 >

GANGSTA RAP (IF YOU'RE WHITE)
Hey, it's a great big world and we should all be allowed to listen to whatever music we like, right? Right. But that doesn't make white kids look any less ridiculous—or more utterly Caucasian—as they sit at traffic lights with N.W.A. or Tupac blasting from the stereo of their parents' car. Still, without these bone thugs from the cul-de-sac, today's hip-hop stars wouldn't be living like pimps. Because the sad truth is that while rap is undeniably about the African-American experience, industry statistics show that a large percentage of the music's buyers are white.

GAP COMMERCIALS Often more entertaining than the shows surrounding them—and with better production values—television ads for the Gap are inevitably oddly watchable. Whether it was L.L. Cool J and Queen Latifah introducing white America to the word "aight," dispassionate slackers singing "Mellow Yellow," or *Matrix*-like dancers freezing mid-motion in the groundbreaking "Khakis Swing" spot, the minds at Gap always seem to know how to mock conformity while, at the same time, pushing it.

GARCIA, CHERRY The most familiar name in the Ben & Jerry's flavor canon, this ice cream dedicated to the Grateful Dead head is proof that all a so-so flavor needs to become a winner is a great name. After all, when was the last time you saw anyone order plain old cherry chocolate at your local ice cream parlor? See also GARCIA, JERRY.

GARCIA, JERRY There are plenty of plausible excuses for missing work. And from the '60s to the mid-'90s, fans of Jerry Garcia and his band, the Grateful Dead, used pretty much all of them. That's because employers tended not to understand if you told them, straight up, that you wanted to take Friday off so that you could drive to three different states to catch a weekend's worth of Dead shows. Jerry Garcia was at the core of the Dead's appeal, a superstar ranked somewhere between the Dalai Lama and Perry Como on the mellowness meter. The teddy-bear–like guitarist and singer led his band to a stand-alone position as one of the top concert draws in the music world, even though only one of its songs ever cracked the Top 10—1987's "Touch of Grey." His death in 1995 left a veritable army of fans all tie-dyed up with no place to go. See also GARCIA, CHERRY and MARIJUANA.

GARLAND, JUDY Gay men long ago deified the former Frances Ethel Gumm. Credit the Kansas native's appeal to her dynamic voice, over-the-top personality,

< 104 >

tortured life, and drag-show-friendly costumes. But when a straight man admits to loving Judy, that's when the eyebrows rise. Enjoying *The Wizard of Oz* and appreciating *A Star Is Born* is acceptable—barely. But owning soundtracks of *The Harvey Girls*, *Summer Stock*, or *Meet Me in St. Louis* is as hard for a hetero to rationalize as membership in a men's chorus. Not that there's anything wrong with that. See also FEMALE IMPERSONATORS; STREISAND, BARBRA (AS ACTRESS); and STREISAND, BARBRA (AS SINGER).

GAS STATION CONVENIENCE STORES See HOT DOGS (CONVENIENCE STORE) and STUCKEY'S.

GATLINBURG There are tourist traps, and then there's Gatlinburg, Tennessee. Positioned just outside the sprawling Great Smoky Mountains National Park, it has for decades served the food and lodging needs of sightseeing tourists—along with their needs for miniature golf, cheap souvenirs, and quickie weddings. Take a slow drive through this tiny town (there's no such thing as a fast drive, because the streets are always clogged with cars), and you can see one of the world's largest collections of lame attractions—everything from Hillbilly Golf (two 18-hole, hayseed-themed miniature courses) to Christus Gardens

(religious statuary, including a sculpture of Christ that not only follows you with its eyes, but *with its entire face*), and both a Ripley's Believe It or Not Museum *and* the Guinness World of Records Museum (home to "the famous Elvis 'Hound Dog' boat," whatever that is, and to the TV Batmobile). What's that you say? You also want roller coasters and giant breasts? Well, Dollywood is just up the road in Pigeon Forge. See also *BATMAN* (THE TV SERIES); GUINNESS WORLD RECORDS; MINIATURE GOLF; and PARTON, DOLLY.

GENERAL HOSPITAL On the air since 1963, ABC's highly rated daytime soap has given us four decades of addictive characters and storylines. Still, much of *General Hospital*'s success can be summed up in two words: "Luke" and "Laura." Played with impeccable star-crossed pathos by Anthony Geary and Genie Francis, the couple shares such enviable chemistry that 30 million viewers witnessed their  1981 TV wedding. The union made rabid fans out of otherwise normal people, many of whom still rush home to their TiVos every evening to find out what sort of crazy stuff happened in Port Charles since they last checked in—

< 105 >

whether that be Bobbie's long-lost daughter showing up to steal her husband, Sonny leaving Brenda standing at the altar, or simply another one of the Cassadine family's wacky plans to put the entire city in a deep freeze by using their high-tech sun-shielding device. See also *DAYS OF OUR LIVES*; *SOAP OPERA DIGEST*; SOAP OPERAS, DAYTIME; and SOAP OPERAS, NIGHTTIME.

GEORGE FOREMAN GRILL, THE In 1993, the former heavyweight boxing champion of the world made American kitchens safe for quickie hamburgers when he attached his name to a tabletop grill. Slanted to drain off excess grease, the product (full name: George Foreman Lean Mean Fat-Reducing Grilling Machine) sold millions. It's difficult to say whether more guilt comes from having an as-seen-on-TV item so prominently displayed in your kitchen or from using it as an excuse to consume even more hamburgers than you did before. See also AS SEEN ON TV PRODUCTS.

GERBILS (DANCING, SINGING) See BIG MOUTH BILLY BASS.

GIANT BUGS (MOVIES ABOUT) There's something about movies featuring humongous, rampaging insects that touches us — and not in a good way.

Maybe, when we see the world terrorized by huge ants (*Them!*), giant mosquitoes (*Skeeter*), or an aircraft carrier–sized spider (*Tarantula*), it makes us think of the payback we deserve for all those bug lights, ant traps, and roach hotels we've deployed. See also RAMPAGING ANIMALS (MOVIES ABOUT).

GIFFORD, KATHIE LEE From 1989 through 2000, Kathie Lee Gifford shared equal billing with Regis Philbin as cohost of an A.M. yapfest. Yet while the curmudgeonly Reege's stock rose over the course of the show (landing him on the *Who Wants to Be a Millionaire?* gravy train), Gifford became an ultra-perky industry joke. But still we tuned in, waiting for the next gush over her kids' cuteness, the next "joke" that only she found funny, or the next attempt to come across as a song stylist (after all, her résumé did include a stint on *Name That Tune*). Gifford's extravagant, made-for-the-tabloids misadventures (including her husband's infidelity and the use of child labor to make her line of signature clothing) became a national obsession that ended only with her retirement from the show. See also *HEE HAW*.

GILLIGAN'S ISLAND It takes a four-year-old's intelligence and about two episodes of viewing experience to realize that the passengers and crew of the

< 106 >

SS Minnow will never get off that island. And it takes a 10-year-old's intelligence (or an open-mic-night stand-up comic) to start pondering the obvious questions: Why did Ginger pack so many outfits for a three-hour tour? If the professor has the savvy to keep the radio batteries going, why can't he figure out how to patch the hole in the boat? Why were the Howells traveling with all that money? And by year three, why didn't the Skipper have his own hut? You'd think there'd be nothing left to mine from this universally-agreed-to-be-lame series (developed by the same folks who brought us the universally-agreed-to-be-lame family sitcom *The Brady Bunch*). And yet we keep watching, like a castaway scanning the horizon for the Coast Guard cutter that will never come. See also *BRADY BUNCH, THE*.

GIMMICKS, MOVIE Producers considering ways to pump up interest in the 1974 Charlton Heston disaster movie *Earthquake* at first considered hiding large Styrofoam blocks in the theater ceilings that would fall during on-screen tremors. That didn't work out, but *Earthquake* (and *Midway*, and *Rollercoaster* after it) *did* get tarted up with Sensurround, a low-frequency sound system that caused objects in the theater to vibrate. It was just one in a pantheon of gimmicks that have been used to attract attention to otherwise dubious films. The master of the form was producer William Castle, who sent a skeleton on a wire out over audiences' heads for 1958's *House on Haunted Hill*; rigged special shock seats to spice up 1959's *The Tingler*; and stopped 1961's *Mr. Sardonicus* in mid-reel so the audience could vote in a "punishment poll." None of these effects caught on, but the most popular gimmick, 3-D, still occasionally rears its right-in-front-of-you head (witness 2003's *Spy Kids 3-D: Game Over*). Then again, we now take for granted two of the biggest—at the time—movie gimmicks: sound and color. See also HESTON, CHARLTON.

GIRL DRINKS From the Brandy Alexander and Pink Lady of yesteryear to the Fuzzy Navel and Flirtini of today, girl drinks have been an embarrassing pleasure for both women and men. Lady drinkers know that they are being treated like second-class citizens of the alcohol world, with assumptions made that their libation needs to be tarted up with fruit, umbrellas, gimmicky names, and other accessories. Meanwhile, barstool-perching guys are forced by their gender roles to order a whiskey and water or a Rusty Nail, when they secretly covet their lady friends' strawberry margaritas or crave a nice white Zinfandel.

< 107 >

GIRL SCOUT COOKIES Begun in 1917 and taken national in 1936, cookie sales used to be an ancillary fund-raising program for the Girl Scouts of America. Now, in many minds, it *is* the Girl Scouts of America, with cookie addicts anxiously awaiting sale time so that they can restock their Samoa stash or satisfy a Thin Mint jones. Just don't let things get out of hand. Each Thin Mint (the most popular of all Girl Scout cookies) contains 40 calories, which means a box (which many aficionados consider to be a single-serving container) weighs in at a staggering 1,440 calories.

GIRLS GONE WILD The television commercials make no, well, bones about the fact that these tapes are filled mostly with scenes of drunk women being begged in the most abject way to reveal their breasts. Yet *Girls Gone Wild* enjoys a large, lucrative following among men wondering why they (A) stayed at the wrong resort; or (B) didn't take a video camera along for the trip. For others who knew how to talk the talk, watching these tapes is a fond remembrance of things past. Either way, they stay at the bottom of the sock drawer. See also SPRING BREAK.

GLADIATORS (MOVIES FEATURING) These films, from *Barabbas* to *Gladiator*, are both the most manly of all cine-matic productions and the most homoerotic. On the one hand, there's all the fighting, gore, and bloody-minded thinking any Joe Six-Pack could want. On the other, all the men wear dresses and seem excessively well oiled, and there aren't many women around. Filmmakers are well aware of this subtext, and in some films even address it—most famously in the male seduction scene between Tony Curtis and Laurence Olivier in *Spartacus*. If this sort of thing troubles you, we advise covering your ears and chanting "la, la, la" whenever the male camaraderie gets a little too intense. See also *AMERICAN GLADIATORS*.

GODZILLA The first installment in this series, 1954's *Godzilla, King of the Monsters*, can rightly be called a classic.

In that film the huge, radioactive dinosaur served as a chilling and very effective parable for nuclear war. But its creator, Toho Co., Ltd., couldn't leave well enough alone. It converted its atomic lizard into a cash cow. The big-gutted, big-butted saurian (really just a guy in a suit) appeared in endless sequels with titles that sounded like second-rate pro wrestling fight cards: *Godzilla vs. the Thing*; *Godzilla vs. the Smog Monster*;

< 108 >

and, inevitably, *King Kong vs. Godzilla.*

Yet through it all, the creature never lost its hold on the imaginations of America's youth. Witnessing the destruction of tiny cardboard cities and legions of radio-controlled tanks was, somehow, mesmerizing. We liked the miniature mayhem so much that in 1998 Godzilla was featured in a big-budget Hollywood film—a flop that stank just as badly as all the previous efforts. Still, not bad for a dinosaur that was named after a hulking stagehand on the Tojo set. His nickname, Gojira (the monster's original Japanese moniker) means, roughly, "gorilla whale." See also RAMPAGING ANIMALS (MOVIES ABOUT).

GO-GO'S If ever there was a band that men should loathe, it's this one. Formed in the late '70s, the Go-Go's brought up-tempo, sugar-frosted tunes such as "Vacation" and "We Got the Beat" to the airwaves. Occasionally their driving guitars and warbling harmonies (courtesy of vocalist Belinda Carlisle) sounded a little like the Beach Boys—if the Beach Boys all had sex change operations. And yet, there's many a male fan who cranks up the Go-Go's when alone in his car. But not before first making sure his windows are securely rolled up.

GOLDEN GLOBES What exactly is the Hollywood Foreign Press Association?

Who cares? What's important is that they stage the annual Golden Globe Awards. Of course we retain the names of the "big winners" for about as long as we remember Teen Choice Award picks, but that's beside the point. These trophies (given in both TV and film categories) are a guilty pleasure not just for the many who enjoy watching any star-studded award show, but also for those who savor unexpected wacky moments, such as 1988's three-way movie actress tie (Jodie Foster for *The Accused*/Sigourney Weaver for *Gorillas in the Mist*/Shirley MacLaine for *Madame Sousatzka*), and Pia Zadora's legendary 1982 win for "New Star of the Year in a Motion Picture." Lately, however, the Golden Globes have become less erratic. Perhaps those halcyon days when Sharon Stone could land an acting award by sending handwritten notes to the entire Hollywood Foreign Press membership are gone. These days, the Globes are billed as a laid-back evening of ass-kissing that fairly accurately predicts each season's Oscar and Emmy winners. See also AWARD SHOWS; OSCAR ACCEPTANCE SPEECHES (EMBARRASSING); *PEOPLE'S CHOICE AWARDS, THE*; and ZADORA, PIA.

GOLDEN TEE Mark Twain described golf as "a good walk spoiled." No telling what he would have said about the

< 109 >

legions of duffers who experience the intense frustration of hooking, slicing, landing in the trees, missing simple putts, and whacking away at sand without even the benefit of a good walk. We're talking about those Tiger Woods wannabes who shove quarters into the addictive Golden Tee golf games. Created by Incredible Technologies and found at any respectable sports bar, the original Golden Tee and its spin-offs take players to the most famous courses in the world without the need for lugging clubs. The company even sponsors tournaments around the country—including an annual world championship with a recent total purse of $57,000. While the game can be intense, the truth is that even if you can birdie your way to the leader board, this is still just a video game. In the real world, you might not be able to putt your way around a wooden windmill. See also MINIATURE GOLF and VIDEO GAMES.

GOLDFISH CRACKERS Since 1962, a handful of smiling, goldfish-shaped crackers has been the quick snack of choice first for kids, and then for adults. Growing to include 25 varieties sold in 40 countries, there are now about 75 billion of the little guppies produced each year.

GONG SHOW, THE Simultaneously spoofing game shows, talent shows, and

variety shows while being itself a variety talent game show, this madhouse of an afternoon program kept audiences glued to their sets from 1976 to 1980. Basically it was a nonstop parade of amateur and sub-amateur acts (including then-unknown Paul "Pee-wee Herman" Reubens and actress/singer Mare Winningham) judged by three borderline celebrities (Rex Reed, Jaye P. Morgan, Jamie Farr, et al.) who could end performances by banging a giant gong if things proved too unbearable. The real kick was its running characters—the bag-over-his-head Unknown Comic, Gene Gene the Dancing Machine (full name Gene Patton), and especially the show's host, game show producer Chuck Barris. His infectious good humor and just-happy-to-be-here attitude kept us watching through many a fat tap dancer, Elvis impersonator, and scantily clad woman sucking popsicles to the tune "I'm in the Mood for Love." If only the two movies based on his exploits, *The Gong Show Movie* and *Confessions of a Dangerous Mind*, were as entertaining as any given half hour of the original series. See also DATING SHOWS; ELVIS IMPERSONATORS; *NEWLYWED GAME, THE*; and VARIETY SHOWS.

< 110 >

GOO GOO CLUSTERS A messy combination of caramel, marshmallow, and roasted peanuts coated in milk chocolate, these calorie bombs (products of the Nashville-based Standard Candy Company) were once advertised as "a nourishing lunch for a nickel!" Now they're a treat you sneak when switching planes at Southern airports. See also SNICKERS.

GOULET, ROBERT This Tony-winning theater trouper first won fame as Sir Lancelot in the original 1960 production of *Camelot*. After that, the baritone-voiced singer gradually devolved into a poor man's Wayne Newton. During the '70s and '80s he appeared in numerous stage productions, but was better known as a TV variety show guest—back when you could build a career out of variety show walk-ons. According to legend, no less a social critic than Elvis Presley saw fit to damn the man's work. One day in 1974 (or so the story goes), the King was eating dinner in front of the tube when Goulet appeared on-screen. Elvis picked up his personal channel changer (a pistol), blew a hole in the TV, announced "That will be enough of that shit," and resumed eating. See also NEWTON, WAYNE and PRESLEY, ELVIS.

GRACELAND See PRESLEY, ELVIS.

GRAVY Bad architects plant vines. Bad cooks ladle on the gravy. This golden broth of forgiveness (in most cases made from meat drippings, flour, and liquids ranging from coffee to wine) can cover a bevy of mistakes, from a dry Thanksgiving turkey to a steak that lingered too long on the grill.

GREATEST HITS ALBUMS These compilations, in which artists repackage previously recorded songs, are the musical equivalent of the sitcom episode where everyone gets trapped in a meat locker/closet/empty missile silo and spends a half hour recalling the funniest and/or most touching moments from the last few seasons. Consider: What fan would say that *1* is her favorite Beatles album? Or that Sinatra's high point was *Greatest Hits Volume 2*? Frankly, if you really liked the particular band or singer, wouldn't you already have all this material anyway? Still, none of this stops these career-spanning retrospectives from flying off shelves. For instance, *Eagles: Their Greatest Hits, 1971–1975* is now the biggest-selling album of all time, surpassing even Michael Jackson's *Thriller*. See also JACKSON, MICHAEL; *THRILLER*; and TIME-LIFE MUSIC.

GREEN ACRES Many children know the tale of the city mouse and the country mouse. Many more adults know the sim-

< 111 >

ilar tale of Oliver Wendell Douglas and his Hungarian-accented bride, Lisa Douglas, nee Gronyitz. The couple escaped the evils of Manhattan—he enthusiastically, she reluctantly—and bought a farm in Hooterville (relax, this was 18 years before the first Hooters opened). Then they spent 170 episodes facing the challenges of country life. Kind of like *Little House on the Prairie*, except that no one ever seemed to learn anything.

For viewers with a countrified bent, *Green Acres* was a chance to laugh at the foibles of city folks. For urbanites, it reinforced the notion that, in a rural town, the smartest resident is likely to be a pig. Like other mid-'60s shows, *Green Acres* blissfully ignored the social upheaval of the time, instead showing a world where the biggest problems involved making a telephone connection or working around the locals' bizarre traditions (i.e., membership in the Hooterville Volunteer Fire Department required the applicant to play a musical instrument). Brought to you by the same folks who produced *The Beverly Hillbillies*. See also BEVERLY HILLBILLIES, THE; BRADY BUNCH, THE; GABOR SISTERS, THE; GILLIGAN'S ISLAND; and HOOTERS.

GREEN BEAN CASSEROLE   At the Thanksgiving pitch-in, you waltz in smug as Martha Stewart and park your snooty-looking brie en croute with cranberry chutney on the buffet table. But nothing awakens your inner hillbilly quite like the sight of a green bean casserole. This murky, grayish-green glob, encrusted with a topping of french fried onions, looks like something you'd see pooled on a frat room floor following a pledge party. Yet it is savored in an estimated 20 million U.S. households during the holidays every year.

The recipe (a can of condensed cream of mushroom soup, milk, pepper, soy sauce, canned green beans, and canned french fried onions) was developed in 1955 in the Campbell's Soup Company test kitchen. The "Green Bean Bake," as it was originally called, is the brainchild of Dorcas Reilly, home economist and manager of Campbell's cooking lab. In late 2002, the then 76-year-old "Grandmother of the Green Bean Casserole" appeared in Akron, Ohio, to donate her original, yellowed 8-by-11-inch recipe card to the National Inventors Hall of Fame. It was commemorated as "a prize invention for its enduring contribution to the holiday meal." The casserole remains Campbell's most-requested recipe, and company officials suspect that about 40 percent of all the condensed cream of mushroom soup they sell winds up incorporated in it. See also CREAM OF MUSHROOM SOUP (RECIPES INCLUDING) and FRENCH'S FRENCH FRIED ONIONS.

< 112 >

GREETING CARDS, DIRTY You know that icky/excited feeling you get when visiting the curtained-off room at the back of the video store? One gets pretty much the same vibe cruising the dirty card aisle at greeting card stores. Here you find naked fat women, horny nuns, and buff gay couples dispensing such subtle witticisms as "Two's company, three's a BLAST!" and "You can't have your cake and Edith, too." Your reaction? Guilty snickers, a quick look to see if you know anyone else in the store, and then a reach to see what the next card says. See also GREETING CARDS, SENTIMENTAL.

GREETING CARDS, SENTIMENTAL Stock photos of adorable puppies. Couplets that read like something from a 100-level English Lit class. And of course, sunsets, sunsets, sunsets. It's easy to be cynical about the greeting card industry, which preys on our guilt over, in the most literal sense, not being there for friends and family. To assuage our conscience they imply we can make everything better by purchasing a $3 folded piece of paper. But then, while trolling the aisle of the Hallmark store, you find that one, perfect card—the one that says, in word and picture, exactly what you'd like to say if you could write from the heart, take better pictures, and had a cuter puppy. See also GREETING CARDS, DIRTY and *HALLMARK HALL OF FAME*.

GRIER, PAM Is there an actress who has had more movies named after her characters than Pam Grier, whose title roles include *Coffy*, *Foxy Brown*, *Friday Foster*, and *Sheba, Baby*? Though she was the queen of '70s blaxploitiation flicks, Grier never seemed all that blaxploited. She was too busy kicking ass— back in the days when such distaff death machines as Angelina  Jolie weren't even born. For women, watching Grier in action was empowering. For men, watching Grier in action was arousing—even the parts (*especially* the parts?) where she got riled and called someone, say, a jive ass m——r. Director/groupie Quentin Tarantino paid homage to her in his 1997 opus *Jackie Brown*. And yes, once again, the movie was named after Grier's character. See also BLAXPLOITATION FILMS.

GUINNESS WORLD RECORDS How appropriate that the book that has settled countless drunken bar bets was invented by a beer company. It all began in 1951 when the managing director of the Guinness Brewery got into an argument over which was the fastest game bird in Europe. It occurred to him that people might enjoy a book that compiled such useless drivel in one place, so a London

< 113 >

fact-finding agency was commissioned to dig up the necessary data and the first Guinness record book was published in 1955. It has since sold some 94 million copies, branched out into TV, and gained regular headlines for the stunts people do in order to gain a mention in its pages. One of the most commonly broken records is for longest disc jockey marathon—well over 60 hours at last count. One of the most painful is for the most clothespins clipped on the face—153. See also STUNTS (INSANE, TELEVISED).

GUM BALL MACHINES As kids, we saw the gum ball machines positioned in the between-doors netherland at the grocery store as our just reward for not being total pains in the asses while mom shopped. As adults we can visit them as many times as we want—if we're willing to block the stream of carts exiting the store while we stoop down, drop in some change, turn the crank, cup our hands, open the metal slot cover, and receive a lot less gum than we remembered getting as a child. Of course the apparatus itself has been dressed up in recent years. The newbies include the Gumball Gizmo (essentially a kinetic sculpture that the candy winds through on the way to your hand) and the Slam Dunk (in which you shoot a basket with your gum ball). See also CHICLETS.

GUYS LOSING THEIR VIRGINITY (MOVIES ABOUT) During the early-to-mid '80s it seemed as if there were almost as many guys-trying-to-lose-their-virginity movies as there were actual guys trying to lose their virginity. The lineup includes *Porky's* (where the objects of lust include Kim Cattrall), *Class* (Andrew McCarthy scoring with his best friend's mom), *Revenge of the Nerds* (with a pre-*E.R.* Anthony Edwards), *Private Lessons* (Sylvia "Emmanuelle" Kristel's stab at legitimacy), *Homework* (Joan Collins gets it on with her daughter's boyfriend), and *Losin' It* (based on the extremely unlikely premise that Tom Cruise couldn't get any tail). And that's just for starters. Far from a creation of the Reagan years, the genre goes back to such respectable films as 1971's *The Summer of '42* (which includes the mother of all condom-buying scenes) and 1969's *Last Summer* (in which Richard "John-Boy" Thomas and *X-Men* senator Bruce Davison have the hots for Barbara Hershey). Today the action continues most famously (and most graphically) in the *American Pie* flicks. Apparently the desire to watch horny kids experience first-time sexual encounters even more embarrassing than yours is timeless. See also COLLINS, JOAN; EMMANUELLE (MOVIES FEATURING THE CHARACTER OF); and *WALTONS, THE*.

< 114 >

H

HAIRSTYLE MAGAZINES Anyone who has ever pondered a major change of coiffure already knows the calming qualities of a dog-eared copy of *101 Celebrity Hairstyles*. Page after page of covetable manes can move a redhead to chunky blond highlights and make a woman with flowing tresses think "pixie cut." Call it overambitious. Call it temporary insanity. Just don't call it misguided, because we know deep down, beneath the hot rollers and touched-up roots, that it's all just a tease. We see the sideways glances every time we fold down a corner of *Soap Star HairStyle Magazine* while waiting our turn in the stylist's chair, and we realize that no step-by-step illustration will ever deliver us to perfectly tousled Meg Ryanhood. But that doesn't mean we won't try. As long as *Hair Flair* and *Braid Masters* keep us follicularly inspired, we'll keep the hot rollers plugged in.

HALFTIME ENTERTAINMENT It's hip to dis the halftime show. After all, you plunked down your hard-earned money to watch a sporting event, not to see the not-ready-for-*The-Gong-Show* players. Yet the step dancers, the quick-change artist, the trampoline-enhanced slam dunkers, and the Frisbee-catching dogs at basketball arenas (not to mention the marching bands, baton twirlers, field goal kicking competitions, and drum lines at football games) have kept many a hardcore sports buff from taking a much-needed trip to the restroom. See also VARIETY SHOWS.

HALL, ANTHONY MICHAEL See *BREAKFAST CLUB, THE* and *WEIRD SCIENCE*.

HALL OF PRESIDENTS, THE Never on the short list of must-see Disney World attractions (for anyone but senior citizens and perhaps Monica Lewinsky), the Hall of Presidents is, basically, a room full of animatronic commanders in chief, featuring a talking Abe Lincoln and George W. Bush. Strangely compelling, in a slightly *Twilight Zone*-ish way, the show is updated (for obvious reasons) after each change of administration. Parents force their kids to attend, in the vain belief that it's somehow educational. But the biggest lesson it inadvertently demonstrates is that even robotic presidents can't stand still during a dull speech. See also LEWINSKY, MONICA.

HALLMARK HALL OF FAME It's hard to tell which makes us cry harder: The high-quality, highly emotional made-for-TV movies presented under the

< 115 >

Hallmark Hall of Fame banner, or the high-quality, highly emotional commercials contained therein. Put them together, and you've got a powerful one-two punch to the tear ducts. The series of specials began in 1951 with *Amahl and the Night Visitors*, the first opera commissioned for TV (no, we can't name another). They continue to this day, attracting such movie folk as Glenn Close (*Sarah, Plain and Tall*), Sissy Spacek (*A Place for Annie*), and James Woods (*My Name Is Bill W*) to prestige projects. George C. Scott, who famously refused his Best Actor Oscar for *Patton*, accepted a Best Actor Emmy just a few weeks later for *Hallmark Hall of Fame's* production of Arthur Miller's *The Price*. In fact, nearly one out of every four actors who have ever won an Academy Award have appeared in a *Hallmark Hall of Fame* special. Yet it's the mini-movie two-minute commercials—only eight of them shown on average during a two-hour broadcast—that really kill us. Example: Couple going through the seemingly endless process of trying to adopt a baby have to go to another meeting. Wife is frustrated. Ready to give up. Husband hands wife a card (Hallmark, of course), that says "To a special Mother." Now she knows what the meeting is about. Admit it, you're kind of welling up right now, aren't you? See also COMMERCIALS (TEAR-JERKING).

HALLOWEEN (ADULT CELEBRATION OF) Remember that last, painful Halloween when you went out trick-or-treating, realized you were the oldest kid in a costume, and ran home in shame? Today's kids need never know that feeling. Halloween (based on the ancient Celtic festival of Samhain) has become an adult function, with Americans dropping $7 billion each year to celebrate it. The reasons are obvious: Any holiday that revolves around dressing up in a costume and behaving like a jackass is way too good to waste on children. Which is why city festivals have devolved into Mardi Gras–like spectacles of debauchery, drunkenness, and (of course) vandalism. But that's okay, because *you're wearing a mask*. See also *HALLOWEEN* (THE MOVIE SERIES).

HALLOWEEN (THE MOVIE SERIES) This massive 1978 hit kicked off, for better or (mostly) worse, a new cinema genre: Movies in Which Teenagers Have Sex and Are Then All Killed by an Unstoppable Masked Psychopath, Except for the Town Virgin, Who Manages, Somehow, to Stop the Unstoppable Masked Psychopath. In this case the psycho was named Michael Myers (wearing a William Shatner mask that was painted white—seriously), and the town virgin was Jamie Lee Curtis in her feature film debut. *Halloween*, directed by John Car-

< 116 >

penter and now considered a classic of sorts, was followed by an avalanche of dreary clones that were hack work in every sense of the word. Remember *Friday the 13th*, *Prom Night*, *My Bloody Valentine*, and *Silent Night, Deadly Night*? Or, for that matter, the seven (so far) *Halloween* sequels? How many teen murders can one sit still for, even if the teens are usually stupid, annoying, and oversexed? See also BARBEAU, ADRIENNE; SERIAL KILLERS (MOVIES ABOUT); and SHATNER, WILLIAM.

HAMBURGER HELPER This product, first marketed in 1970 by General Mills, is basically a box full of powdered ingredients that one dumps onto a pound of ground beef to make a skillet full of tomato-, cheese-, and noodle-laden goo (the original five flavors included Beef Noodle, Chili Tomato, and Potato Stroganoff). Gastronomes have mocked it since its inception, but the sad truth is that a plateful of Helper is baby boomer comfort food of the highest  order—especially when served with its natural accompaniment, Wonder Bread with butter. See also WONDER BREAD.

HAMMER FILMS Bela Lugosi is the actor the general public associates with Count Dracula. But if you had a choice, wouldn't you much rather watch Christopher Lee tear into the throat of a British barmaid? Lee and Peter Cushing were the Lugosi and Karloff of Hammer films, a British outfit that one-upped the classic Universal Studios creatures (Drac, the Frankenstein Monster, the Mummy, the Wolf Man) by adding the key elements of color, sex, and gore. The results offended purists but offered a new generation the guilty pleasure of garish monster movies. That plus endless sequels with eye-catching, marquee-spanning names such as *Frankenstein Must Be Destroyed* and *Taste the Blood of Dracula*.

HANNA-BARBERA CARTOONS Given the utter insipidness of their later work, it's hard to believe that the animation team of William Hanna and Joseph Barbera shared seven Academy Awards, gleaned between 1943 and 1953 for their animated Tom and Jerry theatrical shorts. When the market for movie cartoons dried up, the duo formed their own company in 1957 and flooded TV screens with low-quality "limited animation" cartoons. These were cheap to make, but because fewer individual animation "cels" were used in each cartoon, the finished product tended to have a somewhat jerky feel. Plus, the quality of the drawing (especially in later years)

< 117 >

seemed only slightly better than the pictures high school stoners scrawl in their notebooks during study hall. None of which stopped Hanna-Barbera from creating a string of massively successful shows and characters, including *The Flintstones* (the first prime-time animated series), Yogi Bear, Huckleberry Hound, Scooby-Doo, and *The Jetsons*. True guilty pleasure aficionados, however, savor the team's lesser-known efforts, of which there were scores. Many is the fortysomething executive who, long ago, charged to the TV on Saturday morning to catch the latest episode of *Space Ghost*; *Josie and the Pussycats in Outer Space*; *The Partridge Family: 2200 A.D.*; *Help! It's the Hair Bear Bunch*; *Jonny Quest*; *The Three Robotic Stooges*; *Speed Buggy*; *Captain Caveman and the Teen Angels*; and *Dastardly and Muttley in Their Flying Machines*. See also CARTOONS (ADULT INTEREST IN); *FLINTSTONES, THE*; *PARTRIDGE FAMILY, THE*; SATURDAY MORNING CARTOONS; SCOOBY- DOO; and THREE STOOGES, THE.

HAPPY DAYS Henry Winkler was perhaps the least likely guy ever to become a TV sex symbol. A five-foot-six-inch, 28-year-old Yale grad with next to no real acting credits, he was nevertheless cast as leather-clad, motorcycle-riding high school tough guy Arthur Fonzarelli (a.k.a. Fonzie). By the time Ron Howard,

in theory the star of the show, bailed in 1980, the Fonz was clearly the big dog, managing to turn a simple thumbs-up salute and "Aaayyh" into an embarrassing catchphrase/gesture that everyone seemed to try. Originally produced as a TV pilot (sans Fonzie), the show debuted as a segment of *Love, American Style* before being granted series status. Ironically, *Happy Days* did have a cultural impact of sorts. It soured Ron Howard so thoroughly on acting that he turned to directing, giving us such hits as *Apollo 13* and *A Beautiful Mind*. Even better, it provided the genesis for the phrase "jumping the shark," which is used to indicate the exact moment when a show/band/career begins its downward arc toward oblivion. In this case, it refers to a *Happy Days* episode in which Fonzie water-ski jumped over, yes, a shark. See also LOVE, AMERICAN STYLE and TV CATCHPHRASES (QUOTING OF).

HAPPY GILMORE See SANDLER, ADAM.

HARD ROCK CAFÉ See THEME RESTAURANTS.

HARDING, TONYA The baddest thing about this bad girl of professional skating is that so many people wanted to root for her. She was a big-thighed, rawboned redneck from the trailer park who had succeeded in the la-di-da world of

< 118 >

professional skating. Sure she was a little rough around the edges, but that just made the Oregon native more appealing—until her boyfriend decided to improve her chances of winning a medal at the 1994 Winter Olympics by hiring goons to bust the knees of her chief U.S. competition, Nancy Kerrigan. In no time flat she went from success story to Jerry Springer story. Oh well, at least it helped the sport. When Kerrigan and Harding competed head-to-head a few weeks later at the Olympics, the face-off drew one of the biggest television audiences in U.S. history. See also ICE SKATING SHOWS and SPRINGER, JERRY.

HARDY BOYS, THE Even young teens (the books' core audience) could see that Frank and Joe Hardy, sons of a famous detective, stumbled onto way too many nefarious plots. How many secret coves, smuggling operations, and hidden treasures can one town have? And what self-respecting villain would repeatedly be thwarted by a couple of kids? Still, that's the world created, ostensibly, by Franklin W. Dixon. In reality, the series was the brainchild of Edward Stratemeyer, who put together a team of anonymous scribes to churn out books based on his outlines, then printed them under the byline of the made-up Dixon. Thus it's been since 1927, though after 1959 the first 38 adventures were revised and reissued with changes said to "incorporate the most up-to-date methods used by police and private investigators." In truth, the books were shortened and rewritten to, among other things, remove their most egregious racial stereotyping. More changes came after Simon & Schuster bought the line in 1979. Attempts were made to appeal to older readers (with the Hardy Boys Casefiles series) and to younger ones (with the Frank and Joe Hardy—The Clues Brothers line). But these were to the two-fisted originals what Tiny Toons and Muppet Babies are to authentic Looney Tunes and classic Muppets. See also CASSIDY, SHAUN; DREW, NANCY; and *MUPPET SHOW, THE*.

HARLEQUIN ROMANCES The people who turn up their noses at bodice-ripping Harlequin Romances most likely have never actually *read* one. Those Virginia Woolf worshippers have almost certainly never plowed through five on a rainy day or binge-read a grocery bag full of them while recovering from a tonsillectomy. While no one will ever mistake the likes of *The Pleasure King's Bride* for great literature, that hasn't hurt sales of the paperback novels famous for displaying chiseled Fabios on their covers and using words like "throbbing," "trembling," and "drenched" in love scene after love scene after love scene.

< 119 >

Toronto-based Harlequin, founded in 1949, releases 60-plus books a month and employs more than 1,300 writers. Mass production is a necessity, because loyal readers (average age: 44) can devour a book like *Outback Mistress* in roughly the same amount of time it takes to process a week's worth of dirty clothes at the Laundromat. The volumes are best when read in rapid succession, an experience as indulgently satisfying as eating an entire can of Pringles in one sitting. See also FABIO.

HART, MARY   A former Miss South Dakota as well as a former Regis Philbin cohost, Mary Hart became a pop culture icon of sorts when she joined the staff of the fledgling *Entertainment Tonight* in 1982, quickly rising to the anchor seat. With much-admired legs and a disturbing ability to act as if Hollywood comings-and-goings actually mattered, Hart hasn't used her job as a springboard to some higher spot on the entertainment food chain (although she has played herself on shows ranging from *Frasier* to *JAG*). In fact, her only brush with controversy came when stories surfaced of an epileptic New York woman who started seizing whenever she heard Hart's voice. Kind of like what happens when John Tesh plays the piano. See also BEAUTY PAGEANTS; *ENTERTAINMENT TONIGHT* and TESH, JOHN.

HASSELHOFF, DAVID   His six-year stint as William "Snapper" Foster Jr. on *The Young and the Restless* would have been enough by itself to secure him a place in the guilty pleasures pantheon. But fate had more in store for Hasselhoff. During his stint on the '80s series *Knight Rider*, he became not only a mainstream star, but a mainstream star in a show with a talking car. But was that enough? Not a chance. Hasselhoff topped the European pop charts with the song "Looking for Freedom," then returned to stateside glory as head lifeguard on the TV jigglefest *Baywatch*. Although the show was booted off NBC after only one season, the 6-foot-4-inch hunk boldly helped line up the financing necessary to take the show into syndication, where it became an international phenomenon, launching the careers of Pamela Anderson and Carmen Electra. See also ANDERSON, PAMELA and *BAYWATCH*.

HAWAIIAN SHIRTS   The official uniform of gone-to-seed slobs worldwide, the Hawaiian shirt (also called the "aloha shirt") can conceal a beer gut or a salsa stain with equal aplomb—provided the pattern is busy enough. It evolved at the dawn of the 20th century, incorporating bright, patterned cloth from China and Japan; a traditional untucked shirt from the Philippines called the barong tagalog; the collared shirt style from

< 120 >

America; and block patterns from Hawaii itself. By the early 1930s Hawaii-based clothing manufacturers knew they were onto something. Tourists and celebrity visitors started taking pineapple- and hula-girl-infested clothing back to the mainland, and in no time a phenomenon  was born. In fact, Hawaiian shirts helped usher in casual office attire. In 1947 Honolulu's city and county employees were encouraged to wear the shirts to the office from June 1 to October 31, to help them cope with the summer heat. See also SWEATPANTS.

HEADLINE NEWS When many of us say we "read the newspaper," what we really mean is that we skim the headlines and maybe—maybe—read a few paragraphs. That's the premise, adapted to television, behind CNN Headline News. An overhaul of Ted Turner's CNN2, the cable channel was founded in 1982 with the motto "a whole day's news every half hour," although it could easily be "a whole day's news—for people with attention deficit disorder." The format allows no room for such annoyances as context, perspective, or ambiguity. It is, as promised, real news, real fast—especially after being retooled in 2001 to be even busier, with stock tickers, weather reports, talking-head newsreaders, and separate stories all presented at once. It's perfect for those of us who only have time to learn about current events while riding an exercise bike or walking past an appliance store window.

HEAVY METAL Social critics see it as a metaphor-laden commentary on the bleakness of modern life. Its fans enjoy it as blast-your-eardrums theatrical music where even the ugliest drummer can get a girl. Others treat it like rock and roll's retarded cousin. Yet heavy metal, the musical genre of choice for rebellious adolescent white males, has endured from its Black Sabbath '70s roots to today, overwhelming audiences with music anchored in death imagery, satanic showmanship, and outrageous album covers. Liking it when you are no longer a high school freshman or vocational school enrollee isn't exactly hip, but that doesn't stop some fans. At least metal doesn't take itself seriously. Consider how the genre embraced rather than condemned *This Is Spinal Tap*, a scathing satire not only of the music, but of its bands and fans as well. These days, Spinal Tap is treated with the same reverence as "real" '80s metal gods such as Iron Maiden, Megadeth, and Metallica.

< 121 >

HEE HAW One can argue that *Hee Haw*, kind of a hickified *Laugh-In*, set back country music by decades. On the other hand, one could argue that *Hee Haw* showcased some of the country's best guitar pickers. One could argue all one wants, but that won't change the fact that most guys tuned in to *Hee Haw* just to see Misty Rowe, Barbi Benton, Cathy Baker, Gunilla Hutton, and others strut around in their Daisy Dukes (back before super-short blue jeans cutoffs were *called* Daisy Dukes) and bust out of their woefully too small coveralls. (Note: Only the most diehard fans will admit to watching *The Hee Haw Honeys*, a 1978 spin-off series featuring Kathie Lee Gifford as a truck stop waitress.) See also BENTON, BARBIE and GIFFORD, KATHIE LEE.

HELOISE This pre-Martha domestic goddess is to housework what Julia Child is to cooking—an unattainable ideal of homey tranquility. Famous for offering an easy way to do almost any chore (a slice of bread will keep brown sugar from hardening; a potato will pull the saltiness out of overseasoned soup), the first Heloise, an Air Force wife stationed in Hawaii, started doling out household tips in the *Honolulu Advertiser*. Her equally pragmatic look-alike daughter (full name: Ponce Kiah Marchelle Heloise Cruse Evans) took over in 1977 and built *Hints from Heloise* into the information empire it is today. In addition to her daily newspaper column, syndicated by King Features to more than 500 newspapers across the United States and in 20 countries, the silver-haired authority has penned a stack of books, contributes a monthly article to *Good Housekeeping*, and fills the airwaves with her timeless pearls via the *Heloise Radio Hour*. What makes her stand out—and gives us a twinge of guilt—is the fact that most of her solutions address problems that convenience food–addicted moderns never knew they had. Keep your carrots in a separate drawer from your apples to prevent the carrots from turning bitter? Who has a bag of carrots, anyway? And yet we eagerly read, perhaps hoping that even if Heloise's tips don't help us keep a better house, they might just win us a bar bet someday. See also STEWART, MARTHA.

HENNING, DOUG Combining the age-old craft of prestidigitation with the trendy persona of a droopy-mustached hippy, this wacky Canadian helped bring magic back into the mainstream during the '70s. Adding his bag of tricks to a threadbare plot and Stephen Schwartz *Godspell* music, Henning created *The Magic Show*, whose most amazing feat was that it somehow ran for four years on Broadway. Lucrative TV specials

< 122 >

followed, but after studying with the Marharishi Mahesh Yogi, Henning sold his props (to David Copperfield, among others) and dedicated his life to Transcendental Meditation. Much wackiness followed. His run for the Canadian parliament failed, as did his bid to open a theme park called Veda Land (which was to include a levitating building) and his effort to change the world with the help of 10,000 flying yogis. By then, embarrassed fans had—just like Henning's gear—moved on to Copperfield. See also MAGICIANS.

HERCULES (MOVIES ABOUT) This oily, pumped-up Greek was in many ways the original action hero. Audiences thrilled to his ass-kicking adventures long before movies existed—or technology of any sort, for that matter. A certain subset of film fans likewise digs him, even though he's never translated very well to the big screen. Perhaps it's because directors insist on casting him in such sacrilege as *Hercules and the Captive Women*, *Hercules Against the Moon Men*, and *Hercules in New York* (a low-budget nightmare from 1970 featuring Arnold Schwarzenegger in his first starring role). About the only Hercules project that stayed pumped up over the long haul was *Hercules: The Legendary Journeys*, a series of made-for-TV films that led to a long-running series starring Kevin Sorbo. Why was it so successful? Perhaps because management dispensed with Herc's customary skirt and gave him pants. See also SCHWARZENEGGER, ARNOLD and *XENA: WARRIOR PRINCESS*.

HESTON, CHARLTON Whether you agree with the politics of this former National Rifle Association front man or not, you have to acknowledge his cinematic range. After all, who but Heston has kept a straight face while appearing in so many of the major snicker-inducing cinematic genres? Heston has done biblical epic (*The Ten Commandments*, *Ben-Hur*, *The Greatest Story Ever Told*), futuristic adventure (*Planet of the Apes*, *The Omega Man*, *Soylent Green*), disaster (*Earthquake*), titles that sound like porn (*The Last Hard Men*), airplane-in-distress (*Skyjacked*, *Airport 1975*), horror (*The Awakening*), and movies featuring Tim Matheson (*Solar Crisis*), all with the same chin-out determination that makes us want to shout "Soylent green is people!" whenever we see him. See also PRE–*STAR WARS* '70S SCI-FI FILMS.

HICKORY FARMS A Hickory Farms gift box will never enjoy the cachet of, say, a Gold Ballotin of Godiva Truffles or a Smoked Sockeye Salmon Sampler from Harry and David. But that doesn't stop us from salivating over the sight of a

< 123 >

yellow wheel of rat trap cheese or a Beef Stick Summer Sausage the size of a billy club. Consisting of bits of shrink-wrapped, brightly colored cheese and meat pieced together like a preschooler's puzzle, these boxes are perfect for a Barcalounger-bound pig-out. The Maumee, Ohio–based company has been around since 1951, but sadly, its mall stores were closed in 2000 (except for temporary, holiday-season kiosks) so the company could concentrate on its mail order business. See also BARCALOUNGERS and BOLOGNA.

HIGHWAY TO HEAVEN The third jewel in Michael Landon's triple crown (he previously enjoyed long TV runs with *Bonanza* and *Little House on the Prairie*), this angel-comes-back-to-Earth-to-help-the-rest-of-us series satisfied viewers who longed for an otherworldly force to help fix their problems (as opposed to, say, Dr. Phil). This *Highway* was closed in 1989 after a five-year run. Oddly, Landon and costar Victor French (also of *Little House*) both died within the next two years. See also DR. PHIL; LANDON, MICHAEL; and *LITTLE HOUSE ON THE PRAIRIE*.

HILL, BENNY See *BENNY HILL SHOW, THE*.

HINN, BENNY See TELEVANGELISTS.

HOCKEY FIGHTS Sometimes you just want to haul off and deck a co-worker. If you are, say, an accountant, this impulse must be suppressed, lest unemployment and legal action ensue. In professional hockey, however, pounding on someone will earn you only a few minutes in the penalty box, along with cheers from your adoring, bloodthirsty fans (witness the Philadelphia Flyers in their "Broad Street Bullies" heyday). For every crass spectator who openly cheers hockey brawls, however, there's another who keeps a façade of civility on his face while his guts scream out, "Pound the bastard!"

HOGAN, HULK Born Terry Gene Bollea, this six-foot-six-inch mass of muscle first entered the wrestling world as Terry Boulder, before (we think, wisely) changing his name to Hulk Hogan. As with fellow human cartoon Mr. T, fame found Hogan thanks to an on-screen appearance opposite Sylvester Stallone. After playing a pro wrestler named Thunderlips in *Rocky III*, he became a World Wrestling Federation superstar, helping bring the "sport" to heights surpassing even its 1950s nothing-else-is-on-TV heyday. Hogan tried to parlay his popularity with young chair-throwing fans into gruff-but-lovable movie stardom, but such bombs as *Suburban Commando* and *Mr. Nanny* quickly drove

< 124 >

him back to the wrestling ring. See also MR. T; PROFESSIONAL WRESTLING; ROCKY MOVIES; and STALLONE, SYLVESTER.

HOGAN'S HEROES Who'd have thought being a World War II prisoner of war could be this much fun? This 1965–71 series told of the adventures of a ragtag group of Allies held at Stalag 13, whose security seemed about as lax as that of the average suburban office complex. Each week, Colonel Hogan (Bob Crane) and his cohorts (including future *Family Feud*-er Richard Dawson) got the better of their nemesis Colonel Klink (played  by Werner Klemperer, a Jew who fled Nazi Germany in the 1930s). By season six, the show's last, the number of people Hogan helped save was rising to Schindler-like proportions. The fact that Crane, after his murder in 1978, was revealed to be an amateur erotic filmmaker who had taken photos and home movies of hundreds of women (see Paul Schrader's 2002 movie *Auto Focus*) makes watching this bizarre hit even stranger today. See also *FAMILY FEUD*.

HOLIDAY INNS Thanks to Kemmons Wilson, you are never more than a mile or two from a generic, utterly nondescript hotel. Wilson is the man who, in 1952, lifted the name from a popular Bing Crosby movie and opened the first Holiday Inn. From a single Memphis location, his kids-eat-free empire has expanded to more than 1,500 outlets and tens of thousands of rooms, all equipped with tiny bars of soap. Even the most sophisticated traveler, risking falling asleep at the wheel, has taken comfort in pulling into a parking lot lit by the familiar green Holiday Inn sign, anticipating a restful—if forgettable—night's sleep.

HOLLY HOBBIE Named after the American Greetings artist who created her in the late 1960s, Holly Hobbie worked that whole patchwork country look for all it was worth. In return, her cute little sunbonneted profile graced everything from stationery to bedspreads to commemorative Coca-Cola glasses. But like so many pop icons before and since, Holly's star burned bright and fast. By the early '80s no grade-schooler would be caught dead with a faux gingham lunchbox. But had they known their Holly Hobbie doll would one day fetch a handsome price on the character collectibles market, they might not have chewed its fingers off. See also PRECIOUS MOMENTS.

HOLLYWOOD SQUARES, THE Long about

< 125 >

eighth grade, most of us give up offering wiseass answers to serious questions lest we suffer the wrath of put-upon teachers. But for the celebrities housed in the tic-tac-toe set of *The Hollywood Squares*, wiseass answers weren't just okay, they were encouraged. In fact, they were the reason audiences tuned in during the initial 1966 through 1982 run and then for numerous revivals. We didn't really care if circle got the square or which contestant won. We cared how Paul Lynde, Charley Weaver, Rose Marie, Wally Cox, and the other squares responded to questions posed by toothy host Peter Marshall. So popular were the answers that *Zingers from the Hollywood Squares* became both a paperback book and a record album. Sample: Peter Marshall: "According to the article on dogs in the *Encyclopedia Americana*, the most important single word any dog can learn is . . . what?" Jonathan Winters: "Woof." See also GAME SHOWS.

HOLLYWOOD WALK OF FAME It's easy to spot the tourists on Hollywood Boulevard. They're the only ones looking down. It's nearly impossible *not* to as you prowl either that famous street from Gower to La Brea, or Vine Street from Yucca to Sunset. Festooned on the wide sidewalks are the more than 2,000 names, each in its own manhole-sized star, that together comprise the world-famous Hollywood Walk of Fame. This display is also an unintended object lesson in the shallowness of worldly acclaim, since most of the names honor people you've never heard of (Licia Albanese? Edward Sedgwick? Henry B. Walthall?). The walk has added about two "luminaries" per month since Joanne Woodward received the first star in 1960. The result resembles both a giant trivia contest and a serious pedestrian hazard. Woe to the walker stuck behind fans seeking a particular star, be it Sharon Stone or Slim Summerville. See also OLSEN TWINS, THE.

HOME SHOPPING NETWORK, THE Arguably the biggest waste of time on cable television, the roots of this first all-shopping channel go back to 1977, when a Clearwater, Florida, radio station accepted 112 can openers in lieu of cash to settle a hardware store's advertising bill. Station owner Lowell Paxson tried selling them on the air, and the product, to his amazement, flew out the door. Paxson and a business partner took the idea to a local access cable channel in 1981, then brought it national in 1985. Today the company ships more than 34 million items per year, bringing joy to shut-ins, old folks, and the unemployed all over the country. See also AS SEEN ON TV PRODUCTS; QVC; and RONCO PRODUCTS.

< 126 >

HOOTERS Saying you patronize this restaurant chain for the food is like saying you read *Playboy* for the articles. The first location, which opened in 1983 in Clearwater, Florida, was the brainchild of six middle-aged businessmen. Not surprisingly, the eateries' ambience is a gone-to-seed old guy's idea of paradise: lots of beer, a menu filled with fried things, oldies on the sound system, and, the *pièce de résistance*, a wait staff of "Hooters girls" wearing tight T-shirts and tiny orange shorts. Ask employees if the operation's name refers to the waitresses' ample cleavage, and you'll be told that it really pays homage to an old Steve Martin comedy bit. Right. Perhaps the chain, now with more than 330 locations worldwide (and an airline), could try this motto: Come for the spicy wings, stay for the plump breasts! See also *PLAYBOY*.

HOROSCOPES Google the word "horoscope" and you'll get more than six million hits. Pretty good for a system of nonsense with no track record of accuracy, no basis in science, and no reason for existing except to convince the gullible that their lives are somehow influenced by the positions of the stars in the night sky. And to make horoscope creators a few bucks. Of course, this doesn't keep even the most cynical from occasionally sneaking a glance at the predictions offered in the daily newspaper, then wondering if today might truly offer them a "chance to meet a new love."

HOT DOGS (CONVENIENCE STORE) The old saying "Any port in a storm" is never so sorely tested as when a hungry traveler contemplates eating a convenience store hot dog. But once you get past the unknowable (how long has it been waiting on that rolling steamer grill?) and slather it with the requisite mustard and relish from the condiment-splotched table, such dogs provide a secret thrill when you discover that your sodium sandwich is not just edible, but enjoyable. (Of course, other times you are just thankful when it stays down.) See also HOT DOGS (STADIUM).

HOT DOGS (STADIUM) Unlike the convenience store hot dog, the stadium dog is not purchased in desperation or haste. Rather, it's a game-day rite, as important as downing a beer and cursing an official. The tradition of "dachshund sausages" (as they were once called) being sold at games is said to go back to 1893, when bar owner/team owner Chris Von de Ahe introduced them at a St. Louis Browns baseball matchup. The term "hot dog" has also been linked to the game. Allegedly a *New York Journal* cartoonist, trying to capture a scene in the stands at the New York Polo

< 127 >

Grounds in 1901, wanted to write "Get your dachshund sausages while they're red hot." Unable to spell dachshund, he simply wrote "Hot dog!" However, other stories say that, years earlier, Yale students used the term "dog wagons" to describe sausage carts peddling questionable wares. See also HOT DOGS (CONVENIENCE STORE).

HOT-OR-NOT WEB SITES "Judge not, that ye not be judged" is an often-quoted line from the Gospel According to Matthew. It's not, however, an often-followed tenet. The desire to judge seems hardwired into our system. Witness the new-millennium Web craze for hot-or-not Web sites (and a subsequent short-lived TV series) in which photos of real people are presented for the rating pleasure of you, the person sitting at your home computer. On most such sites, your score is averaged with those of everyone else who voted, so you can see if your score matched the masses (or, at least, the part of the masses that sits at their computers wasting time on silly Web sites). Amihotornot.com started as a lark and went on to attract 3 million page views a day after only six weeks. Of course, that could be three really lonely guys judging a million women each, but that's probably not the case. More likely, this amazingly addictive site (now called simply hotornot.com)

and its copycats have tapped into the guilty kick of anonymously assessing someone's visual allure without putting our own on the line.

HOT POCKETS See MICROWAVED DINNERS.

H. R. PUFNSTUF See KROFFT, SID AND MARTY.

HUGHES, JOHN See *BREAKFAST CLUB, THE* and *WEIRD SCIENCE*.

HUMMEL FIGURES Let the collectors worry about things like backstamps and issue dates. The rest of us will happily admire Apple Tree Girl, Accordion Boy, Kitty Kisses, and Cheeky Fellow from the other side of the curio cabinet. Germany's Goebel Company (absolutely *no* relation) started churning out the rosy-cheeked figurines in 1935, based on paintings by a nun in a nearby convent. People clamored for the company's annual batch of pouty tykes, Goebel  broke a few molds for good measure, and the rest is swap meet history. You have to admit that they *are* kinda cute in their saggy lederhosen and scuffed corrective shoes. But knowing that Umbrella Girl (who sold for $25 when she

< 128 >

first came out in the 1950s) now commands about $1,100 at Hummel trade shows takes away a tiny bit of her charm. See also HOLLY HOBBIE and PRECIOUS MOMENTS.

HUMMER, THE This most formidable of all SUVs was originally developed by the AM General corporation to replace the U.S. Army's Jeep. Called the High Mobility Multi-Purpose Wheeled Vehicle (or HMMWV for sort-of-short), the 6,500-pound behemoth became famous during the first Gulf War. A civilian model was soon offered, with Arnold Schwarzenegger claiming the first one off the assembly line. Comparing it to conventional 4x4s is like comparing Desert Storm to a sorority house pillow fight. Designed to survive 12 years of round-the-clock military operations, it features 16 inches of ground clearance, a 6.5-liter diesel truck engine, and eyelets on the hood to facilitate helicopter transport. In other words, it's more vehicle than a private citizen needs—unless that private citizen happens to be a well-heeled man in the throes of a midlife crisis (73 percent of Hummer purchasers are male, average age 41).

In 2002 AM General, in conjunction with General Motors, released a slightly tamer Hummer called the H2 (the original is now called the H1), which is priced at about half that of its big brother.

However, one feature remains the same: appalling gas mileage. The H2 gets 10 mpg in the city, 12 on the highway. See also RECREATIONAL VEHICLES; SCHWARZENEGGER, ARNOLD; and SUVs.

HUMPERDINCK, ENGELBERT You gotta love a guy who decides to bag his bland-but-record-label-friendly name (Gerry Dorsey) and adopt the sprawling moniker of a 19th-century German composer. Career suicide? Not for Engelbert Humperdinck. Fame found the British singer in 1967 when, with his new name, he filled in at the London Palladium for an ailing singer and wowed the crowd with his new single, "Release Me." It would remain Humperdinck's signature tune throughout his career, which included everything from the Grammy-nominated album *After the Lovin'* to the song "Lesbian Seagull" recorded for *Beavis and Butt-head Do America*. The guy obviously has a sense of humor, as anyone who saw his '70s-era mutton-chop sideburns already knows. Never a critics' darling, Humperdinck, like his contemporary Tom Jones, built his reputation on give-the-audience-all-you've-got live shows. Which is why, while your neighbors may not admit to being fans, Humperdinck has nevertheless played to sold-out crowds for three decades. See also BEAVIS AND BUTT-HEAD; JONES, TOM; and SIDEBURNS.

< 129 >

HUSTLER Begun as a newsletter to help promote Ohio strip clubs owned by Larry Flynt, *Hustler* became a full-color, no-clothes-barred magazine in 1974, positioned as a dirtier, riskier alternative to *Playboy*. Not only did it reach a peak 3 million circulation, it also turned its publisher into a media star—albeit a slimy, Jabba the Hut–like media star. Flynt's colorful history includes a Supreme Court battle with televangelist Jerry Falwell, a $1 million offer for evidence of the extramarital sexual exploits of Washington Republicans (a move that led to the resignation of would-be Speaker of the House Bob Livingston), a Hollywood bio-movie, an assassination attempt that left him in a wheelchair, and a run for the California governors' office. All of which helped *Hustler* readers rationalize that they weren't just buying the magazine to look at not-as-hot-as-*Penthouse* models. They were part of a *political* movement. Who'd have thought you could further the cause of free speech in America simply by masturbating? See also MASTURBATION; *PENTHOUSE FORUM*; *PLAYBOY*; and TELE-VANGELISTS.

< 130 >

I-J

I DREAM OF JEANNIE Created by Sidney Sheldon (of sleazy novel fame), this 1965 to 1970 series tapped into the same adolescent fantasy as *Weird Science* and uncounted porno movies: What if a beautiful woman suddenly appeared out of nowhere and agreed to do your bidding? In this case, the woman was a genie who, the lyricless opening sequence showed us, was released from her bottle by astronaut Tony Nelson (pre-*Dallas* Larry Hagman). While the fantasy is common, the fact that Jeannie displayed a bare midriff, lived with her bachelor buddy, and called him "master" added major guilty kicks to the otherwise innocent proceedings. See also *DALLAS* and *WEIRD SCIENCE*.

ICE CASTLES This 1979 flick can be called, without reservation, the greatest romantic drama about a blind ice skater ever made. In a plot that set the stage for numberless other people-overcoming-handicaps-and-finding-love movies, a 16-year-old Olympics-bound ice skater loses her sight in an accident. She (as would any sane person) figures her competitive skating days are done, but her boyfriend, Robby Benson, gives her the strength to get back on the ice and win. At the time, this premise made perfect sense to girls between the ages of 13 and 16. See also CHICK FLICKS (CINDERELLA FANTASIES).

ICE SKATING SHOWS Combining the glitz of a Vegas revue and the athleticism of a figure skating exhibition, such bygone shows as the Ice Capades and its contemporary "on ice" counterparts (*Disney on Ice: Princess Classics*, *Wizard of Oz on Ice*, et al.) satisfy our desire to see grace, elegance, guys in tights, and/or women in short skirts. More importantly, the arena shows serve as a *Love Boat*–like place for post-peak figure skaters to show off their fading skills, far from those annoying Olympic judges.

IMPOSTOR PERFUMES Who would pay more than $50 for a 3.3-ounce bottle of White Diamonds perfume by Elizabeth Taylor, when you could get the same amount of its impostor, Ice Gems, for $2.50? Certainly not any fake-fragrance aficionados we know. Never mind that the imitators never smell exactly like their uppity originals. You can always blame it on body chemistry. See also DRUGSTORE PERFUMES.

INCREDIBLE HULK, THE This not-so-jolly green giant debuted in Marvel Comics in 1962. (He was originally

< 131 >

gray, but a printing error turned him his famous green.) Since then the Hulk has appeared in numberless comic books, a big-budget feature  film, and, most famously, a CBS television series. Featuring Bill Bixby as scientist David Banner and Lou Ferrigno as his snarling, car-crushing, tiny-pants-wearing alter ego, the program earned muscular ratings by taking the revenge fantasy to new heights—or depths, depending on how you feel about payback. Banner, who was exposed to an overdose of gamma radiation, turned into the Hulk whenever he got stressed. Which meant that if anybody messed with Bixby (and people *always* messed with him), Ferrigno (wearing a fright wig, Billy Bob teeth, and a couple of quarts of Gumby-hued body paint) would suddenly appear and give them flying lessons. And the best part, from the vicariously thrilled audience's perspective, was that all that ass whooping *wasn't Banner's fault.* He wasn't a vigilante nutcase like Rambo or Billy Jack. He was just a regular guy who had a *condition.* See also *BILLY JACK*; RAMBO MOVIES; and SUPERHEROES.

INFOMERCIALS See AS SEEN ON TV PRODUCTS.

INSPIRATIONAL BOOKS No less an addiction than Harlequin Romances, inspirational books are quickly read, quickly abandoned, and just as quickly forgotten. Out of pop psych, out of mind, one might say. Still, books like *Life's Little Instruction Book* and the endless incarnations of *Chicken Soup for the Soul* are addictive and, in some cases, capable of inspiring readers to, if not actually change their lives, at least *think* about changing them. Unlike self-help books, inspirational titles aren't really about the process. They're about simplifying philosophy and theology for the layperson (and by "layperson" we mean anyone who considers Khalil Gibran to be a deep thinker and feels that angels on a cover imply a heavenly endorsement). See also BUSCAGLIA, LEO; *CHICKEN SOUP FOR THE SOUL*; FULGHUM, ROBERT; and HARLEQUIN ROMANCES.

***INSTYLE* MAGAZINE** Launched in 1994, this glossy mag devoted entirely to celebrities and fashion makes its Time Inc. sister publication *People* read like a scholarly journal. Practicing the four W's of journalism (Who Wore What Where), *InStyle* gives its readers a monthly dose of high-quality fluff, including a retrospective of Faith Hill's hairstyles, a tour of Beau Bridges's garden, a peek inside Reese Witherspoon's makeup bag, and a shopping guide full

< 132 >

of dropped names. True, a magazine whose cover lines proclaim "What to Wear Now!" "What's Sexy Now!" and "Debra Messing: The Real Deal" lacks a certain intellectual mien, but no hand-carved antique wood coffee table (like the one in Macy Gray's Los Angeles living room) would be complete without it. See also ENTERTAINMENT TONIGHT and STARS' HOMES.

INTERNET RUMORS It's very easy to check the validity of an Internet rumor. Just plug some key words into a search engine, add the word "rumor," and you'll get plenty of sites created by folks who take it upon themselves to verify or discredit such things. But where's the fun in that? Better to use the awesome technology at our fingertips to tell everyone on our address list that John Denver was an Army sniper, that the FCC pressured *Touched by an Angel* to remove references to God, that Oliver North warned us about Osama bin Laden, and that Charles Darwin renounced evolution on his deathbed. See also DENVER, JOHN.

IRON CHEF A peculiar combination of cooking show and sporting event, this demented Japanese import enjoys a huge U.S. following, even though most viewers would never consider eating the exotic dishes prepared here. The "iron chefs" are four Nipponese culinary masters, each specializing in a different cuisine: Japanese, Chinese, French, and Italian. Each week one of the four, overseen by a bizarre emcee in matador costumes (really an actor named Kaga Takeshi), is challenged to a food fight by an outside chef. The two then spend one hour creating dishes based on a surprise ingredient (anything from cucumber to sea urchin). The resulting fare is sampled by a panel of judges, who then pick a winner.

The show was a huge hit in Japan, where it ran from 1993 to 1999, and where several *Iron Chef* (the literal  translation is *Cooking Iron Man*) specials are still presented annually. The U.S. version (broadcast on the Food Network) draws fans with its Godzilla movie–quality dubbed dialogue, the bizarre ingredients, and the samurai-like seriousness with which the contestants approach each match. The appeal is so strong that UPN even developed a couple of Americanized *Iron Chef* specials, with William Shatner as the host. See also COOKING SHOWS; GODZILLA; and SHATNER, WILLIAM.

IT'S A WONDERFUL LIFE Frank Capra's 1946 classic (unsuccessful on its initial release) makes even the most hard-

< 133 >

hearted guy want to run down the street shouting "Merry Christmas" to the old building and loan. See also TEARJERKER MOVIES (FOR MEN) and *TOUCHED BY AN ANGEL*.

JACKASS At one time or another, all of us (except for maybe Niles Crane and the Queen Mother) had a streak of "Hey, watch this" stupidity in us—a willingness to ride what we shouldn't ride, swing on that which shouldn't be swung on, and race through the halls of hotels on a wobbly-wheeled luggage cart. Of course everyone grows out of that phase—unless you're talking about Johnny Knoxville and his buddies. The stars of the 2000 to 2001 MTV series *Jackass* and the bafflingly successful *Jackass: The Movie* demonstrated both a propensity for tackling dangerous-looking, poorly-thought-out stunts and a remarkably high pain tolerance when those stunts went wrong. The crew "urban kayaks" in city fountains, tests the protective power of an athletic cup by firing paintballs at each other's privates, swallows and then vomits up live fish, and sprays each other in the face with fire extinguishers. Such can-you-top-this acts of idiocy, plus lots of scatological stunts and a steadfast refusal to explain what the point was, made *Jackass* a chance to release the "dare you" clown in us all. See also KICKED IN THE NUTS (WATCHING SOMEONE GET); MORONS (ENTERTAINING, UNTIMELY DEATHS OF); and STUNTS (INSANE, TELEVISED).

JACKSON FAMILY, THE What does it take to found a musical dynasty? If you believe the 1992 ABC miniseries *The Jacksons: An American Dream*, it takes practice, talent, persistence, and a bunch of ass whoopings from your perfectionist, borderline-abusive father. The nine Jackson siblings—Rebbie, Jackie, Tito, Jermaine, LaToya, Marlon, Michael, Randy, and Janet—were born in Gary, Indiana, to Katherine and Joseph Jackson. Dad Joe, a small-time guitarist for a local R&B band, recognized his kids' musical talents and encouraged (and by "encouraged" we mean "forced") them to form a musical act called the Jackson 5. By 1969 they were signed with Motown Records, and by 1971 they were riding the top of the charts with songs such as "ABC." Over the decades, in addition to some fine dance tunes, the Jackson clan has provided connoisseurs of guilty pleasures with enough scandals to fill an entire *Dynasty* season. See also *DYNASTY*; JACKSON, LATOYA; JACKSON, MICHAEL; and JACKSON, TITO.

JACKSON, LATOYA The interesting thing about LaToya, older sister of Michael and Janet, is that she managed

< 134 >

to crash and burn without ever reaching the heights of success. Born in 1956, she cut her teeth on show business by singing occasional backup for the family's bread and butter, the Jackson 5. She signed with Polydor in 1979 as a solo artist, but couldn't score a single hit. So instead of working harder, she posed in the nude for *Playboy*, wrote a nasty, tell-all autobiography in 1991 that alienated her from her family, hitched her name to a "psychic" hotline, then signed to headline at the Moulin Rouge in Paris—a deal that collapsed after only a few months. Saying you're a LaToya fan is akin to saying that Irlene is your favorite Mandrell Sister. See also JACKSON FAMILY, THE; JACKSON, MICHAEL; and JACKSON, TITO.

JACKSON, MICHAEL Remember, in the video for the title song from his album *Thriller*, how Michael Jackson said, "I'm not like other guys"? Well, truer words were never spoken. Yet hard as it is to believe, there was once a time when his fans could proclaim their devotion from the rooftops without drawing a second look. Back when he served as the diminutive front man for the Jackson 5, and during his early 20s as the force behind the albums *Off the Wall* and *Thriller* (which has sold over 50 million copies to date), Jackson may well have been the undisputed King of Pop. But

during the '90s his high-pitched squealing and dance-friendly melodies were muscled off the charts by grunge and rap. Still dressed in what looked like castoffs from the *Beat It* video, he became a Lawrence Welk–like anachronism. That is, if Lawrence Welk had outfitted his home as an amusement park, complete with rides and a petting zoo; "married" one of his groupies and then "fathered" two children via artificial insemination; dangled his son off a hotel balcony in front of dozens of photographers; and underwent so much plastic surgery that his face looked like a waxwork model left under a sun lamp. All of which makes it harder and harder for fans to say, "I like Michael Jackson," without drawing quizzical stares. See also JACKSON FAMILY, THE; JACKSON, LATOYA; JACKSON, TITO; *LAWRENCE WELK SHOW, THE*; and *THRILLER*.

JACKSON, TITO Many of the nine Jackson siblings became known for some distinguishing physical trait. Michael is The Gloved One. Janet is The Cute One. As for brother Tito (Toriano Adaryll Jackson) he was (and remains) The Fat One. A charter member of the Jackson 5, he actually worked on a solo project while at Motown Records, though it was never released. But so what? He still got to ride the rainbow. And while some fans, in the group's hey-

< 135 >

day, probably imagined themselves as Michael, the more realistic no doubt wished they were Tito—just a normal guy of no outstanding ability who by an accident of birth got a seat on the Success Rocket. See also JACKSON FAMILY, THE; JACKSON, LATOYA; JACKSON, MICHAEL; and RINGO.

JAPANESE ANIMATION (ADULT) You live in a strange yet vaguely familiar post-apocalyptic, amoral world. Your girlfriend is an android, an alien, or a demon. And your "job" involves lumbering around inside a big-ass robot, battling other big-ass robots. Welcome to the world of adult Japanese animation, or anime. While most American animation (even the stuff that attracts adult audiences) is inherently kid-friendly, in Japan that's definitely not the case. In fact, the genre, perhaps because of its air of unreality, is home to some of the oddest visions ever committed to celluloid. Nothing, and we mean *nothing*, is off limits. Fans, if they have the stomach for it, can find anything from the atomic bombing of Hiroshima (*Barefoot Gen*) to sex scenes so graphic and misogynistic (*Legend of the Overfiend*) they make a laughingstock of the NC-17 rating. Which is why parents cruising the video store for cartoons for the kids should never, ever snap up an unfamiliar anime without first reading the box. And then,

just to be safe, watching the whole thing before turning it over to junior.

JARED   See DIETS, FAD.

JEAN NATE   See DRUGSTORE PERFUMES.

JELL-O   Believe it or not, this so-easy-it's-embarrassing dessert was once the height of haute cuisine. Gelatin, in case you didn't know (or had banished it from your mind), is usually derived from cow bones, hides, and connective tissue. In the 19th century only the gentry ate enough meat to accumulate the spare body parts needed to make this wobbly treat. But in 1845 American inventor Peter Cooper developed a way to preserve gelatin in a stable, powdered form. Two years later, American inventor Pearle Wait developed a fruit-flavored version of Cooper's gelatin. His wife, May, came up with the name Jell-O. In 1899 Wait, unable to create a market for his invention, sold the formula and name to manufacturer and salesman Orator F. Woodward—for $450. Woodward made it a success by sending out salesman armed with cookbooks explaining how to create fancy-looking dishes just like the rich folks. Shortly thereafter (and forevermore), desserts made from rendered cow parts became staples of picnics, family reunions, and lowbrow wedding receptions. See also AMBROSIA.

< 136 >

JERKY True jerky (dried meat) is usually low in calories, and fairly nutritionally benign for a meat-based snack. Yet no other dish carries such a pronounced if-you-eat-'em-you're-a-hillbilly stigma. Perhaps it's the fact that they're mostly sold in convenience stores, right next to the scratch-off lottery tickets. Or that true jerky is often confused with "meat sticks"—processed, wiener-shaped products chock full of fat and preservatives, and usually incorporating protein from an entire barnyard of different species. Hint: If you're caught at work with some jerky, tell your co-workers that it's pemmican (a Native American snack). Chances are it's probably already called that on the package, because jerky makers are desperate to upgrade their image. See also LOTTERY TICKETS (SCRATCH-OFF); PORK RINDS; and SALT (EXCESSIVE APPLICATION TO FOOD OF).

JERKY BOYS, THE See CRANK PHONE CALLS.

JERRY LEWIS LABOR DAY TELETHON, THE See LEWIS, JERRY.

JETSONS, THE See HANNA-BARBERA CARTOONS.

JIFFY POP POPCORN In the days before microwaves, this snack (created by La Porte, Indiana, native Fred Mennen) was the last word in snack preparation technology. The popcorn was good, but the real fun was watching the foil covering expand to the size of a space alien's cranium as you shook the disposable Jiffy  Pop pan back and forth over the stove burner. The perfect creature feature accompaniment, it even earned a prominent spot as Drew Barrymore's almost-last meal in the 1996 slasher movie send-up *Scream*.

JOKES, BLOND Once mainstream America realized it had no real beef with the Poles, the butt of the classic "isn't that person stupid" joke became blonds. Not only did this prove an effective way of recycling old gags ("Look, deer tracks," says one blond. "No, they're wolf tracks," says the other. "No, deer tracks," says the first. "No, wolf tracks," says the second. After a half hour of arguing, they are hit by a train.), it also gave the teller and the laugher the guilty sense that they were getting away with something in a post-*Ms*. world.

JOKES, DIRTY Like dirty movies, dirty Web sites, and dirty books, dirty jokes not only titillate, but also make you feel like you are getting away with some-

< 137 >

thing. That's why dirty jokes are huge with pre-adolescents still figuring out what goes where. But there's a rich history here. Chaucer, Shakespeare, and other "respectable" writers owe much of their popularity, at least among their contemporaries, to the fact that they had fun with the down and dirty. How different, after all, is Shakespeare's one-liner "Is it not strange that desire should so many years outlive performance?" from the classic joke in which the old man thinks, "My God, if I knew she was a virgin, I would have been much more gentle with her!" and his young lover thinks, "My God, if I knew the old geezer could actually get it up, I would have taken off my panty hose"?

JOKES, ETHNIC The Irish are drunks. The Polish are stupid. The Mexicans dirty. The Jews greedy. The French cowardly. Englishmen are dull. The Chinese can't drive. Such are the basic tenents that built the careers of Don Rickles and other comedians and keep nonprofessional joke-tellers busy during office parties, car pools, and coffee breaks. Sociologists peg the perpetuation of such jokes as a symptom of our desire to classify others. Common folk guiltily put the blame on the fact that many of the jokes are actually funny (e.g., What is a Polish vacation? Sitting on someone else's steps). See also RICKLES, DON.

JOKES, FAXED OR E-MAILED It might be a list of George Carlin one-liners not actually written by Carlin. It might be an anonymous cartoon featuring Osama bin Laden in a compromising position. Anyone with a fax machine or e-mail account knows what it's like to feign annoyance while guiltily sneaking a look at jokes sent from friends . . . and then to forward them along to everyone in your address book.

JOKES, KNOCK-KNOCK If puns are the lowest form of humor, then knock-knocks are the lowest form of joke. Yet no matter how many times your imaginary knocker is knocked on, it's still nearly impossible not to return the requisite "Who's there?" if, for no other reason, than to find out if the joker at the door has come up with a knock-knock joke you haven't heard. For example, "Knock Knock." ["Who's there?"] "Tarzan." ["Tarzan who?"] "Tarzan Stripes Forever." Sure, it sucks—but chances are, you're reading it for the first time.

JOKES, SICK Quadriplegics. Helen Keller. Dead Babies. All are the subject of sick jokes designed not so much to *be* gags as to elicit them. Mysteriously passed from generation to generation of American adolescents, sick jokes show a remarkable ability to adapt to whatever

< 138 >

is in the headlines (What were Christa McAuliffe's last words? "What does this button do?"). And a remarkable ability to get us to repeat them even after we've said, "That's gross."

JONATHAN LIVINGSTON SEAGULL From the dedication ("To the real Jonathan Seagull, who lives within us all") to the final words ("His race to learn had begun"), Richard Bach's slim volume is an exercise in simplistic philosophy. This tale of a free-spirited gull whose narrow-minded fellow birds keep him from maximizing his potential was more than a hit—it was a critic-baffling best seller that made even the most simpleminded reader think semi-deep thoughts.

By the time the 1973 movie was made from this seemingly impossible-to-film book (it used the deadly combination of real gulls and Neil Diamond music), the appeal had diminished, to say the least. The fact that the flick is widely considered to be one of the worst movies of all time might have played a part as well. While the book remains a guilty pleasure, the film doesn't even qualify as "so bad it's fun." See also *BRIDGES OF MADISON COUNTY, THE*.

JONES, DEAN See DISNEY FILMS FEATURING DEAN JONES AND/OR KURT RUSSELL.

JONES, TOM He's got looks, style, and talent, all wrapped up in one very large, very obvious package. Born into a coal mining family in South Wales in 1940, Jones rode to fame on the wings of the worldwide smash (and, now, lounge act standard) "It's Not Unusual." Jones had other hits, but it wasn't his singing that made him an international sensation. It was his good looks and (though few of his '60s-era female fans would admit it) the fact the he appeared to be hauling around a couple of pounds of kielbasa in the front of his extremely tight trousers. Perhaps inevitably, Jones became a Vegas headliner, where his ability to mesmerize his (largely female) audiences was so legendary that Elvis is said to have incorporated some of his moves into his own show. These days, though Jones is in his 60s, he's still an icon of . . . well, we're not exactly sure what. But he's got enough street cred to team up with the alternative band Art of Noise and have his tunes (most often "She's a Lady") sampled for everything from movies (including *Miss Congeniality*) to TV commercials (including Coors Light). See also CHICK FLICKS (CINDERELLA FANTASIES); HUMPERDINCK, ENGELBERT; LAS VEGAS; PRESLEY, ELVIS; and SAUSAGE.

JONNY QUEST See HANNA-BARBERA CARTOONS.

< 139 >

JOSIE AND THE PUSSYCATS See ARCHIE COMICS; HANNA-BARBERA CARTOONS and SATURDAY MORNING CARTOONS.

JUICE BOXES Yes, parents realize that excess packaging creates more landfill clutter. But that doesn't keep them from praising (and using) the juice box. Thanks to this remarkable rectangular creation, annoying Thermos bottles that require regular cleaning have largely vanished from school lunches. In their place are highly disposable, straw-already-attached containers of fruit juice (or, more likely, fruit "drink"). Savvy moms and dads freeze them prior to hot days, and savvy commuters know that juice boxes are safer to drink while driving than other tilt-your-head-back beverages.

JUMBLE Usually parked somewhere south of *The Family Circus*, this daily puzzle, subheaded "that scrambled word game," offers a series of mixed-up words, select letters in which, when unscrambled, give the answer to a cartoon joke. Appearing in more than 600 newspapers, *Jumble* takes a lot less time than the crossword puzzle, but requires slightly more brains than the word search. These days, you don't even have to sully your fingers with newsprint: The game is available online, in books, and in a version for handheld devices.

Getting caught playing it on the subway, though, instantly neutralizes anything you thought was cool about your Palm Pilot. See also *FAMILY CIRCUS, THE.*

< 140 >

K

KARAOKE What began in Japan as an after-work stress reliever has evolved into a cheap way for American bars to avoid hiring entertainers. Instead of paying a singer, just get the karaoke machine going and the crowd will amuse itself by struggling through such classics as "I Will Survive" and "Just a Gigolo." Watching karaoke gives you the chance to mock singers worse than you. Singing karaoke gives you the chance to feel like Whitney while sounding like, well, you.

KC AND THE SUNSHINE BAND The music of Harry Wayne Casey (KC) and his big, loud, horn-intensive band wasn't what anyone would call "complex." No one debated the hidden meaning in lyrics such as "That's the way; uh-huh, uh-huh, I like it, uh-huh, uh-huh." Instead they joyously did what everyone else did during the group's '70s heyday: Put their brains on hold, headed for the dance floor, and tore the place up to tunes like "Get Down Tonight," "(Shake, Shake, Shake) Shake Your Booty," and "I'm Your Boogie Man." The lyrics are vapid, but the tunes still rock—so much so that when disco came back in the '90s, KC (who now, unfortunately, looks like a

pudgy used-car salesman) came back too. If you see him live, don't bother fighting the feeling. Just put on your boogie shoes and dance like no one's watching. See also DISCO (DANCING) and SUMMER, DONNA.

KENNEDY FAMILY, THE Cursed and blessed with more tragedies and triumphs than the complete works of Shakespeare, the Kennedy clan has captured American imaginations ever since Rose started birthing boys in 1915. No need to recap here the specific incidents, but suffice it to say that whether you're a defender of all things Hyannisportian or a closet scandalmonger, there's endless fascination in following the exploits of America's unofficial royal family.

KETCHUP When we say *ketchup*, what we really mean is *tomato ketchup*. Until fairly recently the word referred to an entire family of thick, salty, vinegar-based condiments, only some of which included tomato. The term actually derives from a Chinese term for a fermented fish sauce. Yum. So ubiquitous is modern tomato ketchup that it's estimated to be in 97 percent of American homes. While one can assume that most of that red lead finds its way onto hot dogs, hamburgers, French fries, and the like, true guilty pleasure comes from globbing it onto a good steak. Nixon

< 141 >

reportedly put it on cottage cheese, an embarrassment that rivals his implosion during the 1960 presidential debates.

KICKED IN THE NUTS (WATCHING SOMEONE GET) A man who takes a swift blow to the scrotum will experience severe pain, difficulty breathing, feelings of extreme nausea, and perhaps a fainting spell. A man who *watches* another man take a swift blow to the scrotum will experience a severely puckered facial expression, difficulty hiding his amusement, feelings of extreme mirth, and perhaps a laughing fit. While it's a mystery why so many people find the sight of someone getting kicked in the man sack entertaining, the spectacle is so popular that it is screened repeatedly on everything from *America's Funniest Home Videos* to commercials to numberless martial arts movies. But these films are made by people who have obviously never been kicked in the nuts. Otherwise they wouldn't show antagonists taking one, two, three, or even four swipes at the family jewels before folding. The truth is, one shot to the sperm bank ends a brawl quicker than a bullet to the temple. This move isn't called The Closer for nothing. See also AMERICA'S FUNNIEST HOME VIDEOS and KUNG-FU MOVIES.

KING, LARRY Born in 1933 and chatting away on TV since 1985, this gnomelike broadcaster helped put both CNN and the Ross Perot presidential candidacy on the map. King has also enjoyed a secondary career playing himself in movies, including *Ghostbusters*, *Dave*, *Contact*, *Primary Colors*, and, inexplicably, *The Exorcist III*. But perhaps the most important thing that Larry King has done for media is to provide morning zoo radio personalities with plenty of material—whether it's mocking his sycophantic interview questions, imitating his inane "News and Views" column that ran for years in *USA Today*, or teasing King's penchant for marrying women significantly his junior.

KING, STEPHEN There are a lot of books in the world. There are even a few not written by Stephen King. Not that you'd know it from looking at the best-seller lists. Beginning with 1974's *Carrie*, the master of page-turning-horror-usually-involving-dysfunctional-families-that-are-scary-even-without-the-supernatural-stuff has dominated the market, even when exploiting premises that literally no other big-name novelist could get away with (a killer car in *Christine*, a rabid St. Bernard in *Cujo*). Critics, academics, and *New York Times Book Review* readers like to pretend there's literary merit in his pages, but you know better. This guy just has a bril-

< 142 >

liant ability to scare the piss out of the masses. No wonder his total sales aren't measured in the millions, but in the *hundreds* of millions.

KINKADE, THOMAS The world is complicated. The art of Thomas Kinkade, the self-proclaimed Painter of Light, is not. Kinkade, who markets reproductions of his oil paintings in hundreds of galleries nationwide (along with posters, calendars, nightlights, cards, and figurines at seemingly every other retail outlet on the planet), makes millions each year selling not great art, but escapism. His works are filled with impossibly picturesque landscapes and idealized dwellings with names such as Hollyhock House, Lamplight Manor, and Brookside Hideaway. The point is not to provide fresh insight on the world, but to create an idealized neverland where stressed-out "collectors" can relax and briefly escape. Think of it as visual Valium. But while Kinkade is undeniably the Painter of Light (some of his cottages give off more candle-power than a low-yield nuclear blast), he's definitely not a Painter of People. There are very few humans in his perfect world, perhaps because perfection is impossible with them around. See also ROCKWELL, NORMAN.

KISS Okay, these guys aren't the Beatles—or even Aerosmith. Their songs, most of them stadium rock standards, have all the melodic sophistication of an oil refinery explosion. But when you're thundering down the open road at 2 A.M. in your Trans Am convertible, there's no one you'd rather have on the 8-track player than the self-described "hottest rock band in the world." Best? No. Most talented? Double no. But hottest? Definitely.

When founding members Gene Simmons and Paul Stanley hooked up in the early '70s, that's exactly what they set out to become. The duo brought guitarist Ace Frehley and drummer Peter Criss aboard, worked up bizarre stage makeup and black leather costumes, then went on tour. And they never stopped. Their 1975 live double album, *Kiss Alive*, turned them into megastars with their own action figures, solo albums, and even a 1978 TV movie, *Kiss Meets the Phantom of the Park*.

Through the years, and numerous lineup changes, the band kept pumping out hits. Finally, at the dawn of the 21st century, they entered the realm of nostalgia act—albeit a nostalgia act that can sell out massive arenas worldwide. Sure it's a bit juvenile, but don't keep your

< 143 >

passion for Kiss a secret. Instead, shout it, shout it, shout it out loud. See also CONCERT T-SHIRTS; GREATEST HITS ALBUMS; and TV MOVIES.

KITTEN POSTERS/CARDS Even the most cold, unfeeling, dogcentric person will glance up at the poster above his dentist's chair and grasp the tender "Just hang in there" sentiment of a terrified kitty dangling by a paw from a branch. The point is, a single furry face carries a vast amount of emo-tional information. Plus, nothing warms the cockles like a tabby in a teacup ("May your cup runneth over"), a kitten in a hammock ("Cat Nap"), or a feline wearing sunglasses ("Kool Kat"). Thanks to the work of artists such as Florida photographer Richard Watherwax, who shot the famous three-panel poster "Fat Cat Capsizing" (and who entered his own puss, Willoughby, in the 1989 Key West mayoral race), baby fur balls by the dozen mew out at us from the greeting card racks. Their dewy pink noses, disproportionately cute ears, and knowing cat eyes leave impulse card shoppers with only one question: "How many of these can I take to the register without looking like a freak?" See also

ANGELS (DECORATIVE USE OF); HUMMEL FIGURES; and PRECIOUS MOMENTS.

KNIEVEL, EVEL Watching this man make motorcycle jumps was interesting. Watching him *almost* make motorcycle jumps—which happened pretty often—was fascinating. Knievel, who invented the art of leaping over things with motorbikes, accomplished possibly the most undesirable feat in the *Guinness Book of World Records*. Having sustained 35 documented skeletal fractures, he's listed as the human with the most broken bones in history.

But none of these injuries could keep him from riding. In 1969 he attempted to jump the fountains at Caesar's Palace, crashed, and remained in a coma for 29 days. But his biggest moment came when he attempted to jump the Snake River Canyon in a rocket-powered motorcycle, which malfunctioned at the moment of launch. But this time, by some miracle, the only thing Knievel hurt was his pride.

Though Knievel hung up his helmet years ago, his son Robbie continues the family business. But it's just not the same. Robbie approaches every jump with the practiced, careful eye of a stuntman, doing things that are dangerous, but not suicidal. He seems to have realized that in his profession it's possible to have balls that are *too* big. See also

< 144 >

MORONS (ENTERTAINING, UNTIMELY DEATHS OF) and STUNTS (INSANE, TELEVISED).

KNIGHT RIDER See HASSELHOFF, DAVID.

KOOL-AID The beverage that created a thousand red tongues (and makes an excellent temporary hair dye as well) was invented by Nebraska tinkerer Edwin E. Perkins. He ran a small manufacturing concern called Perkins Products Company, and one of his best-selling products was a soft drink syrup called Fruit Smack. In 1927 Perkins, who shipped by mail and hated paying extra postage to cover the glass Fruit Smack bottle, figured out a way to dehydrate the syrup and package it in envelopes. All that was left was to change the name to Kool-Ade (now Kool-Aid) and a century-spanning tradition was born. These days more than 563 million gallons are consumed each year. There's no word as to how much of that winds up on shirts, car upholstery, and living room couches.

KOURNIKOVA, ANNA For irrefutable proof that life is unfair and that most people are superficial idiots, consider the career of tennis "phenom" Anna Kournikova. She's never won a singles title in her life. After peaking at No. 8 in the women's world rankings, she's slid below 70. Serena Williams, Venus Williams, and probably their *mom* could chase her off the court. And yet, she has legions of fans, has been called the most recognizable face in sports, and makes around $20 million a year in endorsements. That's because she possesses something far more important than skills: looks. Instead of laboring in the obscurity she so richly deserves, Kournikova has parlayed her babehood into lucrative promotional contracts, modeling gigs, even her own calendar. Who cares about making the cover of *Sports Illustrated*? She's on the cover of *Maxim*. See also *MAXIM*.

KRAFT MACARONI AND CHEESE The purpose of a convenience food is to transform something difficult into something easy. Yet one of the world's great convenience foods, Kraft Macaroni and Cheese, achieved enormous popularity by taking an already dead-simple dish (cheesy pasta) and doing nothing more than powdering the cheese, sealing it in a packet, and selling it in the same box with elbow macaroni. Introduced in 1937, it took off during World War II, when it helped bulk up many a rationing-trimmed dinner. Variations—spirals and wheels—were added in 1975 and 1988. All hell broke loose in the mid-'90s when the theme was supplemented with such variations as Super Mario Brothers, Pokémon, and Sponge-

< 145 >

Bob. Meanwhile, the goods became microwavable, cheesier, Alfredo-ized, and fat-reduced in efforts to meet the needs of an I'll-be-damned-if-I'm-ever-going-to-actually-cook public. See also MICROWAVED DINNERS and RICE-A-RONI.

KRANTZ, JUDITH Something of a Jackie-Susann-come-lately to the writing game, Krantz started her first book, 1978's *New York Times* bestseller *Scruples*, when she was 48. That novel, and the titles that followed, sent the message that women of a certain age could have healthy sexual appetites and that a life of adventure and romance could start at any time.

Krantz writes the kind of overwrought romances that smart women don't dare toss into their vacation bags unless they're sure they won't encounter anyone from the office during the trip. Those same fans would probably never fess up to watching her TV movies and miniseries. But blockbuster ratings confirm that everyone's tuning in—maybe because Krantz's name is usually part of the shows' titles (*Judith Krantz's "'Till We Meet Again," Judith Krantz's "Dazzle,"* to name two). These multi-night ratings extravaganzas provide more than escapism. They also provide actresses such as Lisa Hartman, Barbara Bach, Lindsay Wagner, Valerie Bertinelli, and Stefanie Powers with roles worthy of their talents. See also CARTLAND, BARBARA; COLLINS, JACKIE; SUSANN, JACQUELINE; and TV MOVIES.

KRISPY KREME DOUGHNUTS This chain of doughnut depots, founded in Paducah, Kentucky, in 1933, offers what may be the greatest come-on in the history of fast food: a crimson neon sign in front of every location that reads "Hot Doughnuts Now." It lights up when a fresh batch of Krispy Kremes (the vernacular name for the chain's original glazed yeast models) comes off the line. Like White Castle hamburgers, Krispy Kremes are best enjoyed hot, in volume, and while stoned. See also MARIJUANA and WHITE CASTLE.

KROFFT, SID AND MARTY If you think Teletubbies are the product of drug-addled minds, consider the oeuvre of Sid and Marty Krofft. There was *Lidsville*, a live-action series in which hats came to life. Yes, hats. The *Bugaloos* concerned a British band of  winged insects that play in a giant (to them) radio. And then there was *Land of the Lost*, about a family living in a land of dinosaurs while trying to understand a reptilian race known as the Sleestaks. More? What about a snaggle-

< 146 >

toothed sea monster, Electra-Woman and Dyna Girl, and a friendly dragon named H. R. Pufnstuf? Liking such '70s shows was never particularly cool, but they are fondly remembered by a generation that secretly wishes it had a talking flute in its pocket.

Like the Roman one before it, however, the Krofft empire eventually collapsed, undermined in part by such debacles as the Atlanta-based World of Sid & Marty Krofft amusement park, their beating-a-dead-horse *Brady Bunch Variety Hour*, and *Pink Lady and Jeff*, considered by many to be the worst television variety show ever made—after *The Brady Bunch Variety Hour*, of course. See also BRADY BUNCH, THE; LAND OF THE LOST; TELETUBBIES; THEME PARKS (NOT OWNED BY DISNEY); and VARIETY SHOWS.

K-TEL RECORDS Bringing a K-Tel album to a party during the '70s or '80s was tantamount to publicly acknowledging that your ability to discriminate good music from bad was about as finely developed as a blind man's appreciation for painting. For years the company led the world in compilation discs that boasted "original hits/original star"—which in practice meant albums resembling a Super Bowl halftime show from hell. In one true-life example, K-Tel's *Believe in Music*, Donny Osmond, Rod Stewart, Cher, Eric Clapton, and Bobby Vinton were all slapped on the same piece of vinyl. With K-Tel a bankruptcy casualty, the format has more recently been dominated by the *Now That's What I Call Music* series, which might be better titled *Now That's What I Call Teen Music That Next Year You're Going to Be Embarrassed to Admit You Liked*. See also CHER (WITHOUT SONNY) and *DONNY AND MARIE*.

KUNG FU MOVIES These films, which have been around since the 1920s, are made in such numbers that it's possible to find everything from kung fu science fiction (*Zu: Warriors from the Magic Mountain*) to kung fu romance (*Crouching Tiger, Hidden Dragon*) to kung fu comedy (anything by Jackie Chan). It's somewhat tougher to locate fighting flicks that don't bear an unsettling structural resemblance to porn movies. Most begin with a one-on-one encounter, followed by some sort of group thing, perhaps augmented with toys. A little girl-on-girl action is thrown in. Finally, there's a big, loud, sweaty free-for-all. Why? Maybe because movies about people beating each other's brains out are as straitjacketed in their approach as movies about people boffing each other's brains out. Or maybe because both genres are all about fast-forwarding to the good parts. See also MOVIES (PORNOGRAPHIC).

< 147 >

L

LACOSTE SHIRTS There are lots of misconceptions about these '80s preppy icons. First and foremost, they are not "alligator shirts." The reptile featured on the left breast of every knit shirt is a crocodile. It got its name from French tennis star René Lacoste, whose impressive proboscis earned him the nickname "Le Crocodile." In 1934 Lacoste, who must have been an unbelievably good sport, added a reptilian logo to his tennis whites. Thus a legend was born. The "gator" (the U.S. rights to which were purchased by General Mills in 1969) served as a symbol of the highbrow upper crust until the 1980s, when it became a fashion statement for middle-class white kids nationwide—but only if you flipped up the collar. The critter-on-your-shirt trend became so hot that knockoffs featuring everything from tigers to penguins soon surfaced. But with the death of all things preppy, the Lacoste shirt reverted to what it was always meant to be—a high-priced fashion statement for golfers and polo enthusiasts. See also MEMBERS ONLY JACKETS.

LADIES' HOME JOURNAL The editorial lineup at Meredith Corporation's "Heart, Home, Family" publication is so comfortably formulaic that cracking open a fresh copy every month is like meeting the girls for lunch at your favorite café ("Adoption Story, *so nice to see you!* Five Amazing Makeovers, *have you lost weight?"*). Started in 1883 as a supplement to founder Cyrus H. K. Curtis's farm journal, the ladylike periodical has enjoyed one of the longest shelf lives in women's magazine history, mainly because it never lost sight of its demographic. It knows, for example, that any woman careening toward 50 in the carpool lane can't pass up a good first-person piece on eating disorders ("Saving Samantha: One Family Fights a Daughter's Anorexia"); or a health article laced with panic ("Danger at the Pharmacy: Fatal Prescription Mistakes and How to Protect Your Family"). Doesn't it follow that the ads for firming creams and overactive bladder medications are equally dead-on?

LAMBADA, THE Dance crazes are like one-night stands. After a brief, intensely passionate time comes a sudden "what were we thinking" moment followed by intense denial. Such was the case with the Lambada, a salsa offshoot featuring intensely sexy moves when done right and intensely embarrassing injuries when done wrong. The dance hit the

< 148 >

mainstream when a musician and film-maker visited Bahia, Brazil, in 1988, heard a unique sound, returned to France, and cut a record with a band called Kaoma. A craze was quickly born in late 1989 and quickly died less that a year later—leaving behind at least two quickie cinematic cash-in attempts, which opened at the same time: *The Forbidden Dance* and *Lambada: Set the Night on Fire*. Either one could play a double feature with *Breakin' 2: Electric Boogaloo* at the Whoops, Too Late Drive-In. See also ONE-NIGHT STANDS.

LAMBRUSCO When age doesn't matter, undiscriminating drinkers reach for the Lambrusco. This Italian table wine, low in alcohol content and typically possess-ing the shelf life of mayonnaise, comes in red, white, and rosé, but is best known stateside for its pale red version. The most familiar brand may be Riunite, which, in the mid-'70s, was popularized by girls on both sides of the drinking age who, thanks to the bubbles and the can't-get-it-out-of-your-head ads ("Riunite on ice . . . that's nice."), thought they were drinking champagne—an illusion their cash-strapped boyfriends did nothing to discourage. See also BOONE'S FARM STRAWBERRY HILL; WINE COOLERS; and WINE IN A BOX.

LAND OF THE GIANTS See ALLEN, IRWIN.

LAND OF THE LOST Though the show was supposedly for kids, more than a few adults gathered sheepishly in front of the tube for this Saturday-morning classic. *LOTL*, which ran from 1974 to 1976, was possibly the trippiest series ever produced by the brain trust of Sid and Marty Krofft, which is saying a great deal. The live-action show fol-lowed the adventures of forest ranger Rick Marshall and his two kids, Will and Holly. During a routine camping trip the three were sucked into an alternate universe infested with dinosaurs, ape men, bizarre technology, and a race of primitive lizard men called Sleestaks. Remember the time Big Alice the allosaurus and Grumpy the T. Rex fought? Or when Enik, the supersmart time-traveling Sleestak who believed he was marooned in his people's primitive past, finally realized he was actually trapped in their distant *future*? Whoa. Such twists kept the program around for 43 episodes. That's an enormous number for Saturday-morning fare, making *Land of the Lost* the *Gunsmoke* of kiddie shows. A 1991 series with the same name (and starring Timothy Bottoms) attempted to recapture the magic and aired until September 1994. See also *BANANA SPLITS, THE* and KROFFT, SID AND MARTY.

LANDON, MICHAEL This patron saint of family values began his career with the

< 149 >

1957 teen exploitation flick *I Was a Teenage Werewolf*, then moved to the small screen as Little Joe in the '60s oat opera *Bonanza*.

But it wasn't until the premiere of *Little House on the Prairie* in 1974 that America came to know Landon (born Eugene Maurice Orowitz) in all his suntanned, big-haired, G-rated glory. Playing the Ingalls clan's ever-patient "Pa," he became a surrogate dad to an entire generation of latchkey kids. Which is why, even today, sophisticated adults can be stopped in their tracks by the sight of a *Little House* rerun on TV. But the wholesomeness didn't end there. In *Highway to Heaven* (which earned Landon the nickname Jesus of Malibu) he played a problem-solving angel. Even his attempts to bare his "troubled" side seemed inordinately wholesome. Landon wrote, produced, directed, and appeared in a pretty-much-autobiographical 1976 TV movie called *The Loneliest Runner*, about a young boy suffering from a debilitating social problem. No, not drug abuse or alcoholism or even bulimia. The kid was a bed wetter. See also *HIGHWAY TO HEAVEN* and *TOUCHED BY AN ANGEL*.

LAS VEGAS Even if you hate gauche excess, despise gambling, and loathe Wayne Newton, Vegas, a.k.a. Sin City, is still a blast. It's fun precisely *because* it's so lame. Originally a parched, end-of-the-line desert hellhole, it got its big break when Nevada legalized gambling in 1931. Over the decades, thanks to infusions of Mob money, it slowly grew, until it became a parched, end-of-the-line desert hellhole with some of the largest, most lavishly appointed casinos on earth. These days the place has mutated from the semi-sleazy gambling den the Rat Pack made famous into some sort of bizarre entertainment Mecca—like Disneyland would be if they let you drink. And smoke. And gamble. And marry someone you met three hours ago. What's not to like? See also CASINOS; ELVIS IMPERSONATORS; JONES, TOM; NEWTON, WAYNE; and PRESLEY, ELVIS.

LASER SHOWS On May 9, 1969, at Oakland's Mills College, a new entertainment genre—okay, *sub*genre—was born. That's when the first public performance of a laser rock show (in which pure light is synchronized to music) took place. The process was shown to the world at Expo '70 in Osaka, Japan, and in short order planetariums around the world started providing music fans (and by "music fans" we mean "people who like to listen to Led Zepplin and Pink Floyd while stoned") with an entirely new way to get into their tunes. A com-

< 150 >

pany called Laserium started packaging shows, then *Star Wars* debuted, prompting symphonies around the country to do "Music of the Stars" events supplemented, of course, with laser effects. And the rest is head trip history. See also MARIJUANA and *STAR WARS*.

LASSIE   If the dog is man's best friend, then Lassie is man's *bestest* best friend. Debuting opposite a preteen Elizabeth Taylor and Roddy McDowall in the 1943 cinematic release *Lassie Come Home* (the collie was actually a male named Pal who was given to animal trainer Rudd Weatherwax to settle a $10 debt), he/she went on to star in a radio show, then a series of network TV programs running, without interruption, from 1954 to 1971. Since then she's surfaced sporadically in everything from syndicated shows to TV specials to big-screen flicks. The pleasure came from watching a very talented dog (all subsequent "Lassies" are male descendants of the original Pal) repeatedly save its accident-prone owners from disaster. The guilt (sometimes realized years later) came from thinking how much your own flea-bitten mutt suffered by comparison. Well, lighten up. Your Humane Society find is no Lassie, but then you're certainly no *MacGyver*. And consider this. The original Pal, before Weatherwax got hold

of him, liked to chase cars. See also TV SHOWS FEATURING ANIMAL PROTAGONISTS.

LAVA LAMPS   Made in the United States by Lava-Simplex Internationale (a pretty highfalutin name for a tiny manufacturing concern located in a nondescript Chicago neighborhood), the lava lamp (officially called the Lava Lite) works by heating a blob of specially formulated wax that's suspended in a jug of colored fluid. As the wax heats and  expands, its density becomes less than the liquid around it and it rises to the top of the lamp, forming all sorts of cool shapes as it does. Then it cools and drifts slowly to the bottom. Then it gets hot and rises again. On and on and on. This process, mildly interesting to straightlaced folks, can be endlessly fascinating if you've, say, just smoked a great deal of marijuana. Think of it as cable TV for stoners. See also MARIJUANA.

LAWLESS, LUCY   See *XENA: WARRIOR PRINCESS*.

LAWN DARTS   If you still have a set of these steel-tipped missiles (which were tossed high into the air in an attempt to impale them inside a plastic ring), you own a collector's item of sorts. Banned

< 151 >

in the U.S. in 1988 by the Consumer Products Safety Commission, they're possibly the most lethal children's toy ever invented—so lethal that the CPSC advises anyone who still owns a set to destroy them. Of course this doesn't stop a certain segment of society from hauling theirs out on holidays for a few backyard rounds—hopefully sans children. See also MORONS (ENTERTAINING, UNTIMELY DEATHS OF).

LAWRENCE WELK SHOW, THE Few baby boomers who were forced to sit through this show as children have anything nice, or even charitable, to say about North Dakotan Lawrence Welk and his accordion-intensive "champagne music." If you're one of them, then watching an episode as an adult (they run perpetually on PBS stations and other outlets) might prompt a reappraisal. We're not saying that the show's smiling, laughably clean-cut performers and their gelded renditions of everything from show tunes to barbershop standards are great art. Far from it. But *The Lawrence Welk Show*, which ran from 1955 to 1971 on ABC and until 1982 in first-run syndication, wasn't about art. It was about providing refuge. During the show's prime, the real world was full of antiwar protests, street riots, and sexual license—just the sorts of things Welk's core audience (the oldsters targeted by the program's endless Geritol and Sominex commercials) dearly wanted to escape, if only briefly. For one hour each week, Welk provided that escape—bubbles and all.

LEAVE IT TO BEAVER Did we include this classic sitcom, which ran from 1957 to 1963, because it used the same plot (the Beav gets in trouble, then learns an important lesson) in virtually every episode? No. Did we include it because generation after generation has been mesmerized by the antics of the little scamp? Not really. We just felt that there was a spot on *any* list of guilty pleasures for a show where a woman repeatedly says, "Ward, I'm worried about the Beaver."

LEFT BEHIND Almost since the time Matthew, Mark, Luke, and John put down their writing implements, Christian readers have been waiting for a sign— a sign that their faith would spark not just (as with *Ben-Hur*) a best seller, nay, but a *series* of best sellers.

Their prayers were answered with the publication of the *Left Behind* series, a multi-volume saga that begins with the rapture (no, not the Blondie song; the rising of the faithful to heaven) and progresses into an *Omen*-ish battle against the lord of darkness. Even though the books have the depth of a Dick and Jane reader, Christians pore over them, well, religiously. But isn't it wrong—nay,

< 152 >

almost un-Christian—to take such pleasure in the suffering of so many others? See also BIBLICAL EPICS.

LENNY AND SQUIGGY When it came to brain power, Laverne De Fazio and Shirley Feeney weren't the fullest bottles on the brewery line. But they were Rhodes scholars compared to their upstairs neighbors, Leonard Kosnowski and Andrew Squiggmann. During their first appearance on the *Laverne & Shirley* pilot episode, this brain deficient duo tried to lure the titular ladies to a drive-in movie to see "a great make-out picture . . . *The Robe*." From that auspicious entrance, the boys proceeded to malaprop their way into the hearts of television viewers. While they never got their own series (a good idea, since they were best in small doses), Michael "Lenny" McKean did go on to improv success as a member of Spinal Tap. Someday students of television may give these guys their due as the "goofy neighbors" missing link between *I Love Lucy's* Fred and Ethel Mertz and *Seinfeld's* Kramer.

LESBIANS (MOVIE SCENES FEATURING) How did Salma Hayek and Jeanne Tripplehorn save the otherwise unbearable *Timecode*? How did Sarah Michelle Gellar and Selma Blair save the otherwise unbearable *Cruel Intentions*? How have scores of unknown actresses saved otherwise unwatchable Cinemax movies? By participating in lesbian scenes, of course. Whether it's a wet one on the lips or a full frontal attack, hot girl-on-girl action can make all the difference—at least for guys whose wives are asleep upstairs. See also CINEMAX; PRISON MOVIES FEATURING WOMEN; and SPECTRAVISION.

LEWINSKY, MONICA What are we to make of this poor girl who, through no fault of her own, nearly brought down a presidency? To women she was just a hardworking intern trying to get ahead in life by giving a little INSERT LEWD ORAL SEX PUN HERE. To men she was merely a girl placed in an unusual position (actually, several) by her boss. What resulted was a squalid, stupid, decidedly unpresidential scandal that truly saddened us—though of course we felt it was our patriotic duty to read and listen to every word about it, including the Barbara Walters interview. Lewinsky, who graduated with a degree in psychology from Lewis and Clark College in 1995, is now a designer of high-end purses. She also hosted a reality show on Fox (where else?) called *Mr. Personality*. Apparently her time in the White House dissuaded her from entering a career in public service. See also CLINTON, BILL and REALITY SHOWS.

< 153 >

LEWIS, JERRY Given his difficult reputation, his heart-on-his-sleeve charity work, and all the dud flicks mixed in with his hits, being a fan of Jerry Lewis isn't for wimps. But true believers know that it's not just the French who love him. From his first Atlantic City performances with Dean Martin (during which he pretty much redefined the term "manic"), through such classic films as *The Nutty Professor* and *The Bell Boy*, to his "rediscovery" at the hands of Martin Scorsese in the film *The King of Comedy*, then into his starring stint in the Broadway and touring companies of *Damn Yankees* (all the while tirelessly serving as the sometimes-cranky, always profusely sweating host and driving force behind the Muscular Dystrophy Association's Labor Day Telethon), Lewis has proven himself to be a one-of-a-kind entertainer. Trivia note: As if that wasn't enough, he also pioneered the lowbrow sport of phony phone calls. He started recording them in the late 1950s when a Paramount Studios technician taught him how to bug his own phone. See also ATLANTIC CITY and CRANK PHONE CALLS.

LIBERACE In the great big book of unlikely superstars, Wladziu Valentino Liberace warrants his own chapter. An oversized grand piano, a gaudy candelabra and a penchant for smiles not seen this side of the Chesire Cat led Wisconsin's strangest son to nightclub dates, TV gigs, movie roles, and, in 1953, record Madison Square Garden crowds. Two years later, Liberace (he shortened his name in the 1940s, paving the way for Cher, Madonna, and Björk) became the highest paid entertainer in Las Vegas history. Part of the guilty pleasure came from the "Is he or isn't he?" question, which was fueled in large part by Liberace's unmarried status and his devotion to his mother. Okay, and maybe his outrageous costumes (in one show he appeared in pink llama fur trimmed with rhinestones), plus the fact that he came across as the bastard son of Paul Lynde and Carol Channing. The controversy continued after his 1987 death, encompassing legal action with "extremely close friends" and an obligatory TV movie. But there was more to his appeal than mere gossip. Liberace could actually play the piano well. And even if he wasn't to your taste (one critic called him the "biggest sentimental vomit of all time") you had to admire a guy who could offer up "Ave Maria," "Yesterday," and then a little Chopin, all in one evening. See also CHER (WITHOUT SONNY) and LAS VEGAS.

LIFEGUARDS Lifeguards, male and female, have always enjoyed a high standing in the hierarchy of fantasy sex

< 154 >

objects. Not only do they go around rescuing people and watching out for others (a sure turn-on for women), but their job requires them to be buff and pretty nearly naked (a sure turn-on for men). Not that this was always so. The profession began in 1785 when the Massachusetts Humane Society formed a lifesaving service, but it was used mostly to row out during rough seas and try to rescue shipwreck victims. Not until the 20th century, with the rise of beach culture, did the bodyguard lounging in his elevated chair become a tanned, toned, nose-smeared-with-sunblock icon of summer. See also *BAYWATCH*.

LIFETIME Though it calls itself the cable network for women, Lifetime could get even more specific if it wished. Why not call it the cable network for women involved in precedent-setting legal battles; or the cable network for women traumatized by violent crime; or (our favorite) the cable network for women whose no-good husbands get what they deserve in the end? Launched in 1984, Lifetime continues to hit its demographic mark by offering evenings built around movies with names like *A Mother's Justice* (starring Meredith Baxter), *A Mother's Prayer* (starring Linda Hamilton), *A Mother's Revenge* (starring Lesley Ann Warren), and *A Mother's Testimony* (starring Kate

Jackson). Oh, and let's not forget *Mother, May I Sleep with Danger?* Lifetime is perfect background entertainment for folding laundry or dusting knick-knacks—yet compelling enough to make any female between the age of 18 and 80 lose her civility should anyone touch the remote during *Custody of the Heart*. See also CHICK FLICKS (CINDERELLA FANTASIES); CHICK FLICKS (FEMALE BONDING); CHICK FLICKS (IN WHICH SOMEONE DIES); and TV MOVIES.

LILLIAN VERNON Almost everyone has at one time or another perused this diminutive catalog, filled with holiday gewgaws and other cheap, small things. Founded in 1951 by none other than Lillian Vernon, a New York newlywed who used $2,000 in wedding gift money to start selling personalized belts and handbags by mail order, it has blossomed into a juggernaut enjoying $238 million in sales in 2003. A juggernaut built on the sale of such "must-haves" as garden gnomes, hand-painted classic resin stars 'n' stripes, swirling windsocks, and No. 2 pencils with your child's name on each one.

LIMBAUGH, RUSH See CONSERVATIVE RADIO TALK SHOWS.

LIMOUSINES Nothing says "pretentious jerk" quite like riding around in a long

< 155 >

black limo. It certainly doesn't say "classy" anymore. These days the truly wealthy travel in well-appointed but reasonably nondescript luxury sedans—the better to avoid kidnapping. Which means the "high rollers" behind the smoked glass of most stretch Caddies or Lincolns (or oversized SUVs or pickup trucks, for that matter) are probably either drunks traveling from one watering hole to another, a couple of prom-bound kids, or businesspeople sharing a ride to the airport. But still, even though the ride is rented and, often, not all that clean inside, there's nothing like rolling around in a 30-foot land yacht to pump up the ego—even if you're only catching a flight to Newark. See also CADILLACS.

LINE DANCING Offering virtually the only chance for people with two left feet to hit the dance floor without making utter fools of themselves, the concept of the line dance goes back thousands of years. Early American settlers enjoyed a version called the contra dance (two lines, men in one, ladies in the other). Today's versions are mostly country-and-western in nature, with everyone standing side by side, executing carefully choreographed steps at more or less the same time. It's a little bit like waiting in line to music, but you take what you can get. See also ELECTRIC SLIDE, THE; LAMBADA, THE; and MACARENA, THE.

LITTLE, RICH See CELEBRITY IMPERSONATORS.

LITTLE DEBBIE SNACKS The boxed snack of choice for noshers who don't want to fork over the cost of an Entenmann's product, Little Debbie Snacks have been pleasing undiscriminating palates since 1960. That's when O. D. McKee, founder of McKee Foods, cranked out his first hand-held Oatmeal Creme Pie (basically two oatmeal cookies with icing between them). Naming the company after his four-year-old granddaughter—without telling her parents until they saw the first package—McKee and company expanded rapidly, creating (at press time) more than 75 products stressing value over excellence. Most of the Little Debbie treats are individually wrapped in single-serving portions, because eating a Nutty Bar, Star Crunch Cosmic Snack, or Strawberry Shortcake Roll is a private experience, often best savored over the kitchen sink at 2 A.M. See also TWINKIES.

LITTLE HOUSE ON THE PRAIRIE See LANDON, MICHAEL.

LITTLE RASCALS, THE The Little Rascals, a.k.a. Our Gang, appeared in hundreds of short films from the silent era through 1944, leaving millions of kids wishing their neighborhood had

< 156 >

soapbox derbies, that their friendships were as close as Spanky and Alfalfa's, and that their teacher was as nice as Miss Crabtree. Yet, thanks in part to some sequences that are hard to shrug off just as products of the times (a bone-through-his-nose Borneo native chasing the kids, saying "Yum, Yum, eat 'em

up," for instance), questions arose as to whether it was okay for today's tykes to watch the Gang and their exploits. Eddie Murphy's recurring Buckwheat character on *Saturday Night Live* helped play up the perception that *The Little Rascals* were more than a little racist. Yet has there ever been a better picture of a rainbow coalition than this? And is there a better way to relive the childhood you never had than watching an afternoon of *Our Gang* adventures? See also SATURDAY NIGHT LIVE (RECURRING CHARACTERS ON).

LONG JOHN SILVER'S Grilled trout and seared mahimahi are nice, but sometimes we like to see our seafood battered into submission. No one does this better than Long John Silver's. America's No. 1 fast seafood chain (is there a No. 2?) built its fame by offering greasy loads of shrimp, clams, hush puppies, and fish fillets, all doused in the same thick bat-

ter and deep-fried into an undifferentiated mass of golden brown shapes. The chain, opened in 1969 and now headquartered in the ancient maritime community of Louisville, Kentucky, offers a few lighter and trendier menu items, but most entrées are still coated and floated (in hot oil, that is). At some locations, customers can even purchase an order of crusty batter fragments fished out of the deep fryers. Each serving of "Crumblies" contains about 170 calories, about 110 of which are, not surprisingly, derived from fat. See also WHITE CASTLE.

LORD OF THE DANCE See RIVERDANCE.

LORD OF THE RINGS, THE Millions of fans have read J. R. R. Tolkien's *Rings* trilogy since its initial publication in 1954 and 1955. Countless more watched the highly successful movies based on the books. And literary critics have praised *LOTR* not just as great fantasy, but great literature. This means that absolutely anyone should be able to read or watch the story of Middle-earth without a twinge of guilt. There's just one catch. This most perfectly realized of all fantasy worlds is still larded up with the usual cheesy cast of nursery rhyme staples (trolls, elves, wizards, etc.) almost all of whom have silly-sounding names like Elrond, Legolas, Gandalf, and

< 157 >

Éomer. And whether you like it or not, being a fan means you have something in common with the Dungeons and Dragons crowd. Even if you were once *part* of that crowd and all that 10-sided-dice rolling is behind you, there's still that lingering feeling that you should be doing something more adult with your time. See also DUNGEONS AND DRAGONS.

LORDS, TRACI She's of age now, so technically it's okay to lust after her. But an entire generation of porno-watching guys knows that the prime of Lords's career occurred before she could legally drink—let alone do the things she did on screen. The star of such films as *Night of Loving Dangerously*, *Nympherotica*, and *Double Penetration 2* (you don't have to see the first one to follow the plot, or so we've heard), she saw nearly her entire oeuvre (no, that's not a body part) disappear after the FBI raided her home on an anonymous tip.

Her career in adult films over—except for a few scenes shot after she aged a bit—Lords opted for serious acting. She studied at the famed Lee Strasberg Institute and earned ostensibly better roles in such movies as *Plughead Rewired: Circuitry Man II* (you don't have to see the first one to follow the plot, or so we've heard). See also MASTURBATION; MOVIES (PORNOGRAPHIC); and OLSEN TWINS, THE.

LOST IN SPACE See ALLEN, IRWIN.

LOTTERY TICKETS (SCRATCH-OFF) Developed in 1973 by a company called Scientific Games and debuting with the Massachusetts Lottery in 1974, the instant-win scratch-off card has become the impulse buy of choice for convenience store patrons picking up a two-liter bottle of Mountain Dew and a couple of Slim Jims after work. Okay, most of the people who play these games aren't ignorant rednecks, but you can sure *feel* like one when you belly up to the cash register and choose between such no-real-difference games as Break the Bank and Stairway to Riches. Still, in the time it takes to walk to the car, fish a dime out of your pocket, scratch off the numbers, and see that you've lost, you can have fun imagining what you'd do with the cash if you'd won. See also CASINOS.

"LOUIE, LOUIE" The anthem of drunks everywhere, this 1963 Kingsmen's song might have staggered quietly into obscurity if the good folks in Indiana hadn't banned the record (even though the lyrics, which are completely unintelligible in this rendition, are actually pretty innocent). Sniffing a cult hit, its label reissued the tune in 1964. And in 1965. And in 1966. Eventually it landed at No. 2 on the *Billboard* charts. During the '70s it enjoyed a resurgence thanks

< 158 >

to its presence on the *Animal House* soundtrack. Folks in Philadelphia and elsewhere even staged "Louie, Louie" parades. No surprise that their band's official Web site is www.louielouie.org, instead of www.thekingsmen.com. See also GAMES, DRINKING.

LOVE, AMERICAN STYLE Imagine *The Love Boat* without the crew . . . or the boat . . . and you've got some idea of what this anthology show, which aired from 1969 to 1974, was all about. With sketches titled "Love and . . ." (samples: "Love and the Pill," "Love and the Locksmith," "Love and the Hoodwinked Honey"), a cast made up largely of TV game show talent—Dick Gautier, Jo Anne Worley, Mary Ann Mobley, Jo Ann Pflug, and Charles Nelson Reilly, among others—and plots as risqué as the table conversation at your average Little League banquet, *Love, American Style* allowed square audiences to feel "hip," "with it," and "groovy," without being "challenged." The show did leave a legacy. *Happy Days* started as a 1972 segment called "Love and the Happy Days." (To be honest, it was actually an unsold 1971 pilot for a TV series called *New Family in Town* that was squeezed into the *Love* format.) See also *HAPPY DAYS* and *LOVE BOAT, THE*.

LOVE BOAT, THE A sort of nautical *Love, American Style*, this brainchild of überproducer Aaron Spelling ruled the waves from 1977 to 1986. Each week the crew of the *Pacific Princess* (an actual ship of the Princess Cruise Line) welcomed aboard a host of celebrity guest stars seemingly culled from the reject line at Studio 54—everyone from Charo (shown below) to Sonny Bono to an ex-tremely young Tori Spelling. Besides providing work for down-on-their-luck SAG members, the show also reinvigorated the cruise in-dustry and raised the world's awareness of the Mexican town of Cabo San Lucas, where the ship was  forever docking. Sadly, the original Love Boat was scrapped in 2002 and replaced with a new, much larger *Pacific Princess*. One hopes it fares better than *Love Boat: The Next Wave*, a 1998 UPN revival series that quickly foundered. See also CRUISES; *LOVE, AMERICAN STYLE*; SPELLING, AARON; and SPELLING, TORI.

LOVE BUG, THE See DISNEY FILMS FEATURING DEAN JONES AND/OR KURT RUSSELL.

LOVE STORY If chick flicks had a sorority, *Love Story* would be its chapter president. In 1970 there was simply no

< 159 >

escaping this three-hanky weeper, in which rich boy Oliver Barrett IV, played by Ryan O'Neal, falls for poor girl Jennifer (Ali MacGraw). They frolic around together, and then she dies. And that's pretty much it. Yet out of this thin gruel arose an international phenomenon. The book (written at the same time as the screenplay) became a best seller; Andy Williams's overproduced version of the film's theme song ruled the airwaves; and come Oscar time *Love Story* snagged seven Academy Award nominations, including one for Best Picture. Looking at it from the safe distance of more than three decades, it's tough to see what the fuss was about. But be warned. Putting this disc in your DVD player is like doing a line of coke. You may walk away unscathed, or you may be hooked. See also Chick Flicks (In Which Someone Dies).

Lucky Magazine Beauty advice seems so hopelessly vague and theoretical in most fashion magazines—the ones that clutter their pages with articles about women who have overcome, women who have made a difference, women who have *blah, blah, blah*. Not so in *Lucky*, a perky Condé Nast publication that bills itself, in big, unapologetic letters across the top of its cover, as "The Magazine About Shopping." While other glossies merely hint at the truth behind discretionary reading—that all we really want to know about the cover model is where she got her pink leather mules—for *Lucky*, it's the raison d'être.

Not surprisingly, the periodical was nearly laughed off the newsstand—presumably by critics wearing really outdated sweaters from J. C. Penney—when it first appeared in 2001. But *Lucky* laughed last, as its circulation soared and *Adweek* named it 2001's Startup of the Year. Patterned after similar photo-heavy "magalogs" popular in Japan, the magazine even includes a page of peel-off "Yes!" and "Maybe?" stickers to help readers keep track of their materialistic cravings. Frivolous? "Yes!" quoth the sticker. And proud of it.

Luden's Wild Cherry Throat Drops Fans eat this "throat medicine" like candy because it is, for all intents and purposes, candy. Created, appropriately enough, by a turn-of-the-century confectioner named William Luden, the bright red ovals taste more like Lifesavers than medicine. And since their only "active" ingredient is the fruit preservative pectin (a *real* cough drop usually gets its neck-soothing chops from menthol) they're about as helpful with a sore throat as a Hershey's Kiss is with headaches. Appropriately enough, the Hershey Foods Corporation owned Luden's from 1986 to 2001. (Today Luden's is owned by Pharmacia, a division of Pfizer.) Candy fans with a "scratchy throat" should also try the incomparable Mixed Berry flavors.

LUNCH BOXES   From the 1950s to the early 1980s, you never had to ask grade-schoolers what their favorite movie/TV show/cartoon character was. All you had to do was look at their metal lunch boxes. Popularized in the '50s by Aladdin Industries, their vibrant art immortalized everyone from Hopalong Cassidy (the company's first big hit) to TV classics such as *Kung Fu* and cultural phenomena such as skateboarding and CB radios. These days there's a big market for these garishly colored blasts from the past. Some, such as those made for *Star Trek*, sell for hundreds of dollars. Adults can even haul their dinner leftovers to the office inside newly minted, adults-only models that pay tribute to everyone from the rapper Eminem to '50s pinup girl Bettie Page. See also *STAR TREK*.

< 161 >

M

MACARENA, THE   Not since the Hokey Pokey has there been an easier-to-follow dance craze. The song upon which it was based, originally a hit in Spain in 1993, was revamped by a group called the Bayside Boys and became an international musical, and dance, phenomenon. Too bad all those parents teaching it to their five-year-olds didn't pay attention to the lyrics (which, depending on the version, were either in Spanish or nearly unintelligible English). Seems the song is about a girl named Macarena who, when snubbed by her soldier boyfriend, decides to hook up with two dudes she meets while partying. Hey, Macarena! See also LAMBADA, THE and LINE DANCING.

MACGYVER   If you're fighting crime, what could be more useful than an arsenal of weapons? How about a safety pin, or a credit card, or a light bulb? Such were the tools of the trade for MacGyver, the character played by Richard Dean Anderson on this popular adventure series. Audiences might have detected trouble when they saw that the directing credit on the 1985 pilot (in which our resourceful hero fixed a leak using chocolate) went to Alan Smithee, a pseudonym Hollywood folks use when they are too embarrassed to put their name on a project. But loyalists kept the show going for seven seasons, during which MacGyver used a bicycle inner tube as a slingshot, nearly blinded an enemy with a packet of soy sauce, built a baby crib out of hockey sticks, shot cans out of a soda machine to create a distraction, and used a shoe as a grappling hook. In one famous episode called "The Mountain of Youth," he took the not-quite-high-tech approach of using a ladder to clunk a villain. Hey, whatever works.

MACON COUNTY LINE   Beginning with the baldfaced lie that the story audiences—mostly drive-in theater audiences—were about to see was true, *Macon County Line* tells of a pair of reckless good ol' boy brothers and a free-spirited female hitchhiker. The three find themselves in the wrong place at the wrong time when a sheriff's wife (the son of whom is played by soon-to-be-flash-in-the-pan teen idol Leif Garrett) is killed. The sheriff himself is Max Baer Jr. (yes, Jethro of *The Beverly Hillbillies*), who also co-wrote and produced this low-budget 1974 hit, which became the *American Graffiti* of the trailer park set. Credit its success to the fact that drive-in audiences were most likely getting high, drinking heavily, or making out during

< 162 >

much of the action. See also *BEVERLY HILLBILLIES, THE*.

MACY'S THANKSGIVING DAY PARADE

Inevitably during the buildup for the Thanksgiving feast, someone slips into the living room and turns on the Macy's parade. Held since 1924 (in the beginning they displayed real animals borrowed from the Central Park Zoo instead of balloons) and given a popularity boost because of its central role in the 1947 film *Miracle on 34th Street*, it's become a national tradition—and pretty much the only parade that nearly everyone, be they male, female, old, or young, is familiar with. Of course it's somewhat fashionable to make fun of the balloons, the floats, and the elaborately staged musical numbers, but it's still as much a part of Thanksgiving as coats on the bed and leftover turkey. By the way, back in the old days they didn't have to worry about runaway balloons, because the massive creations were intentionally cut loose at the end of the parade. When they finally drifted to earth, whoever found them got a prize.

MAD MAGAZINE

You had to hide it from your parents, your teachers, and pretty much every other authority figure. That's because *Mad*, founded in 1952, was for most of its first quarter century America's leading voice of dissent—or at least the only one available to poor, put-upon grade-schoolers. Everything about the magazine was a hoot, from submoron mascot Alfred E. Neuman to the TV and movie parodies to a seemingly endless string of articles entitled "You Know You're a (fill in the blank) When . . ." Mad lost its cutting-edge feel about the time of *Saturday Night Live*'s 1975 debut. It was still funny and irreverent, but *SNL* (and a horde of imitators) could get the funny bits to the public quicker. Still, if you can't beat 'em, join 'em. A *Mad*-derived show called *Mad TV* debuted on Fox in the mid-'90s. See also *NATIONAL LAMPOON*.

MADONNA (NONMUSIC PROJECTS)

The Material Girl has proved her lack of acting chops in romantic adventure (*Shanghai Surprise*), courtroom drama  (*Body of Evidence*), movie cartoon (*Dick Tracy*), revenge drama/softcore porn (*A Certain Sacrifice*), musical (*Evita*), and just about every other cinematic genre. Yet we continue to, if not buy tickets, at least gravitate to tabloid stories about her latest movie duds. Happily for train wreck fans, she's also branched out into publishing with a line of children's books ("That story's nice, Daddy, but tell me about her lip-lock

< 163 >

with Britney Spears"). And of course, who can forget 1992's *Sex*? That portfolio of Madonna-intensive dirty pictures made an excellent coffee-table book—if the coffee table was in the *Playboy* mansion.

MAGIC EYE These posters, developed by artist Cheri Smith and computer programmer Tom Baccei, may look like a bunch of random squiggles, but in fact they're something called random dot stereograms. The two based their work on that of Dr. Bela Julesz (who created three-dimensional effects with dots back in 1959), and Christopher Tyler (a student of Julesz's who, in 1979, found a way to apply his mentor's techniques to single images). Smith and Baccei added the final, critical step—relentless marketing. Soon, books filled with Magic Eye pictures climbed the *New York Times* best-seller list, syndicated pics popped up in newspapers, and images appeared everywhere from bubble gum packages to telephone cards. The kick of Magic Eye isn't just being able to see 3-D without funky glasses. It's also the fun of watching your friends straining to see what's right in front of their faces.

MAGICIANS Merlin was a lovable old guy who took young King Arthur under his wing. Just about every magician since then has been a jerk who considers making audiences feel stupid to be his life's work. Even "cool" conjurers such as Penn & Teller give off an "I'm smarter than you" vibe. Admit it: Wouldn't you secretly love to punch out David Copperfield, Doug Henning (when he was alive), and/or David Blaine and then disappear under a cloak of invisibility? Yet these guys continue to attract big (and masochistic) audiences. We guiltily watch, knowing that all the mumbo jumbo is just a distraction and that whatever we're looking at—usually the butt of the magician's barely dressed assistant—is exactly where he *wants* us to look while the big switcheroo takes place elsewhere. See also HENNING, DOUG.

MAKEOVERS, MAKEUP COUNTER Whether you're the type of woman who can go for years without so much as buying a new Chap Stick, or a CoverGirl savant who can recite all 12 of the brand's signature LipSlicks from warmest to coolest, chances are good that at some point in your makeup career you have enjoyed the redeeming powers of a free makeover. The secret, as you know, is to succumb. You can't help but feel beautiful and loved when you're getting so much undivided attention, especially once you get past the initial humiliation of perching on a tiny barstool in the middle of a busy mall

< 164 >

while a woman with a China doll complexion studies you like a plumber looking at a broken P-trap.

For better or for worse, those smock bitches know things. Like how to apply Pore Minimizer, and the correct proportion of blush to bronzer. As you sit beneath the department store lights in full, free, moisturized glory, you will begin to imagine yourself as one of *them*: a M•A•C addict, a born-again Laura Mercier, a makeup pro executing flawlessly contoured cheekbones straight from the Bobbi Brown playbook.

Then, of course, you have to get up and guiltily walk away without buying anything. See also AVON and CLINIQUE PORE MINIMIZER MAKEUP.

MALE SINGERS WHO SOUND LIKE WOMEN It's been scientifically proven that high-pitched female voices cut through background noise more effectively than male voices. Perhaps that's why such falsetto superstars as the Bee Gees and Frankie Valli enjoyed huge success. What's harder to understand is how Valli and the brothers Gibb, all of whom have normal speaking voices, decided to take this particular tack. Of course singing like a girl sometimes isn't a conscious career move. Wayne Newton, who must have come late to puberty, sounded like Lesley Gore on "Danke Schoen." As for Michael Jackson, he sounds like a woman on his albums because, well, *he just sounds like a woman*. See also JACKSON, MICHAEL and NEWTON, WAYNE.

MAN, MYTH & MAGIC This massive, 21-volume exploration of everything to do with religion and the occult (originally sold on a mail order installment plan à la Time-Life Books) isn't for lightweights. First marketed in 1970 and still available in an updated form today, it offers not dreamy ruminations about things like pyramid power, but surprisingly erudite, signed articles on everything from astrology to Zoroastrianism. That's all well and good if you're interested in increasing your knowledge of the spiritual. But it's kind of disappointing if, like more than one kid who furtively studied it in the library, you're looking for a spell to turn your brother into a roach. See also HOROSCOPES and TIME-LIFE BOOKS.

MANILOW, BARRY The music of the man born Barry Alan Pincus—and who penned such classic commercial jingles as "Like a good neighbor, State Farm is there" and "I am stuck on Band-Aids" —seemed to blare out of every radio in the world during his reign as the king of ultrasoft pop from the early '70s to the early '80s. Girls enjoyed annoying their boyfriends by turning up the likes of "I

< 165 >

Write the Songs," "Looks Like We Made It," and "Can't Smile Without You" years after Manilow was consigned to the nether regions of fame—including starring in a TV movie of his hit song "Copacabana" (with  a script by *Inside the Actors Studio*'s James Lipton) and releasing an "audio diary" called *Manilow Talks*—even his most ardent enemies sort of miss him. Sure, his 38 Top 40 hits were all pretty schmaltzy. But at least we could understand them.

MANWICH Consider the sloppy joe. Outside of high school cafeterias, it was a little-talked-about delicacy whose ingredients were so finely chopped that it was impossible to discern what lurked between leftover hamburger buns. But then along came this sweet-and-sourish barbecueish tomato sauce with a sexist name that implied a Sloppy Joe on steroids. More importantly, along with the cans came an effective ad campaign ("A sandwich is a sandwich, but a Manwich is a meal"). Suddenly the "dish" became a staple on the dinner rotations of harried households across the fruited plain. Would you consider making it if company was coming over? Not if said company was older than 12. Do you secretly

have a can in your cupboard in case you run out of dinner ideas for your own tribe? Very likely. See also KRAFT MACARONI AND CHEESE.

MARASCHINO CHERRIES They're so red they look like they were made in a lab. Yet these space-age dessert and drink additives have a long and storied history. They were originally grown from the marasca cherry tree and distilled into a powerful cordial called maraschino. Italians used the cordial in desserts and soaked regular white cherries in the beverage to give them more zing. These original maraschino cherries were a true gourmet delicacy. The ones you get at the grocery store are not. Instead of bathing in a rare liquor, they linger for days in sugar water (not to mention food coloring), after which a touch of bitter almond is added to give them a flavor somewhat similar to the traditional maraschino. Of course they taste absolutely *nothing* like the traditional maraschino, but that's beside the point. Hard-core fans eat them right from the jar, even though the rest of the world uses them as nothing but a quickly-brushed-away garnish on everything from hams to grapefruit halves.

MARCHING BANDS It's a mystery how marching bands could enjoy such enduring popularity without ever, for even a

< 166 >

second, being considered cool. (This in spite of such worthy attempts as the movie *Drumline*, and the group Blast!, which took its glorified halftime show to Broadway and on tour in 2001.) The groups, which evolved out of the musical contingents that formerly accompanied fighting forces (hence the uniforms and terms like "drum major") are pretty much the gold standard for geekdom (as seen in such films as *American Pie*). Yet each year, amidst talk of school violence, drug use, teacher apathy, and dropping test scores, learning institutions across the nation manage to field bands filled with silly-hatted musicians sweating in wool uniforms and bleating their way through an Earth Wind & Fire medley. No doubt about it: If there's a geek and nerd heaven, then you know they've got a hell of a marching band.

MARDI GRAS New Orleans's annual orgy has its roots in 1700s African-American celebrations, in the elegant masked balls of French settlers, in Creole parties, and in the insatiable desire of certain drunk women to take their shirts off in public. Also known as Fat Tuesday (and first celebrated in the U.S. in, of all places, Alabama), the parade-and-party-filled celebration always occurs 47 days before Easter, giving its participants plenty of time to atone for the sins committed while in quest of plastic beads.

See also *GIRLS GONE WILD* and HALLOWEEN (ADULT CELEBRATION OF).

MARIJUANA Even though it's been illegal in the U.S. since 1937, the demon weed remains more popular than many WB TV shows. About 6.2 percent of the population say they used it in the past month, placing the American toker population at around 14.6 million. All of which should make Woody Harrelson, Cheech, Chong, and the editorial board of *High Times* magazine very happy. But if you're just a regular guy, you have plenty to feel guilty about, including (but not confined to): (A) The knowledge of how hypocritical you are for making anti-drug speeches to your own children (or for voting Republican); (B) The realization that your sainted mother wouldn't approve (and wouldn't this break her heart?); (C) The difficult-to-avoid fact that you are supporting oppressive foreign regimes with your hard-earned money; and (D) The fact that you're 32 years old and still working at a drive-through. See also CHEECH AND CHONG and WB, THE.

MARSHMALLOW FLUFF This goo makes even peanut butter and jelly sandwiches seem sophisticated. Marshmallow Fluff dates back to 1917 when Archibald Query (a name so quintessentially 1917) whipped up a batch and

< 167 >

started selling it door to door. Shortly thereafter he sold the recipe to H. Allen Durkee and Fred L. Mower, who marketed it first as Toot Sweet Marshmallow Fluff, then dispensed with the Toot and Sweet. The company was so successful that it sponsored a radio show called *Flufferettes*. Not much besides packaging has changed since those days. Fluff still consists of only corn syrup, sugar syrup, vanilla flavor, and egg white. Parents still occasionally throw a jar in the shopping cart to avoid PB&J burnout (and sneak a spoonful themselves when the kids aren't looking). By the way, there's still no such thing as Chocolate Fluff. According to the manufacturer, chocolate's butter fat prevents the Fluff from whipping. See also PEANUT BUTTER AND JELLY SANDWICHES.

MARSHMALLOWS (BREAKFAST CEREALS FEATURING) Part of a balanced breakfast? Not a chance. Part of an I'm-single-and-I-can-eat-whatever-I-want dinnertime travesty? Absolutely. In the 1960s, breakfast cereal, once exclusively the realm of such semi-healthful names as Cheerios and Kellogg's Corn Flakes, was transformed by an onslaught of sugar-heavy monstrosities—some of which had the hubris to include marshmallows in the mix. Those tiny bits of air-puffed goodness made Lucky Charms magically delicious, put the bite in

Count Chocula, and were the raison d'être of such lesser-known brands as Circus Fun and recent additions including Kellogg's Disney Chocolate Mud & Bugs. See also MONSTER CEREALS.

MARTIN AND LEWIS See LEWIS, JERRY.

MARTIN LUTHER KING JR. DAY Abbreviated as MLK Day by the same people who call Christmas Xmas, the third Monday in January is set aside to celebrate the life of one of America's greatest civil rights leaders. Most of us choose to honor his memory (just as we do all other holiday-worthy greats, such as Presidents Lincoln and Washington) by staying up late on Sunday night, sleeping in on Monday, then perhaps meeting friends for lunch and hitting the mall. Still, King has so far received a better shake than Lincoln and Washington. At least he hasn't been forced to share his holiday with anybody else.

MARY KAY COSMETICS It's not easy to separate Mary Kay, the cosmetics firm, from Mary Kay, the well-coifed businesswoman who built an empire upon the principles of "God first, family second, and career third" (along with a collection of skin care formulas derived from animal hide tanning solutions). Using her products is a bit like channeling the perpetually matte-finished entre-

< 168 >

preneur, as if the mere act of applying MK Signature Lip Gloss with microspheres will make you grow big Texas hair and become a motivational speaker. Think what you want. Mary Kay devotees (many of whom, oddly enough, are also Mary Kay *representatives*) wouldn't trade their MK Medium-Coverage Foundations for a million M•A•C Select Tints. They might, however, sell their souls for a pink Cadillac.

MASSAGE CHAIR (AT THE MALL) Gadget-oriented shopping mall retailers such as Hammacher Schlemmer, the Sharper Image, and Brookstone all know how to get customers in the store. Just break out the massage chair. Strategically placed front and center, the therapeutic chair has caused more than one footsore shopper to feign interest in buying a Sonic Bug Zapper, Ten-in-One Emergency Camping Tool, or Heat-Sensitive Foam Neck Support Pillow, just to enjoy a few minutes of mechanical bliss. See also SHARPER IMAGE, THE.

MASTURBATION According to a recent study by the National Opinion Research Center, 63 percent of men and 42 percent of women admitted to masturbating in the last year. This study revealed an important fact: That when it comes to engaging in the guiltiest of guilty pleasures, 37 percent of the men in the study and 58 percent of the women were dirty, stinking liars. Because in spite of fears of everything from hairy palms to blindness to eternal damnation, nothing can stop us, either out of boredom or frustration or simply because we're 16 and home alone, from taking matters in hand. See also CINEMAX; FARRAH FAWCETT POSTER, THE; *PENTHOUSE* FORUM; *PLAYBOY*; and SPECTRAVISION.

MATCH GAME The kick of watching *Match Game* during its 1973 through 1982 heyday was the strong sense that the two-tiered panel was truly having a good time. The game was simple. Host Gene Rayburn read a sentence or two that included a strategically spaced blank (e.g. "The caveman said, 'I just went to a very unusual wedding. A dinosaur _____ed my bride.'"). Six celebs wrote down possible blank-fillers and the people-on-the-street contestants tried to match their answers. It felt like innocent "adult" fun, spiced with the inevitable sexual innuendos insinuated either by the loaded questions or by the smart-mouthed stars, which usually consisted of a subset of any of the following: Brett Somers, Charles Nelson Reilly, Fannie Flagg, Betty White, Nipsey Russell, Gary Burghoff, Richard Dawson, McLean Stevenson, and/or Orson Bean. See also GAME SHOWS.

< 169 >

M*axim* Sophomoric, leering, and highly successful, *Maxim* has climbed to the top of the men's magazine business by admitting that gentlemen really do buy girly magazines just for the pictures. The genius of this publica-tion is realizing that the girlies in question don't have to be totally naked, à la *Playboy*. This strategy has net-ted it a better class of  celebrity T & A. Women who wouldn't dream of sitting for a nude shoot (at least, not yet) don't think twice about doing three *Maxim* spreads wearing nothing but thong underwear and a feather boa. Thus the magazine can snag the likes of Paris Hilton, Shania Twain, Lucy Liu, Jessica Simpson, and even Helena Bonham Carter, while *Playboy* whines and begs to get a couple of scrubs from *Survivor*. See also *P*LAYBOY and T*HONG* U*NDERWEAR*.

M*CHALE'S* N*AVY* From Abbott and Costello's debut flick *Buck Privates* to *Stripes* to Pauly Shore's *In the Army Now*, bungling service personnel have long been cinema and TV staples— which is pretty odd, considering that the fate of the free world rests on the effec-tiveness of these people. One of the genre's most popular representatives is *McHale's Navy*, a television series loosely—and unofficially—based on the popular movie and play *Mister Roberts*. Ernest Borgnine (who not only won a Best Actor Oscar for the movie *Marty* and survived *The Poseidon Adventure*, but also had a sledgehammer fight on top of a moving train with Lee Marvin in *Emperor of the North*) starred as the cap-tain of a World War II torpedo boat who had "crazy" adventures with his "wacky" crew while the rest of the U.S. Navy fought a life-or-death struggle with the Japanese empire. Tim Conway, later to gain attention thanks to his inability to keep a straight face on *The Carol Burnett Show* (and his inability to get anyone to laugh with his *Dorf* videos), stole most of his scenes as Ensign Parker. See also A*BBOTT* A*ND* C*OSTELLO* and S*HORE*, P*AULY*.

M*C*K*UEN*, R*OD* You won't find his poetry taught in many college English departments. In fact, academics give him about as much respect as they would your average rhyming bumper sticker. But the painful truth is that Rod McKuen has sold more books than any other poet in history. Take that, Walt Whitman. The man whose best-remembered feat is adapting a song by Belgian legend Jacques Brel into the 1974 Terry Jacks hit "Seasons in the Sun" touched the hearts—if not the minds—of late '60s, early '70s middlebrow readers with his

< 170 >

best sellers *Listen to the Warm* and *Fields of Wonder* (visit any decent Goodwill store and you'll likely find a battered paperback in the book department). He got so big that Frank Sinatra even recorded an entire album of McKuen material. But the tide turned quickly. In the '80s, facing a no-longer-interested public, he bought back the rights to all of his books and recordings and withdrew them from circulation, a move fans (who no longer admit that they were fans) might perceive as a noble artistic act. Cynics might call it a humanitarian gesture.

MCRIB The McDonald's menu is one long guilty pleasure, from the calorie-packed Big Mac to the deep-fried "apple pie." For years the only thing missing was a pork offering—an oversight the chain remedied with this 490-calorie, boneless, sauce-swathed, onion-topped creation. The creepy part about the McRib is that though it's shaped to look like a tiny rack of ribs, it's really an amalgam of fused pork pieces, à la Chicken McNuggets.

Sadly, McDonalds only offers the McRib periodically. Perhaps corporate headquarters thinks that demand won't support its year-round inclusion on the menu. But if that's the case, they need to spend more time on the Internet. We found several electronic petitions urging McDonalds to sell this sandwich year-round. See also BIG MAC and NUGGETS, CHICKEN.

MEAT IN CANS See SPAM; UNDERWOOD DEVILED HAM; and VIENNA SAUSAGE.

MEAT LOAF (THE FOOD) This dish, first mentioned in print in 1899, has gone from budget-stretching stopgap to cultural icon. The loaf was sort of a prototype Hamburger Helper, designed to make chopped or ground meat go farther. This was accomplished by mixing whatever meat one had with crackers, rice, cornflakes, or some other starchy filler, then bind-ing it all together with one raw egg. These days there are hundreds of recipes for this dish, incorporating everything from turkey to wine. But none, in our opinion, makes the grade unless it's topped with a paste of baked ketchup. See also HAMBURGER HELPER and KETCHUP.

MEAT LOAF (THE SINGER) Like a bat out of hell—an overweight, very sweaty bat out of hell—Meat Loaf pounced on the pop music world like a mastiff going after a Milk-Bone. Loaf (born Marvin Lee Aday) gained minor notice for

< 171 >

singing "Hot Patootie—Bless My Soul" in *The Rocky Horror Picture Show*. But it wasn't until he teamed with songwriter Jim Steinman and producer Todd Rundgren on 1977's over-the-top *Bat Out of Hell* album—still one of the best-selling albums of all time—that Meat Loaf topped the charts. More than a quarter century later, barfly rockers and high school reunion-ites still reflexively sing along with "Paradise By the Dashboard Light"—a paean to sexual pleading in which Meat Loaf was accompanied by Ellen Foley (later a regular on *Night Court*) and Phil Rizzuto (later a regular on ads for The Money Store). See also ROCKY HORROR PICTURE SHOW, THE.

MEAT ON A STICK From the caveman roasting a rabbit on a branch to a waiter plating shish kebabs at a Greek restaurant, there's something about meat on a skewer that rivets the eye—especially if you're a red-blooded American male. Even today, there's an inherent excitement about everything from chicken satay (Thai-style chicken on a stick with peanut sauce) to good old corn dogs. Maybe it's just the wonderful convenience of a food that requires neither plate nor utensils.

MEMBERS ONLY JACKETS There was a time, back in the early '80s, when a stylish man just didn't feel dressed until he'd pulled on his trusty black Members Only jacket—and then shoved the sleeves all the way up to his elbows. These days anyone caught wearing one of these nylon, tab-collared wonders looks like a tool rather than a member. And yet, they're still out there. Old men in particular seem to love this "classic," which is sold under license by New York-based Aris Industries. Go to a bingo hall and you'll see half a dozen, usually in either tan or blue. The line was recently reworked by fashion label Heatherette, but fear not for the traditional jacket. There are plenty for sale on eBay, waiting to make an inevitable comeback. See also EBAY.

MENTALLY IMPAIRED (MOVIES WHOSE STARS PRETEND TO BE) For actors, playing a character with a mental impairment can be a quick ticket to critical praise, audience empathy, and even an Academy Award. Closet fans of the genre (which ranges from Shaun Cassidy in the TV movie *Like Normal People* to Dustin Hoffman's Oscar turn in *Rain Man*) get tear-jerking pleasure watching otherwise faculty-rich thespians play characters who rise above the cruel hand dealt them by fate. Yet mental retardation, autism, or some other

< 172 >

challenge doesn't guarantee a good performance. For every *Rain Man* there's a *The Other Sister*. And for every *I Am Sam* there's a *From Justin to Kelly* (Wait, you mean those characters weren't supposed to be mentally impaired?). See also CASSIDY, SHAUN.

MENTOS COMMERCIALS Is it the jingle, which sounds disturbingly like the theme song from *The Greatest American Hero*? Is it the wacky plotting (example: Guy parks in such a way as to make it impossible for our heroine to move her car. Thanks to her Mentos, she's inspired to get the guys from a construction site to pick up and move her vehicle)? Or is it the smug smirk that at least one character offers up in the final moments? We believe *all* these things make Mentos ads compelling to watch, even though pretty much everyone hates at least one of them—especially the guy hiding from his mom at the mall. And the guy who climbs through the backseat of a stranger's car to get across the street. And the girl who, denied access to the adult dressing room, gets dressed in a teepee in the children's department. And the guy who pretends to be a waiter so he can get drinks for him and his date. And, come to think of it, everyone hates the one about the girl who uses construction workers to move her car, too.

MERV GRIFFIN SHOW, THE He was never Johnny Carson. To some, he wasn't even Mike Douglas. But Merv Griffin managed to hold afternoon audiences for 24 years on his own television talk show.

A big band singer who scored a 1950 hit with "I've Got a Lovely Bunch of Coconuts" (seriously), Griffin segued into television, then parlayed gigs as substitute host on Jack Paar's *Tonight Show* into his own gabfest. What was his enduring appeal? For one, the show was on the tube at a time when stay-at-home moms were making dinner. For another, you could rationalize the guilt of listening to Merv chatting up the Gabor sisters by claiming that what you *really* enjoyed were his serious conversations with the likes of Buckminster Fuller, Gore Vidal, and Bertrand Russell.

Did the show make any lasting impact on America's cultural life? Consider that it was while guesting with Merv that Rip Taylor developed his signature bit: "I was bombing," he said, "so I took Merv's and my script . . . tore it up into little pieces like confetti, then threw it out to the audience." The rest is history. Another bit of history: Merv is the man behind both *Jeopardy!* and *Wheel of Fortune*—and still contributes puzzles and trivia questions to his brainchildren. See also GABOR SISTERS, THE; GAME SHOWS; and TAYLOR, RIP.

< 173 >

MICHENER, JAMES Geography fans, have we got a novelist for you. Michener's first book, *Tales of the South Pacific*, won a Pulitzer Prize and also served as the basis for the musical *South Pacific*. But the dozens of novels that followed cast him as the person to turn to if you want to peruse gigantic, sprawling stories not so much about a person or even a family, but about a piece of real estate. Michener's best sellers include such resonant titles as *Texas*, *Poland*, *Hawaii*, *Iberia*, and *Chesapeake*. Excellent reading for people laid up with broken legs, or who consider Mobil guides to be gripping narratives.

"MICKEY" Boasting nonsensical lyrics and a beat as infectious as Typhoid Mary, Toni Basil's 1982 No. 1 hit "Mickey" was in 2001 named the greatest one-hit wonder of all time by no less an authority than VH1. Though it was Basil's only foray onto the music charts, it capped a career that has spanned decades and brought her, Forrest Gump–like, into contact with some of the greatest guilty pleasures of  the 20th century. An actress and choreographer of considerable skill, she worked on the Elvis vehicle *Viva Las Vegas*; appeared on a *Baywatch* episode in 1992; and choreographed a Gap commercial for khaki pants. Last but not least, her song "Mickey" was parodied as "Ricky" (an *I Love Lucy* spoof) by Weird Al Yankovic. See also BAYWATCH; GAP COMMERCIALS; ONE-HIT WONDERS; PRESLEY, ELVIS; and YANKOVIC, WEIRD AL.

MICROWAVE POPCORN (AS A MEAL SUBSTITUTE) Come lunchtime, at least one worker in every office pops a bag of this stuff into the microwave. And why not? Everyone feels virtuous munching little pillows of popped corn. It makes an ideal meal—that is, unless you read the bag. The first misconception is that each sack only contains one serving. In fact, they usually contain three. So take that nutritional information you only glanced at (something like 180 calories and 13 grams of fat) and triple it. That's 540 calories and 39 total fat grams. Reality check: A McDonald's Quarter Pounder with cheese only sets you back 530 calories and 30 total fat grams. Plus, a Quarter Pounder doesn't contain those annoying stick-in-your-teeth hulls.

MICROWAVED DINNERS On the packaging, it looks like gourmet dining. On the inside it looks like the school lunch from hell. But did you seriously think you were going to get a delicious meal out of a prepackaged microwave dinner? Of course not. What you wanted—and what

< 174 >

you got—is convenience. In this case, convenience being defined as a meal prepared in less than five minutes that can be devoured in another five minutes, and leaves behind nothing that needs to be washed, save a fork (and even that isn't necessary if you opt for a Hot Pocket). That, of course, leaves more time to feel guilty about not remembering the last time you used any of your pots and pans. See also TV DINNERS.

MIDGETS Imagine having a rare, poorly understood, genetic ailment—one that a certain segment of society found *absolutely hilarious*. Welcome to the world of the Little People, formerly known by the now-politically-incorrect term of "midgets." While making fun of literally any other disadvantaged group is uncouth if you're nobody and career suicide if you're famous (heard anything from Jimmy the Greek lately?), it's still perfectly okay for bars to stage dwarf-throwing contests and for *The Man Show* to offer endless skits making fun of the height-impaired. Why do we laugh? Perhaps because we know the little people can't do anything about it. There are only about 200,000 in the entire world—not even enough for a decent march on Washington.

MIDWAYS Sometimes, as with the deep-fried Twinkie, one guilty pleasure can

lurk inside another guilty pleasure. For instance, you might find attending a state fair—with its fried food, 4-H displays and, inevitably, the world's largest pig—to be pretty embarrassing all by itself. But visiting the fair's midway (the term was coined to describe the amusements section of the 1893 Columbian Exposition) takes shame to a different level. The games of "chance" allow you to be outsmarted and fleeced by a guy named Cletus. And the rides will make you cough up whatever money the carnies didn't get—plus those corn dogs you had for lunch. Enthusiasts don't come here for cutting-edge attractions (although some of the rides do have sharp edges). Instead, they board the likes of the Tilt-a-Whirl or Scrambler knowing full well that it was assembled in a matter of hours by people you wouldn't allow to change the oil in your car. See also MEAT ON A STICK; OUTDATED CARNIVAL RIDES; SHOOTING GALLERIES; SIX FLAGS AMUSEMENT PARKS; and STATE FAIR FOOD.

MINIATURE BOOKS Calling these impulse buys "volumes" is a stretch, since many contain only a few more words than an average Bazooka Joe comic. Yet the tiny tomes hawked at bookstore checkout counters are big business for the handful of publishers cranking out such titles as *Cats Up*

< 175 >

Close, *Posh Spice in My Pocket*, and *The Little Book of Voodoo*. However, minis aren't just a contemporary phenomenon. If you happen to have a copy of the 1628/1629 *Novum Testamentum Graecum* miniature Bible, for instance, you can look forward to a comfortable retirement.

MINIATURE CHRISTMAS VILLAGES Lilliputian towns composed of plaster of Paris houses surrounded by a bed of cotton snow have been a part (usually a very small part) of Christmas decorating schemes for generations. But lately they've become the domain of collectors—and thus an embarrassment. Forget about buying a few tiny structures at the dollar store. Instead, how about the Precious Moments Christmas Village, or the Berta Hummel Christmas Village, or Thomas Kinkade's Village, or even better, the Simpsons (yes, you read right) Christmas Village? Of course none of these come cheap, or even moderately priced. Indeed, the cost of some sets, which can contain dozens of houses and figures, is often broken up into installments of, say, $75 for each piece or grouping. It's kind of like buying Time-Life Books—heart-stoppingly expensive Time-Life Books that can only be used once a year. See also DOLLAR STORES; HUMMEL FIGURES; KINKADE, THOMAS; PRECIOUS MOMENTS; and TIME-LIFE BOOKS.

MINIATURE FOODS Ritz Bits. Mini Oreos. Popcorn shrimp. Nutter Butter Bites. Pop-Tarts Snak-Stix. In this over-indulgent age when everything from hamburgers to soft drink cups are super-sized, marketers seem hell-bent on shrinking foods, too. The common denominator, besides size, is that every one of them is an embarrassment to eat in public, making you look like a character out of *Land of the Giants* gobbling regular-size human food. But do these smaller treats mean we eat fewer of them? Nope. We just eat them more rapidly, because bite-sized goodies require less chewing time. See also VIENNA SAUSAGE.

MINIATURE GOLF No golfer ever became famous by hitting a ball through a windmill or into a clown's nose. Yet for many—especially the many who vacation in tourist towns—a round of mini golf is the only chance to experience the thrill of a hole-in-one and the kick of an under-par game. Created in the early 1900s, miniature golf, or garden golf, was played with a swung putter on much longer courses than today's incarnation. It became so popular during the 1930s that Hollywood actors were discouraged from participating, because studio moguls feared the sport would pull customers away from theaters. Of course, it's been a long time

< 176 >

since a movie star had to be talked out of playing miniature golf. These days the courses are filled with sunburned tourists, most of whom know that if they were really any good, they'd be out on the full-sized links. See also GATLINBURG.

MISS AMERICA   See BEAUTY PAGEANTS.

MISS MANNERS   See ADVICE COLUMNISTS.

MISS USA   See BEAUTY PAGEANTS.

MISS WORLD   See BEAUTY PAGEANTS.

MISTER ED   How far can TV milk a single lame premise? *Gilligan's Island* rode the "We're marooned" concept for an amazing three seasons. But that's nothing compared to *Mister Ed*, which ran from 1961 through 1966 on the wafer-thin novelty of a talking horse that would only speak to a hapless guy named Wilbur. Why does the show remain such a kick for audiences? Credit a classic theme song ("A horse is a horse, of course, of course . . ."), amiable support from nice guy actor Alan Young, and the still-imitated horse voice of Allan "Rocky" Lane, a veteran of dozens of now-forgotten screen westerns including *Law West of Tombstone*, *Stagecoach to Monterey*, and *Corpus Christi Bandits*. See also *GILLIGAN'S ISLAND*; TALKING ANIMALS (MOVIES ABOUT); TALKING ANIMALS WHO DIE (MOVIES ABOUT); and TV SHOWS FEATURING ANIMAL PROTAGONISTS.

MISTER ROGERS' NEIGHBORHOOD   Fred Rogers' tortoise-slow program was designed to do one thing: introduce toddlers to the wonders of the world in nonthreatening ways. For example, one episode featured a long, lingering shot of a toilet flushing, so that Rogers could demonstrate the impossibility of being sucked down the pipes.

While tots lapped up this sort of thing, adults found great pleasure in mocking it. Everyone from Eddie Murphy to the lowliest "life of the party" took potshots at Rogers's deliberate speech, his slow, Disney Hall of Presidents movements, those sweaters he always wore, even his show's theme song, "Won't You Be My Neighbor." Well, laugh it up, wise guys, because if there's such a thing as karma, you'll pay for it later. Truth is, Rogers, who died in 2003, *was a living saint*. An ordained Presbyterian minister, he spent  his entire adult life helping children in one way or another, from producing his show to participating in numberless charities. His membership in the Gandhi Club was so widely recognized that when thieves stole his car,

< 177 >

they returned it as soon as they realized whom it belonged to. See also HALL OF PRESIDENTS, THE.

MOISTENED BABY BUTT WIPES They're supposed to make the diaper-changing experience a more gentle one for the baby in your life. Yet many a parent has realized that a moistened butt wipe across the face (a new one, of course) can be a refreshing pick-me-up in the middle of a stressful day. Gulf War troops even used them in lieu of showers. Savvy marketers are already starting to position their product to exploit this niche. But always remember that baby has first call. And never, ever take the last one.

MONKEYS (MOVIES FEATURING) It really isn't a question of whether a movie co-starring a monkey is a good one (*The Barefoot Executive*) or a bad one (all the rest). What matters is that there's a perverse pleasure in watching an actor—be he Matt LeBlanc (*Ed*), Jason Alexander (*Dunston Checks In*), Clint Eastwood (*Every Which Way but Loose*), or Ronald Reagan (*Bedtime for Bonzo*)—try to emote alongside a creature that expresses itself by throwing feces. You can almost hear them (the humans, not the monkeys) cursing their agents as they struggle to escape the proceedings with their dignity. See also DISNEY FILMS FEATURING DEAN JONES AND/OR KURT RUSSELL and *PLANET OF THE APES* MOVIES.

MONSTER CEREALS The classic Universal Studios creatures (including Dracula and the Frankenstein Monster) once struck terror into the hearts of moviegoers. Their ability to truly frighten was seriously diminished by their appearance in Abbott and Costello comedies, then destroyed completely when they were used as thinly disguised shills for marshmallow-enhanced breakfast cereals. FrankenBerry, Count Chocula, Boo Berry, the discontinued Fruit Brute (a werewolf), and Yummy Mummy brought milk-discoloring, oversugared pleasure to millions. Some random observations culled from years of reading cereal boxes over the morning meal: Franken-Berry—who appeared to be more robot-like than his stitched-together-from-corpses semi-namesake—wears strawberry nail polish. Boo Berry looks very, very stoned most of the time. And comparing earlier boxes to later ones, one can't help but think that Count Chocula has gotten a nose job (from crooked to pointy) and had his fangs filed down. Nevertheless, kids keep gobbling this stuff up. See also ABBOTT AND COSTELLO; CAP'N CRUNCH; and MARSHMALLOWS (BREAKFAST CEREALS FEATURING).

< 178 >

MONSTER TRUCKS This curious breed of automotive excess (pickups fitted with gigantic tires, then used to drive over other cars) got its start in 1974 when Missourian Bob Chandler designed a big-wheeled promotional vehicle called Bigfoot. People (*some* people) liked the idea, and started putting bigger and bigger tires on bigger and bigger vehicles, which came to be called monster trucks. Chandler's Bigfoot (constantly upgraded to maintain its supremacy) was the biggest of all, eventually mounting treads so large they dwarfed the truck chassis teetering atop them. In recent years the trend has either lost steam or gone mainstream, depending on your outlook. True, you don't see all that many jacked-up, big-tired pickups anymore, but you do see legions of jacked-up, big-tired SUVs. And while they aren't used to drive over other cars, you can bet some of their owners, stuck in traffic for the umpteenth time, have considered such a move. See also PICKUP TRUCKS and SUVs.

MONTE CRISTO SANDWICH, THE Before the invention of such modern travesties as breaded, deep-fried candy bars, the nastiest, most life-shortening thing you could eat (other than a cyanide tablet) was a Monte Cristo. Basically a ham and/or turkey sandwich dredged in egg batter and fried in a skillet, it inhabits a strange netherworld between breakfast and lunch. Is it a sweet or savory dish? Should it be offered with strawberries, sour cream, maple syrup, a sprinkling of powdered sugar, or mustard? Perhaps, given the fat content, it should be served with a dose of Lipitor on the side. See also STATE FAIR FOOD.

MORONS (ENTERTAINING, UNTIMELY DEATHS OF) Laughing at the antics of idiots is a national pastime. TV networks build entire programs around videos of guys (it's *always* guys) doing everything from attempting insane backyard stunts to leading police on 100-mph car chases just because they want to avoid paying a couple of outstanding parking tickets. But so far only one venue, the Darwin Awards, has had the nerve to chronicle the equally entertaining *deaths* of such individuals. Developed by scientist Wendy Northcutt, the Web site www.darwinawards.com acts as a clearinghouse for colorful tales about people who "eliminate themselves in an extraordinarily idiotic manner, thereby improving the species' chances of long-term survival." How shallow is the gene pool? Let's just say that Northcutt has produced three books (and counting) chronicling morons' ignominious ends, and that her page is always jammed with new stories. It proves the old saw that the last words out of an idiot's mouth

< 179 >

before he dies are usually, "Hey guys, watch this!" See also JACKASS; STUNTS (INSANE, TELEVISED); and URBAN LEGENDS.

MORONS (VENUES THAT FEATURE THE ANTICS OF) See *COPS*; *JACKASS*; *NATIONAL ENQUIRER, THE*; SPRINGER, JERRY; TELEVANGELISTS; and *WEEKLY WORLD NEWS*.

MOTOR VEHICLES (PRETENTIOUS) See CADILLACS; CORVETTES; HUMMER, THE; LIMOUSINES; MONSTER TRUCKS; MUSCLE CARS; and SUVS.

MOUNTAIN DEW The folks who sell this antifreeze-colored beverage work hard to make it seem "radical" and "extreme." But to anyone over the age of 30, it's still the drink of choice for rednecks. In fact, from its birth in the 1940s up to the 1960s, that was its primary market. Created by a Knoxville, Tennessee, bottler, its containers originally featured a picture of a hillbilly shooting at a "revenuer," along with the motto, "It'll tickle yore innards!" In 1973 the company finally switched its focus from the *Deliverance* crowd to "young, active outdoor types." This trend accelerated during the '90s. The tagline "Do the Dew" was introduced, and Pepsi-Cola (Dew's corporate owner) did everything possible to associate their product not with toothless mountain folk, but with

snowboarders, skateboarders, and anyone else who might enjoy a beverage with a "daring, high-energy, high-intensity, active, extreme citrus taste."

Actually, the only truly extreme thing about Mountain Dew is the extremely large dose of caffeine in each 12-ounce serving (55 milligrams compared to only 38 in a can of regular Pepsi). Maybe that's why it's of such interest to active, outdoor types—as well as to rednecks and the occasional all-nighter-pulling college student. See also BIG RED; FRESCA; RED BULL; and TAHITIAN TREAT.

MOVIE REVIEWS (USE OF STAR RATING SYSTEM IN) When it comes to movies, we want to believe we can make our own choices, without guidance from the unelected guardians of pop culture. That's why we're more interested in a critic's reasoned opinion than in a glib, wordless assessment of a film's worth—unless we're in a hurry and our ride to the multiplex is sitting in the driveway, honking his horn. Then all we want to know is how many stars it got. Though few will admit it, the first part of a movie review we study is the number of stars doled out (or, in the case of publications such as *Entertainment Weekly*, the letter grade). It's a guide, but also a weapon. Movie fans beyond number have escaped being browbeaten into watching undesirable flicks by saying, "I heard it

< 180 >

sucks. It only got one star." See also BOMBS (BIG-BUDGET MOVIES THAT TURN OUT TO BE).

MOVIE SEQUELS These days almost every successful movie is considered sequel fodder. It's part of the marketing plan. But what so many studio execs seem to forget is that while making a hit is tough, going back to the well a second time, with the same characters and premise, is like asking to be struck down by the Movie Gods. For every sterling effort such as *Bride of Frankenstein*, *Aliens*, and *The Godfather, Part II*, there are 10 or more stinkers like *Staying Alive* (the sequel to *Saturday Night Fever*); *Grease 2*; *Speed 2: Cruise Control*; and *I Still Know What You Did Last Summer*. Of course, watching an awful sequel can sometimes be awfully entertaining—though not always in the way its creators intended. *Rocky* films, for instance, can't be judged as movie-making—it's more like watching the next episode in a favorite TV series. Another reason to like sequels: They can bypass such first-film technicalities as "character introduction," "plot development," and "suspense," and get quickly down to business. Honestly, do you really want to have DNA explained to you again in a *Jurassic Park* sequel? See also ROCKY MOVIES; *SATURDAY NIGHT FEVER*; and STALLONE, SYLVESTER.

MOVIE SOUNDTRACKS There are two distinct kinds of movie soundtracks. One is, essentially, background music—even when it's big and symphonic. Owning such recordings in any numbers pegs you as either a film snob (Does anyone really sit around the house listening to Bernard Herrmann discs?) or a film dweeb (Do you really want to admit that, just last weekend, you were jamming to your *Star Wars Episode I: The Phantom Menace* CD?). The second type of soundtrack is a collection of songs, original or otherwise, that the producers of the film managed to acquire rights to. Depending on the quality of the flick, these can be either good albums in their own right (*Saturday Night Fever*), interestingly evocative (*American Graffiti*), or lame, lame, lame (Did you really need the disc of the Mel Gibson/Robert Downey Jr. film *Air America*—featuring Aerosmith and the Four Tops—in your collection?). Compilations like this are gathering dust in discount bins through the nation, in part because buying one is about as uncomfortable as buying condoms at your neighborhood pharmacy. See also *SATURDAY NIGHT FEVER* (SOUNDTRACK); TV THEME SONGS (INSTRUMENTAL); and TV THEME SONGS (VOCAL).

MOVIES (PORNOGRAPHIC) Back in the 1970s, when watching a dirty movie meant putting on a trench coat and join-

< 181 >

ing the rest of the perverts down at the local adult theater, producers made valiant efforts to create productions that mimicked "real" films. This golden age of porn spawned such near-mainstream hits as *Deep Throat*, *The Devil in Miss Jones*, and *Debbie Does Dallas*. But the industry changed when videotape technology allowed consumers to ditch their raincoats and leer in the privacy of their homes. It also gave any guy with a sleazy girlfriend and a camcorder the right to call himself a pornographic film-maker. These days, hyperdescriptive titles like *Double Anal Entry* and *Dildo Crazy* occupy as much shelf space as the films that at least try to maintain some semblance of plot amidst the humping and bumping. But thank goodness the industry hasn't lost its sense of humor. A trip into the back room of your neighborhood video store will still reveal that same whimsical zeal that led to such porno classics as *Foreskin Gump*, *Saturday Night Beaver*, and *Blazing Boners*. *The Ozporns*, anyone? See also LORDS, TRACI and SPECTRAVISION.

MOVIES THAT PARODY OTHER MOVIES
Throughout the history of cinema there have always been tiny films that made fun of major projects. But the genre went big-time in 1974 with the premiere of Mel Brooks's western parody *Blazing Saddles*, followed that same year by the even-funnier horror movie parody *Young Frankenstein*. While Brooks (with ever-diminishing success) continues to mine this genre, in 1980 the torch of genius was passed to Jerry and David Zucker and Jim Abrahams, who co-directed the disaster movie parody *Airplane!* Among other things, it launched the comedy career of formerly dead-serious thespian Leslie Nielsen. These days the movies-parodying-movies lineup grows each year, with flicks such as *Scream* (a scary parody of slasher films), *Scary Movie* (a funny parody of slasher flicks that also parodied the parody *Scream*), *Repossessed* (mocks devil films), and *Spy Hard* (does likewise to spy movies) marching onto marquees. Sure, some aren't all that funny, but at least they provide work for Nielsen (look for him in *Spy Hard*, *Repossessed*, and *Scary Movie 3*). See also NIELSEN, LESLIE.

MOVIES TURNED INTO TV SHOWS
Occasionally, a big-screen hit jumps successfully to the small screen. Witness such shows as *M*A*S*H*, *The Odd Couple* (which was based on a stage show that became a movie), and *Buffy the Vampire Slayer*. But far more commonly, the leap to the small screen is followed by a fall, the sound of

< 182 >

expectations deflating, and a quick cancellation. It was only after the shows were canceled that viewers who had hoped to relive the movie magic felt the guilty sting of having been duped into watching *My Big Fat Greek Life*, *Working Girl* (with a then-unknown Sandra Bullock in the Melanie Griffith role), and *Delta House* (in which the *Animal House* antics were sadly cleaned up for TV). See also ANIMAL HOUSE and FAME.

MR. BUBBLE "Take a bath with Mr. Bubble. He'll get you so clean your mother won't know you," boasted the 1963 commercial. Featuring an animated kid whose grandmother mistakes his bubble-covered face first for that of a dog and then a grown man (which makes you wonder if this woman should have been left with kids), the spots helped Mr. Bubble become a household name. Its round pink face is an icon still seen on T-shirts of trendy kids who wouldn't be caught dead buying any tub product not sold at The Body Shop. Now sold in a squeeze bottle rather than the original cardboard box, Mr. Bubble still promises long-lasting bubble fun—something that takes on a different meaning when you're 37 than it did when you were 7. One thing still holds true, however. You should discontinue use if rash, redness, or itching occurs. See also BATH STORES.

MR. T The man who launched a thousand lame "I pity the fool" imitations was born Laurence Tureaud on Chicago's South Side in 1952. He started lifting weights so that he wouldn't get picked on, cultivated a Mohawk after seeing a similar style on a Mandinka warrior in *National Geographic*, and worked as everything from a $3,000-a-day celebrity bodyguard to a gym teacher. Sylvester Stallone spotted him in 1982 and hired him to play his nemesis in *Rocky III*, after which he landed his signature role as B. A. Baracus on TV's *The A-Team*. Interestingly, though T looks like a seven-foot-tall juggernaut in *Rocky III*, in reality he's only 5-foot-11. It's not that he's so big; it's that Stallone is so darn short. See also ROCKY MOVIES and STALLONE, SYLVESTER.

MTV This all-music television network became an instant pop culture icon when it debuted on August 1, 1981 (first song played: "Video Killed the Radio Star"). But though it gained fame by serving up wall-to-wall music videos, these days MTV offers almost none. Instead, its schedule is crowded with reality shows (*The Osbournes*, *The Real World*, *Road Rules*) and damn-near-unclassifiable hits such as *Beavis and Butt-Head* and *Jackass*. Yet pretty much the entire human race, even people who last paid attention to pop music back when Duran

< 183 >

Duran was king, still checks in occasionally. It's a great way to gauge one's age—not in calendar years, but on the maturity scale. When the tunes seem loud, pointless, and insipid, and the kids on the reality shows strike you as vapid, self-absorbed idiots, you've officially become your parents. See also BEAVIS AND BUTT-HEAD; JACKASS; MTV VIDEO MUSIC AWARDS, THE; MUSIC VIDEOS; OSBOURNES, THE; REAL WORLD, THE; and REALITY SHOWS.

MTV VIDEO MUSIC AWARDS, THE Though it likes to bill itself as the coolest of the major award shows, its audience tunes in mainly for the occasional oddball moments, gaffes, and world-class displays of T & A. Sure "You Might Think" by the Cars won Video of the Year during the program's debut broadcast in 1984, but what we really remember is Madonna rolling all over the stage while singing "Like a Virgin." And the highlights that make the national news the next day don't concern the music, but the weird publicity stunts. Say, Michael Jackson playing tongue hockey with his soon-to-be-ex-wife Lisa Marie Presley, or Madonna (there she is again) playing tongue hockey with Britney Spears and Christina Aguilera. See also JACKSON, MICHAEL; MADONNA (NONMUSIC PROJECTS); MTV; and MUSIC VIDEOS.

MUPPET SHOW, THE By 1976, the variety show was dead as a television format. Yet nobody seems to have told Jim Henson and company, who launched *The Muppet Show* that same year. Spun off from *Sesame Street*—and ditching all that "educational" baggage in the process—the syndicated show was packed with bad puns, outrageous characters, and more bad puns. Although it took them a while to admit it, lots of adults loved the show, appreciating the absurdity of glorified puppets interacting—and singing and dancing—with such guest hosts as Charles Aznavour, Lena Horne, Vincent Price, Ethel Merman, and Mummenschanz (all in the first season). *The Muppet Show* was presided over by Kermit the Frog, a *Sesame Street* holdover who didn't host the original *Muppet Show* pilot (that gig went to a long-forgotten hippie Muppet named Wally). The series made stars out of such hand-up-their-rears new characters as Miss Piggy, Fozzie Bear, and the Swedish

Chef, all of whom made the leap to the big screen with varying degrees of success. See also VARIETY SHOWS.

MURDER, SHE WROTE For 12 seasons, mystery writer Jessica Fletcher (Angela

< 184 >

Lansbury) managed to solve a crime a week—often in tiny Cabot Cove, Maine, a picturesque seaside village with a per capita murder rate rivaling Detroit's. The only viewers who didn't feel a bit guilty watching this predictable series were those who had a little dish of hard candies on hand in case the grandchildren stopped by. See also MYSTERIES, COZY.

MURPHY, EDDIE (THE STAND-UP COMEDY OF) America loved him on *Saturday Night Live*. America loved his stand-up act, too, though it wasn't politically correct to admit it. That's because the leather-clad funnyman's first real statement to the world was *Delirious*, a concert recorded in 1983 in which the comic, then only 22, joked about sex, AIDS, and drunken relatives in a show packed with more profanity than Andrew Dice Clay's bachelor party. There was more of the same in 1987's *Raw*, and the debate continued as to whether this man-who-would-be-*Shrek's*-donkey was heir to Richard Pryor (of whom he does an impression), or just a potty-mouthed—albeit very funny—misogynist. See also CLAY, ANDREW DICE and COMEDY ALBUMS.

MUSCLE CARS This uniquely American class of vehicles performs no useful function, save as a male fashion accessory. Unlike classic post–World War II European roadsters, which were nimble and peppy because they were tiny, American "sports cars" had to perform while dragging around a massive steel body and a four-person passenger compartment. In most cases this was accomplished by dropping a hulking V-8 engine under the hood that burned fuel faster than a refinery fire and idled like a washing machine with a bowling ball in it. The near-legendary muscle car stable included the Pontiac GTO, the Firebird, the Mustang, the Camaro, and of course, the Trans Am. As a class they handled horribly, and wore out faster than cheap sneakers. But if you put a mile of arrow-straight road in front of one and stomped on the gas, you understood why no self-respecting high school quarterback could be without one. See also CORVETTES and REYNOLDS, BURT.

MUSEUM GIFT SHOPS It's not that retail establishments tied to cultural institutions are inherently a bad thing. It's just that guilt can easily set in when you realize that you really want to spend more time in the shop than you do in the museum itself—and that you will enjoy buying a Gerhard Richter coffee mug a lot more than you will enjoy looking at one of his paintings. See also PEZ.

MUSIC VIDEOS The "cutting edge" concept of putting pictures to music is actu-

< 185 >

ally more than a century old. As early as 1900, theaters across the nation offered "illustrated songs," in which a musician played a popular tune while glass slides illustrating the lyrics flashed on-screen. Later, performance clips were used as filler at theaters and, still later, on television. But it was the Beatles who truly pioneered music videos in the modern sense, producing conceptual films to go with some of their songs—mainly so they wouldn't have to perform those tunes in person on variety shows. Hell, even Tony Orlando and Dawn featured them on their 1970s program. By the early 1980s quite a few bands filmed clips to go with their music—all of which were gathered up by MTV when it launched in 1981 and then aired non-stop, 24 hours a day. Back in those early days, simply having a bunch of clips in the can could guarantee heavy exposure, followed by fame and fortune. Interestingly, MTV, which started the craze, doesn't play all that many videos anymore, giving its time instead to teen- and tween-themed reality shows. See also MTV; MTV MUSIC VIDEO AWARDS, THE; ORLANDO, TONY (AND DAWN); and VARIETY SHOWS.

MUTUAL OF OMAHA'S WILD KINGDOM The fun of this long-running nature show wasn't listening to host Marlin Perkins ramble about animals from his studio set. It was watching his intrepid sidekick, Jim Fowler, *rumble* with animals. Week after week Fowler would play Tonto to Perkins's Lone Ranger, heading into the field to wrestle with boa constrictors and put radio tags on mountain lions. The show was on the air from 1963 to 1985, but it could have been an even bigger hit if some savvy producer had said, "Lose the old guy and get the young guy a cute girl sidekick. We'll call it, *Mutual of Omaha's Crocodile Hunter!*" See also CROCODILE HUNTER.

MYSTERIES, COZY Also known as Whodunits Featuring Recurring Amateur Sleuth Protagonists. The first adventure can be okay, because it's not too difficult to believe that just about any of us could one day stumble on a murder and maybe even help solve it. The guilty pleasure comes a few books down the line when it becomes clear that the protagonist—whether a Laundromat owner (the "Josie Toadfern" series), a Philadelphia schoolteacher (the "Amanda Pepper" series) or an Amish quilt maker (the "Granny Hanny" series)—lives in a town with both a disturbing number of homicides and a disturbingly lame police force. See also MURDER, SHE WROTE and QUINCY, M.E.

< 186 >

N

NACHOS It should come as no surprise that this ultimate quickie, no-brainer meal started life as a quickie, no-brainer meal. One day Ignacio "Nacho" Anaya was working as maitre d' at a restaurant in the tiny Mexican border town of Piedras Negras when a large party of women arrived, looking for lunch. The cook was absent, so Anaya took matters into his own hands. He headed for the kitchen, put some tostadas on a plate, covered them with grated cheese, slipped them under a broiler for a couple of minutes and then added a jalapeño garnish. Needless to say, there's now a bronze plaque in Piedras Negras commemorating this accomplishment, which has surely had more impact on the average Joe's life (and certainly, waistline) than, say, the space program.

NAKED CELEBRITIES (PHOTOGRAPHS OF) You would think, considering how many paparazzi earn their livings hounding them, that famous people would be extra careful about dropping trou outdoors or near open windows. Yet such is not the case. For whatever reason, everyone from Prince Charles to Jennifer Aniston to Brad Pitt has been caught standing on a hotel balcony or lounging on a yacht in the altogether. Of course anyone who's ever darted down their front steps in their briefs to grab the morning paper at 5 A.M. can sympathize with their plight (while at the same time ogling the shots). However, celebrities who willingly posed nude when they were nobody (including Suzanne Somers, Vanessa Williams, and even O. J. prosecutor Marcia Clark), only to have the photos resurface later, have no right to complain. Neither do actors and actresses whose nude scenes—however important to the plot—end up as Internet downloads. If you plan to go bare assed, be prepared to be bitten in the ass. See also BRITISH ROYAL FAMILY, THE.

NASCAR Though it's been pegged since its inception in 1948 as a redneck sport (a term hard-core fans don't dispute), the National Association for Stock Car Auto Racing is undeniably more exciting than other, more "sophisticated" automotive circuits. Indeed, it's hard to imagine opposing pit crews at a Formula One event getting into fistfights, or a winner doing doughnuts in the infield, or competitors who crash their cars standing on the edge of the track and flipping off drivers still in the race. Besides the mayhem, the other attraction is the vehicles, which resemble the Fords and Chevrolets us civilians can buy in show-

< 187 >

rooms (hence the name "stock" cars). Back in the beginning, NASCAR's rides were truly stock vehicles—old junkers the drivers used because they couldn't get anything better. These days, however, the cars are so heavily modified that the only thing they have in common with street cars is the fact that both run on four wheels. Not that this has hurt NASCAR's fan base, which is 75 million strong. See also MUSCLE CARS and TUBE TOPS.

NATIONAL ENQUIRER, THE If dropping a copy of the *Enquirer* into your shopping cart seems embarrassing today, it must have been excruciating a few decades ago. Founded in 1926 as *The New York Enquirer*, the mag became a rag in the 1950s, when it was renamed *The National Enquirer* and reoriented to focus on car wrecks,

hideous crimes, and other such attention-grabbing mayhem. In 1968 the tabloid (mostly to get into grocery stores) turned on a dime, ditching the gore in favor of celebrity drivel, UFOs, ghosts, tales of woe, psychic predictions, and miracle diets. The new approach pushed its circulation past 4 million. These days things aren't so rosy, with readership declining to around 1.7 mil-

lion. The problem is competition. There was a time when the *Enquirer* had the field of celebrity scandal all to itself. But these days, if the rag hears about an infected pimple on Jennifer Lopez's butt, it must battle everyone from *Entertainment Tonight* to the *Today* show for the scoop. See also ENTERTAINMENT TONIGHT and WEEKLY WORLD NEWS.

NATIONAL LAMPOON People who think that *Saturday Night Live* pioneered ironic, in-your-face humor have obviously never read a vintage issue of *National Lampoon*. Begun in 1970 by three ex-Harvardites as an offshoot of the famous *Harvard Lampoon*, it served up some of the most brutal, politically incorrect parodies ever put to paper (and gave kids who graduated from *Mad* magazine something new to laugh at). Back in the days when Erma Bombeck was considered funny, the 'poon (whose staff of young Turks included conservative political pundit P. J. O'Rourke and future filmmaker John Hughes) published such "groundbreaking" work as an entire issue devoted to hating foreigners, a cover showing a dog with a gun to its head and the line, "If you don't buy this magazine, we'll kill this dog," and, perhaps most famously, a cartoon featuring a legless frog on a cart in front of a restaurant selling frog legs. The magazine changed hands a couple of times

< 188 >

before ceasing publication in 1998, but not before its alumni went on to, among other things, create such cultural landmarks as the movie *Animal House*. See also *ANIMAL HOUSE*.

NEW YORK TIMES BOOK REVIEW, THE (READING, INSTEAD OF ACTUAL BOOKS) What Cliffs Notes are to college students and Classics Illustrated comics are to high schoolers, *The New York Times Book Review* is to faux intellectuals. Too busy (and by "busy" we mean "lazy") to peruse the latest prose? Then a quick scan of this Sunday tabloid over brunch provides just enough information so that you can *sound* widely read. Now all you need is a black turtleneck and some clunky glasses, and you can hold your intellectual ground at any gallery opening or coffee bar. See also CLASSICS ILLUSTRATED and CLIFFS NOTES.

NEWLEY, ANTHONY A Las Vegas staple, a chart-topper in pre-Beatles England, and a former Joan Collins hubby, Anthony Newley was best known for singing—and for being impersonated singing—his signature tune, "What Kind of Fool Am I?" One of those rare stylists who actually put *too much* into his songs, Newley was famous for executing "Fool" with theatrical bravado, inevitably ending each rendition with eyes downcast and right arm held high.

It made Roberto Benigni look like Perry Como. See also COLLINS, JOAN.

NEWLYWED GAME, THE From the mind of Chuck "Gong Show" Barris came this classic that pits couples against one another in pursuit of a prize "chosen especially for them." The foolproof format—which kept the show going from '66 to '74, with revivals later in the '70s and again in the '80s and '90s—was simple: Spouses had to guess how their mates would answer a question. Since these were newlyweds, the questions often had to do with their romantic escapades. One now-infamous moment had longtime host Bob Eubanks ask "Where specifically is the weirdest place that you . . . have ever gotten the urge to make whoopee?" to which a bleeped bride answered, "In the ass." While zingers like that rarely happened, each episode usually featured at least one wife clunking her foolish husband over the head with an answer card. See also DATING SHOWS and GAME SHOWS.

NEWTON, WAYNE In Las Vegas, Wayne Newton is as big as Elvis. Unfortunately (at least, for him), he doesn't enjoy such exalted status in the rest of the world. Still, being the King of Sin City is no small feat—especially when you are known for only one song, "Danke Schoen," that was recorded more than

< 189 >

40 years ago. But like the proceedings at a particularly sordid bachelor party, the fact that you succumbed to temptation and attended one of Newton's sweat-soaked two-hour extravaganzas—and had a great time—is one anecdote you might not want to share with the folks back home. Whatever happens in Vegas, stays in Vegas. See also LAS VEGAS.

NEWTON-JOHN, OLIVIA No self-respecting '70s or '80s hard rock fan could bring himself to say he liked this Aussie import's music. And truth is, they didn't. But that doesn't mean they didn't like *her*. Many was the hard-core Led Zepplin, Van Halen, and/or Kiss devotee who secretly dreamed of saying "I Honestly Love You" to the singer of such immortal classics as "Let Me Be There" and "Have You Never Been Mellow." But though she flirted with a harder image, first slutting it up as Sandy in 1978's *Grease* and then releasing the No. 1 hit "Physical" in 1981, Newton-John seems hell-bent on remaining an angel. In recent years she's written a children's book and become involved in animal rights. See also KISS and *XANADU*.

NFL FILMS You have to hand it to Ed Sabol, the founder of NFL Films. The former overcoat salesman and amateur filmmaker knew a market niche when he saw one. In 1962, back when pro football occupied a place in the American consciousness somewhere just above steeplechase and just below soccer, he offered NFL commissioner Pete Rozelle $3,000 for the rights to film that season's championship game. Just a few years later, Sabol's revolutionary cinematic techniques (ground-level shots, slow motion, loud music, and the rumbling narration of gravel-voiced John Facenda) somehow turned the Sunday afternoon antics of a bunch of huge, sweaty guys into poetry. Today the company Sabol founded films every single NFL match everywhere, and keeps some 20 million feet of footage at its New Jersey headquarters. Not since Leni Riefenstahl managed to make the 1936 Berlin Olympics look sublime has a more lowly subject been elevated to such heights.

NICK AT NITE What, exactly, does a children's channel show in the evening, after its target audience's bedtime? Nickelodeon neatly solved that problem in 1985 when it launched Nick at Nite, a lineup of old sitcoms that plays pretty much from dusk to dawn. These days the schedule might include everything from *Three's Company* to *Family Ties* to *Charles in Charge*. The format is so hot that Nick's parent company, Viacom, launched another network, TVLand, to show reruns around the clock. That's

< 190 >

great news for the entertainment giant's bottom line, but what does it say about people who tune in to catch episodes of shows that weren't worth watching the *first* time around? See also BEVERLY HILLBILLIES, THE; BRADY BUNCH, THE; FACTS OF LIFE, THE; GILLIGAN'S ISLAND; HAPPY DAYS; and THREE'S COMPANY.

NIELSEN, LESLIE There was a time when the star of such films as *The Poseidon Adventure* (he was the ship's captain) and *Forbidden Planet* (again, a ship's captain) was known for doing stone-faced, humorless authority figures. But all that changed in 1980 when he played an inept doctor in the disaster film parody *Airplane!*  From then on, Nielsen (who was always famous for off-screen antics) became, of all things, a slapstick artist and an indispensable part of any movie that mocks other movies. So if you rent, say, *Repossessed* (makes fun of devil movies), *Spy Hard* (makes fun of spy movies), or any of the *Naked Gun* flicks (makes fun of police shows), it's only a matter of time before Nielsen wanders into the scene— and trips over something. See also MOVIES THAT PARODY OTHER MOVIES.

"NIGHT THE LIGHTS WENT OUT IN GEORGIA, THE" There is no logical explanation for how the least-interesting member of *The Carol Burnett Show's* ensemble cast (Vicki Lawrence, selected primarily for her uncanny resemblance to the show's namesake) topped the 1973 charts with this sordid song. Well, actually, maybe there is. It was, after all, penned by her husband, Bobby Russell. Not that his bedmate was his first choice. He ran it past nearly every female singer on the charts at the time, including Cher, before reaching *deep* down the bench for Lawrence. And so the world was treated to one of earth's most squeaky-clean performers belting out one of the nastiest tales of white trash betrayal ever set to music. In just a couple of verses, we learn how the husband of an adulteress tries to kill one of her lovers, is beaten to the punch by another assailant, but still gets hung for the crime. But that's not all. The tune's narrator, the cuckold's little sister (the plot is more twisted than a John Grisham novel), gets away scot free for killing the cheating couple. At least, we think that's what happened. Perhaps reacting to the surprise success of the song-based 1978 movie *Harper Valley P.T.A.*, "The Night the Lights Went Out in Georgia" in 1981 was turned into a less-successful movie starring B-lister Kristy McNichol, one-hit-series wonder Mark Hamill, and yet-to-be-a-star Dennis Quaid. See also DEATH SONGS and TV MOVIES.

< 191 >

NORRIS, CHUCK After battling with the legendary Bruce Lee in *Fury of the Dragon* (a.k.a. *Return of the Dragon*, *Revenge of the Dragon*, and *Way of the Dragon*), this real-life martial arts instructor—who trained Steve McQueen, Priscilla Presley, and the Osmonds—became a star in his own right in a series of flicks beginning with 1978's *Good Guys Wear Black*, in which he played a sort of low-rent Rambo. His run of hits stretched into the '80s, culminating in the *Missing in Action* trilogy. When his cinematic star faded, Norris wisely, and successfully, leaped to television, kicking ass on *Walker, Texas Ranger* from 1993 to 2001. That's quite an accomplishment for an Oklahoma native with an acting range only slightly broader than one of those boards martial artists are forever chopping in half. See also *BILLY JACK*; KUNG-FU MOVIES; and RAMBO MOVIES.

NOVELIZATIONS With the prose largely serving to fill the space around eight or so pages of photos, novelizations—which take a television show or movie and put it between covers—are a godsend to hack writers . . . and to people for whom two hours of movie time just isn't enough to spend with *Jaws 2* or *Kazaam*. Sometimes the writer adapts an original screenplay, allowing a story to see book form for the first time. Thus we have such literary gems as *3 Ninjas Kick Back*, a novelization by Jordan Horowitz from a screenplay by Mark Saltzman based on a screenplay by Simon Sheen. In other cases, the writer adapts a screenplay that was adapted from another book. Thus, the *Little Women* you find at the paperback exchange may be Louisa May Alcott's—or it may be Laurie Lawlor's. The implication? Somewhere there exists a horror movie buff who enjoyed reading *Mary Shelley's Frankenstein* by Leonore Fleischer.

NUGGETS, CHICKEN Possibly the most insidiously unhealthful food since the hot dog, the nugget is both a fast-food staple and an easy, no-brainer meal for parents. It's appropriate for neither role. Composed in most cases of a ground-up slurry of white and dark meat with an artery-clogging infusion of chopped skin, it's bound together with oils and then encased in batter. To get an idea of what this does to the nuggets' nutritional value, consider that a serving of only five Banquet chicken nuggets packs 270 calories and 17 grams of fat (compared to just 10 grams of fat in a plain McDonald's hamburger). And yet, this convenience food is hugely popular with young children—or rather, with the parents of young children who can't be bothered to read the ingredients of the things they feed their progeny.

< 192 >

NUNS (MEDIA REPRESENTATIONS OF) Sally Field takes to the skies, and we watch for three TV seasons. Julie Andrews baffles her fellow nuns and becomes a cinematic icon. A group of convent-dwelling sisters try to raise money to bury one of their own and the result is a huge theatrical hit that spawned a series of sequels. A nun with a guitar sings "The Lord's Prayer" and the result is perhaps history's unlikeliest pop hit. The list of media-friendly nuns goes on and on (and even includes Sister Maria Innocentia Hummel, creator of the cloying Hummel figurines). What is it about these penguin-like creatures of habit that fascinates us so? Why have actresses as diverse as Audrey Hepburn, Whoopi Goldberg, Mary Tyler Moore, and Eric Idle donned habits on screen? Our guess: Even if we didn't suffer the indignities of an old-fashioned parochial school education, we've heard enough tales of stern sisters and knuckle-cracking rulers so that we feel as if we had. Thus, these flicks—as much as we hate to confess it—serve as a form of therapy. See also HUMMEL FIGURES and *SOUND OF MUSIC, THE*.

NUTTER BUTTER COOKIES If cookies had an all-star team, Nutter Butters would probably make only the second-string lineup. And yet, there are times when the only thing that will satisfy a sweet tooth is one (or, more realistically, 10) of these peanut-shaped Nabisco sandwich cookies. More than 34 million pounds are sold annually, and more than 1 billion are consumed each year. Some are eaten "as is," but millions become ingredients in other dishes—either crushed and incorporated into cakes and ice cream desserts, or used intact as the curvy body or face for everything from reindeer cookies to ghost cookies.

< 193 >

O

OCEAN PACIFIC Founded in 1972 by surfboard maker Jim Jenks, Ocean Pacific has been selling laid-back surfer duds to laid-back surfer dudes for more than three decades. Of course it also caters to a much larger market—posers who consider a "big wave" to be the splash made by the fat guy when he cannonballs into the apartment complex swimming pool. Perhaps that's why OP clothing is available at such well-known surfer hangouts as J. C. Penney.

OFFICER AND A GENTLEMAN, AN See CHICK FLICKS (CINDERELLA FANTASIES).

OLD SPICE COLOGNE A more appropriate name for this long-lived toiletry might be "Old *Man* Cologne." Splash some on, and you risk reminding female friends not of the stud monkey you think you are, but of grandpa's cardigan. And here's an interesting bit of trivia: Remember the Old Spice commercials from the 1970s that featured a sailor walking around in a peacoat, looking for action? The sailor was played by John Bennett Perry, father of Matthew Perry from *Friends*. See also DRUGSTORE PERFUMES.

OLD YELLER See TEARJERKER MOVIES (FOR MEN).

OLIVE GARDEN Offering dishes just slightly more authentic and complex than the contents of a Chef Boyardee can, Olive Garden (which debuted in 1982) was originally conceived as a nonthreatening place for rubes to try Italian (pronounced "eye-talian") food. It possessed a wait staff who, if you asked about the calamari, would first explain what calamari *was* before answering your query. These days the chain claims to operate a "culinary institute" for its cooks in an 11th-century Tuscan village. Whatever. For most diners the entrées are just an excuse to suck up the all-you-can-eat breadsticks. See also CHEF BOYARDEE and RED LOBSTER.

OLSEN TWINS, THE Mary-Kate and Ashley Olsen arrived on the Hollywood scene playing, in turns, Michelle Tanner on *Full House* (1987–1995). Their careers could have gone the way of other wisecracking TV kids such as Tina Yothers, Emmanuel Lewis, and whoever it was who played Chris and Tracy on *The Partridge Family*. Instead, they became a marketing empire through the magic of such made-for-video extravaganzas as *The Adventures of Mary-Kate and Ashley*: *The Case of the Sea World Adventures* (early period), *You're Invited*

< 194 >

to Mary-Kate and Ashley's Mall of America Party (mid-period), and the now-interested-in-boys teen adventure *Passport to Paris* (post-first period). The twins are so popular they've even received a star on the Hollywood Walk of Fame. Women guiltily pretend that these flicks are enjoyable only in an ironic way. Guys hide the fact that they counted down the days to the Olsens' 18th birthday (June 13, 2004). See also HOLLYWOOD WALK OF FAME.

ONE-HIT WONDERS It's easy to be a fan of such long-running hit makers as the Rolling Stones, Stevie Wonder, and Elvis. It's much more difficult, not to mention embarrassing, to be the fan of a one-hit wonder—as pretty much everyone has been at one time or another. Remember the slowly dawning horror when you realized, after weeks of waiting for Frankie Goes to Hollywood's follow-up to its smash hit, "Relax," that there wouldn't *be* a follow-up? If you do, then you share a sad-but-special bond with the frustrated fans of Big Country ("In a Big Country"), the Divinyls ("I Touch Myself"), Tommy Tutone ("867-5309 (Jenny)"), and the Hillside Singers ("I'd Like to Teach the World to Sing (in Perfect Harmony)"). See also DEATH SONGS; "MICKEY"; "ONE NIGHT IN BANGKOK"; "SAFETY DANCE, THE"; and "YOU LIGHT UP MY LIFE."

"ONE NIGHT IN BANGKOK" One of the few hit songs since "Hello Dolly!" to come from a stage musical, this walk on the Thai wild side also holds the distinction of being the only pop song to utilize the words "cloister," "cerebral," and "Somerset Maugham." A disco staple sung to a pulsating beat by Murray Head, "One Night in Bangkok" emerged from the Cold War tuner *Chess*, written by the gentlemen of ABBA. A huge hit in London and a bomb on Broadway, the show told the story of a chess match between an earnest Russian and a petulant American. The catchy song had little to do with the action, but did get the show away from the game for a little while and into the realm of writhing prostitutes. See also ABBA.

ONE-NIGHT STANDS These days they're called hookups, and if you believe such shows as *Friends* and *Sex and the City*, they're as common a form of social interaction as exchanging business cards. So why are people still reticent to discuss them? Perhaps because, while just about everyone has a couple of these on their sexual résumé, making a habit of them can still hurt one's marketability. Setting aside the whole disease thing, people who spend Sunday mornings stumbling around dark bedrooms, looking for their shoes, risk being pegged as either low-order sexual predators or (even worse)

< 195 >

having their names written on bathroom stalls, usually in association with the phrase, "For a good time . . ." See also SEX (IN UNUSUAL AND/OR INAPPROPRIATE PLACES).

ONLINE GAMBLING The average casino gambler, even when going solo, encounters a series of people—doormen, cashiers, fellow big spenders, dealers—on the way to losing his money. Online gamblers dispense with these undesirable interactions and can focus entirely on deciding whether or not to take a blackjack hit. Technically, the games are the same when you play online. But it takes a seriously focused player to avoid thinking about the fact that you're a long way from Monte Carlo. In fact, you're sitting in front of the same computer you've used for online porn and e-mailing your mother. See also ONLINE GAMES.

ONLINE GAMES Maybe we just naturally lose interest in games as we get older. But more likely we give them up because we can't talk our friends into playing anymore. That theory is supported by the thousands of players who can be found at any one time at pogo.com, Yahoo!Games, and many other online sites. Here, there's always someone willing to sit down for a round of backgammon, chess, checkers, or euchre, with ongoing scores and/or the possibility of

cash prizes to keep players playing. This worldwide game room is incredibly convenient, but also dangerous. After all (as more than one deadline-missing cubicle drone has learned), when there's always a game, there's always the temptation to play. See also EUCHRE and ONLINE GAMBLING.

OPRAH If she did nothing else, Oprah Winfrey would rate a spot in this book simply for driving sanctimonious Phil Donahue from the airwaves. She began this great work when her syndicated program debuted in 1986, booting Phil from the No. 1 talk show slot within weeks. Over the years she's flirted  with sleazy, Jerry Springer–like topics; suffered numerous attacks of Shares Too Much Syndrome (offering gory details about everything from her relationship with Stedman to her battles with weight loss/gain/loss/gain); and, most fatefully, unleashed Dr. Phil upon an unsuspecting world. But on balance, hers is an inspiring story of how a woman with nothing followed her dreams and worked hard to build a vast fortune and a media empire. That's something for her fans to consider as they sit on their living room couches in the middle of a workday, watching the

< 196 >

show. See also DIETS, FAD; DR. PHIL; and SPRINGER, JERRY.

ORANGE JULIUS What, exactly, is this foamy, fruity beverage made of? The company itself won't say. All they'll share is that it was first served by California orange juice stand owner Julius Freed in the late 1920s (the name allegedly comes from customers incessantly shouting "Give me an orange, Julius").

Recently the chain started pursuing the burgeoning "fruit smoothies" market. Hit any location and you can get such beverages as Muscle Peach, Blueberrathon, and Strawberried Treasure—along with the good old Orange Julius (which, experts contend, gets its shake-like consistency from nothing more exotic than powdered egg whites).

ORLANDO This central Florida town was just a mosquito-infested dot on the map until the arrival of Walt Disney World in 1971. Now it serves as the front porch for the world's biggest collection of amusement parks, including Universal Studios Florida and SeaWorld. But it's also something else: a Gatlinburg-esque tourist trap that's not nearly as relentlessly G-rated as Disney. For one thing, Orlando seems to have more (and more aggressively promoted) strip clubs than any other city its size. For another,

its environs still offer the kinds of off-kilter "attractions" that characterized Florida in its pre-Disney days. Oddities include Gatorland (an alligator park featuring a politically incorrect gift shop filled with scorpion key chains and stuffed frogs playing saxophones); the palatial Tupperware World Headquarters (yes, there's a museum); and Splendid China (60 famous Chinese landmarks, including a half-mile length of the Great Wall, recreated at scale model size). It's great to know the Magic Kingdom hasn't cornered the market on all things dopey and goofy. See also GATLINBURG; SEA-WORLD; and THEME PARKS (NOT OWNED BY DISNEY).

ORLANDO, TONY (AND DAWN) At first, it was only Dawn. That's because Tony Orlando, the general manager at a music company, didn't want his name attached to a song he secretly sang for a rival studio. That tune turned out to be "Candida," which rose to No. 3 on the pop charts. Bye bye, anonymity. Hello, embarrassingly catchy gimmick songs. With "Tony Orlando and" quickly added to the front, the trio went on to create the through-the-ceiling-love-story "Knock Three Times," the surprise ending-ed "Tie a Yellow Ribbon Round the Ole Oak Tree," the verbosely titled "Say, Has Anybody Seen My Sweet Gypsy Rose," and the grammatically challenged "He Don't

< 197 >

Love You (Like I Love You)." The group took the Sonny & Cher route and tried to turn music stardom into variety show popularity (George Carlin was a regular on the program during its second—and last—season, when it was renamed *The Tony Orlando and Dawn Rainbow Hour*). The inevitable post-cancellation breakup took Orlando and backup singers Telma Hopkins and Joyce Vincent in different directions: He to casino shows, the ladies to, respectively, sitcoms (*Family Matters*) and who the hell knows. See also FAMILY MATTERS; LAS VEGAS; and VARIETY SHOWS.

OSBOURNES, THE The first episode of this MTV reality series pulled in 3.2 million households for its 2002 premiere—not too shabby for a cable network. But why was America so interested in the antics of a former heavy metal god turned doting (and doddering) father? The reason was as obvious as the numerous piles of dog poop on the  Osbourne family's living room floor. Watching them cursing and flailing through what passed for a typical day put our own troubled lives into perspective. We might not be model mates or parents, but compared to the Osbournes

we're f——ing Ward and June Cleaver. See also LEAVE IT TO BEAVER; MTV; and REALITY SHOWS.

OSCAR ACCEPTANCE SPEECHES (EMBARRASSING) Just as a certain sick segment of the stock car community attends races primarily to see wrecks, so a hefty portion of the billion-or-so humans who watch each Oscar broadcast wait breathlessly for someone to deliver a truly humiliating acceptance speech. Seeing a major performer reduced to a blubbering mess is interesting (Sally Field's "You like me, right now, you like me!" comes to mind), as are overlong speeches eventually drowned out by "wrap it up" music from the studio orchestra. (Oscar hint: The more insignificant the category, the longer the speech. So when Best Dubbed Film with Out-of-sync Dialogue is announced, that's a good time to hit the restroom).

Premeditated "political statements" are also good, mean fun. Richard Gere, though only a presenter, stuck his foot in his mouth when he asked viewers to use meditation to help the leadership of China see the error of occupying Tibet. But the award for Best Diatribe undoubtedly goes to documentary maker Michael Moore. His ham-handed rave against George W. Bush during the 2003 broadcast drew boos even from Hollywood

< 198 >

liberals. No doubt about it, a truly muffed speech can be as big an embarrassment as the musical production numbers. See also AWARD SHOWS and GOLDEN GLOBES.

OUTDATED CARNIVAL RIDES They visit a new town each week, transported on flatbed trucks and set up in no time flat in locations ranging from shopping center parking lots to fairground midways. Sure those old, obsolete-looking carnival rides don't hold a candle to exciting, state-of-the-art theme park attractions. However, they do offer thrills that are uniquely their own. Instead of screaming through a half-dozen 5-g barrel rolls, you can wonder if the rust spots you spied as you boarded indicate structural damage; or if the stringy-haired, hung-over carnie who took your ticket is the same guy who put the ride together; or if child welfare would take your kids away if they knew you let them near such a piece of junk. Now *that's* thrilling. See also MIDWAYS and ROLLER COASTERS (ENORMOUS).

OUTLET CENTERS Go to any second-rate tourist trap and you'll find a nearby "outlet mall" allegedly selling discontinued merchandise and factory seconds direct to the consumer at huge discounts. However, the large number of such places (from the Pigeon Forge Outlet Malls in Tennessee to the Shipyard Shops Outlet Center in Wilmington, Delaware) begs a couple of questions. First, how can retail companies such as Van Heusen, Bass Shoe, and Carter's Childrenswear (to name a very few) have enough excess inventory to stock so many locations? Haven't they heard of just-in-time manufacturing? And secondly, how inept must their manufacturing staff be to produce so many seconds? Still, we'll waste a tank of gas driving hours to get there—just to say we saved 20 percent on a pair of slacks. See also WHOLESALE CLUBS.

OUTTAKES See BLOOPERS.

< 199 >

P-Q

PAC-MAN Developed in Japan and originally called Puckman (the name was changed to prevent vandals from substituting an "F" for the "P" on arcade machines), this 1980 game swallowed up oceans of discretionary income, one quarter at a time. Everything from a breakfast cereal to a Saturday-morning cartoon was trotted out to feed our insatiable desire for more information about its minimalist protagonist—a little yellow circle with a wedge chopped out of it. Pac-Man was also the first video game to become popular with women—perhaps because it was pretty much the only one that didn't feature a gun-toting character ejaculating—oops, we mean shooting—at everything in sight. To hammer home this deeply Freudian point, Ms. Pac-Man was offered in 1982. See also DOOM; PONG; and VIDEO GAMES.

PAINT-BY-NUMBERS PAINTINGS Artist and designer Dan Robbins earned the eternal thanks of hobbyists and psych ward inmates everywhere when in 1949 he developed the concept for paint-by-numbers paintings. Figuring that anyone could make a masterpiece if they were provided with an outline of the finished product, a set of paints, and numbers on the template to show where each shade went, he took the concept to his boss at the Palmer Paint Company in Detroit, and in short order the first Craft Master Paint-by-Numbers kits hit the market. Within a year or two they were as big a hit as the Davy Crockett coonskin cap. By the way, if you've hidden yours away somewhere, you might want to fish it out. Finished 1950s paint-by-numbers pieces are becoming hot collectors' items, with some selling for more than $100. But remember that the ones done on canvas are generally worth more than the ones on cardboard. See also PLASTIC MODEL KITS.

PAINTBALL This two-decade-old sport wouldn't exist without one piece of peculiar technology: CO_2-powered pistols that fire plastic balls filled with paint. Originally used by cowboys and foresters to mark cattle for slaughter and trees for cutting, they gained a new function in 1981, when the first recorded paintball match was played in New Hampshire. Basically a version of the kids' game capture the flag (except that participants dress in camouflage and shoot each other with paintballs), it quickly grew into a phenomenon. Paintball parks now operate across the country, celebrities such as Ozzy Osbourne

< 200 >

endorse new gear, and corporations use the game to teach teamwork. There's just one problem. If you're that infatuated with small-unit military tactics, why not join the armed forces? Perhaps because paintballers are about as interested in real feats of arms as are their kissing cousins, the renaissance fair geeks who stage fake sword fights. See also OSBOURNES, THE.

PAJAMA BOTTOMS (WEARING INSTEAD OF PANTS) Worn around the house on a chilly Saturday morning, a comfy pair of flannel jammies is as quaint as a the-touch-the-feel-of-cotton commercial. Wear those same drawstringed britches to a matinee, on the other hand, and you're playing a dangerous game of chicken with the fashion police. Nevertheless, pajamaistas didn't need to read it in the "Tastes and Trends" section of the 2001 *Old Farmer's Almanac* (which predicted both the return of the mustache and a pajama-bottoms-in-public movement) to proclaim, "PJs! They're not just for the Laundromat anymore!" You can roll out of the sheets and go straight to the deli, the post office, even the mall. It's as easy as throwing on a pair of flip-flops.

Comfort accounts for only part of the pajama pants allure. More socially acceptable cozies such as cargo shorts and sweatpants feel just as free-flowing and relaxed, but they lack a certain rebelliousness, a certain *"Yeah, I'm wear-ing my pajamas. You got a problem with that?"* That's why, if you're going to attempt the slothlike look favored by college coeds and the Lost Boys of Never Land, you have to wear it like you mean it. Tie off the waist low and lazy; put a little extra drag in your step; and never, ever second-guess your wardrobe decision. Hey, if it works for Hugh Hefner . . . See also SWEATPANTS.

PARADE Though it bills itself as the most widely read magazine in America (with a circulation of about 37 million, mostly because it's distributed in roughly 350 newspapers nationwide), it's difficult to find people who are bona fide fans. Mostly, *Parade* is the thing you shake out onto the dining room table (along with the color ads) while searching for the sports section. Still, there are some amusing spots. For instance, the cartoons are a nice, straight-out-of-the-'50s diversion, as is the usually celebrity-intensive cover story, complete with questions as incisive and probing as the ones offered by softball champ Larry King. It's perfect for people who want their celebrities treated like fresh peaches: carefully packaged and never bruised or manhandled. See also KING, LARRY.

PARTON, DOLLY From the time she partnered on television with country legend Porter Wagoner in the late '60s,

< 201 >

this big-hearted blonde has been in the public eye. After storming the hats-and-boots circuit, she crossed over into mainstream pop success in the mid-'70s with a string of hits including "I Will Always Love You" and "Here You Come Again." She hit it big at the movies with *9 to 5* and *Steel Magnolias*, while somehow managing to emerge unscathed from such atrocities as *Rhinestone* (for those who never miss a Sylvester Stallone musical) and *The Best Little Whorehouse in Texas* (ditto Burt Reynolds). Through it all, she's recorded an impressive array of albums, including acclaimed collaborations with Emmylou Harris, Linda Ronstadt, Loretta Lynn, and Tammy Wynette. She also founded an amusement park, Dollywood, and put Pigeon Forge, Tennessee, on the map. She even inspired a "tribute" album with contributions from Melissa Etheridge, Norah Jones, Joan Osborne, and Sinéad O'Connor.

Did we miss anything? Oh, yes, there's the reason why she gets an entry here: She's got big, big breasts. We're talking "Oh, the humanity" zeppelins fairly bursting from her inevitably tight top. We're talking getting-stopped-at-customs-because-it-looks-like-she's-smuggling-two-bald-guys-across-the-border bazooms. So overwhelming are her endowments that Jay Leno, in explaining his TV hosting style to a reporter, said, "I don't do wife jokes and I don't do Dolly Parton jokes," a statement that clearly shows the hold these twin peaks have on the national consciousness. See also CHICK FLICKS (FEMALE BONDING); CHICK FLICKS (IN WHICH SOMEONE DIES); GATLINBURG; REYNOLDS, BURT; STALLONE, SYLVESTER; and THEME PARKS (NOT OWNED BY DISNEY).

PARTRIDGE FAMILY, THE The premise of this unlikely sitcom smash—a mom, played by Shirley Jones, forms a rock band with her five kids—was in its own way just as harebrained as those of *Gilligan's Island* or *The Beverly Hillbillies*. But the plot was only the start of the weirdness. After the show debuted in 1970, Partridge Family songs started topping the charts in the real world. Of course it wasn't the actual TV family belting out such massive hits as "I Think I Love You," and "I Woke Up in Love This Morning." David Cassidy (who played No. 1 son Keith Partridge) indeed sang lead while his TV mom (and real-life stepmom), Shirley Jones, handled backup vocals, but the rest of the show's keyboard fingering, tambourine-shaking, lead guitar–holding clan was jettisoned in favor of session players. The Family pranced around in their frilly shirts and velvet jumpsuits until the show was canceled in 1974, leaving its devotees feel-

< 202 >

ing like they would after a passionate one-night stand: tired and just a little creeped out. Especially the 12-year-old boys who wondered if they might be perverts for lusting not for Cassidy's TV sister, Susan Dey, but for Shirley Jones. See also *BEVERLY HILLBILLIES, THE*; CASSIDY, DAVID; CASSIDY, SHAUN; *GILLIGAN'S ISLAND*; ONE-NIGHT STANDS; and TV MOMS (LUSTING AFTER).

PARTY OF FIVE A mother and father die in a car crash and their five children must fend for themselves. Let's party! For six seasons, we watched this Fox network soap, a sort-of *Boxcar Children* update in which the whining Salinger clan had to prove that love would keep them together week after week after week. Why was it so addictive? Perhaps we all were once angst-ridden teens who secretly wondered what life would be like without Mom or Dad. Or maybe it was just that we lusted after Jennifer Love Hewitt and Neve Campbell, or Scott Wolf and Matthew Fox. See also SOAP OPERAS, NIGHTTIME.

PEANUT BUTTER AND JELLY SANDWICHES Here's what food historians figure happened: American soldiers shipped overseas during World War II found peanut butter in their ration kits. They also found jelly. And bread. One day (doubtless with *Also Sprach Zarathustra* playing in his head) some unknown culinary genius put all three together. This would explain why even though there's no record of the PB&J before the 1940s, sales of both PB and J skyrocketed after our boys came home. Today, even though the pictures on the lunch boxes have changed, the sandwich remains a staple in school meals. And if you're too lazy to prepare these easy-to-make sandwiches, you can now buy them ready-made. See also JUICE BOXES; LUNCH BOXES; and MARSHMALLOW FLUFF.

PECAN LOGS Next to a triple latte, nothing provides an illicit energy boost faster than one of these nut-covered calorie bombs. A Southern staple for more than a century, they were popularized (and nationalized) by the Stuckey's convenience store chain. For decades the company's rolls were manufactured in Eastman, Georgia, home of the very first Stuckey's. They're still available at that chain's locations, plus by mail order from numerous other candy stores. You can even, without too much trouble, locate recipes for them on the Internet. Be warned: You'll need lots of corn syrup. See also STUCKEY'S.

PEEL-OFF MASKS Long before SPF, UVA, and UVB were part of the vernacular, we had sunburns—blistering, skin-singeing sunburns. But as consola-

< 203 >

tion for all that pain and itching, we enjoyed the sick pleasure of peeling dead skin off our faces. Don't pretend you didn't do it. Who can forget the twisted fascination of carefully picking off onion-skin-thin sheets of, well . . . skin? The trick was to see just how big a piece you could shuck without tearing into live tissue. For adults who are smart enough to come in out of the sun, peel-off masks provide that same molting merriment, without the threat of skin cancer.

For millennia, women have glopped mud on their faces to remove dirt and debris from their pores. Today's mud packs are made from purified earth and clay, go on wet, and harden as they dry. In theory, when they're rinsed and wiped away, these facials take excess dirt, dead skin cells, and oil with them. (Though some experts believe they do little more than provide psychological benefits, making the face *feel* tighter.) Peel-off masks, composed of such not-so-down-to-earth ingredients as polyvinyl alcohol, latex, and vinyl acetate, are used in the same manner as mud preparations — but they're a whole lot more fun. First, slather your mug with gelatinous goo. Then wait 10 minutes or until the goo dries into a clear, shiny mask. Then peel off the Saran Wrap-like covering as if it were the worst sunburn you've ever had. And if your face feels all tingly afterward, well, consider it a bonus.

PEEPS Even though these chick-shaped marshmallow treats are possibly the most inconsequential thing one could receive in an Easter basket, they've been a holiday staple since their invention in 1953. These days their maker, Just Born, Inc., turns them out year round in a variety  of shapes, including bats for Halloween and hearts for Valentine's Day. The company's Bethlehem, Pennsylvania, plant produces Peeps at the rate of 3,800 per minute, or 1 billion each year. Which means there must be a huge demand for a confection that tastes like a sugar-coated packing peanut. True connoisseurs freeze them before eating. See also MARSHMALLOW FLUFF.

***PENTHOUSE* FORUM** *Penthouse*, which debuted in America in 1969, positioned itself as a blue-collar porno glossy. Whereas *Playboy* touted its high-class articles, lifestyle advice, and, oh yeah, pictures of naked women, *Penthouse* did away with the preaching and offered a double serving of boobies. One of its most interesting non-pictorial staples is the "Forum" section, in which readers describe their own sexual experiences. And what sexual experiences they are. Some sound so much like porno movie

< 204 >

set pieces (three-ways in college dorms; getting it on with limo drivers; sex in public places) that it's tempting to believe they contain about as much truth as the typical *Weekly World News* cover story. And yet, decade in and decade out, the *Penthouse* editors swear these missives are legit. What does that mean to the average reader? Only that there are lots of people out there having more sex, and in more interesting scenarios, than they are. See also ONE-NIGHT STANDS; *PLAYBOY*; and *WEEKLY WORLD NEWS*.

PEOPLE Though it's not as cloying as *Us Weekly* and certainly not as goofy as the *National Enquirer*, *People* still isn't the sort of publication one fans on the living room coffee table. Nevertheless, lots of people read it—more each week, the magazine asserts, than watch even the most highly rated TV shows. *People* draws such crowds by giving readers exactly what they want, even if they can't bring themselves to admit they want it: celebrity fashions, celebrity marriages, celebrity divorces, celebrity kids, sick celebrities, celebrities in rehab . . . on and on and on. Since the first issue debuted on March 4, 1974 (Mia Farrow was the cover girl), the magazine has printed some 40 billion copies—enough to circle the earth about 30 times. Over the decades some topics have always been big sellers (the "Most

Intriguing People" issue, which debuted in 1974, and the "Sexiest Man Alive" report, which kicked off in 1985 with cover guy Mel Gibson), but none has matched the star power of Diana, Princess of Wales. The special commemorative issue after her death sold some 5 million copies—pretty good, even for *People*. See also DIANAMANIA; *NATIONAL ENQUIRER, THE*; and *US WEEKLY*.

PEOPLE'S CHOICE AWARDS, THE First aired in March 1975, the People's Choice Awards was conceived as a populist answer to the Oscars and the Grammy Awards. Since then it's devolved into an opportunity to marvel at how the public taste (as polled by Gallup) is both numbingly predictable and startlingly perverse. Consider that Burt Reynolds has won more than Robert De Niro. And that while *Will & Grace* won for Best New Comedy Series of 1998, it tied with *Jesse* (with *Jesse's* Christina Applegate taking Best Female Performer in a New Television Series). Want more eyebrow-raisers? Kirstie Alley won one for *Veronica's Closet* and Tony Danza scored for *The Tony Danza Show* (Does anyone even remember *The Tony Danza Show*?). And to hell with categories like Best Director, let alone writers, designers, or sound effects engineers. The People want to see stars and nothing but. And the winners usually

< 205 >

show up to accept—mainly because they're told beforehand that they've got it locked.

PEOPLE'S COURT, THE Presided over by tough-but-fair retired judge Joseph A. Wapner (with the able assistance of Bailiff Rusty Burrell), *The People's Court* offered small-claimers the chance to have their disputes mediated on television. Viewers—many of whom would have done anything to avoid real jury duty—fell hard for this courtroom drama. The original show ran from 1981 to 1993, spawning not only a host of copycats (*Judge Judy*, *Judge Mills Lane*, *Animal Court*, etc.), but also returning just a few years later with former New York City mayor Ed Koch on the bench. He was followed by Jerry Sheindlin (husband of Judge Judy) and then Miami judge Marilyn Milian. Applying the same format to bigger trials might help alleviate our clogged court system. *Supreme People's Court* anyone? See also COURT TV.

PETER, PAUL & MARY Bob Dylan sang "Blowin' in the Wind" and moved on to other things. Peter, Paul & Mary sang "Blowin' in the Wind" over and over again—for decades. That and other hootenanny favorites such as "If I Had a Hammer," "Lemon Tree," and "Puff (the Magic Dragon)" throughout their more than 40 years together. You can admire them for being dedicated to their ideals or criticize them for being stuck in a '60s time warp. But whatever the case, Peter, Paul & Mary (these days you could call them Two Bald Guys and a Big Mama) still get audiences to sing along. Once the house lights are turned up, though, embarrassment sets in. You are more likely to find your boss doing macramé than you are to find anyone you know donning PP&M tour shirts or listening to the trio's "I Dig Rock and Roll Music" or their cover of "This Land Is Your Land."

PEYTON PLACE Published in 1956, Grace Metalious's steamy novel about the bedroom-hopping residents of a fictitious New England town exposed the dark side of American family values. Populated by characters driven by a grab bag of unseemly motivations (mainly lust), *Peyton Place* brimmed with the kind of trashy content that a school librarian might pronounce unsuitable reading material—after devouring every last word while hiding behind the card catalog. "If I'm a lousy writer, then an awful lot of people have lousy taste," the outspoken author once said of her blockbuster tome, which quickly surpassed *Gone With the Wind* as the top-selling novel of all time (it was later surpassed by another trashfest, *Valley of the Dolls*).

< 206 >

The *Peyton Place* phenomenon continued for decades in various formats: two cinematic films, a couple of TV series, and a handful of made-for-TV movies. Most importantly, a legion of "town with a secret" shows, from *Twin Peaks* to *Dawson's Creek*, owe the novel a huge debt. Those guys wouldn't have known the first thing about dragging skeletons out of closets if Grace Metalious hadn't shown them how. See also *DALLAS*; *DYNASTY*; SOAP OPERAS, NIGHTTIME; SUSANN, JACQUELINE; and TV MOVIES.

PEZ   Developed in the 1920s by an Austrian candy maker (and named Pez because it was short for Pfefferminz, the German word for peppermint), this rather infantile candy was originally marketed as a sophisticated adult breath mint. The

first Pez dispenser was a sleek-looking contraption (without a novelty head) that was unveiled in Europe in 1948. But when the candy came to America in 1952 (today it is manufactured in Connecticut), it did so in fruit flavors and with colorful Pez dispensers originally topped with cartoon characters such as Popeye and Mickey Mouse. Of course the lineup has since expanded to include well over 1,000 characters.

Inevitably, collectors have created a robust secondary market for old dispensers. If you'd like to see some of the rarest, you can visit the Burlingame Museum of Pez Memorabilia in the San Francisco Bay Area. Yes, you can buy Pez in the gift shop.

PHONE SEX   The unknown person who invented this "service" is a genius for getting men to pay to masturbate. As for all you guys who shell out $2.95 a minute for the privilege of flogging your fun puppet while balancing a phone on your shoulder—you're paying to masturbate! And that woman on the other end of the line who sounds like Anna Kournikova could just as easily look like *Sanford and Son*'s Aunt Esther. Surely there are less costly ways to let your fingers do the walking. See also KOURNIKOVA, ANNA; MASTURBATION; and *SANFORD & SON*.

PICKUP TRUCKS   These utilitarian vehicles have been around almost as long as the internal combustion engine. Henry Ford pioneered the concept when he removed the back half of his famed Model T and replaced it with a cargo bed. For most of its lifetime, the pickup truck was a rugged, no-frills wagon used primarily for farm work, construction, and little else. That is, until the 1980s, when city folk decided *they* needed a

< 207 >

rugged, no-frills vehicle—even if all they wanted to haul was a load of garden mulch. Which brings us to today's pickups, which are available with the very frilliest of frills, including elaborate sound systems, leather interiors, multiple cup holders, and chrome, chrome, chrome. Even Cadillac makes one. Of course you wouldn't want to take them anywhere *near* a farm or construction site, but the odds of that happening are pretty slim. These urban cowboys are all about looking good, not working hard. See also SUVs and *URBAN COWBOY*.

PICTIONARY Created by a 24-year-old Seattle waiter named Rob Angel and first marketed in 1986, this game (an iteration of charades in which participants try to guess a word or phrase based on pictures their partners draw) became a brief phenomenon—as well as the cop-out entertainment of choice for parties that are going stale. The game even made it into the 1989 comedy W*hen Harry Met Sally . . .* , which gave us the immortal phrase, "Baby fish mouth! Baby fish mouth!" See also *WHEN HARRY MET SALLY . . .*

PINBALL Pinball has been around since 1931, but in its original incarnation it was about as exciting as, well, being around in 1931. Early versions lacked tilt control, and flippers didn't arrive until 1947. Yet prior to the creation of mass market video games in the early '80s, it dominated arcades. Tommy wannabes played not to win prizes, but merely for a free game—and, perhaps, to ogle the artwork on the housing. Those cleavage-intensive salutes to male yearning were as garish as the posters for British vampire flicks or Russ Meyer movies. Did we mention that teenage boys were the games' prime audience? See also MIDWAYS and VIDEO GAMES.

PINK FLAMINGOS See WATERS, JOHN.

PIPES Not too long after Sir Ralph Lane brought clay tobacco pipes back to England from the New World, Queen Elizabeth impressed her court by blowing smoke rings. Such was the addictive appeal of this in-your-face nicotine delivery system. Significantly less popular now than just a few generations ago (during WWI, the U.S. Army sent corncob versions to the troops), pipes demand time and patience from the smoker. And unlike the disposable vice of cigarettes, they encourage participation. Half the pleasure comes from searching for the perfect tobacco blend or just the right bit (that's the mouthpiece). But despite its rich history, pipe smoking is now an affectation best savored privately, where your friends won't notice that you look like a parody

< 208 >

of a Norman Rockwell painting—or that your favorite "blend" smells like a fire at a Log Cabin Syrup plant. See also CIGARETTES and ROCKWELL, NORMAN.

PISTACHIOS (RED) Even though they stain your fingers and even though you now know that they're dyed red not for taste but to mask imperfections and to draw more attention on shelves and in vending machines, you still like them. Think of them as the savory yin to the maraschino cherry's cloyingly sweet yang. See also MARASCHINO CHERRIES and STRIP CLUBS.

PIT BULLS Why are these vicious dogs so popular? Blame a foible of male character. Many men think they can absorb the traits of objects simply by possessing them. For instance, a cool car will make *me* cool. A sophisticated cell phone will make *me* sophisticated. Likewise, a tough, intimidating dog will make *me* tough and intimidating.

Sadly, nothing could be further from the truth. Pit bulls (a mongrelized offshoot of a well-known breed called the American Staffordshire terrier) may add to your street cred if you're, say, a soldier for the Crips. But if you're a 19-year-old high school dropout living with your parents, getting a big, strong, well-nigh uncontrollable fighting dog simply confirms your status as someone with

very poor judgment. It's the pet equivalent of walking around with a pistol in your belt with the safety off. Plus, owning one *won't make your penis one bit bigger.* See also MORONS (ENTERTAINING, UNTIMELY DEATHS OF) and RAMPAGING ANIMALS (TV SPECIALS ABOUT).

PIXY STIX As bubble gum cigarettes were the child's version of tobacco products, so Pixy Stix are the kiddie version of crack. These paper tubes filled with tart, fruit-flavored sugar are eaten by biting off one end of the container and draining the contents into your mouth. For a truly shameful indulgence (not to mention a truly righteous sugar buzz) try the 21-inch Giant Pixy Stix, containing enough sugar to send an entire elementary school into diabetic shock.

PIZZA, FROZEN Where did all those pepperoni-decked, cheese-encased slabs of frozen dough come from? The perhaps-apocryphal origin story goes like this: During World War II, an Italian-American marine on Iwo Jima wrote his stateside brother saying how much he'd love to have a pizza like mama made. So his Newark, New Jersey–based bro set to work creating the first frozen (and, thus, shippable) pizza. When the happy and well-fed marine returned home, he and his family started the frozen food company Nino Foods. But regardless of

< 209 >

whether the brothers actually froze the very *first* pizza, one fact remains: Since the 1940s, marketers have tried their damnedest to convince the public that the stuff you get in a box from your grocer's freezer is just as tasty as the stuff delivered from your local pizzeria. Someone must believe it, because the American Frozen Food Institute says annual sales of the frozen discs total approximately $2.5 billion. See also TV DINNERS.

PLACEMATS, EDUCATIONAL Whether featuring the signs of the Chinese zodiac, a map of Italy, the natural wonders of the U.S., or an illustrated history of schooners, the restaurant placemat is an underrated medium for communication. Sure, the space is limited, but who can resist the novel idea of soaking in a little information from an object designed to soak up excess pancake syrup? See also PLACEMATS, INTERACTIVE.

PLACEMATS, INTERACTIVE Grab a pen, it's puzzle time—at least, until the waitress shows up. Used by restaurateurs to help keep hyperactive kids from building sugar packet houses and hanging spoons from their noses, preprinted interactive placemats, filled with not-too-hard crossword puzzles, fairly simple mazes, and absurdly easy word search puzzles, are also a favorite of

bored solo diners, drunks, and couples with nothing to say to each other. See also PLACEMATS, EDUCATIONAL.

PLANET HOLLYWOOD See THEME RESTAURANTS.

***PLANET OF THE APES* MOVIES** Sure, you can make a case that it's sharp social satire. Or you could argue that it's one of the headier pieces of screen science fiction. But in your heart of hearts you know that there's perverse pleasure in seeing Charlton Heston go  bare assed and monkeys ride horses in the same flick. See also HESTON, CHARLTON and MONKEYS (MOVIES FEATURING).

PLASTIC MODEL KITS There was a time when model airplane kits were excruciatingly complicated affairs made of balsa wood. To build one, you had to cut out dozens of individual wing struts and fuselage supports, glue everything together, then coat it all with a paper skin held in place by a foul-smelling shellac called dope. Of course, these models were popular in the years before TV. These days kids (or, more likely, middle-aged men with time on their hands) use less messy, less complex plastic models made by such companies as Revell-

< 210 >

Monogram and including everything from 1957 Chevrolets to the aircraft carrier USS *Kitty Hawk* to the B-2 Stealth Bomber. The models are still tough enough to give one a sense of accomplishment, but nowhere near as demanding as the old balsa wood nightmares. And for today's even more effort-averse kids, there are snap-together models that don't require the sticky, finger-coating glue. None of which answers the age-old question of what to do with the model once you finish it.

PLATES, COLLECTIBLE See FRANKLIN MINT, THE.

PLAYBOY Sure, it contains lots of high-falutin articles and information on the latest in consumer electronics, but most Americans never bought into Hugh Hefner's assertion that *Playboy* is a lifestyle publication rather than a nudie book. Since its inception in 1953 (centerfold No. 1: Marilyn Monroe), Hef has pitched the idea (extremely novel in the '50s, but passé today) that sex is fun and healthy and part of the everyday man's swinging, sophisticated lifestyle (like the bowl of Count Chocula that's "part of a complete breakfast"). But as the years passed, his competitors (chief among them, *Penthouse*) beat him at his own game by offering raunchier pictures and a "streamlined" philosophy that

could be summed up as "Me like sex." These days *Playboy* is getting its clock cleaned by sophomoric titles such as *Maxim* that offer nearly naked celebrity tail.

So who buys *Playboy* now? Doubtless there are actually people who read the articles. But perhaps, just perhaps, most of its base is composed of men who still feel the need to hide their love of naked ladies behind a fig leaf of intellectualism. See also *MAXIM* and *PENTHOUSE* FORUM.

PLAYBOY ADVISOR, THE See ADVICE COLUMNISTS AND *PLAYBOY*.

PLAYGIRL A funny thing about naked men: The harder they try to look sexy, with their clean-shaven pecs and intense come-hither stares, the harder women giggle when they see pictures of them. This doesn't seem to inhibit the seductive efforts of *Playgirl*, the New York–based magazine that has featured a new batch of steamy nude models every month since its 1973 debut, 20 years after Hugh Hefner published *Playboy*'s first issue. *Playgirl*'s inaugural centerfold, Lyle Waggoner of *The Carol Burnett Show*, stopped just short of full frontal nudity. Readers complained. So the featured model in issue No. 2, George Maharis of *Route 66* fame, left nothing to the imagination. When Burt Reynolds

< 211 >

appeared as a centerfold in the '70s, the hirsute actor concealed his private parts with a strategically placed hand (or "Arm!" as he contended on *The Tonight Show* shortly after publication). But these days, the magazine gets more press when someone *doesn't* want the fawning attention of *Playgirl's* sexually aggressive female (and gay male) readership. Leonardo DiCaprio, Brad Pitt, and Antonio Banderas have all sued the monthly over unauthorized photos. See also *PLAYBOY* and REYNOLDS, BURT.

POLICE ACADEMY MOVIES Suffice it to say that enough people saw *Police Academy 5: Assignment: Miami Beach* (one of the few films in movie history whose title included two colons) to justify the making not only of *Police Academy 6: City Under Siege*, but also *Police Academy 7: Mission to Moscow*. In fact, a new entry in the series appeared every year from 1984 to 1989—with another added in 1994 and two TV series (one animated, one live action) in 1988 and 1997. Starring Steve Guttenberg for the first four flicks and football great Bubba Smith for the first six, the series about wacky police recruits also featured visits from *Sex and the City's* Kim Cattrall in the original and Sharon Stone in the fourth.

PONG Released in 1972, Pong was the world's first commercially successful video game. It was popular for a couple of reasons, neither of which reflected well on the people who played it. First, it was simple enough even for half-drunk bar patrons to quickly grasp; second (and perhaps most important), it was the first and only video game that the average schmuck could not only get good at, but *master*. That's right, youngsters. This simple game, based on ping-pong (its maker, Atari, couldn't call it that because the word was copyrighted), didn't churn out ever-more-complicated challenges until players screamed for mercy. At a certain point its tiny CPU simply gave up the ghost, and *you won*. That's why veteran gamers occasionally miss its lame graphics and glacial pace, in the same way retired playground bullies sometimes miss the fat kid with glasses. See also DOOM; PAC-MAN; and VIDEO GAMES.

POPCORN SHRIMP Like potato chips and cocktail weenies, popcorn shrimp is one of those dishes that diners simply can't stop eating. Diets and cholesterol counts be damned—when these tiny, batter-fried, comma-shaped treats hit the table, the feeding frenzy won't end until there's nothing left on the plate but a lemon wedge and a paper cup half-filled with cocktail sauce. Introduced to America by Red Lobster in 1974 (and now as ubiquitous at chain eateries as

< 212 >

the omnipresent chicken nugget), it features tiny, battered, deep-fried shrimp with their tail shells removed—the better for quick consumption, usually three or four at a time. See also LONG JOHN SILVER'S; NUGGETS, CHICKEN; and RED LOBSTER.

POP-TARTS Designed to expand the range of items that could be cooked in a toaster, Kellogg's Pop-Tarts debuted in 1964 with a name inspired by the pop-art movement. The treat, shilled by an animated mascot named Milton the Toaster, was a rectangular pastry with filling and (later) an optional sweet exterior coating on one side. The flavor lineup, which originally consisted of strawberry, blueberry, brown sugar cinnamon, and apple currant, has been augmented in recent years by Frosted S'Mores, Frosted Wild Magicburst, and other iterations. Hardcore fans can expand their Pop horizons with recipes from the Kellogg's Web site, which includes such "delicacies" as Easy Pop-Tarts Crumble, Pop-Tarts Trifle, and Pop-Tarts Parfaits. Today they continue as a kids-are-late-for-school lunch box staple, even though in the mid-'90s experimenters discovered that the strawberry variety caught on fire if left in the toaster too long. (Humorist Dave Barry later corroborated—and popularized—these tests, which are said to have generated flames up to 18 inches in height.) Linguistic note: Pop-Tarts, like overalls and eyeglasses, are always plural.

PORK RINDS These crispy bits of fried pigskin are the most politically incorrect thing you can put in your body, short of having sex with Bill O'Reilly. And yet, sales have risen strongly since the mid-'90s. Maybe it's because the low-carb, high-protein Atkins Diet favors them as a snack. Rudolph Foods, the world's largest pork rind manufacturer, turns out around 100 million pounds annually. But if pig parts are diet food, how come we don't ever see skinny people pounding them down? Perhaps because what pork rinds lack in carbs they more than make up for in fat (five grams in each half-ounce serving). Even if you're not a fan, it's worth visiting the Rudolph Foods Web site just to see the company's mascot—a pink hog wearing a bow tie, chef's hat, and Snidely Whiplash mustache. See also BAC~OS; DIETS, FAD; and SPAM.

PORKY'S See GUYS LOSING THEIR VIRGINITY (MOVIES ABOUT).

POTATO CHIPS (BARBECUE) What's more addictive than deep-fried potato slices? How about deep-fried potato slices coated in tomato powder, paprika, dehydrated onions and garlic, MSG, and

< 213 >

other fun stuff? Sure, the concept of barbecued potatoes makes absolutely no sense, but is it any less goofy (or delicious) than corn chips covered with essence of ranch dressing?

PRACTICAL JOKES Though no one particularly enjoys being the butt of a practical joke, almost everyone loves pulling them. That's why stores such as Spencer Gifts make a killing keeping the world knee-deep in Billy Bob Teeth and fake vomit. Lately, however, spoofing people has become an industry of sorts, with a new crop of *Candid Camera*–like shows (only more mean-spirited) taking to the airwaves. These days, with programs like MTV's *Punk'd* seeking to turn celebrity's lives upside down; *The Jamie Kennedy Experiment* flummoxing civilians by attacking them with men in giant rat costumes; and the Sci Fi Channel's *Scare Tactics* staging fake alien abductions, landing in the crosshairs of Allen Funt is the least of your worries. See also SPENCER GIFTS; VOMIT (FAKE); and WHOOPEE CUSHIONS.

PRECIOUS MOMENTS A little girl pulls a cart full of puppies. A little boy in fishing garb holds up his catch of the day. A pair of itty-bitty two-steppers "Praise the Lord and do-si-do." In the porcelain bisque world created by Christian artist Samuel Butcher (no relation to *The Brady Bunch*'s Sam the Butcher), there's a sweet, teardrop-eyed child to correspond with every one of life's moments, precious or otherwise. The Precious Moments figurine empire dates back to 1978, when the president of collectibles manufacturer Enesco Corporation spotted Butcher's illustrations on a small line of greeting cards. He took the artwork to a master sculptor in Japan, had it translated into clay models, and created the vanguard for the pastel army of darlings lining the shelves of Hallmark stores everywhere.

How many ways are there for cherubim to look adorable? At least 1,500 and counting. That's how many statuette models are on the market. Collectors not only collect, they also join clubs and make pilgrimages to Carthage, Missouri's Precious Moments Inspiration Park (complete with a music revue, a Fountain of Angels, and a Precious Moments Chapel). And they buy them as gifts. After all, what better way to tell someone "I wuv you" than by sending a tiny statuette of a child clutching a bouquet of tulips? See also *BRADY BUNCH, THE;* FRANKLIN MINT, THE; and HUMMEL FIGURES.

PRESLEY, ELVIS During his 42 years of life, the King of Rock and Roll was both the coolest and un-coolest person on Earth. At the start of his career, his rock-

< 214 >

abilly attitude, rockin' tunes, and swinging hips challenged mainstream America and made him a hero to kids. Trouble was, he didn't age gracefully. By the 1960s Elvis was squandering his street cred by making terrible movies, playing Vegas, dressing in ever-more-outlandish stage costumes, and changing his physical appearance almost beyond recognition not through plastic surgery, but through overeating. Which means that if you blast "Hound Dog" out of your sound system, you better be ready to explain that you're a fan of Elvis's hardcore period—not of his bloated, jumpsuit-wearing, "American Trilogy"–singing twilight years. See also ELVIS IMPERSONATORS and PRISON MOVIES FEATURING MEN.

PRE–*STAR WARS* '70S SCI-FI FILMS The release of 1977's *Star Wars*, with its state-of-the-art special effects, made it easy for the masses to like science fiction. But it also made it difficult for diehard fans to admit they enjoyed the cinematic offerings of the pre-*Wars* '70s. This was an era of dark, special effects–starved apocalyptic and post-apocalyptic visions such as *Soylent Green*, *A Boy and His Dog*, *Death Race 2000*, *Westworld*, *The Omega Man*, and *Logan's Run*. True, the production values could be spotty and the effects awful, but these films often had something many a

CGI-laden 21st-century space opera lacks—a serviceable script. That's something to mention the next time someone disses your *Beneath the Planet of the Apes* DVD. See also *DEATH RACE 2000*; HESTON, CHARLTON; *PLANET OF THE APES* MOVIES; and *STAR WARS*.

PRETTY WOMAN See CHICK FLICKS (CINDERELLA FANTASIES).

PRICE IS RIGHT, THE If you know the rules to Plinko, can name two of Barker's Beauties, and had your pet spayed or neutered simply because Bob Barker said it was the right thing to do, you must be one of the millions addicted to *The Price Is Right*. Not only is it the longest running game show in the history of the medium, its host is also the proud owner of more Emmy Awards (15) than any other television performer. That's a lot of recognition just for prodding an endless herd of middle Americans into guessing the prices of various consumer items. And it's not as if the show ever made anyone (besides Barker and its producers) a millionaire. Although more than $200 million has been given away during its decades-spanning history, the biggest single *Price* winner was a Pepperdine student who cleared a mere $88,865 (most of which, we assume, was in the form of Lovely Dinette Sets and Broyhill

< 215 >

Furniture). Patriotic trivia note: *The Price Is Right* only gives away American-made cars. See also GAME SHOWS.

PRINCE (GIRLFRIENDS OF) Say what you will about the music and fashion sense of His Purpleness. What cannot be debated is his fabulous taste in sidekicks. Starting in the early '80s, a seemingly never-ending series of women glommed onto his coattails (and, perhaps, other parts of his anatomy). The only requirements to be a Prince protége (besides a hot body) seemed to be big hair, the fashion sense of a streetwalker, and, of course, a goofy name. The all-time favorites include lingerie-wearing Vanity (now an evangelist, of all things), Apollonia (Prince's love interest in the movie *Purple Rain*), and Sheila E. (who managed to make pounding away on a drum kit look sexy). What were all these women being groomed for? Who knows. All we can say is that whatever they were getting ready for, they sure looked good doing it. See also PRINCE (MOVIES OF).

PRINCE (MOVIES OF) Of these there are three: 1984's *Purple Rain* (which ruled, in a dance-intensive, big-haired, 1984 sort of way), followed by 1986's *Under the Cherry Moon* (which sucked wind), and 1990's *Graffiti Bridge* (a sequel to *Purple Rain*, but without hit songs, production values, or a believable plot). All

three are guilty pleasures, though for different reasons. *Purple Rain* because it's a delicious slice of '80s nostalgia that is absolutely indecipherable to  anyone who wasn't actually there. For fun, try making your kids watch it with you. As for *Moon* and *Bridge* (both of which were directed by Prince, which explains a lot), there's the sheer, cruel joy of watching an egotistical celebrity wander, Nero-like, through monstrous, flaming disasters of his own making. See also PRINCE (GIRLFRIENDS OF).

PRISON MOVIES FEATURING MEN As with gladiator movies, films about men in prison offer an undeniably dramatic situation (surviving in a tough environment filled with caged desperados) fraught with homoerotic overtones. But while prison movies featuring women usually go out of their way to exploit those overtones, flicks about men's prison for the most part ignore the gay subtext in favor of chaste camaraderie—along with plenty of danger and violence. The limited choice of locales (the exercise yard, the chain gang, the laundry, the cell block, the warden's office, and, of course, The Hole) helps create taut storytelling. That might explain why

< 216 >

this relatively small subgenre has produced a relatively large number of very good films, including *Cool Hand Luke*, *The Shawshank Redemption*, *The Birdman of Alcatraz*, *Papillon*, *Midnight Express*, and *Kiss of the Spider Woman*. There are even prison comedies (*Ernest Goes to Jail*, *Stir Crazy*) and a prison musical, *Jailhouse Rock*. However, should you ever find yourself in a real prison, we recommend you refrain from dancing around like Elvis. See also GLADIATORS (MOVIES FEATURING); PRESLEY, ELVIS; PRISON MOVIES FEATURING WOMEN; and VARNEY, JIM.

PRISON MOVIES FEATURING WOMEN We're sure someone, somewhere, has made a movie that examines the lives of incarcerated women in a realistic manner. Good luck finding it. Ask at your local video store for flicks on the subject and you'll likely be steered to *Caged Heat*, *Chained Heat*, *Girls in Chains*, *Naked Cage*, *Women Unchained*, or any number of other R-rated films, almost all of which include the words *Caged*, *Chained*, *Naked* and/or *Heat* in their titles. Most dispense with realism in favor of a more idealized (if you're a porn fan) view of women's prison: one in which the inmates wear skimpy outfits, are all 18 to 25, take frequent group showers, and live in fear of a dominatrix-like warden. If you rent one (and we're certainly not implying that you ever would), be sure to check the cast for B-list, D-cup celebrities. For instance, Linda Blair in *Chained Heat*, and Brigitte Nielsen in *Chained Heat 2*. See also BLAIR, LINDA; LESBIANS (MOVIE SCENES FEATURING); MASTURBATION; and PRISON MOVIES FEATURING MEN.

PRIVATE LESSONS See EMMANUELLE (MOVIES FEATURING THE CHARACTER OF) and GUYS LOSING THEIR VIRGINITY (MOVIES ABOUT).

PRIZES (CEREAL BOX) Though it shames us to think about it now, few among us haven't rushed home with a box of cereal, ripped it open, then stuck in our arm down to the elbow in search of the prize inside—usually a plastic gewgaw that was even more fragile and poorly made than the crap sold in the grocery store toy aisle. And yet, cereal prizes have been around almost as long as cereal. Bowls made with the new miracle product "plastic" were big in the 1930s, while tiny metal license plates caught on in the 1950s. Today the cereal companies are very interested in software, dropping CDs loaded with computer games or music tracks into their Smacks and Flakes. What's next, copies of TurboTax in boxes of Fruity Pebbles? See also MARSHMALLOWS (BREAKFAST CEREALS FEATURING).

< 217 >

PROFESSIONAL WRESTLING As the century turned, the Connecticut-based World Wrestling Federation finally admitted (mostly for tax reasons) what everyone with an age above five and an IQ above 70 already knew—pro wrestling is fake. As if to drive the point home, the WWF even changed its name to the WWE (World Wrestling *Entertainment*). This after a half century of telling America that goofy personas from Gorgeous George to Rowdy Roddy Piper and Hulk Hogan were on the level, and that all those sleeper holds and body slams were legit.

But the truly shameful part is that America keeps watching, just as we have since the invention of television. Believe it or not, before the boob tube, this was actually a real, semi-unrigged sport. The funny business started when early wrestling broadcasts drew boffo ratings. Figuring they needed more than just a bunch of big, sweaty men in tights to keep drawing crowds, producers soon added story lines, garish personas and costumes, and "good" wrestlers facing "bad" wrestlers. Basically, a soap opera with jock straps. See also HOGAN, HULK and MR. T.

PSYCHIC HOTLINES It's an obvious point that's been milked by comedians the world over, but we still feel compelled to bring it up. If the psychic hotlines fronted by LaToya Jackson, Miss Cleo, and Dionne Warwick really worked, then *why do you have to call them*? Why don't they know you need help and call *you*? And why can't these psychics keep their parent companies from getting into legal trouble? Just a little something to contemplate while adding up those $2.95-a-minute charges on your phone bill. See also HOROSCOPES and JACKSON, LATOYA.

PUDDING CUPS Pudding is practically a guilty pleasure in and of itself. But when you devour it in a form that's designed for a kid's lunch box—and where a grownup's spoon barely fits into the container—then you've crossed some sort of line. See also LUNCH BOXES.

PULP NOVELS The name comes from the fact that these tomes were printed on the cheapest available paper—the kind the folks at Charmin wouldn't touch. The guilt came from the fact that the sleazy cover art and attention-grabbing titles made them not quite proper for, say, your local book club. These days, some masters of the genre, including James M. Cain (*Double Indemnity*), Jim Thompson (*The Grifters*), and Mickey Spillane (the Mike Hammer series) have been welcomed into the pantheon of great American writers. But though the pulps produced a handful of diamonds,

< 218 >

most were simply fill dirt. Remember *Marijuana Girl* or *The Oversexed Astronauts*? Neither do we.

PU PU PLATTERS Those Asian-themed appetizers ringing the pu pu platter's charcoal-fueled hibachi may look exotic, but this popular Japanese/Hawaiian/Chinese fusion dish is really as American as apple pie. Based on the Hawaiian word for hot or cold appetizers, it's applied to the trays of heat-and-eat treats (everything from beef on a stick to bacon-wrapped chicken livers) that are served as meal starters both in Chinese restaurants and in Polynesian-themed establishments—most famously at Trader Vic's, which is also the original home of the pu pu platter's preferred accompaniment, the Mai Tai. See also MEAT ON A STICK.

QUEEN OF ENGLAND, THE You can't help but get misty about the woman who has sat on the throne of the United Kingdom since 1952. Maybe it's because Elizabeth Alexandra Mary Windsor sort of reminds us of our own grandmother— if our own grandmother rode around in a gilded carriage and never left the castle without putting on a pair of full-length white gloves. And let's not think too deeply

about the fact that we probably know more about Her Majesty's royal likes and dislikes than we do about those of our own grannies. Sure, she's had some bad press, and maybe she wasn't the best mother-in-law, but after 50+ years on the throne, she still has a hat to match every outfit, savors her gin and tonics, and speaks perfect Queen's English. But then, how could she not? Every monarch should be so cool. See also BRITISH ROYAL FAMILY, THE.

QUINCY, M.E. It's hard to believe there once was a show about a medical examiner that didn't involve gallons of fake blood and buckets of cow innards. *Quincy M.E.*, starring Jack Klugman and running from 1976 (when it was part of the *NBC Sunday Mystery Movie* lineup that included *Columbo*, *McCloud*, and *McMillan and Wife*) to 1983, told the story of a Los Angeles County Coroner's Office employee who managed to do his job without ever making a single on-camera Y incision. Call us prudes (or wimps) but this TV version of the cozy mystery was a lot easier on the eyes— and the stomach—than its more graphic progeny, such as *CSI*. See also AUTOPSIES (TELEVISION) and MYSTERIES, COZY.

QVC Begun in 1986, it's the "other" order-now channel that came along after the Home Shopping Network. Created

< 219 >

by Joseph Segel (founder of the Franklin
Mint), today it employs some 12,000
people, selling everything from garden
doodads to scary-looking, high-priced
dolls. Should you feel the need to visit
the company's West Chester, Pennsylvania, headquarters, you can actually
take the QVC Studio Tour. Last stop is
the gift shop, where you can enjoy the
novel experience (for home shoppers, at
least) of purchasing things without having to use the phone. See also AS SEEN
ON TV PRODUCTS; FRANKLIN MINT, THE;
and HOME SHOPPING NETWORK, THE.

< 220 >

R

RAMBO MOVIES In the 1970s Sylvester Stallone created Rocky, a lovable-loser-turned-winner who captured that era's zeitgeist. He captured a less-endearing aspect of America's character in 1982's *First Blood*, which introduced John Rambo. An embittered Vietnam vet, Rambo seemed less interested in getting respect than in getting payback. As anyone familiar with this film, or any of a hundred other films just like it, already knows, the plot goes like this: (A) Hero is introduced; (B) bad people repeatedly vex the hero; (C) rat-tat-tat-tat! Whoosh! Boom!

The difference with Rambo was that, unlike earlier vigilantes such as Billy Jack, who usually kept their revenge killings in the low double digits, these movies featured body counts rivaling those of Civil War battles. Nevertheless, the public ate it up. *First Blood* was followed by two sequels, one set in Vietnam and the other in Afghanistan, both of which were denuded of buildings, bridges, and men of military age by the time the credits rolled. These vestiges of the late Cold War blazed the trail for that other pumped-up action-hero-turned-action-figure, Arnold Schwarzen-egger. See also *BILLY JACK*; ROCKY MOVIES; SCHWARZENEGGER, ARNOLD; STALLONE, SYLVESTER; and WAR MOVIES.

RAMEN NOODLES Since the 1980s American college students have subsisted on ramen, a Chinese-style wheat noodle that's as popular in Japan (indeed, perhaps more so) as in America. The big difference is that while the Japanese enjoy freshly prepared noodles served in restaurants, Americans eat them in deep-fried blocks whose chief advantages are speed of preparation (drop them in boiling water and you're dining in three minutes), flavor (anything containing approximately 8 grams of fat per serving and 900 mil-  ligrams of salt can't taste bad), and low, low price (costing as little as 10 cents per plastic-wrapped portion, ramen noodles can keep a student alive for a week on change scrounged from the dorm lobby's couch). Living on a diet of these during college is like drinking yourself blind every weekend: It's a rite of passage. See also SALT (EXCESSIVE APPLICATION TO FOOD OF).

RAMPAGING ANIMALS (MOVIES ABOUT) Before *Jaws*, there had already been plenty of films about animals consuming humans. But this 1975 megahit about a great white shark depopulating a New England town one swimmer at a time is the *Citizen Kane* of its kind. It deftly exploited humanity's fears about the primal creatures lurking on the edges of civilization, causing thousands of terrorized moviegoers to cancel their beach vacations.

The movie should have been the last word in ravening beast flicks, but for some reason *people wanted more*. This infatuation with all things fanged and finned was doubly odd because, when a film's star can't talk or even think, there's not much chance for character development. But just as this difficulty hasn't stopped the makers of slasher movies, it also hasn't slowed the Scary Animal franchise. The near-numberless post-*Jaws* releases include *Grizzly*, *Orca*, *The Swarm*, and the more recent *Lake Placid*, which starred a giant crocodile. See also ALLEN, IRWIN; *HALLOWEEN* (THE MOVIE SERIES); and SHARKS.

RAMPAGING ANIMALS (TV SPECIALS ABOUT) Just about anyone who watches *When Good Pets Go Bad 2* or *When Animals Attack 3* at some point feels like a traitor to his species. Admit it. When Fox (it's always Fox) trots out grainy footage of pea-brained Spanish bullfight "enthusiasts" being turned into human piñatas by angry ungulates, or of a department store Santa getting kicked in his toy sack by a reindeer, one's first thought isn't "Oh, those poor people." It's more like, "Payback's a bitch when Mother Nature's your banker." See also *CROCODILE HUNTER*; *MUTUAL OF OMAHA'S WILD KINGDOM*; PIT BULLS; and RAMPAGING ANIMALS (MOVIES ABOUT).

"RAPPER'S DELIGHT" Rap had been around for a few years already, but it was the Sugarhill Gang's 1980 hit that brought it—albeit in a sugarcoated, neutered form—out of the ghetto and into the mainstream. All the essential elements (except for anger) were there: lyrics spoken, not sung, with a background melody lifted from another tune (in this case, Chic's "Good Times"). It was danceable, and who cared if the words (sample: "I said a hip hop the hippie the hippie / to the hip hip hop, a you don't stop") were a bit vapid? The more authentic "kill the police" genre would arrive shortly. See also VANILLA ICE.

RAZZLES Its disc shape and nubby, anti-skid surface were enough to make Razzles unique in the candy aisle. But there was something bigger at work in the thin packet. The trick? Razzles started out as a candy, then turned into a gum. This transformation briefly made it a baby boomer favorite, until the product

< 222 >

suddenly vanished from the candy shelf. But anyone who enjoyed Razzles knew it wouldn't stay away for long. Recently relaunched by Canadian company Concord Confections (the folks behind Dubble Bubble), Razzles now sport a new lineup of flavors.

READER'S DIGEST A magazine that debuted in 1921 and whose first office was in a basement under a Greenwich Village speakeasy has become one of the most staid institutions in journalism. The Reader's Digest Association publishes both the *Digest* and its myriad foreign editions, along with those famous compendiums of condensed books and a slew of other magazines. Lately, however, in the face of falling readership, it has taken steps to "jazz up" the pocket-sized pamphlet with diet stories and more celebrities. That's fine, but there was a certain weirdness about the old *Digest* that we miss. Who remembers "I Am Joe's Spleen"? And who hasn't taken the edge off a stint in the dentist's office waiting room by perusing "Life In These United States"? Some things should be sacrosanct. See also READER'S DIGEST CONDENSED BOOKS.

READER'S DIGEST CONDENSED BOOKS Forget the "If a tree falls in the forest" query. The more relevant modern question is, "If you've read the Reader's Digest Condensed Book version of Mary Higgins Clark, Judith Krantz, or Michael Crichton, have you really read the book?" Quietly devoured by cost cutters and time savers everywhere—and now known as Reader's Digest Select Editions—these "skillfully edited" volumes are perfect for people who want to do more than just read a review but can't handle the work required to conquer every word of Nicholas Sparks's latest. See also CLIFFS NOTES; CRICHTON, MICHAEL; and KRANTZ, JUDITH.

REAL WORLD, THE Imagine if *Friends* wasn't funny and had no sympathetic characters. That was the formula for one of American TV's first reality shows, *The Real World*. It launched in 1992 by following a group of "typical" young adults living together in a New York City flat. Every room was bugged, the phones were tapped, and camera crews lurked 24/7 to capture every moment of their lives. The results, condensed into 30-minute shows, featured twentysomethings whining about their interpersonal relationships and dating quandaries as if the fate of the world hung in the balance.

Nevertheless the program, created by MTV, became a massive, long-running hit, with a new group of typical kids thrown into a house in a different locale every season. Except, as the years went by, the kids seemed less and less typical.

< 223 >

Or even normal. Some looked like professional models, while others seemed to have been picked strictly for their intractable psychosocial problems—the better to stir up photogenic discord.

MTV, milking the concept for maximum profit, debuted another long-running hit called *Road Rules*, in which a group of dysfunctional young people shared not a house but a camper. Then it created a sort of ersatz *Battle of the Network Stars*, in which ex–*Real World* and *Road Rules* cast members faced off against each other in athletic contests— that is, when they weren't whining about their interpersonal relationships. See also BATTLE OF THE NETWORK STARS; MTV; and REALITY SHOWS.

REALITY SHOWS When we first heard the words, "This is the true story of seven strangers picked to live in a house …" during the opening credits of MTV's inaugural season of *The Real World* in 1992, the idea of watching ordinary people caught in the act of being themselves seemed novel—even a bit naughty. While reality-based programs such as *Candid Camera*, *COPS*, and PBS's 1973 miniseries *An American Family* had blazed the trail for such gawkumentaries, *The Real World* took the genre to new highs (or lows), existing for no other reason than to service viewers' most voyeuristic needs. Gladys Kravitz

Fever spread quickly as the networks cooked up batch after batch of evermore-indulgent slices of real life, from *Survivor* to *Big Brother* to *Who Wants to Marry a Millionaire*. It was only a matter of time before reality wasn't real enough. These days fans want conflict, tight dramatic arcs, and twist endings. And most importantly, they want people to hook up. Highbrow viewers complain that the TV listings are starting to read like a mockery of entertainment (witness *I'm a Celebrity, Get Me Out of Here!*). But even the naysayers tuned in weekly to see if Kelly would outwarble Justin on *American Idol*, or if that bitch Jerri would get voted off *Survivor*. And when critics write scathing reviews practically blaming *Joe Millionaire* and his ilk for the fall of civilization, all it proves is that they watch too. Sure it's crap, but it's entertaining crap. See also CANDID CAMERA; COPS; and REAL WORLD, THE.

RECREATIONAL VEHICLES As soon as there were cars powerful enough to pull them, travelers started buying campers —first tent-topped trailers, then shiny Airstreams, then hulking Winnebagos big enough to accommodate the touring company of *Les Miserables*. There's just one problem with this sort of vacationing. Remember the old saying "No matter where you go, there you are?"

< 224 >

With recreational vehicles, it's worse. No matter where you go, there you are—and there's your house, your spouse, your kids, your pet(s), and every other nagging detail of your day-to-day domestic existence. Of course there is an upside. If your adventure on the open road gets a bit *too* adventurous, you can always retreat  to your big chair, satellite TV, and fridge packed with Bud. See also BARCA-LOUNGERS.

RED BULL An Austrian-made beverage designed, according to its promotional materials, to "boost your energy and concentration," Red Bull gets its name from one of its active ingredients—1000 milligrams of the amino acid taurine. The taurine is supposedly a natural pick-me-up, but it gets help from a couple of tried-and-true stimulants—27 grams of sugar, plus 80 mg of good old caffeine in each slim blue-and-silver can. As if to emphasize the air of misplaced invincibility that imbibing so much sugar/caffeine/taurine can create, Red Bull sponsors an annual U.S. event called Flugtag (or "flying day" in German). Participants, no doubt fueled with the sponsor's beverage, are invited to try to fly human-powered machines. The first edition, held in San Francisco in 2002, allowed participants to launch their craft off a ramp, soar (briefly) over the ocean—and then crash into it. See also MOUNTAIN DEW.

RED DAWN A survivalist's wet dream, this action flick was a real embarrassment to anyone else who saw it during theatrical release in 1984. Ironically, this bit of Cold War paranoia, in which the Red Army (assisted by the Cubans and that early '80s enemy du jour, the Nicaraguans) invaded America, came out just as the Soviet Union neared collapse. Today it's interesting mostly as a cultural artifact—and because it stars Patrick Swayze and Jennifer Grey, three years before they got together in 1987's *Dirty Dancing*. See also DIRTY DANCING.

RED LOBSTER Begun in 1968 in Lakeland, Florida, this operation brought mahimahi to the masses and popcorn shrimp to the proletariat. Considered by generations of fast fooders to be the "fancy" chain restaurant, it started life serving combo dishes with names such as the Neptune Platter. Almost everything on the menu was loaded down with hush puppies, slaw, a baked potato, and three or four (or five or six, depending on how much you spent) different ocean delicacies, almost all of them fried.

< 225 >

Telling clams from scallops was tough, because in an era when dark restaurants were considered to be fancy restaurants, Red Lobsters were darker than mine shafts. Still, you couldn't beat the Cheddar Bay Biscuits.

Today's Red Lobsters (run by Darden Restaurants, the brains behind that other great middlebrow chain, Olive Garden) resemble a Key West shrimp house rather than a dark New England lobster joint. Even the menu has changed beyond recognition, with most of the fried things tossed overboard in favor of grilled and broiled items. But purists, take heart. You can still get the Admiral's Feast—an all-fried platter of shrimp, scallops, clam strips, and fish fillets. See also OLIVE GARDEN.

RED SHOE DIARIES (A.K.A. *ZALMAN KING'S RED SHOE DIARIES*)   Followed by his dog, *X-Files* star David Duchovny wanders around reading a letter. Dissolve to a dramatic retelling of the contents of the letter—a retelling in which the protagonists, inevitably, boink. Such was the formula for Showtime's soft-core hit series that ran for 67 episodes from 1992 to 1999. Class points were earned for George S. Clinton's original soundtrack. Class points were erased by the paint-by-numbers plots, including one in which a hottie investment banker is kidnapped by a rugged cowboy. Somehow, name-above-the-title creator Zalman King (whose own acting career included such flicks as *The Ski Bum* and *Galaxy of Terror*) managed to lure a pack of Hollywood middleweights onto the show, including Brenda Vaccaro, Steven Bauer, and Matt LeBlanc, the latter as a bike messenger who, ahem, goes down in an elevator. See also CINEMAX.

REDDI-WIP   See WHIPPED CREAM IN A CAN.

REED, REX   See *GONG SHOW, THE*.

REEVES, KEANU   A man of few words and even fewer facial expressions, Reeves first piqued moviegoers' interest in the 1989 hit *Bill & Ted's Excellent Adventure*, surfing through time as the classic Everydude, Ted. While the actor's chiseled good looks haven't exactly hurt his career (which has included such blockbusters as *Speed*, *Bram Stoker's Dracula* and, of course, the *Matrix* trilogy), we believe it is Reeves's economy of emotion—his flat, stoic delivery of lines like "Trinity? The Trinity?"—that keeps us going back to the cineplex for more.

REMINGTON STEELE   From the first notes of Henry Mancini's instrumental opening theme to the final cheesecake

< 226 >

shot of Laura and Remington as the credits rolled, this weekly TV detective series had us hooked for five seasons in the 1980s, then returned in reruns on A&E during the mid-1990s. Would you expect anything less from a sleuth show whose title character (played by a pre-007 Pierce Brosnan) spoke with an English-Irish accent and based his deductive skills on the plots of old movies—and whose female lead (Stephanie Zimbalist) exuded such sexy-smart confidence that her young male fans developed secret crushes on her? Throw in a little romantic tension between the two, and producers had an instant cult following. Fans ate it up—even though they secretly knew they should be watching *Moonlighting* instead.

RENAISSANCE FAIRS While turning a blind eye to the rampant disease, lack of civil rights, and other atrocities typical of this era, Renaissance fairs extol the virtues of tall pointed hats, turkey drumsticks, and broadswords. As such, they offer a chance for common folk to play dress-up in a cleaned-up version of another world—one where a person is judged not by the color of his skin, but by the size of his lance. See also *STAR TREK* CONVENTIONS.

RERUN See *WHAT'S HAPPENING!!*

RERUNS See NICK AT NITE.

REUNION SHOWS It's stupid to feel all warm and fuzzy about make-believe people. Yet we do, which is why staging reunion shows for long-gone TV programs is nearly always a ratings winner. These fall into two broad categories: narratives that catch up with the fictional characters in the present day (as was done for, among many others, *The Andy Griffith Show*, *L.A. Law*, *The Wild, Wild West*, *Baywatch*, and *Growing Pains*), and pseudodocumentaries in which the cast talks about the good old days and watches clips (*Laverne & Shirley Together Again*; *Mary Tyler Moore Reunion Special*; *M*A*S*H: 30th Anniversary Reunion Special*, and *The Cosby Show: A Look Back*). Both have their advantages and drawbacks. It's always somewhat sad to behold a favorite performer at the end of his career. On the other hand, it can also be somewhat amusing to see how hard Father Time has bitch-slapped, say, Loretta Swit. See also *ANDY GRIFFITH SHOW, THE*.

REVENGE FANTASIES See *BILLY JACK*; *DEATH WISH*; *INCREDIBLE HULK, THE*; NORRIS, CHUCK; RAMBO MOVIES; RAMPAGING ANIMALS (TV SPECIALS ABOUT); SCHWARZENEGGER, ARNOLD; SUPERHEROES; and *WALKING TALL*.

< 227 >

REYNOLDS, BURT Sure, most of his movies leave a lot to be desired, but there are few men who wouldn't switch lives in a heartbeat with Reynolds. A Florida State University football player, he was scouted by the Baltimore Colts but had to quit football due to injuries. So he went into acting, landing one TV role after another  until his breakthrough performance as The Guy With the Hunting Bow in 1972's *Deliverance*. After that, Reynolds rode the success rocket throughout the '70s, appearing in such hits as *Starting Over*, *The Longest Yard*, *Cannonball Run*, and his masterpiece, 1975's *Smokey and the Bandit* (his costar was nominally Sally Field, but in fact was his tricked-out Trans Am). In his spare time he also married (and then dumped) '80s ultrababe Loni Anderson. Since then his star has dimmed, though he seems to be positioning himself for some sort of elder statesman role in films, à la Sean Connery. He even earned a Golden Globe and a Best Supporting Actor Oscar nomination for his role as a pornographer in the 1997 film *Boogie Nights* (a movie he thought would ruin his career). See also UNBELIEVABLE SPORTS COMEBACKS (MOVIES ABOUT) and MUSCLE CARS.

RICE, ANNE Born Howard Allen O'Brien (!), this New Orleans native bumped around the literary world for years before hitting on a unique formula for success: Write about a bunch of immortal gay guys flouncing around Europe and New Orleans, then substitute the word "vampires" for "gay guys." Voilà! You've got Rice's long-running "vampire chronicles" novels. Beginning with 1976's *Interview with the Vampire*, they tell the story of impeccably dressed bloodsuckers who make their way through time, draining the bodily fluids from unlucky humans. The books are big with goth kids and with people who want something undemanding to read on long plane flights. Besides lots and lots of supernatural novels, Rice has written several "dirty" books, including *The Claiming of Sleeping Beauty* and *Exit to Eden*. The latter was made into a film featuring Rosie O'Donnell wearing a dominatrix outfit. Now *that's* horror. See also VAMPIRE NOVELS.

RICE-A-RONI The San Francisco Treat really was developed in San Francisco in 1958 by pasta manufacturer Vince DeDomenico. Based on an Armenian-style pilaf, it was half rice and half pasta—hence the name. Over the years the DeDomenico family's firm, the Golden Grain Company, added new varieties to the lineup, including, in

< 228 >

1964, the first Noodle Roni flavor, Parmesano (basically fettuccine Alfredo). For decades it and the Kraft Macaroni and Cheese Dinner were America's last-minute side dishes of choice. Rice-a-Roni also became a famous game show booby prize ("and for our other contestants, a year's supply of Rice-a-Roni . . ."). See also GAME SHOWS and KRAFT MACARONI AND CHEESE.

RICE KRISPIES TREATS This quickest of all scratch-made snacks can be prepared by a seasoned hand in less than 10 minutes. First gather the marshmallows, butter, and Rice Krispies. Melt the butter and marshmallows in the microwave (this can also be done on top of the stove if you've got an extra few moments), then mix in the Rice Krispies. Turn out into a greased pan to set. Then eat. And eat. And eat. Granted, these supersweet snacks are right down there with Chex mix on the scale of culinary difficulty. But if you bring a plate to any—and we mean *any*—gathering, they'll disappear faster than pens out of the office supply room.

RICKLES, DON Ever since his attention-grabbing first appearance as a guest on *The Tonight Show* in 1965—and his legendary trashing of Frank Sinatra during a club date—Don Rickles has earned such nicknames as "The Merchant of Venom," "The King of Insult," and the ironic "Mr. Warmth." A mainstay on *The Dean Martin Celebrity Roasts*, Rickles built a four-decade career by thumbing his nose at political correctness long before the term even existed. Lashing out at all ethnic groups with equal glee, he created an act that was described by author Gay Talese as "too offensive to be offensive." Rickles also made notable movie appearances in *X: The Man With the X-Ray Eyes*, *Kelly's Heroes*, and, vocally, *Toy Story*. Throughout his long career, there's no record of anyone being able to explain why Rickles calling someone a "hockey puck" is insulting. See also CELEBRITY ROASTS; CLAY, ANDREW DICE; and JOKES, ETHNIC.

RINGO It took a spine of steel (something rare among teenage groupies) to admit that Mr. Starr was your favorite Beatle. It takes an even stronger spine to say that you like his post–Fab Four music (remember "Wrack My Brain"?). Don't weep for Ringo, though. He did, after all, score the hottest Beatle wife, Barbara Bach.

RINGWALD, MOLLY See *BREAKFAST CLUB, THE* and *FACTS OF LIFE, THE*.

RIVERDANCE This *Cats* of dance revues originated in 1984 as a seven-minute intermission performance at a

< 229 >

Dublin, Ireland, song contest. That's probably how long it should have stayed, but the standing ovation it received gave troupe member (and Chicago native) Michael Flatley delusions of grandeur. Was there, perhaps, a vast, untapped demand for Irish step dancing?

Apparently so. Flatley and company turned their intermission bauble into a two-hour travel-  ing stage production loaded with traditional Irish dancing and featuring a bare-chested, baby-oiled Flatley tapping, twirling, and sweating amidst a clogging army of lycra-swathed step-dancing men, and wig-wearing, mini-skirted, step-dancing lassies. Flatley, who choreographed the show, tapped his way through 15 weeks of *Riverdance* before being canned for "artistic differences" in October of 1995. Unfazed, the world's fastest tapper (according to the *Guinness Book of World Records*) went on to create and star in *Lord of the Dance*. Debuting in 1996 and telling the story of a bunch of "good" dancers battling a bunch of "evil" dancers (you know they're evil because they wear Lone Ranger masks), it has grossed more than $400 million since its Dublin debut. Flatley starred in the production for two years, but now

holds the less-sweaty position of creative director. See also GUINNESS WORLD RECORDS.

ROAD RULES See *REAL WORLD, THE* and REALITY SHOWS.

ROAD RUNNER No wisecracks. No wordplay. No social satire. Just a bipedal coyote chasing a really fast bird through a stylized American Southwest landscape. The first Road Runner cartoon was made by Warner Bros. in 1949 and the last in 1966, with nary a plot difference from episode to episode. Why do we keep sitting still for them? The shameful truth is that everyone who ever watched Road Runner cartoons secretly longed for Wile E. Coyote to *wring that bird's beep-beeping neck.*

ROBBINS, HAROLD A best-selling author who wrote about the raw pursuit of power, money, and sex, sex, sex, Harold Robbins lived his life like a character in a Harold Robbins novel. The high school dropout from Hell's Kitchen made his first million before he turned 20 (selling sugar for wholesale trade), blew through it as quickly as it came, then moved to Hollywood to climb the ranks at Universal Pictures and write his first novel, *Never Love a Stranger*, on a $100 bet. It was the first of more than 20 books penned by the self-proclaimed

< 230 >

"greatest writer in basic English." Literary critics weren't particularly keen on Robbins's graphic, swaggering prose, but readers were usually hooked within the first sentence, as in "The sun was beginning to fall from the sky into the white Nevada desert as Reno came up beneath me," or "It was pissing rain at eleven o'clock in the morning in front of St. Patrick's Cathedral." When Robbins died in 1997 at the age of 81, he left us with 50 years worth of toe-curling raunch and a legacy that showed Sidney Sheldon, Jackie Collins, and Jacqueline Susann how it's done. See also COLLINS, JACKIE; KRANTZ, JUDITH; and SUSANN, JACQUELINE.

ROBBINS, TONY This former school janitor has become the biggest thing in motivational speaking—literally the biggest thing. At 6'7", Robbins has made millions by "modeling" the behavior of successful people. That means he examines their strategies, distills them into simple steps that even the sorts of people who listen to motivational speakers can understand, and then sells that knowledge in everything from videos to audio tapes to CDs. So how does one succeed the Tony Robbins way? Basically by working hard, focusing on your goals, not getting discouraged . . . the same pap your parents handed you when you were 12. Yet for some reason

it sounds so much more reasonable coming from a giant who vaguely resembles the James Bond villain Jaws.

ROCK CITY This Chattanooga, Tennessee, tourist trap owes its national reputation to a publicity department of one: Clark Byers, who for decades traveled the country painting some 800 barns with the famous "See Rock City" message. We'll never know how many millions of kids, spying the slogan repeatedly while on family trips, whined about it enough to convince their parents to take them. And what did they find there? Basically a rocky oucropping offering a legitimately breathtaking view of seven surrounding states, along with a bevy of naive-looking attractions that are fun if you're 5 years old, mildly amusing if you're 40, and incredibly disappointing if you're, say, 8 to 12. There's Fairyland Caverns (a rock grotto filled with fluorescent fairy tale characters), Mother Goose Village (more fairy tale characters), and Lover's Leap (from which you can see the aforementioned seven states). If you forced your parents to make a special trip to this place, you owe them an apology—or, perhaps, you should return the favor and take them to Branson. See also BRANSON.

ROCKWELL, NORMAN The painter responsible for 321 *Saturday Evening*

< 231 >

Post covers (and whose biography was modestly titled *My Adventures as an Illustrator*) is the most recognizable American artist since, well, ever. Yet admitting you like him is like saying you really dig Muzak or TV dinners—it pegs you as irretrievably lowbrow. Still, is there anyone who isn't touched by the picture of the baseball umpires searching a threatening sky for rain; the mother and her soldier son peeling potatoes; or the little boy taking his dog to the vet? And does, say, Robert Mapplethorpe have a Presidential Medal of Freedom? We didn't think so. See also KINKADE, THOMAS and TV DINNERS.

ROCKY HORROR PICTURE SHOW, THE It's no surprise that *The Rocky Horror Picture Show* tanked. After all, it starred Tim Curry. But *Rocky Horror* was no ordinary Tim Curry bomb. Unlike *Clue* and *Annie* and *Oscar* (and *The Shadow* and *Passed Away* and *Congo* and *McHale's Navy* and . . .), this outrageous

musical science-fiction horror spoof got a second chance. A gutsy ad exec named Tim Deegan convinced his bosses at Twentieth Century Fox to book the show for a midnight run at the Waverly Theater in New York on April Fools' Day 1976, and the rest is cult flick history. What started as

simple booing by a few giddy audience members evolved around Labor Day into talking back to the screen and, by Halloween, into a dress-as-your-favorite-character event. Seeing a balls-out midnight showing of *Rocky Horror* was a must-do pleasure in the late '70s and early '80s, whether you got into it with People's Temple–like devotion or were just a dilettante stumbling through your first "Time Warp" and unsure when to damn Janet or fling your toast. See also MEAT LOAF (THE SINGER).

ROCKY MOVIES Over the last couple of decades moviegoers have watched Sylvester Stallone slowly drain every last ounce of life out of his original 1976 blockbuster, *Rocky*. So far there have been four sequels, each with the same recycled story. First we meet a new boxing villain; then Rocky doubts his ability to whup the new guy; then he decides to fight; then he trains while "Gonna Fly Now" (or one of its clones) thunders in the background; then he fights and wins, but not before getting pounded like a piece of veal scaloppine. And yet, even though the proceedings are as formulaic as a Thai temple dance, we still buy tickets in the millions—except for *Rocky V*, which tanked, perhaps because it deviated slightly from the classic dogma. We do it for the same reason junkies keep taking drugs. We want to catch some

< 232 >

faint echo of that incredible rush we felt the first time the Italian Stallion ran up the art museum steps and raised his arms in victory—even though we are too wimpy to ever even think about setting foot in a boxing ring. See also RAMBO MOVIES and STALLONE, SYLVESTER.

ROLLER COASTERS (ENORMOUS) Anyone who screams on a roller coaster feels slightly embarrassed afterward, because the sense of danger they inspire is just an illusion. But *what* an illusion. Modern models top out at more than 300 feet in height.

Of course it's all downhill from there. For instance, anyone riding the Millennium Force at Cedar Point in Sandusky, Ohio, faces an initial 310-foot drop down an 80-degree slope at 93 mph. That's basically the same as jumping from the Statue of Liberty's torch. How much higher can they go? It depends on how much riders can stand, and how much parks are willing to spend. Coaster experts contend there's no reason why these thrill rides couldn't go 200 mph and tower 600 feet high. Loops are another matter. Physiologists report that the average human can take only about seven or eight of these before tossing his corn dogs. Which is why you'll never see coasters with more than seven or eight loops. See also THEME PARKS (NOT OWNED BY DISNEY).

ROMY AND MICHELE'S HIGH SCHOOL REUNION While the Two Male Idiots on an Adventure genre has been a cinematic staple for decades (witness everything from the Abbot and Costello films to more recent "triumphs" such as *Dumb & Dumber* and *Bill & Ted's Excellent Adventure*), there's been no distaff counterpoint (Thelma and Louise driving over the cliff doesn't count). The strongest attempt was this 1997 film starring Mira Sorvino and Lisa Kudrow as two dumb-as-dishwater blondes attending their 10-year high school reunion in Arizona. In spite of sometimes-scathing reviews, the movie (based on characters from the Robin Schiff play, *The Ladies' Room*) has built a *Rocky Horror*–like cult following. And why wouldn't it, with such immortal dialogue as, "I was so lucky getting mono. That was like the best diet ever," and "Let's fold scarves!" Plus, it contains one of the funniest three-person dance scenes ever filmed. See also ABBOTT AND COSTELLO; CHICK FLICKS (FEMALE BONDING); *DUMB & DUMBER*; MENTALLY IMPAIRED (MOVIES WHOSE STARS PRETEND TO BE); REEVES, KEANU; and *ROCKY HORROR PICTURE SHOW, THE*.

RONCO PRODUCTS If you're under 30, you know Ron Popeil—namesake of the famous Ronco company—because you've no doubt sat through his half-

< 233 >

hour pitches for the Showtime Rotisserie Oven and BBQ. If you're over 30, you remember him using breathless, omnipresent, 30-second commercials to sell such "miracles" as the Veg-O-Matic, Mr. Microphone, and the Buttoneer. And if the number of Ronco devices laid out at garage sales is any gauge, the sad truth is that almost all of us have, at one time or another, purchased something from this man. See also AS SEEN ON TV PRODUCTS.

ROTH, DAVID LEE How great a rock and roll front man was David Lee Roth? In 1985, during the height of his fame as the long-haired, Fabio-like singer for the supergroup Van Halen, he released a solo album, *Crazy from the Heat*, that contained such potentially career-killing missteps as a cover of the Beach Boys' "California Girls" and an utterly out-of-character medley of "Just a Gigolo" and "I Ain't Got Nobody." Any other singer would have been a laughingstock, but since it was Roth (who was already sort of a laughingstock, except that he was in on the joke), they both became huge hits. Shortly thereafter he left Van Halen to launch a successful-at-first solo career that, sadly, seemed to dwindle and fade at approximately the same rate as his hairline receded. Today, though he's an aged anachronism, we treat him like an old high school buddy. Even if he's not

the man he once was, he's welcome to crash on our couch. See also FABIO.

ROURKE, MICKEY John Waters released his film *Polyester* in Odorama—which meant that scratch-and-sniff cards were issued to the audience for use at key points in the show. No such gimmick was necessary when watching Mickey Rourke films—you could smell the stink all the way from the back row. Justly acclaimed for his work in 1982's *Diner*, the former boxer known for his difficult on-set behavior (he's said to have walked off a set because the director wouldn't give a part to his pet Chihuahua) snagged a string of leading roles in such films as *Angel Heart* and *Nine 1/2 Weeks* (written by Zalman King, who would go on to *Red Shoe Diaries* fame). The quintessential Rourke experience, though, remains 1987's take-a-shower-afterward epic *Barfly*, which was penned by the equally nutty Charles Bukowski. See also GIMMICKS, MOVIE; *RED SHOE DIARIES*; and WATERS, JOHN.

RUSSELL, KURT See DISNEY FILMS FEATURING DEAN JONES AND/OR KURT RUSSELL.

< 234 >

S

"Safety Dance, The" Not since "Mairzy Doats" has such an utterly nonsensical song burned itself so thoroughly into the public consciousness. Nothing about this 1983 one-hit wonder made sense. Not the lyrics (including "We can dress real neat from our hats to our feet / And surprise them with the victory cry"), nor the video (the lead singer roaming a medieval village accompanied by a lute-playing midget and a female village idiot), nor the name of the band—a group called Men Without Hats (formed by Canadian brothers Ivan, Stefan, and Colin Doroschuk). Perhaps its appeal springs from the fact that because it was incomprehensible, there was nothing to hate. That certainly wasn't the case for Men Without Hats' follow-up music—politically conscious drivel that dropped off the charts. "We can dance if we want to," indeed. See also Midgets and One-Hit Wonders.

Salad in a Bag In 1989 the Salinas, California-based produce processor Fresh Express debuted the greatest advance in culinary laziness since the invention of the TV dinner: retail packaged salads. Since the '70s the company had provided pre-cut roughage to several fast-food chains, but it took years to develop the bagging technology necessary to keep sacks of salad fresh on grocers' shelves. Before long, Dole and several other produce companies began shelving similar products, including baby spring greens and Caesar salad mixes. By 1995, salad in a bag revenues had reached $800 million—which is a lot of lettuce. Not surprisingly, other ultra-convenient veggies followed, from pre-sliced, pre-boiled potatoes to bags of julienned, slaw-ready cabbage and carrots. Now, if they could just get someone to chew it for us. See also TV Dinners.

Salt (Excessive Application to Food of) Restaurant servers willfully wave their magical wooden wands over your salad, cranking out clouds of peppery pixie dust. However, you never see one haul out a giant salt cellar and ask if you'd like some extra sodium. That's because salting an entrée, like putting ketchup on a steak, is considered an insult to the chef. You should be satisfied with the savory zest of lime or the bouquet of fresh herbs seasoning on your fish, beef, or fowl. Yet everyone knows that some foods (pastas and potatoes in particular) benefit from a blast of salt. The same goes for tomatoes, turkey, and fried fish and chicken. Is that so wrong?

Actually, according to the United

< 235 >

States Food and Drug Administration, it is. The FDA recommends we consume no more than 2,400 milligrams of sodium daily (about a heaping teaspoon's worth). Yet Americans typically suck down more than 4,000 milligrams per day, most in processed foods and restaurant fare. Which means that you're already over the limit (and jacking up your chances for everything from high blood pressure to stroke) before you even reach for the shaker. Still, if you're scarfing down a box of batter-fried fish from, say, Long John Silver's, too much sodium is probably the least of your worries. See also LONG JOHN SILVER'S and RAMEN NOODLES.

SAM'S CLUB See WHOLESALE CLUBS.

SAMOAS See GIRL SCOUT COOKIES.

SANDLER, ADAM If you'd been asked in 1991 to pick the two *Saturday Night Live* regulars who would become break-out stars, chances are you'd have guessed Mike Myers and Dana Carvey. But while Myers has certainly done well for himself (at least when he plays Austin Powers) and Carvey also did okay (though only when playing opposite Myers in the *Wayne's World*  flicks), their lesser costar Adam Sandler became the unlikeliest A-lister since Esther Williams. Why? Because he makes guys laugh, whether they admit it or not. Say what you will about Sandler's range. It takes skill to make a golf comedy (*Happy Gilmore*) that's now quoted nearly as often as the leader of the genre, *Caddyshack*. Another secret of Sandler's success: He never tried to turn one of his SNL characters into a feature film. See also CADDYSHACK and SATURDAY NIGHT LIVE (MOVIES BASED ON CHARACTERS FROM).

SANFORD AND SON Most guilty pleasures know no social boundaries. A Twinkie, for instance, is a lowbrow calorie bomb to every race, creed, and gender. Not so with *Sanford and Son*. Originally aired from 1972 to 1976, the show gave an illicit thrill to both blacks and whites, but for different reasons. Based on the British series *Steptoe and Son*, it offered African-American viewers the guilty pleasure of laughing at a show that they knew was written by an all-white staff and that its star, Redd Foxx (real name John Elroy Sanford), was unhappy with. For Caucasians, the guilt came from enjoying a sitcom filled with people the likes of whom they'd never meet (Grady, Aunt Esther) and set in a place (Watts) they'd never visit. See also TWINKIES.

< 236 >

SATURDAY MORNING CARTOONS During the '60s and '70s, watching Saturday-morning cartoons was as big a childhood tradition as going to a movie matinee in the '30s and '40s. Once upon a time, when there were only three networks, Saturday became, by common consent, the ghetto into which kiddie programming was consigned. Thus, between the hours of, say, 7 A.M. and noon, baby boomers could dig into a bowl of Sugar Smacks while watching everything from old Road Runner cartoons to such Hanna-Barbera "classics" as *Josie and the Pussycats*, *Scooby-Doo, Where Are You?* and *The Funky Phantom*. But these days, thanks to cable television, Saturday morning has lost its tawdry magic. With Nickelodeon, the Disney Channel, and Cartoon Network serving up 'toons around the clock, today's minors needn't wait for the weekend to get eyestrain from staring at Shaggy and Scooby. See also HANNA-BARBERA CARTOONS; ROAD RUNNER; and SCOOBY-DOO.

SATURDAY NIGHT FEVER Like *Rocky*, this 1977 blockbuster is about a loser from the neighborhood who tries to make good. Except instead of punching his way out of obscurity, Tony Manero (John Travolta) tries to dance his way out. The movie, based loosely on a *New York* magazine article, never got a lot of respect from critics. And yet, this is one of those films that makes us pause when we happen to channel surf past it. Sure the clothes and the dancing are dated (sometimes hilariously so), but it's touching to watch Tony try to wrap his 10-cent brain around the idea of doing something with his life. Also, the Bee Gees–intensive soundtrack remains as crisp and colorful as a new polyester shirt. See also ROCKY MOVIES and *SATURDAY NIGHT FEVER* (SOUNDTRACK).

SATURDAY NIGHT FEVER (SOUNDTRACK) Plenty of disco haters are closet fans of this album. Who wouldn't be, with such monster hits as "Stayin' Alive," "More Than a Woman," "Boogie Shoes," and "Disco Inferno" all on one disc? Just pop it in the 8-track—oops, we mean CD player—and in no time you're grooving like a no-name schmuck from Brooklyn. Of course disco haters have another reason to carry a torch for the soundtrack. This biggest of all dance records was instrumental in killing the genre it celebrated. Disco, at least among the cool, was already dying when *Saturday Night Fever* came out, flaming it back to life like lighter fluid poured on smoldering charcoal briquettes. But finally, after the general public got as sick of the *Fever* soundtrack as the trendsetters were, the entire fad collapsed into a cultural black hole, dragging disco, and the '70s itself,

< 237 >

into oblivion. Thus was the world made safe for boy bands. See also BOY BANDS; DISCO (DANCING); DISCO (FASHIONS); KC AND THE SUNSHINE BAND; and *SATURDAY NIGHT FEVER*.

***SATURDAY NIGHT LIVE* (MOVIES BASED ON CHARACTERS FROM)** There are few things that most film buffs agree on, but one of them is this: Movies based on characters from *Saturday Night Live* almost invariably suck. Personas that are tolerable in seven-minute sketches just don't warrant ninety minutes of celluloid. Of course there are a handful of moderately interesting successes (*The Blues Brothers*, *Wayne's World*, *Gilda Live*), but they're the exceptions to the rule. Still, the same reflex that makes us slow down as we drive past car wrecks also tempts us to stop channel surfing whenever we come across such Irwin Allen–worthy disasters as *Coneheads*, *A Night at the Roxbury*, *Superstar*, *Stuart Saves His Family*, *It's Pat*, *The Ladies Man* . . . and on and on and on. See also ALLEN, IRWIN and *SATURDAY NIGHT LIVE* (RECURRING CHARACTERS ON).

***SATURDAY NIGHT LIVE* (RECURRING CHARACTERS ON)** John Belushi hated the famous bees that kept popping up during the first season of *Saturday Night Live*. Likewise today's comedy snobs complain about the show's increasing reliance on recurring characters. Yet if we made a list of them—say, the Wild and Crazy Guys, the Cheerleaders, Todd DiLaMuca and Lisa Loopner, Pat, Stuart Smalley, Tommy Flanagan, Wayne and Garth, Chico Escuela, Nat X, the Church Lady, Goat Boy, and the Samurai, you'd no doubt say, "Wait, what about the Blues Brothers . . . or the Land Shark . . . or Fernando . . . or the Roxbury guys . . . or . . . " As much as we hate to admit it, the recurring characters are one of the reasons the show has lasted as long as it has. Which is still no excuse for "I Married a Monkey." See also *SATURDAY NIGHT LIVE* (MOVIES BASED ON CHARACTERS FROM).

SAUSAGE Though folks have stuffed ground meat into the intestinal tracts of dead animals at least since ancient Roman times, they only started feeling guilty about it fairly recently. While there's no denying the pleasure of pepperoni on your pizza, andouille in your jambalaya, or a hot dog at the baseball park, sausage's typically high fat content and sometimes-unorthodox ingredients (which many suspect includes the bits not quite good enough for cat food or Spam) make this a guilty pleasure staple. How many foodstuffs are so vile that they actually rated their own muckraking exposé (Upton Sinclair's *The Jungle*)? Plus, if you're a Jew, there's the added

< 238 >

guilt of someday having to face irate ancestors demanding to know why you were eating *traif*. See also HOT DOGS (CONVENIENCE STORE); HOT DOGS (STADIUM); SPAM; and VIENNA SAUSAGE.

SAVED BY THE BELL Every generation has to have a mediocre high school sitcom to call its own. Those watching TV in the late '80s had two. Just as *Head of the Class* was winding down, *Saved by the Bell* was ramping up. Running for four years, *Bell* grew out of the Disney Channel's show about junior high school called *Good Morning, Miss Bliss*, which featured three of *Bell's* students (if you must know, they were Zack, Lisa, and  Screech). In hindsight, one of the reasons for this show's success was the eye-candy casting. For girls, there was Mario Lopez and Mark-Paul Gosselaar. For the boys, there was Tiffani Thiessen, Elizabeth Berkley (of *Showgirls* infamy), and Lark Voorhies. For everyone else, there was Dustin Diamond. See also *SHOWGIRLS*.

SCHOOLHOUSE ROCK Truth be told, most of what we learned (or, more importantly, retained) about math, science, grammar, and American history was gleaned from *Schoolhouse Rock*—

three-minute musical cartoons that aired during ABC's weekend kids' shows. They debuted in 1972 with the *Multiplication Rock* series (remember "My Hero, Zero" and "The Good Eleven"?), followed by *Grammar Rock* in 1973 (including "Lolly, Lolly, Lolly, Get Your Adverbs Here"), then bicentennial-inspired *America Rock* in 1974 (featuring the legendary "I'm Just a Bill," voiced by *Merv Griffin Show* trumpeter Jack Sheldon). A science and health edition appeared shortly thereafter. During the '70s the various episodes were broadcast roughly 300 times each season. Today the segments are available on CDs and even in songbooks. Perhaps modern parents figure if it worked for them, it can work for their kids, too.

SCHWARZENEGGER, ARNOLD There are plenty of reasons to laugh at this guy. He talks funny. He looks like a cartoon character. He has a goofy, spell-check-defying name.

But there are plenty of reasons not to laugh at this Austrian import. For one thing, if he hears you he might pound you flatter than a schnitzel. For another, he personifies the American dream. A dirt-poor (albeit well-built) U.S. immigrant, he became a bodybuilding superstar, then parlayed his fame into a movie career studded with hits ranging from

< 239 >

1982's *Conan the Barbarian* to 1994's *True Lies*. Mostly by playing monosyllabic killer cyborgs and monosyllabic killer mercenaries, he became one of Hollywood's hottest box office draws. Though many of his most recent films have been disappointments (primarily because, in flicks such as *End of Days* and *Collateral Damage*, Schwarzenegger actually tried to *act*), he's far from a has-been. In October 2003, through a controversial "recall" election that made headlines around the world, Ah-nold became the governor of California.

Truth is, lots of people see Schwarzenegger (whose name means "black plowman" in German) as a role model. And why not? If you want to realize your dreams on a monumental, pumped-up, steroid-soaked scale, you could have worse guides.

SCOOBY-DOO Most classic, long-lived cartoons earn their success by serving two audiences. They provide slapstick for the kids, plus sly puns aimed squarely at the old-enough-to-drive crowd. Not so, Scooby-Doo. This longest-running of all network TV animated series caters to kiddies and no one else. The animation is crude, the dialogue lame, and the premise downright bizarre. Four teenagers—beatnik Shaggy (voiced by Casey Kasem), debutante Daphne, brainy Velma, and hunky Freddy—plus a talking Great Dane (the aforementioned Scooby-Doo) drive around in a tricked-out van named the Mystery Machine, investigating spooky occurrences. Kind of like an *X-Files* for the *Romper Room* set.

The saga started in 1969 with the debut of *Scooby-Doo, Where Are You?* During the '70s, '80s, and '90s nearnumberless incarnations emerged, including (but by no means confined to): *The New Scooby-Doo Comedy Movies*, *The 13 Ghosts of Scooby-Doo*, and *A Pup Named Scooby-Doo*. One of the most fascinating aspects of the show was that even as time marched on, the cartoon kids continued to wear '60s-vintage bell bottoms and miniskirts. Then, in the summer of 2002, came the most improbable development of all: a big-budget Hollywood film that, though only slightly more sophisticated than the cartoon, nevertheless earned better than $100 million in the United States alone. That buys a lot of Scooby Snacks. See also HANNA-BARBERA CARTOONS and SAT-URDAY MORNING CARTOONS.

SCREEN SAVERS, WACKY This bit of computer technology has outlived its usefulness, yet survives because people love it. Years ago, leaving the same image on a computer monitor for long periods could cause a problem called burn-in. The monitor's glass surface

< 240 >

would actually become discolored, creating a ghost image that never went away. Screen savers (random images that take over the screen if the computer is left unattended for a certain amount of time) prevented this problem. Modern monitors are immune to burn-in, but people still love personalizing their computers with screen savers: the odder the better. Almost anything is available (often for free) on the Internet, from a program that helps SETI sift through space noise for signs of intelligent life (visit www.setiathome.ssl.berkeley.edu to sign up), to aquarium fish, to pretty much any sex act you would care to name. We don't recommend that last category for office use. Unless you're Larry Flynt. See also *HUSTLER*.

SEA MONKEYS A staple in comic book ads, the Sea Monkeys of real life shocked millions of kids by not holding hands, not having big smiles, and not wearing bows or crowns. They were—and are—brine shrimp eggs that hatch when tossed into water laced with a secret solution (mostly salt) that comes with the Sea Monkeys kit. Their Dr. Frankenstein was inventor Harold von Braunhut, who "created" them in 1957. He first slapped the hapless eggs with the name Instant Life, but then modified it because the creatures sort of, kind of had something that looked like a monkey's tail—if you looked really, really hard. And most kids did look at them really, really hard—for about an hour, after which they flushed the "monkeys" down the toilet and got on with their lives.

SEAWORLD The dolphin shows are fascinating. The killer whale performances are awesome. The sea lions are hilarious. And you are a bastard. That's the icky feeling more than one visitor to the SeaWorld water parks (or, for that matter, any water park or aquarium) gets when he sees so many intelligent, energetic sea creatures penned up and performing for the amusement of a bunch of sunburned, souvenir-T-shirt–wearing nimrods. You don't have to be a card-carrying Greenpeace member to realize that dolphins probably could think of better ways to amuse themselves than by leaping out of the water after a mackerel and that, given their druthers, they probably wouldn't spend their lives doing endless laps around a glorified swimming pool in Orlando, Florida. And yet, there they are. And there *you* are, paying the admission money necessary to keep them there. See also ORLANDO.

SEDAKA, NEIL Perhaps the least-macho guy ever to come out of Brooklyn, Neil Sedaka may also be the least macho guy

< 241 >

ever to have a string of Top 10 hits. After co-writing "Stupid Cupid" and "Where the Boys Are" for Connie Francis, he climbed the charts on his own from 1959 to 1962 with "Oh! Carol," "Happy Birthday Sweet Sixteen," "Breaking Up Is Hard to Do" and "Stairway to Heaven" (No, not *that* "Stairway to Heaven." What's wrong with you?). An inexplicable resurgence in popularity occurred in the early '70s when Sedaka's "Laughter in the Rain" hit No. 1 and his song "Love Will Keep Us Together" was covered by Captain & Tennille (the result won a Grammy for Record of the Year). Now well into his sixties, Sedaka continues to tour in venues ranging from casinos to Carnegie Hall.

SERIAL KILLERS (MOVIES ABOUT) It says something about the mental state of our society that movies featuring serial killers have become a popular and much-lauded genre. From Fritz Lang's 1931 *M* to Alfred Hitchcock's *Psycho* to such modern "masterpieces" as *The Silence of the Lambs* and *Henry: Portrait of a Serial Killer*, they not only win critical acclaim, but also sell tickets by the millions. The best of these productions try to analyze the inner workings of the criminal mind. But things get icky when these human buzz saws become stock characters, à la *The Bone Collector*, *Seven*, and *Manhunter*. Truth is, no matter how nasty traditional horror films get, we can always tell ourselves that we're watching outlandish fiction. Serial killers, on the other hand, are real. Which means the guy sitting next to you in the theater could be watching the screen, thinking, "Hey, they stole my bit." See also *HALLOWEEN* (THE MOVIE SERIES).

SEX (IN UNUSUAL AND/OR INAPPROPRIATE PLACES) For some, discreetly doing the nasty in public (be it on a plane, in a nightclub restroom, an elevator, the ocean, or even a moving car) provides the ultimate sexual thrill. Unfortunately, the presence of ever-smaller cameras and Inspector Gadget–like cell phones with digital imaging means these semiprivate trysts can sometimes go public (thanks to Internet porn sites) in a big way. Who can forget the two "baseball fans" who had their bleacher tryst taped by a bored cameraman—and then broadcast to computer screens across America? Of course, since the danger of discovery is what makes this so exciting, perhaps the threat of lurking cameras will only make it *more* enticing. See also NAKED CELEBRITIES (PHOTOGRAPHS OF).

SEX (WACKY THINGS NERDS WASTE THEIR TIME ON INSTEAD OF HAVING) See *BATTLESTAR GALACTICA*; *DR. WHO*; DUNGEONS AND DRAGONS; *LORD OF THE*

< 242 >

RINGS, THE; SHATNER, WILLIAM; *STAR TREK*; *STAR TREK* CONVENTIONS; and *STAR WARS*.

SEX (WATCHING OTHER PEOPLE HAVE) See CINEMAX; *HUSTLER*; LESBIANS (MOVIE SCENES FEATURING); LORDS, TRACI; MASTURBATION; MOVIES (PORNOGRAPHIC); *PENTHOUSE*; SEX (IN UNUSUAL AND/OR INAPPROPRIATE PLACES); and SPECTRAVISION.

SGT. PEPPER'S LONELY HEARTS CLUB BAND (THE MOVIE) Purists reacted to this cinematic adaptation of the famous Beatles album as if someone sprayed graffiti on the ceiling of the Sistine Chapel. Today's fans of bad cinema, enjoying a clinical distance from both the film and the Beatles, can take a more charitable view. Filmed in 1978, it features the Bee Gees, then at the height of their fame, plus Peter "Talking Guitar" Frampton as the four members of the Pepper band. The supporting cast includes everyone from Alice Cooper to Steve Martin to George Burns, none of whom seem to have any clue what's going on. These days plenty of people (unaware that this titanic bomb destroyed the career of Frampton and severely wounded that of the Bee Gees) see it simply as a so-bad-it's-funny example of '70s excess—and a worthy companion piece to those two other disco-era musical nightmares, *Can't Stop the Music* and *Xanadu*. See also BEE GEES, THE; *FRAMPTON COMES ALIVE!*; H. R. PUFNSTUF; MALE SINGERS WHO SOUND LIKE WOMEN; NEWTON-JOHN, OLIVIA; VILLAGE PEOPLE, THE; and *XANADU*.

SHAKE 'N BAKE Launched in 1965 in two versions (chicken and fish), Shake 'n Bake quickly became the pretending-to-actually-cook default setting for moms who felt guilty shoving TV dinners in front of their tykes. Nothing more than a disposable bag of flour and spices, this cornerstone in the Kraft Foods lineup now offers variations for pork chops, chicken nuggets, and teriyaki whatever. See also TV DINNERS.

SHARKS Ever since the movie *Jaws* debuted in 1975, the world has been fascinated by these ocean predators. Books on the subject fly off the shelves, and documentaries get top ratings on the Discovery Channel. Everyone, it seems, is interested in, and more than a little afraid of, sharks.

Well, "everyone" is an idiot. The truth is, dreading an encounter with these creatures is like fearing a UFO abduction. It just isn't going to happen. According to the Florida Museum of Natural History's International Shark Attack File, there were only 60 unpro-

< 243 >

voked shark attacks worldwide in 2002. Each year elephants, hippos, and even *bees* claim more lives. You have a far better chance of choking to death on that hot dog you bought at the beach concession stand than of falling victim to a great white. See also RAMPAGING ANIMALS (MOVIES ABOUT) and RAMPAGING ANIMALS (TV SPECIALS ABOUT).

SHARPER IMAGE, THE Since the first one opened in San Francisco in 1981, Sharper Image stores have established themselves as the premier spot for men to bum around while their wives cruise the mall. And why not? From day one the stores, catalog business, and burgeoning Web site have offered everything men crave: jukeboxes, karaoke machines, electronic nose hair shavers; robotic floor vacuums; stereo systems the size of a thermos; and vibrating chairs that do everything but cook you breakfast in the morning. The name was developed by founder Richard Thalheimer, who originally applied it to his copier company (get it, sharper image?). Thalheimer quickly branched out into doodads, opened stores, and went public in 1987. Today the chain provides a vital service to shoppers worldwide—if you consider selling pith helmets with built-in solar fans to be a vital service. See also MASSAGE CHAIR (AT THE MALL) and SKYMALL.

SHATNER, WILLIAM It's hard to think of another actor whose personality contains such an entertaining mix of arrogance, cluelessness, and bizarre likability. Canadian-born Shatner knocked around Hollywood during the late '50s and early '60s, mostly doing bit parts but also appearing in Broadway productions, the occasional A-list film (including *Judgment at Nuremberg*), and some surprisingly interesting TV roles—most famously as the flying nutcase in the scariest of all *Twilight Zone* episodes, "Nightmare at 20,000 Feet."

Then came *Star Trek*. The show only ran from 1966 to 1969 and was never a hit in its initial run, but for years it typecast Shatner as Captain Kirk. Not that Shatner didn't do everything (including some very ill-advised things) to break that mold. Though he can't sing a note, he nevertheless released an album, which includes his immortal, proto-rap rendition of "Lucy in the Sky with Diamonds."  Finally he managed to break out of "set phasers on stun" mode, landing the TV series *T.J. Hooker* in 1982 and then hosting duties on the reality show *Rescue 911*—all while appearing in a seemingly never-ending stream of *Star Trek* movies.

These days Shatner exploits his goofy image in a very Leslie Nielsen–esque

< 244 >

way. He's played a smarmy, glad-handing version of himself on everything from the movie *Miss Congeniality* to the sitcom *3rd Rock from the Sun*. He also served as the real-life (sort of) host of the Americanized version of the Japanese cooking show *Iron Chef*. See also *IRON CHEF*; NIELSEN, LESLIE; *STAR TREK*; and *TWILIGHT ZONE, THE*.

SHOCK JOCKS These dirty-minded, boob-obsessed morning deejays are the flip side of conservative talk radio hosts. Instead of freaking us out with their extreme right-wing views, the likes of Howard Stern, Mancow, and Don Imus titillate us with dirty jokes and sexual innuendo. But while millions listen during their morning commutes, few fans dare to recite what they've heard during a meeting, lest they draw cold stares or, even worse, a lecture from someone in Human Resources. But politically incorrect though they may be, the truth (as ratings prove) is that plenty of people listen in the privacy of their cars, where no one will ever know how un-PC they really are. See also CONSERVATIVE RADIO TALK SHOWS and STERN, HOWARD.

SHOOTING GALLERIES Shooting galleries were developed as a place where cowboys and other rough-and-tumble types could practice with their firearms. During the Civil War they were even used to teach women how to protect themselves. Today, shooting galleries are staples of third-rate amusement parks where guys who don't know an M-16 from an M&M can blaze away at targets. Why is this most politically incorrect of all carnie attractions still around? Because, as one Midwestern shooting gallery employee put it, "It's fun to shoot a gun." See also MIDWAYS.

SHORE, PAULY When *Encino Man* proved a surprise movie hit in 1992, two careers were launched. Brendan Fraser went on to mix big-budget blockbusters with art house fare and silly comedies. His costar, however, managed only to make silly comedies—and the "comedy" part is in several cases debatable. The son of comedy club maven Mitzi Shore and comic Sammy Shore, Pauly (who got his start on MTV) defied critics by seeming blissfully unconcerned about the fact that he had no noticeable talent. Still, there were closet fans who smiled through *Son in Law*, *In the Army Now*, *Jury Duty*, *Bio-Dome*, and other, lesser (yes, there were lesser) films. See also MTV.

SHOWER MASSAGERS These devices are marketed as a stress-relieving way to soothe tired or tense muscles with pulsing jets of water. But as various stand-up comedians and numerous sitcoms

< 245 >

(including *Will & Grace* and *Friends*) have implied, they can also be used for other things. Nasty things. Things that make us not want to touch the shower massagers in hotel bathrooms.

SHOWGIRLS An absolutely terrible film that everyone makes fun of, yet everyone seems to have seen. *Saved by the Bell* alumna Elizabeth Berkley plays a stripper who wants to become a Las Vegas showgirl and will do anything and anyone to make it. Unlike most high-profile train wreck movies (*Ishtar*, *Howard the Duck*, *Heaven's Gate*), *Showgirls* offers something to compensate for the bad acting and bad script: legions of naked and near-naked females (which explains why the copy at your local video store is always checked out). *Showgirls* is like a beautiful, sexy date with a horrible personality; you have to deal with a lot of crap to get to the good stuff. Try watching it with the sound off. See also *SAVED BY THE BELL*.

SHOWTIME AT THE APOLLO Ella Fitzgerald. James Brown. Stevie Wonder. Michael Jackson. Lauryn Hill. All got early breaks when they played amateur night at Harlem's legendary Apollo Theater. Since 1987, that same stage and a similar format has been brought to TV audiences who somehow manage to locate this unheralded syndicated show in its circa 1 A.M. time slot. Featuring a parade of familiar hosts—Sinbad, Mark Curry, Mo'Nique, Steve Harvey, and others—*Showtime at the Apollo* is *American Idol* without the annoying theme song, squabbling judges, and self-congratulatory interviews. It's a fun alternative to all of the bizarre infomercials and televangelists who share its time slot, thanks not only to the talent on display (quality varies) but also to the rowdy spirit of the crowd, which ultimately decides each amateur entertainer's fate. Just don't expect anything but blank stares when you ask, "What did you think of that guy who won on *Apollo* this weekend?" See also JACKSON, MICHAEL and *STAR SEARCH*.

SIDEBURNS Wacky sideburns are a coming-of-age statement for young men who finally achieve the hormone levels necessary to sprout them. Little can these guys imagine their embarrassment when, years later, spouses or children stumble across old college photos of Dad looking like a Civil War officer. Incredibly enough, the world owes this dubious fashion statement to just such an officer: General Ambrose Burnside. He was so famous for his jaw hair that the look became known as burnsides—and then, for reasons unknown, got switched to "sideburns." The rest is hair history. See also HUMPERDINCK, ENGELBERT.

< 246 >

SILLY STRING Introduced in 1969 by a company called Julius Samann, Ltd., Silly String has risen from children's toy to cultural icon. Basically a plastic-like compound that hardens when exposed to air (the exact formula is a trade secret), Silly String has found its way into everything from weddings (where it has replaced rice as the missile of choice to aim at the departing bride and groom) to themed fraternity parties. The only problem is, while blasting it all over the place is fun, getting it out of your hair and off your living room walls is not.

SIMMONS, RICHARD Just what we need; fitness tips from someone who looks like the kid everyone made fun of in gym class. Yet for more than three decades Americans (or, rather, Americans who are so far gone physically that more-demanding mentors aren't an option) have grunted, sweated, and starved at the behest of this permed pixie in short shorts. Born in 1948, Simmons was a little butterball until he invented his own diet system and  workout regimen. They allowed him to become, if not exactly a strapping lad, then at least a skinny one. Over the decades he's marketed his products and exercise videos (most famously, *Sweatin'*

to the Oldies) to the too-fat-for-the-gym crowd. See also AEROBICS PROGRAMS.

SINGERS (WHO MUST HAVE MADE DEALS WITH SATAN IN ORDER TO GAIN FAME) See GOULET, ROBERT; NEWLEY, ANTHONY; NEWTON, WAYNE; SEDAKA, NEIL; and STEVE & EYDIE.

SIX FLAGS AMUSEMENT PARKS Positioned as Disneyland with balls (a good advertising slogan might be "*They* have animatronic presidents, but *we* have roller coasters that make you hurl"), this national chain began as a single park. Six Flags Over Texas opened in 1961 and was named for the flags of the six nations that have flown over that state at various times in its history. The brainchild of Texas oil baron Angus Wynne, the company expanded to include 39 parks in eight countries. Though they may not offer the stuff of memorable family vacations, they're certainly easy to reach on short notice. After all, 98 percent of the U.S. population lives within eight hours of one. See also THEME PARKS (NOT OWNED BY DISNEY).

SIX MILLION DOLLAR MAN, THE Remember how kids, circa 1975, used to run around the playground in slow motion? Most likely they were pretending to be Colonel Steve Austin, the electronically enhanced protagonist of this

< 247 >

ABC series. An astronaut who suffered a calamitous flight test accident (the footage of which was as ubiquitous in its time as the ill-fated ski jumper on ABC's *Wide World of Sports*), Austin was the inspiration for 90-pound weaklings everywhere. Who, after all, wouldn't want a limb or an organ (in Austin's case, an eye, an arm, and both legs) enhanced by the wonders of science? And what bionic boy wouldn't want a sidekick like Jaime Sommers (a.k.a. the Bionic Woman) to fight crime with?

If you feel a strong sense of nostalgia for this show, *never, ever watch a rerun.* Like a week-old bologna sandwich in a third-grader's lunch box, it hasn't aged well. The special effects, such as they are, seem absurd, and star Lee Majors (who wears almost nothing but leisure suits) displays the acting range of an anatomy class cadaver. No wonder the series, which ran from 1974 to 1978, became ever more cartoonish. Toward the end there was even a bionic boy and a bionic dog, and Austin, instead of fighting the commies as he originally did, was facing off against Bigfoot. No doubt about it—they pulled the plug just in time. See also ABC's *WIDE WORLD OF SPORTS* (THE GUY ON THE SKI JUMP WIPING OUT DURING THE OPENING CREDITS OF).

SKEE-BALL Invented in 1909—but not hugely popular until the alleys were cut down from 36 feet to 14 feet in length in 1928—Skee-Ball (a variation on bowling where you roll balls up an alley and into score-specific holes) is an arcade staple that, unlike pinball, has maintained its popularity generation after generation. Anyone over the age of seven knows that the value of the prize you get when you cash in your Skee-Ball tickets can't possibly come anywhere near the value of the money you put in. Instead, the attraction is about landing the highest score and the kick of seeing and hearing the tickets spit out of the bottom of the machine. For a select minority, it's also about the ability to cheat by positioning a friend along the side of the last alley so that he can toss the ball into the 50-point hole. See also MIDWAYS and PINBALL.

SKYMALL Many a weary airline traveler has been tempted to make an ill-considered purchase from SkyMall, the colorful catalog full of Home Shopping Network–quality gewgaws that lurks in the passenger compartments of nearly 75 percent of U.S. domestic flights. It seduces its captive audience by offering items that look appealing only after, say, a long pre-takeoff wait at Denver or a six-hour transcontinental flight. Those tired, cranky, slightly airsick flyers suddenly find themselves longing for, say, a

< 248 >

Frolicking Frog Water Fountain ($54.95), Air Massager Headband ($69.95), Pop-up Hot Dog Cooker ($49.95), or an eight-foot-tall resin giraffe ($895 plus $79 shipping). But that's not where the guilt comes in. If you want to actually buy something from SkyMall, you either have to hit a Web page or fill out and mail an order blank located in the back of the book. Which means you have to get off the plane, rest, gather your wits, and then *still* think buying an eight-foot-tall resin giraffe is a good idea. See also HOME SHOPPING NETWORK, THE and QVC.

SLIM-FAST If you have a set of scales in your bathroom, chances are you also have a canister of Slim-Fast in your cupboard. You're not alone. Since its 1977  launch, this powdered meal replacement (later offered in a premixed, liquid form) has gone hand in hand with high school reunions, bathing suit season, wedding dress fittings, and other aesthetically demanding milestones. Expect some sympathetic stares when you hoist a 24-pack of Chocolate Royale out of your cart at the checkout counter.

A diet program that lets you drink milkshakes *and* lose weight sounds a little too good to be true. But at roughly 200 calories and one gram of fat per serving, this gritty chocolate libation has plenty of before-and-after pictures to back up its claims. The trick is to drink Slim-Fast exactly as directed (a shake for breakfast, a shake for lunch, and a sensible meal at dinner). Not as a post-cheeseburger chaser, or as part of an ice cream float. See also BEFORE AND AFTER PHOTOS.

SLOT MACHINES Originally, one-armed bandits were considered a sideshow—something for the girls to play with while their husbands hit the blackjack and craps tables. Today, however, slot machines rake in about two-thirds of all U.S. casino income. Gamblers like them for one pretty obvious reason: When you play the slots, there's no one to see you lose. Go bust at roulette, craps, or any other table game, and you do it in front of an audience. But a machine won't give you so much as a dirty look as you piss away your kids' college fund. See also ATLANTIC CITY; CASINOS; and LAS VEGAS.

SLURPEES This beverage, like youth, is wasted on the young—which is why you see so many adults hurriedly filling huge cups with this semi-frozen concoction. Slurpees got their start in 1959, when the technology for chilling beverages to 28 degrees and turning them into slush was

< 249 >

developed by a Texas company. The 7-Eleven chain bought into the idea in 1965 (at the time the beverages were called Icees), then renamed the product "Slurpees" in 1967 (a play on the sound the ice-filled morass makes when sucked up a straw). Something like a mania followed, with the introduction of commemorative Slurpee cups, a short-lived *Slurp Magazine*, even a dance step called The Slurp. Today some 11 million Slurpees are sold monthly, in flavors such as Memphis Melon, Banana Split, Crystal Light Pineapple Orange, and good old Classic Coke. Sorry, there's still no cure for brain freeze. See also SOFT DRINKS (GIANT PLASTIC CUPS FILLED WITH).

SMITH, ANNA NICOLE If you like your supermodels on the chubby side, here's your gal. Likewise, if you take sick pleasure in watching a gone-to-seed celebrity self-destruct before your eyes, here's your gal. Smith (real name Vickie Lynn Hogan) was born in the small town of Mexia, Texas. In a sense, she never left. Early on she put her zaftig figure to work at a strip club, where she was spotted by a photographer, started modeling, and in 1993 became *Playboy*'s Playmate of the Year. She went on to become a model for Guess? jeans. Then the weirdness started. In 1994 Smith married 89-year-old oil magnate J. Howard Marshall

II. The very next year Marshall died, igniting a huge inheritance fight with his heirs that saw Smith walk away with a cool $450 million—more than enough to pay the court costs from a 1994 sexual harassment suit filed by a female former assistant. Since then she's devoted herself to what seems to have become her life's work: bloating up to the size of a Macy's Thanksgiving Day Parade balloon. This plus-sized Pamela Anderson even allowed the public to watch her decline by doing a reality series on E! Thanks, Anna. The Osbournes were getting a bit dull. See also ANDERSON, PAMELA; MACY'S THANKSGIVING DAY PARADE; *OSBOURNES, THE*; REALITY SHOWS; and STRAWBERRY QUIK.

SMOKEY AND THE BANDIT See REYNOLDS, BURT.

SNICKERS Long before anyone thought of Slim-Fast, this candy bar became the meal replacement of choice for harassed office workers. And why not? Crammed with 14 grams of fat, 35 grams of carbs, and 30 grams of sugar (not to mention 280 calories), it packs enough punch to carry a cubicle drone through even the toughest afternoon. Could its creator, Mars founder Frank C. Mars, have foreseen its utility as a clandestine pick-me-up for grunts when he debuted it in 1930? Perhaps. Why else would he name

< 250 >

it after his family's horse? See also SLIM-FAST.

SOAP OPERA DIGEST For more than 25 years, America's best-selling soap magazine has taken its beat as seriously as *Time* and *Newsweek* take theirs, delivering the goods 52 times a year on *GH*, *GL*, *ATWT*, and *OLTL* (that's *General Hospital, Guiding Light, As the World Turns,* and *One Life to Live,* for those not in the loop). The *Digest*'s cover, always a busy collage of stills arranged around incendiary text, is designed to get readers keyed up before they even crack open the book. "Look Who's Making Love!" and "Psycho Sami Returns!" hint at juicy stuff indeed, but one of the best features of the bantam periodical is its brevity. Anyone who doesn't want to part with $3.50 for a copy can easily skim it from cover to cover while standing in line at the grocery store checkout. See also *DAYS OF OUR LIVES; GENERAL HOSPITAL;* and SOAP OPERAS, DAYTIME.

SOAP OPERAS, DAYTIME In the beginning, soap operas were a solitary addiction. People hooked on the daily melodramas (which were already on the tube as far back as 1946) kept their passion to themselves, eschewing fan clubs, chat rooms, special interest magazines, or any of the other support systems available nowadays. But modern fans seem rather proud to announce that they grew up on *Days of Our Lives,* or that they've taped every episode of *Passions* for the past four years. They're taking their entertainment compulsion out in the open, huddling up at cocktail parties to puzzle over Isabella's mysterious disappearance on *The Young and the Restless,* or to discuss the pros and cons of Sheila's return to *The Bold and the Beautiful.* Let's get something straight, though. Even the genre's staunchest supporters admit that escapism, pure and simple, is the main appeal of Luke and Laura's hollow, overlit world of evil twins, men with eye patches, and happenin' ICUs. Scholars (including a group of University of Dayton academics who analyzed 14 years of daytime serials and found that—can you believe it—soap operas *don't offer a representative view of women's health issues*) can write about their questionable impact on the American psyche until their pens run dry. All they're doing is missing the point: It's only make-believe. See also *DAYS OF OUR LIVES; GENERAL HOSPITAL;* SOAP OPERAS, NIGHTTIME; and *SOAP OPERA DIGEST.*

SOAP OPERAS, NIGHTTIME No matter where our day takes us, evening always brings us back to familiar territory: Dallas, Dawson's Creek, Melrose, Beverly Hills. At these hip locales, the

< 251 >

cool people don't mind us staring at them while we slouch around in sweatpants, eating peanut M&M's from a one-pound bag. Nighttime soap operas (a genre pioneered by *Peyton Place* in the '60s and perfected by *Dallas* in the '80s) provide an alternate reality, an exciting real-time world that runs parallel to our own—until reruns start. All the rules of addiction apply to the compulsive watching of shows like *Beverly Hills 90210*, *7th Heaven*, *Falcon Crest*, *Dynasty*, and *Dallas*. You know you have it bad when you still care about the characters' lives long after they cease to bear any resemblance even to a plasticized version of reality. Why else would we have obsessively watched Fox's *Melrose Place* for seven seasons, even when the plot grew so thin that Kimberly finally simply blew up the apartment complex where they all lived? Maybe because it's always sad to see friends—even annoying and sometimes evil friends—go away. However, as long as Aaron Spelling has a wallet and Heather Locklear has a SAG card, nighttime soaps can keep on churning out the suds. See also *SOAP OPERA DIGEST*; SOAP OPERAS, DAYTIME; and SWEATPANTS.

SOFT DRINKS (GIANT PLASTIC CUPS FILLED WITH) The loathsome trend of "super sizing" food portions is at its most grotesque and shameful when applied to beverages. These days most convenience stores offer a half-gallon-sized (64-ounce) plastic cup into which patrons can pour an entire day's supply (or what, in a sane world, *should* serve as a day's supply) of their favorite soft drink. If the beverage of choice happens to be sweetened with sugar, that's about 620 calories in one Double Gulp (the 7-Eleven chain's term for the product). Yet we happily go for the big drum, knowing that for, say, an extra quarter, we can nearly double the size of our drink. About the only brake on the growth of these cups seems to be the relatively small size of car drink holders, most of which only accommodate more sanely proportioned receptacles. To get around this problem, cup makers pinch the bases of even their most gigantic vessels to holder-friendly dimensions.

SOFT SERVE ICE CREAM See DAIRY QUEEN.

SOLITAIRE Despite the fact that Napoleon Bonaparte, Franklin Roosevelt, and Leo Tolstoy all played it, solitaire is still a red flag to the rest of the world that you have too much time on your hands. Dating back to the 16th century, this game (and its countless variations) seems important only when you're in the middle of it. Afterward comes the inevitable "What was I thinking?" guilt.

< 252 >

SORRY! Whether you're playing against your 8-year-old niece or your 80-year-old grandfather (either of whom can learn the game in minutes), you still feel a perverse sense of pleasure when you pull a Sorry! card and send your opponent back to start. Created in 1934, this Parcheesi-esque board game requires a lot of luck, a bit of strategy, and a take-no-prisoners attitude. No wonder it was famously used in a particularly vicious "Mama's Family" segment of *The Carol Burnett Show*.

SOUL TRAIN Basically an R&B-fueled version of *American Bandstand*, *Soul Train* was big with black kids, and even bigger with white kids. Begun in 1970 by Chicago deejay Don Cornelius, it soon won national syn-dication by offering hot tunes, hot dancing (courtesy of the Soul Train Gang), and hot fashions. But perhaps most importantly, it provided a peek at the funked-up urban scene to the pasty denizens of Wonder Bread Land. Who cared if most of its white viewers would have died of fright rather than shake their junk on the Wacky Line? They could dance in the privacy of their parents' shag-carpeted living rooms and pretend that they, too, were fly. Today, even though Don Cornelius, who hosted for 27 years, has given up his on-air duties, *Soul Train* chugs on—albeit without the Afro-Sheen commercials. See also *AMERICAN BANDSTAND* and WONDER BREAD.

SOUND OF MUSIC, THE Its songs are so familiar they're almost as ubiquitous as "Happy Birthday." The image of Julie Andrews spinning around atop an Austrian mountain is as famous as Dorothy skipping down the Yellow Brick Road. But while cynics may call it "The Sound of Mucus" and mock its wholesomeness, you can bet they've sat through Rodgers and Hammerstein's syrupy musical masterpiece at least once—and probably more than once. So it should come as no surprise that the highly fictionalized story of how the Von Trapp family sang and danced its way out of Nazi-held Austria became the subject of a campy, *Rocky Horror*–like sing-along. Audience members not only wore habits, but also dressed as such "characters" as Ray, a Drop of Golden Sun, and Lonely Goatherds. See also NUNS (MEDIA REPRESENTATIONS OF), and *ROCKY HORROR PICTURE SHOW, THE*.

SOUTH PARK Everything about this Comedy Central cartoon is crude, from the language to the animation. Yet you've got to admire the Horatio Alger–like pluck of its creators, former University

< 253 >

of Colorado film students Matt Stone and Trey Parker. Their saga began when they created a holiday cartoon called *Jesus vs. Frosty*, in which a homicidal snowman battled the Savior, who eventually cut the snowman's head off by throwing his halo at him. This novel take on the holiday season caught the attention of executives at the Fox network (what a surprise), who commissioned Stone and Parker to create a video Christmas card called *The Spirit of Christmas* (in which Jesus battles Santa Claus). The video made it onto the Internet, and the duo soon had a deal to do a cartoon series, which became *South Park*. A masterpiece of raunchy humor that mines everything from Presbyterianism to pedophilia for laughs, it once featured the voice of George Clooney (who was instrumental in getting the duo noticed) as a gay dog.

SPAGHETTIOS Jimmie Rodgers sang a bunch of 1950s hits like "Kisses Sweeter Than Wine" and "Honeycomb." But his best-known lyric may be the one he convinced Campbell's executives to add to their commercial for canned pasta in 1965. That line, "uh-oh, SpaghettiOs," coupled with spokesperson Oscar Robertson's "the neat round spaghetti you can eat with a spoon," helped make this brand a kid favorite and a can't-think-of-anything-else-to-eat dinner choice for harried parents. They're surprisingly low in fat, surprisingly high in protein, and, not surprisingly, through the roof in sodium content.

SPAM Who among us hasn't eaten this dish while wondering, darkly, just what it might contain? Invented in 1937 (it was originally called Hormel Spiced Ham, but the name was shortened to Spam), it's been the meat of last resort for everyone from soldiers (Soviet leader Nikita Khrushchev said it kept Russian troops from starving during World War II) to hungry stoners searching for something to stop the munchies. So far, more than 5 billion cans have been sold. What's in it? Even the official Spam Web page leaves room for speculation. "Pork shoulder and ham, mostly," it says. And what exactly does "mostly" mean? Best not to think about it. See also SAUSAGE; VELVEETA; and VIENNA SAUSAGE.

SPEARS, BRITNEY (VIDEOS FEATURING) No adult has any excuse for voluntarily listening to this borderline jailbait's music. But men should be forgiven—*have* to be forgiven—for staring transfixed at such music videos as "Oops! . . . I Did It Again" and " . . . Baby One More Time." Think of it as pining for lost youth. Or, perhaps, a certain unobtainable youth. See also MUSIC VIDEOS and OLSEN TWINS, THE.

< 254 >

SPECTRAVISION Available in close to 1 million hotel rooms, Spectravision supplies lonely travelers with first-run movies, video games, and Internet access. It also supplies *really* lonely travelers with porn. We'll never know how many dreary business trips have been enlivened by a quick look at the NC-17 antics on this cable service, owned by Liberty Media (the parent company of the shopping network QVC). By the way, in case you're worried about your comptroller looking at you funny when you hand in your travel receipts, the title of the film you watch doesn't appear on your hotel tab. Which means that as far as the rest of the world is concerned, you could have been watching *Divine Secrets of the Ya-Ya Sisterhood*. See also CINEMAX; MOVIES (PORNOGRAPHIC); and QVC.

SPEED RACER Japanese animation has produced many interesting, thought-provoking, and downright cool programs. *Speed Racer* isn't one of them. Available in syndication throughout the United States, this 1960s "classic" followed the exploits of a teenage driver with the improbable moniker of Speed Racer (given his name, his career choice was probably predestined). He and his car, the Mach 5, followed a racing circuit that seemed like a mix between Formula One and *Death Race 2000*. The Mach 5 featured all sorts of *Knight Rider*–like extras (buzz saws to cut down approaching trees, special jacks to help it jump, etc.) that came in handy when, inevitably, some villain tried to win by foul play.

The most interesting thing about the Japanese-to-English version was that Speed and all the other characters (including car designer Pops Racer, annoying little brother Spridal, and a monkey named Chim Chim) spoke with breathtaking rapidity, as if they'd had one too many triple lattes. Add to that the superabundance of violent, extreme hand gestures and you'd be forgiven for thinking this was a piece of Italian, rather than Japanese, animation. Watching just one frenetic episode could leave kids longing for naps. See also *DEATH RACE 2000* and JAPANESE ANIMATION (ADULT).

SPELLING, AARON It's not the man himself who we guiltily care about. It's the creations that bear his name (usually as some sort of producer). A short list: *The Mod Squad*, *The Rookies*, *Satan's School for Girls*, *S.W.A.T.*, *Starsky and Hutch*, and *Family*. Pretty impressive—in a cheesy way—so far? Well, we've just grazed 1976, when Spelling was beginning to hit his stride. His glory days included *Charlie's Angels*, *The Boy in the Plastic Bubble*, *The Love Boat*,

< 255 >

Fantasy Island, *Friends* (sorry, not that *Friends*, this is the one that lasted five episodes in 1979), *Hart to Hart*, *Dynasty*, *T.J. Hooker*, *Glitter*, *Beverly Hills 90210*, *Melrose Place*, and *7th Heaven*. Without him, this book might not exist. See also BEVERLY HILLS 90210; BOY IN THE PLASTIC BUBBLE, THE; CHARLIE'S ANGELS; DYNASTY; FANTASY ISLAND; LOVE BOAT, THE; and SPELLING, TORI.

SPELLING, TORI We knew she got her *Beverly Hills 90210* gig because her dad, Aaron, was the producer. We knew after watching a few episodes that she couldn't act to save her pampered life. But we watched, and we inexplicably cared about what the show's writers had in store for her character, Donna Martin. And we knew—

don't ask how, we just knew—that Shannen and Jason and Luke and even Gabrielle would leave the show at some point but that Tori would endure to the end. And we were right. After all, where else did she have to go? See also *BEVERLY HILLS 90210* and SPELLING, AARON.

SPENCER GIFTS For a while, your local mall's Spencer Gifts seemed like the only place to pick up a lava lamp, the drinking game Passout, or an inflatable Edvard Munch *The Scream* dude. Ready to jump on any slightly irreverent bandwagon that comes America's way (witness the recent emphasis on Austin Powers and SpongeBob merchandise), Spencer Gifts is still *the* place to sneak to when your companion is spending too much time trying on shoes in another store. See also LAVA LAMPS and MARIJUANA.

***SPORTS ILLUSTRATED* SWIMSUIT ISSUE, THE** No one batted an eye back in 1964 when, for no particular reason, unknown model Babette March, wearing a white bikini, graced *Sports Illustrated*'s January 20 cover. What red-blooded subscriber wouldn't like looking at chicks, even if it seemed slightly out of place in a sports rag? But though we've allegedly had our consciousness raised since then, this particular cultural icon just keeps hanging around.

Occasionally the magazine's management has offered hilarious arguments "justifying" its place in the editorial mix. The real justification is that *SI*'s babe issue is a huge moneymaker, inspiring spin-off videos, calendars, and even trading cards. Before *Maxim*, this was the premier venue to see famous women (Christie Brinkley, Cindy Crawford) with almost all their clothes off. Today it seems almost quaint. Photographers, out

< 256 >

at the beach for the umpteenth time, shoot "new" poses that look almost identical to previous years: standing in thigh-high water at sundown; reclining on sand; top off, back to camera; etc. Yet every year American men line up to buy it—though occasionally hidden behind a copy of *Newsweek*. See also *MAXIM*; *PLAYBOY*; and SUPERMODELS.

SPRING BREAK Like a bachelor party without a wedding to worry about the next day, spring break is an "I won't tell if you won't tell" event where one's character is tested . . . usually to the breaking point. Of course this doesn't matter if, the following morning, you don't remember what (or who) you did. Built around college vacations and the schedules of *Girls Gone Wild* cameramen, spring break is seen by many to be a rite of passage much like the Aborigine's walkabout, only with a bigger bar tab. See also *GIRLS GONE WILD* and WET T-SHIRT COMPETITIONS.

SPRINGER, JERRY He was a campaign aid to Robert Kennedy and mayor of a major U.S. city (okay, so it was only Cincinnati). But his day of infamy arrived when his issues-oriented talkfest *The Jerry Springer Show*, on the brink of cancellation, was re-imagined by a new producer hired from the *Weekly World News*. The result: Jerrymania. These

days staffers troll the trailer parks to bring us such programs as "My Boyfriend Is a Girl," "My Brother Is My Lover," and "Brawlin' Broads" (all offered in the same week), followed by Springer's too little, too late moralizing at the end. It's no surprise that Springer became daytime's No. 1 show. His parade of white trash panelists makes the folks on *COPS* seem functional. See also *COPS* and *WEEKLY WORLD NEWS*.

SPRINKLES Apply a coat of this chocolate or multicolored candy topping to your otherwise standard ice cream treat and it feels like you've become a kid again. Some say they're the creation of a Russian immigrant named Sam Born—the same guy who developed a machine to attach sticks to lollipops (he's also the founder of Just Born Candy, the company that brings you marshmallow Peeps). Others contend that sprinkles go back at least to the early 19th century. For the record, "jimmies," a common synonym for sprinkles, is a trademarked term for a specific brand. See also PEEPS.

STALLONE, SYLVESTER It just isn't cool to say you love the Italian Stallion. It's okay to enjoy Rocky or even Rambo, but not the man who brought both characters to life. Why? Maybe it's because the Manhattan-born hard body has made so many questionable cinematic decisions,

< 257 >

including starring in some of the goofiest bombs ever committed to celluloid. His personal Hall of Shame includes *Rhinestone* (in which Sly plays a country music singer), *Cobra* (one of the most over-the-top vigilante movies ever made), and *Stop! Or My Mom Will Shoot* (which won Stallone the 1992 Golden Raspberry Award for Worst Actor). And yet, the man still gets leading roles—perhaps on the forlorn hope that this proven heavy hitter will one day smack another one over the fence. If he does, then perhaps we'll even forgive him for *Staying Alive*, the nearly-impossible-to-watch sequel to *Saturday Night Fever*, which Stallone not only wrote but directed. See also BOMBS (BIG-BUDGET MOVIES THAT TURN OUT TO BE); RAMBO MOVIES; ROCKY MOVIES; and *SATURDAY NIGHT FEVER*.

STAR SEARCH A spiritual descendant of Ted Mack's *Original Amateur Hour* (a televised talent show that hooked audiences from 1948 to 1970), *Star Search* proved a syndicated success from the mid-'80s to the mid-'90s. In the categories of comedy, music (solo and group), dance, and, to much at-home mockery, spokesmodel (read: attractive person with no real talent), the show pitted unknowns against one another for prizes and potential fame. The word "unknown," of course, is time sensitive.

Looking back, the amateurs now seem like an all-star cast. They included Justin Timberlake, Rosie O'Donnell, Drew Carey, Britney Spears, LeAnn Rimes, Ray Romano, Christina Aguilera, Alanis Morissette, Martin Lawrence, and Dennis Miller. Kids today would more likely say "Who's he?" about host Ed McMahon. The pleasure (which translates with varying degrees of success onto more recent shows such as *American Idol*, *Last Comic Standing*, and the revived *Star Search*) comes from trying to figure who has real star potential—and then making fun of those who don't. See also SPEARS, BRITNEY (VIDEOS FEATURING).

STAR TREK In this age of big-budget science-fiction productions, it's hard to remember why so many kids (and so many nerds) found the old *Star Trek* television series interesting. The special effects were only marginally better than those in Flash Gordon serials. But it did have one important advantage. The program actually took science fiction sort of seriously. Instead of  rolling around the galaxy blowing up planets, Kirk, Spock, and the rest of the crew philosophized about racial intolerance, war, and pretty much every other

< 258 >

1960s hot button issue. There was even Nichelle Nichols, a black woman, as part of the bridge crew. She was just a glorified switchboard operator, but she was *there*.

After its undistinguished, low-rated three-year run, the show vanished from network TV. But when the original 79 episodes aired in syndication, something unprecedented happened. Ratings soared. Fans started gathering to hold conventions. And *Star Trek* became The Show That Wouldn't Die. Today, after four follow-on series, almost a dozen big-screen films, and numberless other commercial tie-ins, it's The Media Franchise That Wouldn't Die. Which still doesn't mean you can wear your Star Trek tunic to the company picnic. See also SHATNER, WILLIAM.

STAR TREK CONVENTIONS The first *Star Trek* conventions were a pre-Internet way to connect with a few hundred people sharing a similar passion. Of course, the fact that those people often dressed as Klingons, Andorians, and Romulans—and were willing to buy William Shatner's albums—caused many a raised eyebrow among folks who didn't know the difference between Mr. Spock and Dr. Spock. Still, as the *Trek* franchise expanded to movies and spin-off series, the conventions grew exponentially. What was once a small cult became so familiar to the masses that the convention world could be satirized on *Saturday Night Live*, gently mocked at the movies in *Galaxy Quest*, and even subjected to documentary treatment in *Trekkies*. As far as conventioneers are concerned, the masses can go ahead and mock. *Star Trek* conventions remain a place where one can, if properly costumed, partake of a world where all creatures are respected regardless of race, creed, color (even if it's blue or green), species, or whether they've ever been on a real date. See also SHATNER, WILLIAM and *STAR TREK*.

STAR WARS For many adolescents who came of age in the *Star Wars* era, their most potent memory (next to their first sexual encounter or, in the case of hardcore fans, *in lieu* of a first sexual encounter) is seeing the words, "A long time ago in a galaxy far, far away . . . " scroll across a darkened screen, followed by Wagnerian music and a monstrous, thundering starship.

Why did this 1977 space opera come out of nowhere to become one of the biggest films of all time? Perhaps because its creator, George Lucas, thought so carefully about the plot. He'd studied the works of scholar Joseph Campbell, who believed certain myths, and mythic types, are universal throughout human history. Figuring that anything that

< 259 >

could hold the attention of neolithic cave dwellers would also appeal to 20th-century moviegoers, Lucas tried to insert as many archetypes as possible into his film. There was the Lovable Rogue (Han Solo); the Reluc-tant Hero (Luke Skywalker); the Princess in Distress (cinnamon-bun-coifed Leia); and many more. So there's lots more going on than meets the eye (as any hard-core fan will explain, usually at great length, unless you tell him to go play with his lightsaber and leave you alone).

Which leads to a delicate question many an aficionado has faced. Are you just a *Star Wars* fan or a *Star Wars* geek? Here's how to find out: If you know what a Wookie is, you're okay. But if you know what a Bantha is, you've got a problem.

STARS' HOMES With all due respect to Robin Leach, the real reason why we can't get enough of lifestyle programs like MTV's *Cribs*, E! *Celebrity Homes*, and *Famous Homes & Hideaways* has nothing to do with "champagne wishes and caviar dreams." No, what we really want is a glimpse at stardom's dark, embarrassing "ugly-tile work wishes and shoddy-crown-molding dreams." Doritos crumbs on the sofa. Tennis shoes piled in a walk-in closet. PlayStations in the formal living room. Now *that's* good stuff.

You can ooh and ah all you want over John Leguizamo's tasteful mid-century modern digs, but be honest enough to admit that it is the interior design train wrecks—the B2K Denim Rooms, the Mariah Carey hot tubs—that keep you glued to the set, hungry for more, more, more. After all, MTV's hit *The Osbournes* was only supposed to be an episode of *Cribs*. See also *INSTYLE* MAGAZINE and *OSBOURNES, THE*.

STATE FAIR FOOD There are certain places where the laws of dietary sanity don't apply. Places like the ballpark (you've *got* to have a hot dog because it's part of the experience), and the New Year's Eve party (of *course* you drink a little too much). But that culinary anarchy reaches its zenith at state fairs. In this universe of funnel cakes, pork chop sandwiches, smoked turkey legs, elephant ears, and foot-long corn dogs, Jenny Craig takes a holiday. Carnival concessionaires seem well aware of this fact and have pushed the envelope by offering ever more outlandish abominations, including the battered, deep-fried Twinkie (about 425 calories each) and the battered, deep-fried candy bar. What's next, batter-dipped Vienna sausage poppers? See also HOTDOGS (STADIUM); MEAT ON A STICK; MONTE CRISTO SANDWICH, THE; and VIENNA SAUSAGE.

< 260 >

STEAK SAUCE (A1) For more than 140 years, A1 has been the douse of choice for disguising the taste of tough T-bones and funky filets. Its marketing company, Kraft Foods, says the recipe goes back to Henderson William Brand, chef to King George IV during the 1820s. Would you use it at a high-end steakhouse? Only if you were out of town on a business trip without a colleague in sight. See also GRAVY.

STEEL MAGNOLIAS See CHICK FLICKS (IN WHICH SOMEONE DIES).

STERN, HOWARD If so many people hate Howard Stern and his morning radio show, how come he's been so popular for so long? And how come so many people have found themselves late for work because they were sitting in their cars listening to the self-proclaimed "King of All Media" interview a stripper, a homeless man, an irate dwarf, or Alec Baldwin? His rise to fame is a story told in both his best-selling book *Private Parts* and in the very well-received self-starring film that followed. You could argue that he jumped the shark and lost his charm when he and his wife divorced. You could argue that his antics aren't as original as he seems to believe they are. But, as irate callers and uncomfortable guests have learned, you can't win an argument with Howard. See also SHOCK JOCKS.

STEVE & EYDIE They're not quite hip enough for the Rat Pack, and not quite smarmy enough for Robert Goulet–level mockery. But that hasn't stopped Steve Lawrence and Eydie Gorme from doing their thing for more than 40 years, ever since they met as guests on Steve Allen's original *Tonight* show. What exactly is that thing? Imagine the most effortless lounge singers you've ever seen and you're in the ballpark. Better known as one of those rare long-lasting entertainment industry couples than for the virtues of any particular song, the pair recently retired from touring. Somewhere, a theater-in-the-round talent booker weeps. See also GOULET, ROBERT.

STEWART, MARTHA America's doyenne of home decor was a target for wisecracks long before she got in trouble with the law. Since then, however, making fun of her near-obsessive (actually, there's nothing "near" about it) devotion to The Good Life has grown from a cottage industry into large-scale manufacturing, including a warts-and-all 2003 TV movie *Martha Inc.* The truth, however, is that lots of people still respect this woman's cooking skills and design acumen, even if they would just as soon ignore her stock tips. So go ahead and make fun of Martha when you're with your friends, because when it's time to make that special canapé for your next

< 261 >

cocktail party, faux finish an end table, or pull off the perfect wedding reception, everyone knows who you'll turn to. See also HELOISE and TV MOVIES.

STRAWBERRY QUIK Introduced in the United States in 1948, Nestlé Quik (now Nestlé Nesquik) was the first powdered chocolate milk. We didn't really care— after all, chocolate milk is chocolate milk—until Nestlé introduced Strawberry Quik. Maybe it was the fact that Quik's mascot rabbit looked even more bizarre when it was turned pink to push the new product. Or that, in a pinch, Strawberry Quik served, milkless, as a substitute for Pixy Stix. Whatever the case, there's a reason why Anna Nicole Smith called Strawberry Quik her favorite beverage. See also CARNATION INSTANT BREAKFAST; PIXY STIX; and SMITH, ANNA NICOLE.

STREISAND, BARBRA (AS ACTRESS) In order to watch a Barbra Streisand movie, you must enter into a make-believe world where EVERYTHING IS ALL ABOUT BABS. That's true for her Hollywood debut, 1968's *Funny Girl*, true for her latest work, 1996's *The Mirror Has Two Faces*, and also true for everything in between. What closeted Streisand fans (both gay and straight) understand is that it's just that me-me-me egomania that makes her so compellingly watchable.

After all, who really cares about costars Mandy Patinkin, George Segal, Kris Kristofferson, and Ryan O'Neal, et al.? Even the worst of her films (*The Main Event? A Star Is Born? Nuts?*) are bizarrely compelling—like viewing news footage of Latin American dictators surrounded by terrified commoners. And you can't beat the guilty pleasure of watching a 40-ish Streisand playing a young girl trying to pass herself off as a young boy in *Yentl*. Need ego evidence? In that 1983 musical, producer/director Streisand allows no one in the cast other than herself to sing. See also STREISAND, BARBRA (AS SINGER).

STREISAND, BARBRA (AS SINGER) Selling a phenomenal number of albums, charting a phenomenal number of hit singles, charging phenomenal prices for her phenomenally rare concerts, and pissing off a phenomenal number of conservatives, Barbra Streisand has been an entertainment force for four decades. With an appeal initially derived from her unattractive-girl-who-rises-to-the-top-on-chutzpah persona (and amazing voice), Streisand became a gay icon—which is one of the reasons why straight men are hesitant to call themselves fans. And

< 262 >

even if the discs within them are winners, there's also the embarrassing album cover factor. Just try deciding which is more dorky, the picture of Babs on *Streisand Superman* or the one on Barry Gibb–era *Guilty*. See also STREISAND, BARBRA (AS ACTRESS).

STRIP CLUBS The lights are dim at strip clubs for the same reason red pistachios are red—to hide blemishes and imperfections. It's equally good camouflage for customers who don't want to be seen by friends and neighbors. (Though being spotted isn't necessarily a disaster, because the standard reply to a self-righteous "What are you doing here?" is an even louder "What are *you* doing here?") In recent years these "gentlemen's clubs" have worked valiantly to shake this stigma by positioning themselves as classy places for adult entertainment. Dream on. The day polite society accepts ogling naked women in a bar is the same day regul ar folk start referring to pole-straddlers as "dancers." See also PISTACHIOS (RED); *SHOWGIRLS*; and SMITH, ANNA NICOLE.

STUCKEY'S For generations of family vacationers, this odd gift shop/gas station/souvenir stand hybrid was a welcome roadside oasis after a day trapped in the backseat of Dad's station wagon. The first store, which opened in 1937 in Eastman, Georgia, made its reputation by selling pecans and pecan candies, including the company's soon-to-be-signature item, the pecan log. By 1964 there were more than 100 blue-roofed locations nationwide, and by the '70s some 375. This was the place to go for "To Hell with Psychology" cedar paddles, Indian war bonnets, states of the Union shot glasses, and, of course, pecan logs. While time has passed—and the glory of Stuckey's is somewhat faded—you'll be happy to know that all of the above gadgets are still on sale. In fact, they're probably the very same ones (with the possible exception of the pecan logs) that were languishing there when you last passed through. See also PECAN LOGS.

STUNTS (INSANE, TELEVISED) In 1974, when stunt king Evel Knievel tried to jump Idaho's Snake River Canyon in a rocket-powered motorcycle, television viewers were transfixed. But that bit of insanity was just a hint of the craziness to come. Over the last quarter century, we've been privy to a parade of *World's Most Dangerous Stunts* specials, David Blaine encasing himself in a block of ice, and even Knievel's own son, Robbie, jumping a motorcycle from the roof of one Las Vegas hotel tower to another. But perhaps the most interesting development has been the entry of the

< 263 >

common man into the world of loony stunts. Whereas playing dice with death was once the stuff of pay-per-view specials, now we can watch people just like us on *Fear Factor* lying in pits of snakes, eating animal penises, and collecting dead skunks from pitch-black tunnels. See also *JACKASS*; *KNIEVEL, EVEL*; and MORONS (ENTERTAINING, UNTIMELY DEATHS OF).

STYX In the land of elaborately produced, pushing-back-the-frontiers-of-musical-pretension stadium rock bands, Styx knew no peer. From early hits such as "Lady" through their late '70s peak with such pop stalwarts as "Come Sail Away" and "Babe," through the high-concept *Paradise Theater* disc to the what-the-hell-were-they-thinking world of "Mr. Roboto," Styx not only kept audiences entertained (or at least, mystified), it also provided enough backstage battles to make it the subject of one of the more entertaining editions of VH1's *Behind the Music*. Lead singer Dennis DeYoung later released an album of Broadway show tunes. God help us all. See also VH1's *BEHIND THE MUSIC*.

SUGAR (EXCESSIVE APPLICATION TO FOOD OF) See BIG RED; BUBBLE YUM; CAP'N CRUNCH; CHARMS BLOW POPS; CINNABON; COTTON CANDY; DILLY BARS; DUNKIN' DONUTS; FANNIE MAY CANDIES; GARCIA, CHERRY; GIRL SCOUT COOKIES; JELL-O; KOOL-AID; KRISPY KREME DOUGHNUTS; LITTLE DEBBIE SNACKS; LUDEN'S WILD CHERRY COUGH DROPS; MARASCHINO CHERRIES; MARSHMALLOWS (BREAKFAST CEREALS FEATURING); MONSTER CEREALS; MOUNTAIN DEW; NUTTER BUTTER COOKIES; PECAN LOGS; PEZ; PIXY STIX; POP-TARTS; PUDDING CUPS; RAZZLES; RICE KRISPIES TREATS; SLURPEES; SNICKERS; SOFT DRINKS (GIANT PLASTIC CUPS FILLED WITH); SOFT SERVE ICE CREAM; SPRINKLES; STRAWBERRY QUIK; TAHITIAN TREAT; TOOTSIE POPS; TWINKIES; and YOO-HOO.

SUMMER, DONNA In the private sanctum of many a car stereo system, the former Ladonna Gaines still reigns as the queen of disco—even though it's been a couple of decades since her prime (1975's "Love to Love You Baby," consisting of an infectious beat melded with Summer's orgasmic moans, followed  in 1978–79 by four No. 1 hits, including "MacArthur Park" and the roller rink standard "Hot Stuff"). Around 1980 Summer became a born-again Christian, which put a damper on her club credibility, to say the least. Still, even now, the first notes of "Bad Girls" can send a horde of unrepentant fans

< 264 >

stampeding toward the dance floor. Disco may be dead, but Summer never ends. See also DISCO (DANCING) and DISCO (FASHIONS).

SUMMER OF '42, THE See GUYS LOSING THEIR VIRGINITY (MOVIES ABOUT).

SUPER BOWL, THE Often the only thing "super" about this game is the name. As history has proven, the matchup on the field usually begins with a tense, error-prone first quarter. After that, one of the teams cracks under the pressure of playing in front of the entire straight male population of the United States and gets run out of the stadium. Of course none of this stops the aforementioned entire straight male population of the United States from tuning in each January, or from depleting every supermarket snack aisle in North America in preparation for the festivities—the better to lay down a new coat of salsa and beer stains on the rec room couch. Oh well, at least the commercials are entertaining. See also SUPER BOWL COMMERCIALS.

SUPER BOWL COMMERCIALS More than a few "football fans" have tuned into this biggest of all games not to see the contest for the NFL title, but to watch international corporations vie for their money. When it comes to launching attention-grabbing ad campaigns, the Super Bowl, with a viewership of around 90 million, is the venue of choice. But it's only the venue of choice if you can afford to drop around $2 million for a 30-second spot. Thank God someone does. Considering that most Super Bowls are uninteresting routs, one can be excused for looking forward not to the next big play, but to the next Nike spot. See also SUPER BOWL, THE.

SUPERHEROES When superhero comics debuted in the mid-'30s (the very first was *The Phantom* in 1936, followed in 1938 by *Superman*, who premiered in *Action Comics* No. 1), they tapped into something powerful and primal in the human psyche. For whatever reason, drawings of men in brightly colored skintight outfits and flamboyant capes who wore their underwear over their clothes became incredibly popular. So popular that the biggest names from the early days of DC Comics—Batman, Green Lantern, Wonder Woman (who started out as *secretary* for the Justice Society of America), and the aforementioned Superman—all became part of America's culture. Of course the dirty little secret of these books is that they've always been as big with adults as kids. The grown-ups have even turned vintage books into hot investment items. The original Spider-Man comic, valued at just a few hundred dollars a couple of

< 265 >

decades ago, is now approaching $100,000 in price. See also BATMAN (THE TV SHOW).

SUPERMARKET SWEEP Contestants on this heart-pounding test of shopping proficiency can walk away with a couple thousand dollars if they play their carts right. Even so, the term "game show" only loosely applies to this PAX network no-brainer in which frenzied shoppers crash their way through a grocery store, filling their baskets with all the turkeys, disposable diapers, and loaves of pumpernickel that the laws of physics will allow. Strip away the mystery envelopes, rhyming couplet clues, and all the blinking studio gewgaws, and the show (which ran on ABC and Lifetime in various incarnations from 1965 to 1990) is nothing more than physical comedy at its finest, as excitable contestants dressed in matching sweatshirts scramble down the aisles in goofy desperation, oversized packs of Wrigley's spearmint gum tucked under their arms. Factor in host David Ruprecht, looking exactly like a grocery store clerk in his rolled-sleeve ensembles, and you have a TV gem as deliciously cheesy as those giant rounds of Gruyère in the deli section. See also LIFETIME and PRICE IS RIGHT, THE.

SUPERMODELS There's no clinical def - inition for what separates a supermodel from a plain old ordinary run-of-the-run-way model. But like court definitions of pornography, you know a supermodel when you see one. She's the one named Cindy or Claudia or Kate. She's the one who sells magazines just by appearing on the cover and who stretches reporters' skills to the breaking point by forcing them to have to write stories about her. While a handful of these glorified coat hangers had previously burst into the national consciousness (e.g., Twiggy), the era of the supermodel essentially lasted through the '80s to the late '90s, roughly from the point where we started saying "Hey, that's Cheryl Tiegs" to the point when *Vogue* labeled a Naomi Campbell story "The Last Supermodel." See also MASTURBATION; SPORTS ILLUSTRATED SWIMSUIT ISSUE, THE; and VICTORIA'S SECRET CATALOGS.

SUPER SOAKERS Does it come as a surprise that the man who invented the Super Soaker water gun worked at the Jet Propulsion Laboratory? An engineer on the Galileo Jupiter mission, Lonnie Johnson started tinkering in 1982 but didn't launch his creation, first dubbed the Pneumatic Water Gun, until 1989. Its hand-pumped, high-pressure water delivery system revolutionized the squirt gun industry, with recent versions able to shoot a stream of water 40 feet. Sure they're designed for kids, but much pleasure has also been had by adults retal-

< 266 >

iating against a rugrat onslaught or exercising a preemptive strike on a battalion of unsuspecting preteens. Plus, it's more dignified than running through a sprinkler.

SURGERIES (TELEVISED) You could watch some cutup on Comedy Central, or you could click over to the Learning Channel or PBS and actually watch someone get cut up. Thanks to the magic of patients and their families signing waivers, voyeuristic viewers can now tune in for a doctor's-eye view of an open head, a peeled-back face, or the delicate details of a nose job. The appeal is difficult to explain to someone not of the surgery-enjoying persuasion. Yet watching doctors do what they do under life-and-death (except for the nose job) circumstances can be more compelling than the real-life-ish activities of *ER* or lesser medical dramas. Like watching *COPS* or *Court TV*, it's a chance to actually see why these professionals make the big bucks (except for cops). However, it's lousy dinner hour viewing. See also AUTOPSIES (TELEVISION).

SUSANN, JACQUELINE Back in the 1960s Susann was to trashy novels what P. T. Barnum was to circuses. She singlehandedly created the market for thick paperbacks filled with celebrities, millionaires, family strife, and, of course, sex, sex, sex. Interestingly, her first work contained few of these elements, though the protagonist was a bitch. The volume that made her a household name was 1963's *Every Night, Josephine!*, a nonfiction account of life with her poodle. Susann, a former starlet and master promoter, toured relentlessly to push it. Her husband, former press agent Irving Mansfield, was even more aggressive. When he and his wife visited the former home of *Gone With the Wind* author Margaret Mitchell, who had been killed in an automobile accident just outside, he advised Susann to run into traffic and get hit by a car, too.

Her second book was her real tour de force. *Valley of the Dolls* told the story of three vaguely disguised starlets trying to make it in Hollywood and having plenty of sex and drugs along the way. It spent more than 20 weeks at No. 1 on the *New York Times* best-seller list and (according to most sources) remains the top-selling novel of all time.

Other formulaic, R-rated blockbusters followed until Susann's death in 1974. Her fame proved as fleeting as the careers of the starlets she wrote about. But though her books are ancient history, a flock of Susann wannabes, from Jackie Collins to Judith Krantz, pay her homage with every second-rate potboiler doorstop they author. See also CARTLAND, BARBARA; COLLINS, JACKIE; and KRANTZ, JUDITH.

< 267 >

SUVs In 1983 AMC General debuted a new, improved Jeep Cherokee—the first true sport utility vehicle, or SUV. That same year the Chevy S-10 Blazer hit the market, changing the face of conspicuous automotive consumption.

By 2002, roughly 50 percent of the vehicles on America's highways were either SUVs or trucks. Some 4 million were sold in that year alone, with every car company worth its hood ornament (including Lexus, Porsche, Cadillac, and Saturn) offering at least one. Why are they so favored? It isn't for their gas mileage. The Natural Resources Defense Council asserts that the U.S. uses 5 billion more gallons of gas yearly than if the balance of cars to trucks were the same as in pre-SUV 1975. And it isn't for their off-road capabilities. Only about 5 percent of SUV drivers ever take their massive rigs off the pavement.

It's about status, pure and simple. For their money, SUV drivers get to command a 3,000-pound hunk of metal that gives them the same view of the highway semi drivers enjoy. And of course there's the bully factor. Rare is the sedan driver who hasn't been cut off by a gigantic SUV piloted by a tiny woman talking on an even tinier cell phone.

It's not surprising, therefore, that some drivers purchase SUVs not just for status, but for self-defense. Yet fatality rates for the big rigs aren't all that different from those of conventional cars—in part because SUV drivers killed in fatal accidents often didn't bother to buckle up. They should have remembered that driving an off-road vehicle only makes you *feel* invulnerable. See also HUMMER, THE.

SWAGGERT, JIMMY (AMUSING SEXUAL ANTICS OF) See TELEVANGELISTS.

SWEATPANTS It is a testament to the staying power of cotton blend fabric and stretchy waistbands that sweatpants have managed to survive several public relations nightmares, ranging from a general association with obesity (Russell Athletic, a leading manufacturer of heather gray slouchwear, offers sizing up to 4XL) to an out-and-out mockery on an episode of *Seinfeld*—the one in which Jerry told a dressed-down George, "You know the message you're sending out to the world with these sweatpants? You're telling the world, 'I give up.'" Maybe so. But when it comes to watching videos, sleeping in, or eating ice cream directly from the carton, no other garment will do but a pair of sweats—the rattier the better.

< 268 >

SWEEPSTAKES We may have already won? Yeah, right. You can afford to give away millions as a way to promote selling magazine subscriptions? Sure. Yet even though we can't figure out how Publishers Clearing House and other sweepstakes manage to balance their books, we still catch ourselves searching, licking, and sticking our way through packet after packet, imagining that prize patrol showing up on our doorstep. See also LOTTERY TICKETS (SCRATCH-OFF).

SWEET CAROLINE See DIAMOND, NEIL.

SYBIL It seems a bit goofy now, but at the time of its release in 1976, this TV movie scared the wits out of many a strong man and woman. It told the mostly true story of a girl named Sybil (played by Sally Field) who manifested 16 different personalities, and the psychiatrist (Joanne Woodward) who tried to figure out why. Hint: Sybil's mother wouldn't win any Parent of the Year awards. The movie won an Emmy for Field, and blazed the path, for better or worse, for a zillion other "socially relevant" small-screen flicks exploring every medical/psychological problem from bulimia to narcolepsy. See also LIFETIME; MENTALLY IMPAIRED (MOVIES WHOSE STARS PRETEND TO BE); and TV MOVIES.

< 269 >

T

TABLOIDS See *NATIONAL ENQUIRER, THE* and *WEEKLY WORLD NEWS*.

TAHITIAN TREAT When it comes to carbonated beverage consumption, we have been trained to consider only colas, clear lemon-limeish drinks, and maybe root beer and Dr. Pepper. But in the dog days of summer, something lures us inexorably toward bright red drinks such as Tahitian Treat. Like malt liquor, Tahitian Treat is often labeled a "ghetto drink" whose charms have been referenced by rappers and hip-hop artists. But it's also a nostalgia trip for upper and upper-middle classers who taste a warm glass of Tahitian Treat and remember the bug-juice-fueled glory days of summer camp. See also BIG RED.

TALKING ANIMALS (MOVIES ABOUT) Animals may be lovable. Animals may be smarter than we give them credit for. But barring a few members of the parrot family, animals cannot talk. Except in Hollywood, that is, where chatting creatures are often more articulate than Arnold Schwarzenegger, Sylvester Stallone, and Vin Diesel combined. Back in the 1950s the live-action genre was upheld mostly by *Francis the Talking Mule* (clearly the model for TV's *Mister Ed*), while Disney cornered the market on animated anthropomorphic animals. In the past twenty years, however, membership in this freakily popular category has swelled to include everything from a stock-market-savvy horse in *Hot to Trot* (opposite Bobcat Goldthwait), to Danny DeVito– and Diane Keaton–voiced dogs in *Look Who's Talking Now*, to a semiliterate computer-animated dog in *Scooby-Doo*, to entire menageries of babbling beasts in *Babe*, *Dr. Dolittle*, *Stuart Little*, and their sequels. Which all begs the question: If animals could really talk, wouldn't we be terrified of what they had to say? See also TALKING ANIMALS WHO DIE (MOVIES ABOUT).

TALKING ANIMALS WHO DIE (MOVIES ABOUT) What's more embarrassing than enjoying a movie featuring a talking animal? How about crying at a movie featuring a talking animal? From Bambi's weeping for his plugged mamma to the title spider buying the farm in *Charlotte's Web* to the Lion King senior getting trampled, many a guilty tear has been shed for beasts that not only don't exist but *could not* exist. See also TALKING ANIMALS (MOVIES ABOUT) and TEARJERKER MOVIES (FOR MEN).

TAMBOURINES Kids who receive

< 270 >

tambourines in music class know exactly what it means; they can't sing and they can't handle a real instrument. It's a sad legacy for a device that was played in ancient China, India, and Egypt. When Miriam celebrated the Israelites' escape from Egypt, she did so by banging on her tambourine. In the 19th century, composers such as Berlioz even wrote parts for it in some of their works. The instrument has truly come down in the world since the birth of rock and roll, when tambourines were given to singers so they could look busy during instrumental bridges.

TANG Possibly the orangest beverage ever invented, Tang was introduced by the General Foods Corporation in 1959. But it really took off (in the most literal sense) when it was selected for use on manned space flights. Not because it was better-tasting than real orange juice, but because the just-add-water powder was (A) easy to store and (B) easy to store. Kids promptly clamored for the astronaut-approved mix, which parents reluctantly provided. It was basically sugar and food coloring, but at least, Mom and Dad rationalized, it was chock full o' vitamin C (a 100-percent daily supply in each Day-Glo-colored glass). Tang peaked when *Apollo 11* astronauts Neil Armstrong and Buzz Aldrin carried it all the way to the moon (along with

other culinary gems such as bacon squares and freeze-dried ice cream). They might as well have left it there. As the glory of space exploration faded, so did its signature beverage.

TANNING, ARTIFICIAL A tan used to be a sign that you were back from a holiday in a tropical climate—or, at least, returning from a week at the Jersey shore. These days, however, tanning salons are as omnipresent as Starbucks, despite the fact that excessive use has been linked to skin cancer (and is an excellent way to give yourself the hide of a 70-year-old). Still, the alternative (buying self-tanning bronzing lotion) is more embarrassing than picking up a pack of Trojans. Is the George Hamilton look really worth so much humiliation?

TATTOO See *FANTASY ISLAND*.

TATTOOS Who would willingly allow a needle to be stuck in their arm 3,000 times each minute, for minutes on end, without any sort of painkiller to take the edge off? The answer is: about 15 percent of the U.S. population. Made by injecting pigment under the skin, tattoos probably predate human civilization. Yet like getting pregnant in high school or partying too hard in college and flunking out, getting tattooed is one of those youthful lapses in judgment that can

< 271 >

follow you for the rest of your life. Today's modern primitives use them as a way to record their feelings. The problem, of course, is that our feelings change over time (art celebrating an ex-wife no longer feels quite right, tribal patterns no longer jibe with a thirtysomething junior exec's worldview)—which is why an-other big business is tattoo removal.

TAYLOR, RIP Taylor, along with such luminaries as Milton Berle and Steve Allen, belongs to a very elite group of performers: People Your Mom Thinks Are Funny. At one time he was just a stand-up comedian. But sometime between 1962 (when he did a career-making turn on *The Ed Sullivan Show*) and now, he morphed into one of those all-purpose troupers who can  be found, depending on the day of the week, either spicing up a daytime talk show, taking the lead in a touring Broadway musical, headlining a Vegas review, or serving as a Very Special Guest on a TV sitcom. This "versatile" thespian has shown up everywhere from the kiddie show *Sigmund and the Sea Monsters* to that randy cinematic classic *The Happy Hooker Goes to Washington*. He also served on Chuck Barris's *Gong Show* follow-up *The $1.98 Beauty Show*.

What does he do during his appearances? Mostly, he acts very flamboyant and wired—like Charles Nelson Reilly on a three-day crystal meth binge. But then, you already knew that, didn't you? Because at one time or another you've watched him—probably with your mom (or grandmom, depending on how old you are). See also BARRIS, CHUCK; *GONG SHOW, THE*; and *MERV GRIFFIN SHOW, THE*.

TEARJERKER MOVIES (FOR MEN) Hollywood expends a great deal of effort getting women to cry tears of either sadness or joy. Fortunately for directors, that isn't very difficult, as movies such as *Beaches*, *Love Story*, and even *Pretty Woman* (not to mention more than a few Very Special Episodes of sitcoms) prove. What's tougher is getting men to cry. Males prefer to get angry during movies and then see someone take revenge. At least, that's what they say. But the truth is, guys like to cry, too—only on their own terms.

A few things can get them to well up, including tales of selfless heroism and friendship (*Saving Private Ryan*), explorations of the father/son relationship (*Field of Dreams*), and, first and foremost, stories in which dogs are in danger. If you'd like to test this theory, tell a man that you've rented a copy of *Old Yeller* and ask if he'll watch it with you.

< 272 >

When he refuses, offer him $20. When he refuses again, offer him $50. Chances are he still won't do it, even if you offer him a Benjamin. See also CHICK FLICKS (IN WHICH SOMEONE DIES) and TALKING ANIMALS WHO DIE (MOVIES ABOUT).

TELETUBBIES There's nothing wrong with watching this PBS program if you're part of its target audience: one-year-olds. There's something *very* wrong with watching it if you're a teenager, college student, or, even worse, a full-fledged adult. Being addicted to the antics of four furry, bulbous creatures named Po, Laa-Laa, Dipsy, and Tinky Winky, who each day wander around a psychedelic playground uttering mono-syllabic squeaks, can mean only one of two things. Either (A) at some point during your childhood you spent a great deal of time unconscious at the bottom of a swimming pool; or (B) you smoke way too much weed. And since you have to be home in the middle of the day (as opposed to at school or working) to be an adult Teletubbies fan, we're picking (B). See also MARIJUANA and MISTER ROGERS' NEIGHBORHOOD.

TELEVANGELISTS Sunday morning heathens always have a great time making fun of the folks who bring us the word of God via the idiot box. There's so much to mock, you just have to pace yourself.

Start by savoring the white trash accents and the convoluted pronunciations of even the simplest words. For instance, in preacherspeak Jesus becomes Ja-EEEEEZ-us. Next, revel in the appalling clothing and hairstyles that only a Savior (and, perhaps, Porter Wagoner) could love. Finally, if you have the patience, there's the sublime delight of watching folks such as Jim Bakker and Jimmy Swaggart slowly paint themselves into ideological corners (Ja-EEEEEZ-us says no to the fornicator! No to the homo-sexual! No to the pornographer!), and then, inevitably, get caught in a hotel room with either a hooker or a hooker-like follower. Such are the wages not of sin, but of hypocrisy. See also MASTUR-BATION; MOVIES (PORNOGRAPHIC); and PHONE SEX.

TEMPLE, SHIRLEY (THE ACTRESS) The star of *Bright Eyes*, *Little Miss Marker*, and *Baby Take a Bow* wasn't your average adorably packaged prodi-gal. If you doubt that assertion, just *try* to flip the channel during her stairway scene with Bill "Bojangles" Robinson in *The Little Colonel*. Just try.

America's favorite kid sister didn't become one of the most recognizable people of our time by just sitting around drinking ginger ale splashed with grenadine and topped with a maraschino cherry. Gosh, no. The child star had a

< 273 >

serious work ethic. By the age of 11, she had appeared in more than 40 films (including an astonishing *eleven* in 1934, the year she received a special pint-sized Academy Award in recognition of her outstanding contribution to screen entertainment). And then, cue a fast pan across puberty, Little Curly Top wasn't so little anymore. The grownup Shirley Temple, with her lipstick and boobs, didn't sell in Hollywood. Not that it mattered. The future ambassador to Ghana had already step-ball-changed her way into the entertainment pantheon, not to mention our hearts. And her cutie-pie legacy lives on today in auditoriums across the land—every time a stage mom stands up and shouts, "*Jazz hands, Alexia! Jazz hands!*"

TEMPLE, SHIRLEY (THE DRINK) Mix grenadine with ginger ale, garnish with a maraschino cherry, and you've got the perfect nonalcoholic kiddie cocktail. Named after the famous child star, it has for decades been the drink of choice for children who want to emulate adults at cocktail parties. Which begs a couple of questions: Is *this* the sort of behavior you want your kids to emulate? More importantly, what are kids doing at your cocktail party, anyway? See also MARA-SCHINO CHERRIES.

TEQUILA Derived from the spiny agave plant, tequila, unlike its snobbier dis-

tilled cousins, is used primarily for just one thing: messing people up. So if you want to impress your friends with your taste in spirits, buy something else. But if you're planning a really ugly bachelor party, or just a quiet evening of getting wasted on the couch, we've got the beverage for you.

TERMINATOR, THE See SCHWARZENEGGER, ARNOLD.

TESH, JOHN Mix the musical credibility of Kenny G with the holier-than-thou preachiness of Anita Bryant and you've got the six-foot-six-inch guy Howard Stern relentlessly called the "blond Frankenstein." So what's to like? We have no idea. And we perfectly understand the moti-  vation behind the creation of the National Anti-Tesh Action Society (a tongue-in-cheek—we think—organization that claims Tesh is an alien). Yet the former *Entertainment Tonight* cohost and New Age recording star fascinates us, whether playing himself (badly) in such movies as *Soapdish* and *Love Affair*, hawking gospel CDs on QVC, pushing self-help infomercials, or telling TV audiences that he and wife Connie Sellecca didn't have sex until they got

< 274 >

married. Must make image stop. See also *ENTERTAINMENT TONIGHT*; G, KENNY; HOME SHOPPING NETWORK, THE; QVC; and STERN, HOWARD.

T.G.I. FRIDAY'S Much-mocked for its flair-bedecked uniforms, brass bar railings, cluttered wall hangings, and ubiquitous presence in every town with a decent-sized hotel, T.G.I. Friday's was once, believe it or not, a trendsetting New York restaurant. Opened in 1965 on the Upper East Side, it helped anchor the singles bar scene. These days, however, any breath of originality in the 700-location chain has long since fled. Still, there's something irresistible about a place with a novella-length menu, perky wait staff, Jack Daniel's–enhanced entrées, and a good chance that the bar is peopled with easy pick-ups. See also ONE-NIGHT STANDS.

THEME HOTELS Who remembers the differences between the last three nondescript Holiday Inn rooms they spent nights in? Yet who could forget the evening they spent at the Antony & Cleopatra room at Lake Tahoe's Fantasy Inn or the Doctor's Office room of Van Nuys' Eros Station? Of course, this doesn't mean you'd want either to show up on your business expense form. See also HOLIDAY INN; LAS VEGAS; and THEME RESTAURANTS.

THEME PARKS (NOT OWNED BY DISNEY) During a visit to an old-school theme park, Walt Disney (the man, not the corporation) allegedly looked around in disgust and decided he could build something better—a place that was clean, safe, and full of life-affirming fun. Thanks, Walt. But while the "It's a Small World" ride is neat and all, a part of us pines for places that are just slightly less clean and calculating, and perhaps a touch more spontaneous, quirky, and (dare we say it?) scary. Other parks, forced to compete with the Disney juggernaut, have exploited this one-and-only chink in the Magic Kingdom's armor. For instance, Coney Island doesn't have year-round shirtsleeve weather, but it has a coaster (the Cyclone) that people have been carried off of in stretchers. And Holiday World (just outside Santa Claus, Indiana) doesn't have Minnie or Mickey, but it does have Saint Nick, in full costume, from May through October. Even bigger operations, from Knott's Berry Farm to Universal Studios, have climbed onto the we're-not-as-nice-as-Disney-and-proud-of-it bandwagon. Sure they can't offer flying Dumbos or a Hall of Presidents, but when it comes to rides that make you scream like your little sister, they lead the way. See also PARTON, DOLLY; ROLLER COASTERS (ENORMOUS) and SIX FLAGS AMUSEMENT PARKS.

< 275 >

THEME RESTAURANTS Why simply have dinner when you can have dinner in a rainforest? Or on board a submarine? Or surrounded by Hollywood props? Written off by epicureans as pathetically proletarian—understandable when the gift shop is often bigger than the kitchen—such eateries are a magnet for tourists and for people who get a guilty kick out of playing tourist. Of course, the chance of actually seeing Arnold Schwarzenegger eating Cap'n Crunch Chicken at a Planet Hollywood or Keith Richards devouring a burger at the Hard Rock Cafe is about as likely as spotting a turkey-leg chomping Henry VIII at Medieval Times. See also THEME HOTELS.

THIN MINTS See GIRL SCOUT COOKIES.

THIS OLD HOUSE Like watching chefs on the Food Network making extravagant dinners you'll never cook, there's something satisfying and a little sad about following the miraculous renovation work on this show (or in the pages of its sister magazine) yet steadfastly refusing to replace the burnt-out light bulbs by the garage.

THONG UNDERWEAR Frederick Mellinger—the same famed Fred who *is* Frederick's of Hollywood—wedged his way into lingerie history on August 2, 1981. The butt-floss revolution began when Mellinger mass-marketed his "scanty panty," now known simply as the thong. Formerly worn only by trashy hos and exotic dancers, his creations are now crammed up the cracks of mainstream soccer moms and socialites alike, making these tiny T-shaped drawers the fastest-growing segment of the $2 billion-a-year women's panty business. Frederick's alone sells about 75,000 pairs a week, but the bottomless bloomers are also sold everywhere from Bergdorf's to Wal-Mart. So why have women tossed their traditional undies for these skimpy skivvies? If you'd ever spent a day at the office (or a night on the town) trying to nonchalantly dig a pair of cheek-creepers out of your derriere, you'd know. With thongs, it's Destination Butt Crack as soon as you slip them on. However, their dearth of posterior fabric actually makes them comfortable, unlike full-bottomed panties that bunch up into a wicked wad. An even bigger advantage: Thongs eliminate V.P.L. (visible panty lines). When wearing them under snug-fitting pants or skirts, your tush remains smooth and naturally rounded—unlike the "rump roast tied in twine" look created by V.P.L.

It seems the only thing women don't like about the dinky drawers is buying them. As you wait in the checkout lane with these naughty-looking unmentionables, you can't help feeling like a skank.

< 276 >

See also COTTON PANTIES (ENORMOUS); FREDERICK'S OF HOLLYWOOD; and VICTORIA'S SECRET CATALOGS.

THORN BIRDS, THE (THE MINISERIES) While such late '70s video events as *Roots* and *Holocaust* sent the message that the television miniseries could make important statements, early '80s efforts such as *The Thorn Birds* reminded everyone that they could also serve another purpose: getting big stars to do glorified soap operas. The story line was larded with racy plot lines executed by such respectable actors as Richard Kiley, Barbara Stanwyck, and Christopher Plummer. Everything centered around priest Richard Chamberlain, who ditched his vows of celibacy to get with Rachel Ward. The then-novel suggestion that priests might not only think nasty thoughts, but act on them, earned the show plenty of press, as did the fact that ABC debuted the 10-hour series on Palm Sunday and ran it through Holy Week. See also TV MOVIES.

THOUSAND ISLAND DRESSING This tangy condiment with the distinctive coral hue dates back to the early 1900s, when the wife of a fishing guide in the Thousand Island region of upstate New York introduced it as a dinner staple. Over the years, the enigmatic sauce has expanded its culinary horizons.

Variations of the original recipe—mayonnaise and chili sauce studded with finely chopped pickles, onions, olives, and hard-boiled egg—have graced the buns of fast food hamburgers, sealed the deal on Reuben sandwiches, and shared the appetizer plate with deep-fried vegetables. The beauty of Thousand Island dressing, it seems, lies not so much in its own salty/sweet, creamy/crunchy mélange as it does in its ability to bring out the best in other foods—though at a price. One serving equals about 70 calories.

THREE STOOGES, THE To hell with Rodney Dangerfield, it's the Three Stooges who, in the world of comedy, don't get any respect. Credited with teaching generations of kids how to slap faces, pull hair, and poke eyes, Larry, Moe, and Curly (or, in lesser work, Shemp, Joe, or Curly Joe) made about 200 short films, many of them still remembered fondly by regular guys, if not by snooty critics. You could, if you really wanted to, analyze these guys as representing three distinct personality types. Moe was the bossy control freak. Larry was the perpetual guy-in-the-middle. And Curly was the out-of-control id. Put them together, along with a frying pan, a pair of pliers, and plenty of "Nyuk, nyuk, nyuks," and the results were classic.

< 277 >

THREE TENORS, THE What do you do if you'd like to be an opera fan but simply can't stomach actual opera? You join the masses who either caught live concerts or (far more likely) tuned in to PBS pledge break specials featuring that dreamed-up-in-marketing-heaven opera star triumvirate, Luciano Pavarotti (whose attempt at movie stardom in the flick *Yes, Giorgio* was so misguided it doesn't even rise to the level of guilty pleasure); José Carreras (who laughably tried to play "Romeo" in a misguided *West Side Story* disc and televised recording session); and Plácido Domingo (who has managed not to do anything spectacularly stupid in his lengthy career). Thanks to their act, arena audiences and TV viewers can experience opera without having to face the fat lady.

THREE'S COMPANY For seven seasons, without ever being too proud of it, we accepted the theme song's invitation to knock on the door of Jack Tripper (John Ritter) and his two female roommates, who encouraged him to pretend to be gay so they could all live together (back when people still worried about a guy living with two girls). The show went through two landlords (Norman Fell and Don Knotts) and three blondes (Suzanne Somers, Jenilee Harrison, and Priscilla Barnes) before calling it quits in 1984. Could be that they just ran out of double

entendres? Or excuses to put Joyce DeWitt and Somers/Harrison/Barnes in skimpy outfits? See also TV THEME SONGS (VOCAL).

THRILLER Don't bother denying that you owned this album. Or that you watched the videos it inspired or danced to the seven Top 10 U.S. singles it spawned. After all, this best-selling record has moved  an incredible 45 million units since its 1982 release. That's enough to provide one for every citizen of Canada, with Cuba thrown in. But more to the point, it's enough for every American who happened to be in their teens or early 20s during the early 1980s.

By now the songs are so overplayed that they're dance floor clichés. But at the time, tunes like "Billie Jean," "Beat It," and "Thriller" were as cool as it got. And so were the fashions sported by their creator, Michael Jackson. The bright red leather jacket in the "Thriller" video became a vintage '80s statement. Its only serious challenger in the men's outerwear category was the ubiquitous wrap produced by Members Only.

Perhaps inevitably, the album's overwhelming success cast a pall on Jackson's future work. After all, when you sell 45

< 278 >

million of *anything*, whatever comes next is bound to be a letdown. The Gloved One's record sales inevitably fell, and his image and music became appallingly dated. In no time those *Thriller* albums were relegated to the back of the closet, right next to all those red leather jackets. See also JACKSON FAMILY, THE; JACKSON, LATOYA; JACKSON, MICHAEL; JACKSON, TITO; and MEMBERS ONLY JACKETS.

TIC TAC DOUGH Presided over by Wink Martindale (and, later, Jim Caldwell, who went on to become the voice of the Roto Zip Solaris infomercial), *Tic Tac Dough* took the basic three-in-a-row game and added quiz show questions . . . and nine Apple II computers for high-tech gosh-wow effect. Known as the Fort Knox of game shows, the addictive *TTD* had a reputation for giving out piles of cash. Take contestant Lt. Thom McKee, for instance. Over the course of 46 episodes, the good lieutenant knocked off 43 challengers, amassing cash and prizes worth more than $300,000 (including eight cars)—and that's in late-'70s/early-'80s, pre–*Who Wants to Be a Millionaire* dollars. See also GAME SHOWS and *HOLLYWOOD SQUARES, THE*.

TILT-A-WHIRL See OUTDATED CARNIVAL RIDES.

TIME-LIFE BOOKS These mammoth, multivolume book sets, which explored everything from World War II to the occult, first hit the market in 1961. Ordering them was like buying a magazine—albeit one that kept harping on the same subject and that you never threw away. In most cases a new volume would arrive each month, sometimes for years on end. Buying them wasn't exactly a sign of intellectual prowess. In fact, displaying a shelf-snapping set in public was akin to framing a GED certificate. Sadly, this particular road to mail-order smarts is now closed. Time-Life Books shut down in 2000. See also TIME-LIFE MUSIC.

TIME-LIFE MUSIC After the death of Time-Life Books several years ago, bibliophiles could no longer purchase multivolume book sets covering everything from the Civil War to home repair to Civil War home repair. However, Time-Life Music still offers multidisc song compilations surveying everything from specific decades (*'60s Gold*) to specific genres (*The Folk Years Collection*). This is definitely the place to visit when you're deep in a nostalgia funk—or have been seduced into watching one of Time-Life's half-hour infomercials. More than one late-night viewer has sat through the pitch for *The Ultimate '70s Collection*, tapping his foot to sound

< 279 >

bites from everything from "He Ain't Heavy, He's My Brother" to "Heart of Glass." Quick question: If you're enough of a folk music fan to take John Sebastian's pitch and buy this many discs, wouldn't you already have most of these songs in your collection? See also GREATEST HITS ALBUMS; *MAN, MYTH & MAGIC*; and TIME-LIFE BOOKS.

TOMB RAIDER See CROFT, LARA.

TOOTH WHITENERS It never occurred to us, before the onslaught of commercials for products such as Simply White, Truly White, Opti-White, and Brite White, that a dull smile could sabotage our lives. All those botched job interviews and aborted dance floor pickups? Apparently they were caused by our yellowish teeth. Thank goodness for the redemptive powers of carbamide peroxide, the magic ingredient in most over-the-counter tooth whiteners that, even when doctored up with mint, still taste pretty much like model airplane glue smells.

Still, with visions of the Osmonds dancing in our heads, we brush it on, paint it on, and squirt it into rubber retainers that we wear around the house for 30 minutes, all the while drooling like Saint Bernards. Things could be worse, of course. One wonders what kind of *I Love Lucy* catastrophe com-

pelled the makers of Crest White Strips, a product that adheres directly to the teeth in the form of gel tape, to issue the following warnings to users: Do not swallow plastic strip. Do not get gel material in eyes. See also BIORÉ STRIPS.

TOOTSIE POPS Named after the daughter of Austrian immigrant/confectioner Leo Hirshfield, the Tootsie Roll was introduced to the public in 1896 in a small New York store. It took another 35 years, though, for the powers that be at the Sweets Company of America to hide it away inside hard candy and attach it to a stick, making Tootsie Pops the first soft-centered lollipop. It turned out to be a brilliant move. The company grew and, once TV emerged as a tot tastemaker, kids became obsessed with the question asked on its commercial: "How many licks does it take to get to the Tootsie Roll center of a Tootsie Pop?" In the '70s, the Pop engrained itself further into pop culture when TV detective *Kojak* started mouthing them on his show. These days 20 million Tootsie Pops roll off the assembly line each day, proving that the old saying that there's a sucker born every minute was a gross understatement.

TOP GUN This formulaic 1986 film allegedly concerns a lone wolf fighter pilot who learns about teamwork while

< 280 >

attending the Navy's Fighter Weapons (Top Gun) School. In truth, it was one of the 1980's slicker salutes to cinema's dynamic duo, sex and violence. Guys enjoyed the aerial dogfights and ogling Kelly McGillis. Gals checked out the famous volleyball scene and the shots of Val Kilmer and Tom Cruise lounging, post-mission, in towels in the locker room. Interestingly, there aren't any shower facilities for pilots at the real Top Gun school.

In addition to launching a lot of planes, this film kicked plenty of careers into afterburner, including those of Cruise, Kilmer, Anthony Edwards, and Meg Ryan (Remember? She was Goose's wife). One of the stranger beneficiaries was antiwar activist and Susan Sarandon consort Tim Robbins, who played a pilot "extra." See also *COCKTAIL* and *WHEN HARRY MET SALLY* . . .

TOUCHED BY AN ANGEL From Clarence in *It's a Wonderful Life* to Michael Landon in *Highway to Heaven*, the Lone Angel Sent to Help a Hapless Human is one of Hollywood's most well-worn plot staples. But this CBS series took the concept one step further by offering the services of not just one minor deity, but a veritable heavenly

host. *Touched by an Angel*, which aired for nine seasons (and will, we surmise, remain in syndication forever), featured head angel Della Reese overseeing a veritable SWAT team of winged wonders who helped wayward mortals find their way back to the straight and narrow. Sure it was heartwarming, but after watching an episode more than a few viewers felt slightly sick—as if they'd eaten too much divinity. See also *IT'S A WONDERFUL LIFE* and LANDON, MICHAEL.

TOURS (GUIDED) Travel scribes make a big deal about the difference between traveling and touring. The clear implication being that traveling—making it up yourself—is much preferable to touring—following a guide's predetermined plan. Yet sometimes you don't want to blaze new trails, take risks with untested eateries, and have to strike up acquaintances on your own. And you don't want to keep flipping through tour books to explain why the church you just passed is of historical significance. Guided tours eliminate those risks, making sure your trip is close to exactly that of everyone else's. When you finish, you really will have been there, done that, bought the T-shirt—because chances are the T-shirt is part of the package. See also T-SHIRTS (SOUVENIR).

< 281 >

TOURS (MUSICAL NOSTALGIA) There are a couple of clear ways to find out if the band you are watching on stage is coasting on its nostalgia value: (A) the audience goes dead silent during any song written or recorded in the past decade; (B) the performers on stage are 20 years older than your mental picture of them; (C) the act is touring on a double bill with the Turtles, the Association, the Four Tops, or the Temptations; (D) the act *is* the Turtles, the Association, the Four Tops, or the Temptations. None of which should dampen your pleasure at hearing has-beens come close to hitting all the notes of your old favorites. See also TRIBUTE BANDS.

TRANS AMS See MUSCLE CARS.

TRIBUTE BANDS Just one step removed from celebrity impersonators, tribute bands exist because your favorite musicians can only be in one place at a time. And chances are, that place isn't a nightclub near you on a Monday night. Whether covering the works of the Grateful Dead (Dark Star Orchestra, Uncle John's Band), Kiss (Hotter Than Hell), Jimmy Buffett (B2B), Led Zeppelin (Fred Zeppelin, Whole Lotta Led, White Summer), or Pink Floyd (too many to name), tribute bands have to be admired for their willingness to put their own aspirations on hold so you can pretend they're someone else. And fans have to be excused for wanting to hear their favorite music live without waiting for, say, the Rolling Stones to roll through town. See also GARCIA, JERRY and KISS.

TRIVIAL PURSUIT (WINNING AT) Okay, smarty-pants, so what if you were the most intimidating Trivial Pursuit player in your neighborhood/dorm/family? It's not like it got you into a better school or helped you land a better job. After all, it's not called Useful Knowledge Pursuit. But that didn't stop you from feeling really, really good when you nailed a question, especially a History one. Kicking butt at this game was a major guilty pleasure in the mid-'80s and gloating was as much a part of the fun as filling up your pie with colorful slices. The game was created by two Canadian journalists, who tried to market it themselves, failed, and then wisely sold their creation to Selchow and Righter, the company that pushes Scrabble. The year after the sale, 20 million copies were sold, and soon imitators and extra editions flooded toy stores, reintroducing adults to the pleasures of board games. Now the property of Parker Brothers, Trivial Pursuit continues to turn friends into rivals and otherwise intelligent people into mumblers of the phrase "Wait, I know this. It's on the tip of my tongue." See also PICTIONARY.

< 282 >

TRUMP, DONALD In 1988 it seemed as if every businessperson and wannabe businessperson in America was lugging around a copy of Donald Trump's *The Art of the Deal*. Almost everyone *wanted* to be like Trump, even though almost no one *liked* Trump. A poster child for corporate greed and shameless self-promotion, this NYC-based real estate mogul slapped his name on casinos, hotels, and high-rises across the country. In short, he did everything possible to paint himself as an overleveraged ass straight out of *The Bonfire of the Vanities*. Sure he got on our nerves, but the truth is, if we were in his place we probably wouldn't have done it any differently. And just when we thought the spotlight had moved on to Bill Gates, boom! Trump returned to the national eye with *The Apprentice*.

T-SHIRTS (SOUVENIR) In visiting just about any destination, whether it's a Caribbean island or the nearest Hard Rock Cafe, it's common practice to pick up a (usually overpriced) souvenir shirt. Yet, rarely do we consider why we make such an extraneous purchase. Surely we have enough torso coverings at home. And the experience is unlikely to have been so great that we just *have* to spend additional money to commemorate it. Perhaps we get them because buying and wearing such a garment is a public announcement that you are a worldly person. And buying one for a friend or family member who didn't make the journey—especially one that offers some variation of "My Grandpa Went to New Orleans and All I Got Was This Stinkin' Shirt"—is a sign that you really *didn't* want to buy a souvenir but felt the nasty pull of obligation. See also THEME RESTAURANTS.

TUBE TOPS If ever there were an article of clothing designed *for* a woman *by* a man, the tube top (or "boob tube," as the Brits call it) is it. Consisting of a band of rib knit fabric hovering around the bosom, these strapless, one-size-fits-all garments neither lift nor support, leaving breasts with no other option but to hang in limbo with public exposure just inches away. No wonder they've been the bane of official dress codes since the moment they appeared on the fashion scene in the 1950s, stylishly paired with matching shorts and skirts for the beach. Always a hit at stock car races, Grateful Dead concerts, and on *Girls Gone Wild* videos, tube tops are the perennial wardrobe choice for women who want to get noticed at any cost and girls who want to get sent home from school early. See also *GIRLS GONE WILD* and NASCAR.

TUPPERWARE PARTIES History is filled with what-ifs. What if the battle of

< 283 >

Normandy had gone the other way? What if Ronald Reagan had taken the lead in *Casablanca*? And in a case relevant to this item, what if Earl Silas Tupper, inventor of Tupperware, had succeeded with an earlier creation? If that were the case, perhaps thousands of entrepreneurial housewives today would have parties selling Tupper's device that performed appendectomies through the anus. Ah, but that was not to be. Instead, for more than 50 years, folks just like you have been invited by "friends" to Tupperware parties—opportunities to be lectured for an hour on how burpable plastic containers can change your life. The parties actually saved the company from obscurity. When business was bad, Tupper noted a Detroit saleswoman who was hosting "parties" to sell his products. He promptly pulled his goods from stores (they didn't return until recently), made the lady a vice president, and made his moniker a household name.

TV Catchphrases (Quoting of) We all have mental filters to strain out useless stimuli, but they aren't foolproof. For instance, sometimes, often without realizing it, we lift dialogue straight out of TV shows and use it in day-to-day conversation. Painful as it is to admit, rare is the person who has never replaced their standard discourse with such tube-ified nuggets of wisdom as "Watchu talkin' 'bout, Willis?" (*Diff'rent Strokes*), "Dy-no-mite!" (*Good Times*), "Kiss my grits" (*Alice*), "Sock it to me" (*Laugh-In*), "Stifle it" (*All in the Family*), "Survey says" (*Family Feud*), "Sit on it" (*Happy Days*), or "Nanu Nanu" (*Mork & Mindy*). See also COMMERCIAL CATCHPHRASES (QUOTING OF).

TV Dinners Though the Swanson company stopped calling its heat-and-eat meals TV dinners back in the '60s, the name has become a generic term for all frozen, minimum-effort meals. Originally developed in 1953, they addressed two issues: the boom in television viewing and the fact  that Swanson had more turkey than it knew what to do with. The company developed a segmented metal tray into which such items as chicken, meatloaf, and the aforementioned turkey were placed, along with various side dishes. The whole works was covered with aluminum foil, frozen, and pushed out the door to eager *I Love Lucy*–watching consumers. This instant winner sold more than 10 million units in its first year of national distribution. And why *wouldn't* they be huge? The meals rode three of the hottest modern American lifestyle

< 284 >

trends: excessive television consumption, low standards, and inhuman laziness. See also DINNERS, MICROWAVED; JIFFY POP POPCORN; KRAFT MACARONI AND CHEESE; and PUDDING CUPS.

TV MOMS (LUSTING AFTER) Lonely is the TV watcher ashamed and confused by the odd stirring caused by Shirley Partridge, Carol Brady, Clair Huxtable, Elyse Keaton, Debra Barone, or Carmela Soprano. Needing serious help, however, is the one who has those same feelings for Edith Bunker, Florida Evans, or Marge Simpson. See also *PARTRIDGE FAMILY, THE*.

TV MOVIES This genre was born in 1964, when NBC teamed up with Universal to produce long-form teleplays. But it hit its stride in 1969 when the *ABC Movie of the Week* debuted. For years this venue, as well as its competitors, churned out low-budget, 90-minute (sans commercials) wonders that dealt with, literally, every topic under the sun. The most popular formula was to write a script around a controversial topic, then cast a well-known TV trouper against type (say, Elizabeth Montgomery) in the starring role.

Most TV movies were mindless pap (remember *Killdozer* and *Trouble Comes to Town*?), but occasionally the format approached greatness. *The Night Stalker* (penned by horror legend Richard Matheson) was one of the highest-rated small-screen flicks of all time and served as the inspiration for the series *The X-Files*. Other small gems included *Duel* (also penned by Matheson, this was one of Steven Spielberg's earliest directorial efforts, in which Dennis Weaver was pursued by a homicidal trucker); the male bonding film *Brian's Song*; and such unclassifiable classics as *The Boy in the Plastic Bubble*.

As the '70s turned into the '80s, TV movies delved ever more deeply into social issues and, to the detriment of the industry, diseases. Everything from bulimia (in 1981's *The Best Little Girl in the World*) to, well, bulimia (1986's *Kate's Secret*, starring Meredith Baxter-Birney) was trotted out for examination. The illness mania has receded, but only to be replaced by true crime tales (the Amy Fisher/Joey Buttafuoco tryst) and scandals (such as *Martha Inc.*, which savaged Martha Stewart). But whatever the topic, a trashy TV movie is still a good excuse to plop down on the couch with a bag of microwave popcorn—and to see how Valerie Bertinelli is looking these days. See also *BAD RONALD*; *BOY IN THE PLASTIC BUBBLE, THE*; FISHER, AMY; MICROWAVE POPCORN (AS A MEAL SUBSTITUTE); and STEWART, MARTHA.

< 285 >

TV Shows Featuring Animal Protagonists The plot of every episode of *Gentle Ben*, *Flipper*, *My Friend Flicka*, and *Lassie* (especially *Lassie*) was pretty much the same: Stupid humans get into trouble; smart animal bails them out. Why did these shows hold such fascination? Perhaps because we knew there were damn few people we could rely on as completely as these folks did their pets. Let's face it: A dog doesn't count how many guys you're up against in a bar fight before deciding whether to admit he knows you. See also *Lassie* and *Mister Ed*.

TV Theme Songs (Instrumental) TV themes that lack vocal accompaniment are slightly (but only slightly) less infectious than the ones with words. For some reason, though there is no scientific evidence to support it, they usually seem to start rattling through our brains as we drive. Who among us, while sweating out a stoplight or tooling down the open road, hasn't felt the *Miami Vice* theme tickling his cerebellum, or unconsciously hummed the "Theme from *S.W.A.T.*"? See also TV Theme Songs (Vocal).

TV Theme Songs (Vocal) They welcome us into our favorite sitcoms or TV dramas with a recap of the backstory (*The Brady Bunch*), an introduction to the characters (*The Jetsons*), a statement of theme (*Baretta*), or some combination of the above. Some, such as "Welcome Back" (the theme to *Welcome Back, Kotter*) and "Closer to Free" (*Party of Five*), even become hit singles. Of course, when they are spun to the radio there's always that awkward moment when, in an effort to stretch the song to a radio-acceptable length (no station would play a 30-second song), the vocalist chimes in with a second, previously unheard chorus—or a guitar bridge from nowhere. "All those nights when you've got no lights / The check is in the mail"? Whaddaya mean there's another *Cheers* verse? See also *Brady Bunch, The* and *Party of Five*.

TVLand See Nick at Nite.

21 Jump Street Airing from 1987 to 1991 and centered around a bunch of extremely young-looking police officers who do undercover work in high schools (and, later, colleges), one of the Fox network's first hits featured grown men and women forced to relive all their high school traumas—but with a twist. During the final act, star Johnny Depp would inevitably flash his badge at a hood, classroom bully, or (best of all) teacher, and say something to the effect of, "*I'm* going to detention? No buddy, *you're* going to detention." Sweet.

< 286 >

TWILIGHT ZONE, THE From its debut in 1959 to its final broadcast in 1964, this show, hosted by Rod Serling (who also wrote the majority of the 156 episodes), took the art of the twist ending to new heights. Want to see people make extremely ill-advised bargains with Satan? Or travel back in time to change history for the better, only to screw things up even worse? How about extraterrestrial encounters in which the "aliens" turn out to be cannibals, microscopic in size, a thousand feet tall, or — most mind-blowing of all — us? Well then, this is your show. Though the *Zone* long ago devolved from cutting-edge television into a cultural cliché, it's still fun to look for all the soon-to-be-celebrities who appeared there. Omigod, is that Robert Duvall in love with a miniature doll? Is that William Shatner getting spooked by a fortune-telling machine? And look, here comes Burt Reynolds! See also REYNOLDS, BURT; SHATNER, WILLIAM; *STAR TREK*; and *STAR WARS*.

TWINKIES Americans gobble up about 500 million of these golden snacks each year, even though they're universally decried as the junkiest of junk food. Indeed, a popular urban legend claims they have an unlimited shelf life because they contain no organic substances. If only that were so. Each year the Hostess company uses 1 million eggs, 7 million pounds of flour, and *8 million pounds of sugar* to make its half-billion golden treats, each of which contains 160 calories. Though they can't sit on the shelf forever, they can loiter for almost a month — an unheard-of length of time for a baked product. The Twinkie achieves this not because it's loaded with preservatives, but because it contains no dairy ingredients. See also STATE FAIR FOOD; URBAN LEGENDS; and WONDER BREAD.

TWISTER Debuted by Milton Bradley in 1966, it was called "sex in a box" by detractors. Consisting of a plastic sheet dotted with rows of colored circles, Twister's rules call for contestants to follow the directions of a spinner and place a hand or foot on appropriate spots. In no time participants get tied up in entertaining and (if you're with the right person) suggestive knots. Johnny Carson and Eva Gabor demonstrated the erotic potential of the game, and sent sales soaring, when they played a round (or played around, depending on your perspective) on *The Tonight Show*. Overnight, Twister became (and remains) a college favorite. See also GABOR SISTERS, THE and GAMES, MAKE-OUT.

< 287 >

U-V

UFOs (BOOKS AND TV SPECIALS ABOUT) It's a great big universe out there, so it's not such a stretch to believe that our lonely little planet may not be the only one supporting intelligent life. It is a stretch, however, to believe that creatures from some other world are anus-probing back-woods folk and creating

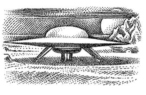

elaborate designs in cornfields. Yet television specials such as *UFOs: Best Evidence Ever Caught on Tape* and *Alien Autopsy: Fact or Fiction* (which Fox TV ultimately admitted was a hoax), and books including *Chariots of the Gods* continue to find audiences. Why? Because beyond the hard-core believe-anything yokel, there's a large group of people who may not admit it publicly, but privately wish for a world as interesting as the ones in science-fiction novels and movies. Plus there are a few people who like the idea of surprise anal probes. See also AUTOPSIES (TELEVISION); *NATIONAL ENQUIRER, THE*; and *WEEKLY WORLD NEWS.*

UNAUTHORIZED BIOGRAPHIES Apart from a handful of shameless stars (we're talking about you, Shelley Winters), few autobiographers reveal as much dirt as we really want from a life-of-the-rich-and/or-famous story. For that, we have to turn to unauthorized biographers such as Kitty Kelley, who slung the mud on Frank Sinatra, Jackie Onassis, and the British Royal Family. How much of what she said was true? Do you really care? See also BRITISH ROYAL FAMILY, THE and KENNEDY FAMILY, THE.

UNBELIEVABLE SPORTS COMEBACKS (MOVIES ABOUT) This hoary cinematic genre is the Y-chromosome version of the chick flick. First take the typical romantic tearjerker plot: boy pursues girl; boy almost loses girl; boy finally wins girl. Now substitute the word "championship" for "girl" and you've got the rationale for everything from *Knute Rockne, All American* to *The Fish That Saved Pittsburgh.* The story is of course formulaic, but the male response to either a lone warrior battling for respect (*Rocky*) or a bunch of guys working hard to become a team (*Hoosiers, The Longest Yard*) is so Pavlovian that it's almost impossible to screw up (though the stinky sailing "epic" *Wind* comes to mind, as does *Dreamer*, an attempt to make a bowling championship seem interesting). Done

< 288 >

right, a good sports comeback movie makes even the most sedentary male want to hit the gym for a few sets of bench presses—even if the heaviest thing he's ever lifted is a can of beer. See also ROCKY MOVIES; STALLONE, SYLVESTER; and TEARJERKER MOVIES (FOR MEN).

UNDERWOOD DEVILED HAM This meal of last resort (try it spread on Club Crackers) was developed by the Underwood Company, founded in 1822 and famous throughout the 19th century for its tinned goods. For decades, one wouldn't think of, say, jumping on a California-bound wagon without first stocking up on cans of Underwood mackerel, pickles, oysters, and other such delicacies. But it wasn't until 1868 that the sons of the company's founder, William Underwood, developed a special ham spread using a process they called "deviling." These days that spread (and its logo, the Underwood devil, which at more than a century of age is the oldest trademark still in use in the United States) is the company's sole claim to fame—not surprising, considering that its other offerings include liver pate, liverwurst, and roast beef spread. See also SPAM and VIENNA SAUSAGE.

UNSOLVED MYSTERIES There are people who guiltily flip to the end of mystery novels to find out whodunnit. There are others who watched this show knowing that they might *never* get the answers. This series, hosted by Robert Stack, offered fugitive-on-the-lam stories similar to *America's Most Wanted*, mixed with supernatural mysteries à la *In Search of . . .* , with a few *Finders of Lost Loves* heartwarmers thrown in. Plus there were some real head-scratchers along for the ride, like the one about the Brit pub-dwellers who believed that sitting in a particular 300-year-old chair caused death. At its best, *Unsolved Mysteries* could be more terrifying than standard horror films because it could do scary scenes without ever having to worry about resolving the plot or developing characters. Plus there was always Stack, telling us with utmost credibility that the killer *was still out there somewhere*.

URBAN COWBOY The success of this 1980 cinematic salute to all things country (imagine *Saturday Night Fever* with chewing tobacco and twangy accents) inspired millions of Americans to acquire such ill-advised fashion accessories as pointy boots and big hats. All to emulate a young Texas hick (played by literally the last person you'd expect to see in such a role, John Travolta) who moves to Houston, marries a hickette played by Debra Winger, then almost

< 289 >

loses her to a guy who rides the mechanical bull at the local roadhouse. But everything turns out okay when Travolta learns to ride the bull better, beats up the other guy, and reconciles with Winger. See also ELECTRIC SLIDE; LINE DANCING; and *SATURDAY NIGHT FEVER*.

URBAN LEGENDS Urban legends are nothing new. The compulsion to pass fictional weird/scary/funny tales off as factual is as old as the human race. Remember the one about the fisherman who lost his ring at the beach, then found it years later while cleaning a fish he caught? Check the work of the Greek historian Thucydides and you'll find almost the exact same tale attributed to Croesus, king of Lydia, in roughly 550 B.C. And Thucydides, just like the guy at work who told you about the family who adopted a chihuahua that turned out to be a rat, swore it was true. Such whoppers never go away; they just get updated. For instance, the lead character in the story of the tall black man in the elevator who says, "Sit, Lady" to his dog, only to terrify an elderly white woman in front of him, has morphed over the years from Reggie Jackson to Eddie Murphy to Puff Daddy.

How do you spot an urban legend? If you hear slightly different versions of the story from several people, if the teller can't say exactly where it hap-

pened or who it happened to, or, most importantly, if the tale sounds like the plot of a *Twilight Zone* episode, you're probably hearing a whopper. Not that this makes them any less fun. See also *TWILIGHT ZONE, THE*.

URKEL, STEVE See *FAMILY MATTERS*.

US WEEKLY Light and malleable enough to roll up and tuck inside a handbag, this rag full of tiny, bite-sized stories gives star trackers exactly what they want— the scoop and nothing else. Crammed with photos showing Hollywood's "it" crowd in various stages of candidness, *Us* has its finger on the pulse of America's stargazing public . . . and another finger on its f-stop. What started out as *People* lite evolved into the *National Enquirer* (only with fewer lawsuits) by throwing every rule of tasteful magazine design out the window. Snapshots bump against each other, overlap, and multiply across the page in a manner reminiscent of high school yearbooks. Even the "feature articles" seem more like glorified captions, which means a cute shot of Reese Witherspoon coming out of Starbucks with a gingerbread latte in hand is enough grounds for a major story. See also *INSTYLE MAGAZINE*; *NATIONAL ENQUIRER, THE*; *PEOPLE*; and *WEEKLY WORLD NEWS*.

< 290 >

VALLEJO, BORIS If you've ever read a novel with the word "barbarian" or "conqueror" in the title, the flesh-intensive cover art you ogled was probably done by Vallejo. A classically trained artist and native of Peru, he's built a reputation as the world's foremost painter of pumped-up guys with swords; semi-nude women with gravity-defying bosoms; monsters; and (by far his most popular category) pumped-up guys with swords trying to rescue semi-nude women with gravity-defying bosoms from monsters. His near-ubiquitous work can be seen everywhere from the covers of old heavy metal albums to the sides of numberless customized vans to the poster for *National Lampoon's Vacation*. Recently Vallejo married Julie Bell, a fellow artist, female body builder, and former model for some of his paintings. He's still cranking out his highly realistic work. Well, realistic to the same degree that Arnold Schwarzenegger (who portrayed one of Vallejo's favorite subjects, Conan) is realistic. See also SCHWARZENEGGER, ARNOLD.

VAMPIRE NOVELS When Bram Stoker's novel *Dracula* was first published in 1897, it became a huge hit by broaching (albeit obliquely) topics that Victorians didn't usually talk about: sex, rape, xenophobia, homoerotica, women's liberation, and so on. Today's vampire novels, though not as groundbreaking as *Dracula*, lurk in that same psychosexual netherworld. Want homoerotica? Anne Rice's "vampire chronicles" will oblige. There are even subgenres of lesbian vampire novels, action/adventure vampire books, and "romantic" neck biter novels. Maybe it's the fact that, unlike the Frankenstein monster, a mummy, or a werewolf, the reader can imagine him or herself hanging out (or at least holding a conversation) with one of these suave guys. Or maybe it's just the sex thing that makes neck biters by far the most popular literary monsters. Try to name another semi-mainstream book category with so many penetration scenes and (usually one-way) exchanges of bodily fluids. See also RICE, ANNE.

VAN DAMME, JEAN-CLAUDE Belgium's answer to Chuck Norris once said "I am the Fred Astaire of karate." Unfortunately, he's also the G.I. Joe of acting, showing all the emotional range of a plastic doll. Mercifully, this was perfectly adequate for his roles in such films as *Cyborg*, *Universal Soldier*, *Street Fighter*, and *Sudden Death*. Still, being better-looking than most of the guys battling their way to fight-movie stardom and willing to crank out an average of two movies a year, regardless of quality, earned the "muscles from Brussels" a loyal following. So what if he was called

< 291 >

one of the world's worst actors by Leonard Maltin? We'd pay to see Van Damme kick Maltin's critical ass. See also KUNG FU MOVIES and NORRIS, CHUCK.

VANILLA ICE Like your rap music served with a cracker? Then you probably grooved to this young, blond, tough-as-an-Avon-lady superstar's one-and-only 1990's hit, "Ice Ice Baby." Mainstream America ate up this tune, which offered all of the groove of regular rap, with none of the rage. Vanilla Ice was even named Favorite New Artist at the American Music Awards. Ice mooned the audience after receiving his trophy, then walked offstage and, for all intents and purposes, right off the edge of the planet. Today, if goofball posers had a god, he'd be it. But that doesn't change the fact that millions of people bought—and, even more horribly, danced to—his music. See also "RAPPER'S DELIGHT."

VARIETY SHOWS Admit that you long for the days of television variety shows and you might as well admit that you give Werther's butterscotch candies to your grandson. In other words, you're old. Yet there was something exciting about an evening of TV spent with Carol Burnett, Dean Martin, the Smothers Brothers, or especially Ed Sullivan— something rarely seen in today's demo-

graphics-obsessed media market. Before the segmented world of cable television, a variety show's audience could appreciate (without a hint of irony) a classic crooner, a storytelling comic, a magic act, a ventriloquist who uses his hand as his puppet, and the latest hit band from Liverpool, all on the same show. It was like a multivitamin for your senses. See also CHER (WITH SONNY); MAGICIANS; STEVE AND EYDIE; and VENTRILOQUISTS.

VARNEY, JIM Every second-rate office comedian who's uttered the phrases "Hey, Vern," or "Knowhadimean?" owes a debt of gratitude to this classically trained actor from Lexington, Kentucky. Varney knocked around Hollywood for  years before being tapped in 1979 for a series of commercials in which he played a moron in a baseball cap named Ernest P. Worrell. Ernest's sole function was to harangue an unseen neighbor named Vern about an advertiser's product. The bits were so successful that over the years Varney did some 4,000 spots for companies ranging from radio stations to dairies. The character of Ernest stuck in people's craws the way bubble gum sticks to carpeting. In 1987 Touchstone Pictures released the movie *Ernest Goes to Camp*, which was fol-

< 292 >

lowed over the years by eight more. A Saturday-morning kids' show called *Hey Vern, It's Ernest!* even earned Varney an Emmy for "Outstanding Performer in a Children's Series." Varney attempted to diversify his career (he played Jed Clampett in the 1993 big-screen remake of *The Beverly Hillbillies*), but lung cancer took his life in 2000, at the age of 50. But while the man is gone, Ernest—and, more irritatingly, the catchphrase "Knowhadimean?"—lives on. See also *BEVERLY HILLBILLIES, THE.*

VELOUR There are certain risks associated with wearing clothing made out of a fabric so soft and plush you can't resist running your hands up and down its soothing nap, sometimes at inopportune moments. If this ever happens, simply explain to the people staring at you that it's not your fault a velour jogging suit feels like an irresistible cross between satin sheets and kitten fur. Invented in Lyons, France, in 1844, velvet's laidback cousin owes its unique tactile qualities to a special arrangement of closely woven fibers of various lengths. That pebbled effect of light and shaded areas can turn an ordinary pair of running shorts into luxury wear and make a sofa feel like a seat in heaven's waiting room.

VELVEETA This spongy, orange-ish brick is to dairy products what Spam is to meat. Processed from a mix of cheeses (Swiss, cheddar, Colby) plus several other milk-based ingredients, it's been a Kraft Foods staple (and the very symbol of lowbrow fare) for decades. But though many see it as an oddity, it's the rare home cook who hasn't made use of it. Fact is, it melts better and more thoroughly than almost any "real" cheese. Cube one brick, then toss it in the microwave for a minute or two with the contents of a can of salsa, and you've got a kick-ass dip. Try that with your fancy Brie or Stilton! Also, it's the perfect topper for grilled Spam sandwiches. See also NACHOS and SPAM.

VENTRILOQUISTS Occupying a rung on the ladder of entertainment respectability somewhere between celebrity impersonators and mimes, ventriloquists spend their careers feeding straight lines to dummies. Yet while most people aren't willing to admit it, there's a reason why acts as varied as Paul Winchell (with Jerry Mahoney), Wayland Flowers (with Madame), and Willie Tyler (with Lester) all had their days in the variety show sun. A good ventriloquist delivers the laughs of a comedy act combined with the awe inspired by an

< 293 >

expert juggling team. Of course, none of that explains how Edgar Bergen (with Charlie McCarthy) became a huge star by performing *on the radio*. See also CELEBRITY IMPERSONATORS and VARIETY SHOWS.

VH1's *Behind the Music* Let magazines from *Rolling Stone* to *People* report on the band of the moment. Since 1997, VH1's *Behind the Music* series has been the place to turn to for career-spanning postmortems of yesterdays hitmakers. The musical equivalent of the *E! True Hollywood Story*, it's a program as addictive as the illegal drugs that wrecked the careers of many of the show's subjects. The more the band is a guilty pleasure in and of itself—M.C. Hammer, Meat Loaf, Milli Vanilli, Styx—the better the *Behind the Music* report. That's because the clips, interviews, and anonymous narration of host Jim Forbes (a.k.a. James Jude) remind us that we actually took these acts seriously once upon a time. The format is now so familiar that the show was subjected to spoofs on *Saturday Night Live* (*Behind the Music: Fat Albert*), *The Simpsons* (*Behind the Laughter*), and some guy on the Internet (*Behind the Music: Alvin and the Chipmunks*). See also *E! TRUE HOLLYWOOD STORY*; MEAT LOAF (THE SINGER); *PEOPLE*; and STYX.

VIBRATING BEDS/MAGIC FINGERS "Put in a quarter/Turn out the light/Magic Fingers makes ya feel alright." So sang Jimmy Buffet in his recording of the Steve Goodman song "This Hotel Room." And while the most recent generation of hotel-dwellers may not get this reference, more seasoned travelers remember the private pleasure of keying into a room and finding a bed equipped with a Magic Fingers unit. That meant, as long as your pocket change held out, you'd be vibrating your way to under-the-covers relaxation. In a pre-cable, pre-Internet, pre-Spectravision world, who could ask for anything more? See also SPECTRAVISION.

VIBRATORS There's a really good reason why your Bel Ami Lukas uncut with removable foreskin, your reflective gel veined 18-inch Double Dong, your Chasey Lane Slimline G, and your Rhythm Master Bouncing Cannon are kept hidden in your underwear drawer. 'Nuff said.

VICTORIA'S SECRET CATALOGS Intimate Brands, the parent company of the lingerie chain Victoria's Secret, mails about 394 million copies of its catalog to shoppers each year. Female consumers (if you've bought so much as a thong at Victoria's Secret, you're probably on the mailing list) can peruse the book with an

< 294 >

eye toward buying, say, a cotton knit chemise, ruffle lace V-string panties, or a crystal beaded fishnet tee. Male consumers (buy your *girlfriend* so much as a thong, and you're probably on the list, too) like the catalogs not so much for the naughty underwear but for the big color photos of supermodels lounging around in that underwear. Which is why VC wish books can be found in sad little bachelor pads nationwide—and why a guy who can't locate his birth certificate or Social Security card can lay hands on, say, "Fall Fashion 2004" in seconds. See also FREDERICK'S OF HOLLYWOOD; THONG UNDERWEAR; and WONDERBRA, THE.

VIDEO ARCADES See VIDEO GAMES.

VIDEO GAMES Technically, this high-tech waste of time was born in 1971 when a game called Computer Space, which included its own 13-inch black-and-white monitor, was put in play. Problem was, the few people who could figure it out weren't terribly interested. But a year later, Pong arrived with its simple paddle control and any-moron-could-understand-it rules, and an industry was born. Soon, thanks to such early hits as Space Invaders, Galaga, and Asteroids, pinball games were relegated to the nether regions of arcades and video games were given the prime spots. Unlike pinball—where skill and luck could win you free games—video games were essentially nihilistic. Eventually, you died. No way around it.

The games didn't just suck quarters out of the pockets of kids. Adults, too, found themselves guiding Pac-Man on his fruit-gulping quest and playing track-ball football until their palms ached. The games came home, courtesy of Atari and its imitators, and the rest is mind-sucking, money-vacuuming, time-wasting, "Oh my God is it already 1 A.M.?" history. See also PONG.

VIENNA SAUSAGE One wonders why God reserved such a terrible fate for these finger-sized treats. When it began life in the 18th century, the Vienna sausage was a spicy little number not too different in size and flavor from the frankfurter and other thin-skinned European sausages. Yet for some reason the Armour company chose to sunder the poor things into two-inch links and pack them in water. Since then they've lost all cachet, becoming a bottom-of-the-barrel snack choice that's only called on when there's no more bologna or Kraft Macaroni and Cheese. Interestingly, the Armour company has tried to kick their bland reputation up a notch. These days Jalapeño, Hot & Spicy, and Barbecue versions are available, along with an Internet recipe page offering such dishes as Vienna Sausage Bake; South-of-the-

< 295 >

Border Viennas; and Sausage Fried Rice. Or you can just eat them out of the can with a toothpick, as the Lord intended. See also BOLOGNA and KRAFT MACARONI AND CHEESE.

VILLAGE PEOPLE, THE So how long did it take you to figure out this was a gay thing? It's a measure of America's naiveté that when this group (conceived by record producer Jacques Morali as a spoof of homosexual stereotypes) broke big in 1978 with "Y.M.C.A." and "In the Navy," many in the mainstream didn't realize the songs were about *having gay sex* at the Y.M.C.A and in the navy. Indeed, the U.S. Navy was so clueless that

it lent the group a destroyer to use in a video. And it wasn't as if they were trying to keep it a secret. The People danced around dressed as construction workers, cowboys, and pretty much every other gay archetype you'd care to name, short of Judy Garland. Like the Spice Girls after them, the guys took a shot at movie stardom only to have their film, *Can't Stop the Music* (directed by Rhoda's mom and Bounty spokeswoman Nancy Walker), released just as the band fell out of vogue. See also GARLAND, JUDY.

VOMIT (FAKE) In the world of prepackaged practical jokes—the joy buzzer, the impossible-to-open sugar packet, the bug in the ice cube—fake vomit reigns supreme. Why? Because it actually does what it is designed to do. Just drop it on the floor and an unsuspecting victim may well gasp with the sudden belief that someone heave-hoed. The best models (including Whoops, Vomit, and Vomit Oops!) are crafted with the understanding that the right mix of chunks and liquid-like areas makes all the difference. *Grossology*, a book, CD-ROM program, and touring museum exhibition, included lessons in making edible fake vomit, which seems to imply that this gagging gag will likely be pulled on your grandchildren's grandchildren. See also PRACTICAL JOKES and WHOOPEE CUSHIONS.

< 296 >

WALKING TALL With a name like Buford Pusser, you'd better be tough. And he certainly was, if the cinematic portrayal of this small-town Tennessee sheriff is remotely accurate. *Walking Tall*, released in 1973, told the "true" story of Pusser's war against corruption after mobsters killed his wife. Of course there was plenty of shooting, but the real fun started when the sheriff (played by Joe Don Baker) pulled out his weapon of choice, a thick length of wood. Inevitably, *Walking Tall 2* appeared in 1975, sans Baker, followed by *Walking Tall: The Final Chapter* in 1977, a TV series in 1981 and a remake in 2004 starring The Rock.

Not that Joe Don Baker, the original Pusser, was done playing big, scary rednecks. Indeed, he specializes in portraying them (check his appearances in *Cool Hand Luke*, *The Natural*, and the James Bond flick *GoldenEye*). The only "stretch" of his career was his presence, for some reason, in *Braveheart*. Does anybody recall seeing a big, gone-to-seed hillbilly in a kilt? See also *BEVERLY HILLBILLIES, THE* and *BILLY JACK*.

WAL-MART It's easy, and oh, so fash-ionable, to hate Wal-Mart (founded in 1962 in Rogers, Arkansas). You can despise the company's merciless destruction of mom-and-pop stores. Or decry its brutal focus on the bottom line. Or simply loathe the inhuman scale of its so-big-they-create-their-own-weather-systems stores. But here's the dirty truth: You shop there. You and all your friends. And here's how we know. In 2002 the 41-year-old discount retailer accounted for *2.3 percent of the gross national product of the United States*. That's about $240 billion in annual sales. Indeed, its haul during one particularly good day—$1.43 billion—was larger than the gross domestic product of 36 separate countries. None of which could happen if most of those Wal-Mart bashers didn't, in the words of the immortal Cher classic "Gypsys, Tramps & Thieves," "come around and lay their money down."

WALT DISNEY WORLD Since its 1971 opening, this mother of all theme parks has served as the default vacation choice for people who want to take an exotic trip without actually taking an exotic trip. Encompassing 47 square miles of central Florida real estate (that's twice the size of Manhattan), the "World" features everything from a sanitized slice of Africa (Disney's Animal Kingdom) to a hooker-free Hollywood (Disney-MGM Studios) to the original Magic Kingdom,

< 297 >

home of such famous rides-turned-into-movies as Pirates of the Caribbean and the Haunted Mansion. But though it will never make the cover of *Conde Nast Traveler*, this hermetically sealed, *Westworld*-like complex does offer certain advantages. Parents can, if so inclined, shove their progeny out the hotel door first thing in the morning, then hit the links or relax by the pool while Cody and Mandy exhaust themselves waiting in interminable lines. The management seems to tacitly acknowledge this option by offering six on-grounds golf courses, numerous shopping centers, two spas, and liquor-friendly eateries pretty much wherever you turn (booze is readily available everywhere except in the Magic Kingdom). See also CRICHTON, MICHAEL and HALL OF PRESIDENTS, THE.

WALTONS, THE Begun in 1971 as a tear-jerking Christmas TV movie, this story of a Depression-era family made millions of tube-watchers jealous for the good old days of abject poverty. With a folksy opening theme (by Jerry Goldsmith who, in a display of freakish versatility, also wrote the music for *The Twilight Zone* and that really weird horns-without-mouthpieces sound for *Planet of the Apes*), a multigenerational cast, and messages of love and tolerance, *The Waltons* kept us entranced from 1972 through 1981. Well, except when the one sister's husband who was supposed to have died at Pearl Harbor turned up in Florida. *Then* we were just annoyed. The show, Energizer-bunny-like, kept going and going despite a stroke suffered by Ellen Corby (Grandma Walton), the death of Grandpa Will Geer, the 1977 departure (and subsequent career disappearance) of Richard Thomas (John-Boy) and Michael Learned (his mother, Olivia), and the Hail-Mary-pass replacement of Richard Thomas with a different John-Boy (Robert Wightman). See also PLANET OF THE APES MOVIES and TWILIGHT ZONE, THE.

WAR MOVIES The problem with war films is that to enjoy them you have to be somewhat blasé about seeing other people get shot. And not just a few people, but thousands. The other problem with war films is that most glorify (some intentionally, some unintentionally) what is without argument the most vile situation in which human beings could ever find themselves. The *other* other problem is that even "realistic" pictures such as *Saving Private Ryan* don't come close to authenticity. Sure the THX-enhanced flying lead sounds real and the torn bodies bleed in a very lifelike (deathlike?) manner, but every ticket buyer knows he or she is going to walk away from the experience with life and

< 298 >

limbs intact. Which is, needless to say, not the case on an actual battlefield.

Viewers who feel bad about getting off on the mayhem have several options. They can avail themselves of politically correct, mostly Vietnam-era flicks such as *The Deer Hunter* and *Platoon*; or they can watch goofy, cartoonish efforts like the Rambo movies, but recognize them for what they are: entertainment that's about as realistic as a video game. See also RAMBO MOVIES and TEARJERKER MOVIES (FOR MEN).

WATER BEDS Once used as a treatment for ulcers, water beds are said to be more therapeutic than a standard mattress. But even Charles Hall, the guy credited with perfecting the concept while a student at San Francisco State University in 1968, knew that such benefits weren't the water bed's prime selling point. Why else would he have initially called them "pleasure pits"? He made millions of dollars off this sex-toy-pretending-to-be-furniture, bounced on one on *The Dinah Shore Show* (a piece of videotape that wound up as evidence in a lawsuit—long story), and helped waterbeds reach their 1987 zenith, when one trade group said they accounted for more than a fifth of the American mattress industry. Alas, the business sprung a leak. These days, having a water bed is about as cool as having a rumpus room.

WATER PARKS We're not sure where water sliding began. One source says the first such contraption was Coney Island's Chutes at Luna Park, while the *Bill & Ted's Excellent Adventures* cartoon series traces it back to 1849 at Sutter's Mill. But we do know that if you visit any water park in the country—whether it's a single-slide relic or a can-you-top-this collection of multistory plastic tubing—you'll find otherwise sane adults gleefully flopping down onto a foamish mat and letting a steady flow of water careen them through chutes, around bends, and into the pools below. Warning: Make sure your swimsuit is securely fastened before shooting the pipe. See also WISCONSIN DELLS.

WATERS, JOHN Now an icon of the independent film world, director John Waters was once just a dirty-minded cult filmmaker out to make theatergoers barf in their popcorn. He came close to achieving that with 1972's *Pink Flamingos*, in which a "who's the most disgusting" competition climaxed with the on-camera consumption of dog feces. Now that's entertainment! Yet the notoriety of that film led to more commercial efforts, including the scratch-and-sniff-enhanced *Polyester*, the surprisingly joyful *Hairspray* (the basis for the hit Broadway musical), and such movies as *Serial Mom* and *Cecil B. DeMented*,

< 299 >

which featured respectable actors such as Kathleen Turner and Melanie Griffith (though admittedly, both had already exceeded their "Best If Used By" dates). See also GIMMICKS, MOVIE and JOKES, SICK.

WAX MUSEUMS Even if you visit New York or Las Vegas or London, home to many a celebrity, there's little chance you'll see an honest-to-goodness star on the street. But if you are in any of those towns—or Amsterdam or Hong Kong for that matter—you can hit Madame Tussaud's and ogle wax figures of famous people. This most notorious of all wax museums was begun by Marie Grosholtz (later Tussaud). Having learned her trade in Paris—including a stint molding guillotine victims' heads—she inherited her mentor's collection, toured them around the British Isles, then settled in on London's Baker Street and opened up her permanent display in 1835. One can only imagine what the museum's namesake would think of the place now. Transplanted to larger digs and to other locations, it includes a talking Simon Cowell (of *American Idol* fame), a wax Michael Caine who looks disturbingly like Charles Nelson Reilly; and a squeeze-the-bum Brad Pitt.

WAYNE, JOHN America's prototypical action hero (born Marion Morrison)

built his career playing the sort of men Dr. Phil would call repressed: quiet, self-assured, more comfortable with horses and firearms than women. Of course, today's male knows how important it is to express himself, open up to the ladies in his life, get in touch with his feminine side, blah, blah, blah. And  yet, when he watches *Rio Bravo*, *The Searchers*, *True Grit*, or pretty much anything else from the John Wayne cinematic canon, he can't help wishing *he* could be that tough under pressure. Because let's face it, when the poop hits the fan, very few people, male or female, find themselves desperately thinking, "Damn, I wish Alan Alda were here." See also DR. PHIL; RAMBO MOVIES; ROCKY MOVIES; SCHWARZENEGGER, ARNOLD; and STALLONE, SYLVESTER.

WB, THE If you are a teen or preteen *Dawson's Creek* and/or *7th Heaven* addict, a parent who has sacrificed a good portion of your kids' college fund feeding their *Pokémon* and *Yu-Gi-Oh!* addictions, or the sole member of the *Sister, Sister* fan club, you've got the WB to thank. Launched in 1995 with a not-quite-powerhouse Wednesday night lineup of sitcoms (*The Wayans Bros.*, *The Parent 'hood*, *Unhappily Ever After*,

< 300 >

and *Muscle*), its retinue of shows grew (some would say metastasized) into an every-night-but-Saturday lineup. What can you say about a network that takes pride in getting higher ratings than shows on UPN?

WEATHERMEN (FAT AND/OR JOLLY) Nothing makes a hurricane easier to take than a Willard Scott wannabe yukking it up in front of the Chroma Key. Sure *Today*'s Al Roker made headlines by undergoing bariatric surgery and shrinking to the size of a garden gnome, but we still prefer that our weather wizards shop in the Big and Tall department.

WEBBER, ANDREW LLOYD Go on. Say you hated *Cats* and feel all superior. Even among much-mocked musical theater buffs, it's safe to trash it. But just remember that *someone* kept the feline follies running in New York for nearly 18 years. And *Cats* is only the most obvious target of Andrew Lloyd Webber–bashing. The prolific theater composer has been taking shots ever since he offered up a high-pitched *Jesus Christ Superstar* to Broadway audiences in 1971—a show once labeled sacrilegious and now treated like a fifth gospel. Since then, his music has graced (or disgraced, depending on your bent), such long-running New York and/or London hits as *Evita*, *Starlight Express*, and *Phantom*

of the Opera. A lot of it is overblown. A lot of it is goofy. But some of it is, admit it, rather catchy. See also *CATS*.

WEDDING STORY, A This show gets to viewers in several different ways. For some, it's when the starry-eyed couples recount the moment they knew they were in love. Others lose it during the climactic walk to the altar, or when the father dances with his just-married daughter at the reception. Even if you make it all the way through an episode of TLC's documentary-style drama without welling up, you're not officially out of the emotional woods until you've endured the previews for the next episode. Just thinking about it makes our chins quiver—real-life people baring their souls to the TLC cameras as they prepare for this one life-defining moment, conveniently edited down to a half-hour show. The cable network bills its you-are-there programming as "Life Unscripted," which sounds a little like reality television that has gone to film school. The big difference is that in the copacetic world of *A Wedding Story*, flower girls don't throw tantrums; bridesmaids don't do shots of tequila before stumbling down the aisle in hunter green taffeta; best men don't make inappropriate toasts about ex-girlfriends; and nobody ever throws up. See also RE-ALITY SHOWS.

< 301 >

WEEKLY WORLD NEWS You're standing in line at the grocery store when a tabloid catches your eye. The usual lurid headlines span the black-and-white cover, but everything, from the "news" stories ("Feminists Want Robots to Replace Men!" "Miracle Carp Says the End Is Near!") to the self-help pieces ("How You Can Tell If Your Neighbor Is a Time Traveler!" "Improve Your Sex Life Tonight—The Amish Way!") seems too weird even for a supermarket rag. Congratulations, you've just entered the twisted alternate universe of the *Weekly World News*. Published by American Media (the same folks responsible for the *National Enquirer*), *WWN* peddles UFO and conspiracy theory–laced hokum so bizarre it would make Barnum blush. While morons may take it as gospel, the intelligentsia (there are many among the rag's roughly 1 million readers) chuckle appreciatively at (what they perceive to be) ironic, self-referential humor of the highest order. Sales spike when there's a cover story about Bat Boy, a half-human, half-bat creature that *WWN* has reported on for years—and that was the subject of a well-received off-Broadway musical. Of course to enjoy all this, you have to commit the socially questionable act of buying a tabloid at the grocery store. Perhaps, so that no one misunderstands your motives, you should loudly state, "I love this magazine for its naive yet sophisticated, almost dadaist take on modern culture." Or you could just toss it face-down on the conveyor belt and try not to make eye contact with the cashier. See also *NATIONAL ENQUIRER, THE*.

WEIRD SCIENCE It had to happen eventually—a movie that revolves around teens who, thanks to those newfangled things called *computers*, create the perfect woman. Kind of a cross between *Bride of Frankenstein* and *The Last American Virgin*, this John Hughes film—who are we kidding, it really was a Kelly LeBrock film—could be the reason why armies of geeks turned from Dungeons and Dragons to the Internet. Many remember LeBrock's over-the-top, 17-year-old's-idea-of-va-va-voom entrance. Fewer remember that her character ends up behaving more like a mom (okay, maybe a hot aunt) and less like a sex toy. See also *BREAKFAST CLUB, THE*.

WESTHEIMER, DR. RUTH She looks like your grandmother, she's about the size of Yoda, and she knows more about sex than Larry Flynt. A creepy combination, to be sure, yet this German-born former Israeli freedom fighter, Sorbonne student, and kindergarten teacher somehow found her way onto New York's WYNY at the age of 52, becoming the de facto sex therapist for an entire nation.

< 302 >

Why did her heavily accented advice catch on? Well, it's one thing, intellectually, to feel that masturbation is probably okay. It's another to have Grandma  Yoda Flynt give you the official palms up. See also *HUSTLER* and MASTURBATION.

WESTWORLD See CRICHTON, MICHAEL and PRE-*STAR WARS* '70S SCI-FI FILMS.

WET T-SHIRT COMPETITIONS Something remarkable happens when moisture is applied to a standard men's cotton undershirt being worn by a standard drunk coed. Just ask any guy who spent spring break in Florida. But apart from the obvious reasons why wet T-shirt competitions are popular, there's one you may not have thought of: The results are easily rigged. All a bar owner has to do is lure contestants with the promise of big prize money, hold the contest, then anoint a predetermined champ who takes a fee rather than collects actual prize money. Voilà . . . a bar gets a cheap evening of entertainment and a couple of drunken girls get chest colds.

WHAT'S HAPPENING!! Not much, really, just teenagers Roger, Dwayne, and Rerun hanging out at Rob's Place, an eatery that, on this 1976–79 series, served as the lower-middle-class African-American version of *Happy Days'* Arnold's Drive-In. Okay, it was a little different—Shirley Hemphill, the sassy waitress, was big enough to have eaten both Pat Morita and Al Molinaro in one sitting. The series returned with most of the same cast as *What's Happening Now!!* in 1985 for another three seasons, a remarkable feat considering few people admitted to watching the first one. See also *HAPPY DAYS.*

WHEN HARRY MET SALLY . . . Of all the world's chick flicks, this one is the easiest for men to bear—not that they'd ever admit it. Though the formula is standard romance movie pap (two people dance interminably around the issue of hooking up), it does have several important things going for it. For one, female lead Meg Ryan has never looked hotter. And for another, director Rob Reiner imparts a refreshing male sensibility to the proceedings. This is the movie to suggest when your wife or girlfriend wants to rent a DVD. You'll score sensitivity points, and you won't be constantly tempted to hit the fast forward button on the remote. Just don't get suckered into the rest of the Meg Ryan oeuvre. See also PICTIONARY.

WHERE ARE THEY NOW? In a world where fame can dry up quicker than a slug on a sun-baked patio (just try naming the

< 303 >

winner of the second season of *Survivor*), it's no wonder that newspapers, magazines, and television shows can guarantee an audience when they promise to tell us what happened to yesterday's familiar faces. While we couldn't have cared less about, say, *Family Ties'* Tina Yothers or *Happy Days'* Donny Most while they were making weekly appearances on our living room TV, if a *People* article or *E! True Hollywood Story* offers a retrospective, we're there. See also *E! TRUE HOLLYWOOD STORY*; *PEOPLE*; and VH1's *BEHIND THE MUSIC*.

WHERE'S WALDO? These accursed volumes, laboriously painted by Martin Handford (it takes him years to create enough for a single book) are a bane to adults' self-image. The object is to locate a stripe-shirted fellow named Waldo, who hides in plain sight in huge pictures jammed with hundreds of other figures. They're designed for children aged five and up, which makes it particularly embarrassing for adults who stare at the pages for 15 minutes and *still can't find the skinny bastard*. During the early '90s Waldo books were all the rage, though a cartoon based on the character flopped. Maybe no one could figure out which channel it was on.

WHIP, THE See OUTDATED CARNIVAL RIDES.

WHIPPED CREAM IN A CAN Equally at home on a delicate plate of strawberries or as a prop in an episode of *Red Shoe Diaries*, Reddi-Wip and other, lesser whipped-cream-in-a-can products take a great taste and make it as convenient as (and much more palatable than) foam insulation. Credited with being the first aerosol foodstuff, Reddi-Wip launched in 1947. It taught a generation of not terribly creative burnouts how to "do whippets" by sucking the propellant out of unused cans. It's also useful in a pinch as shaving cream. See also COOL WHIP and *RED SHOE DIARIES*.

WHITE, VANNA We were so hip. Collectively, we got together and decided to take the television personality —using the term "personality" loosely—with the most minimal job description and  turn her into a big-time celebrity. This *My Fair Lady* trick (you were in on it, weren't you?) worked almost too well. Suddenly the former Vanna Marie Rosich, who did nothing but turn letters on *Wheel of Fortune*, became a household name, appearing on talk shows, "authoring" a best-selling autobiography in 1987, and playing herself on shows ranging from *Gimme a Break* to *L.A.*

< 304 >

Law. No matter what you think of her (if you think of her at all), you have to give the South Carolina native credit for one thing: She never quit the *Wheel*. Unlike Shelley Long, David Caruso, Suzanne Somers, and a parade of other here-today-gone-tomorrow TV stars, Vanna knew that the nation would stop caring as soon as she ditched her meal ticket. See also GAME SHOWS.

WHITE CASTLE The greasy, microscopic burgers made by this first-ever fast-food chain were once touted as healthy. In 1930, nine years after its first store opened, White Castle hired a food scientist to see what would happen if a medical student lived on nothing but its burgers and water for *13 weeks*. "Studies show conclusively that the student maintained good health," crows the official White Castle Web page.

He must have had bowels of iron, because Slyders (also known as "Belly Bombers" and "Rectum Rockets") are famous for their laxative effects. Nowadays they're the meal of choice for binge eaters, the very depressed, and the very, very drunk. Getting caught with a brimming White Castle bag is like being busted coming out of the video store with porn. Everyone knows that, as soon as you get home, something very unsightly is going to happen.

WHITE ZINFANDEL See GIRL DRINKS.

WHOLESALE CLUBS The theory behind wholesale clubs such as BJ's, Sam's Club, and Costco is a sound one. Small business owners who may not do enough business to get wholesale prices can use their collective shopping strength to keep their costs in check. That's fine, but it doesn't explain why armies of suburbanites who haven't operated their own business since they last peddled lemonade on the sidewalk make hitting the club an every-weekend ritual. The appeal? This is shopping writ large: boxes containing enough tampons to insulate your attic; side-by-side gallons of fruit drink shackled together like Tony Curtis and Sidney Poitier in *The Defiant Ones*; and enough candy to have some to spare even if the trick-or-treaters line up around your block. While one impulse buy—say, a tub of Bavarian Dutch-style pretzels—is enough to destroy any accrued savings, you can always rationalize that you also got a free lunch from all the sample stations. See also OUTLET CENTERS.

WHOOPEE CUSHIONS Even after outgrowing the fake vomit, the joy buzzer, and the string-in-a-ketchup-squirter, there's still pleasure to be had when amateur, unimaginative practical jokers successfully surprise a victim with a fictional fart. See also VOMIT, FAKE.

< 305 >

WHO'S THE BOSS? Even after Tony Danza (the former Antonio Iadanza) caught a major break when discovered in a New York City boxing gym and cast as the dumb guy on *Taxi*, conventional wisdom held that this Stallone wannabe couldn't carry his own series. But like Michael Landon before him, Danza proved to be one of those guys that television audiences—albeit, television audiences that would never, ever admit it—just seem to love. Exhibit A is the sitcom *Who's the Boss?* which took the standard "unlikely nanny" premise and milked it from 1984 to 1992. Of course it had other selling points besides Mr. Danza. There was costar Judith Light (whose pointy, overprocessed hairdo became an '80s icon); the soon-to-be babe-a-licious Alyssa Milano; and the pixie-like *Cujo* costar Danny Pintauro (who came out of the closet roughly 10 seconds after the show went off the air). As with many sitcoms, interest built as the two principals danced interminably around the idea of Doing It, then plummeted when they actually did. After the show, Light went on to do Proactiv Solution infomercials; Milano went on to become a soft porn icon; and Danza went on to perform on Broadway in Arthur Miller's *A View from the Bridge* and Eugene O'Neill's *The Iceman Cometh*. Go figure. See also LANDON, MICHAEL and STALLONE, SYLVESTER.

WILD ON Essentially *Girls Gone Wild* without the exposed nipples, *Wild On* began as a series of *Sex on . . .* specials for E! Entertainment Television (*Sex on South Beach*, *Sex on the Great Barrier Reef*, et al.) hosted by former vice presidential daughter Eleanor Mondale. The premise has since evolved into a flagship show for the celebrity-obsessed cable channel, although with a few changes. Mondale was replaced by bikini-clad Jules Asner, who was replaced by bikini-clad Brooke Burke, who was replaced by bikini-clad Cindy Taylor. But through it all, *Wild On* has retained its screaming-at-the-camera, finding-new-ways-to-drink, Cinemax-for-people-who-can't-afford-Cinemax character, leaving a nation to wonder, "Gee, why wasn't my Carnival Cruise like this?" See also CINEMAX; CRUISES; *GIRLS GONE WILD*; and SUPERMODELS.

"WILDFIRE" See FOGELBERG, DAN.

WINE COOLERS As with wine in a box, coolers are a California creation—making one wonder if the state doesn't harbor some secret hatred for the product it sells in such quantity. Mixing citrus fruit with white wine and a shot of carbonation, these single-serving, beer-bottle-sized concoctions experienced a vogue in the '80s, thanks in large part to a pair of fictional guys named Bartles and

< 306 >

Jaymes. Appearing in 230 separate ads, David Joseph Rufkahr and Dick Maugg actually had nothing to do with the company that made the product. Rufkahr (the talkative one) even admitted in an interview that he only drank the beverage once. Coincidentally, that's the same thing many high school students told their skeptical parents. See also WINE IN A BOX.

WINE IN A BOX Sometimes bouquet doesn't matter. Neither does age, color, taste, or what your party guests think of you. Sometimes it's just about ease and quantity and keeping the wine fresh over the course of a long evening without having to bother with recorking. That's where boxed wine (actually bagged wine inside a box) comes in. Introduced in the 1980s by California wineries and predicted by some to be the beginning of the end for bottles (in the future, these prognosticators say, we will imbibe from the grown-up equivalent of juice boxes), wine in a box is still perceived by snobs as barely a step above Boone's Farm Strawberry Hill. But it's still the vino to buy when stackability and accessibility trump vintage and vineyard. See also BOONE'S FARM STRAWBERRY HILL; JUICE BOXES; LAMBRUSCO; and WINE COOLERS.

WISCONSIN DELLS Remember the U.S./Soviet arms race? Now, imagine that rather than countries, those rivals were middle-of-nowhere Midwestern hotels. And instead of weapons of mass destruction, they were trying to outdo each other by building the largest indoor water parks ever seen by humankind. That should give you some idea of the competition that helped transform Wisconsin Dells, about an hour north of Madison, Wisconsin, from a mere summer honky-tonk of a resort into a year-round destination. Since the mid-'90s, off-season visitors have laughed at the cold while riding eight-story water slides, tubing in wave pools, and otherwise splashing their way toward a never-see-the-outdoors getaway. And why not? Hell, kids usually say their favorite thing about a vacation was the hotel pool anyway. See also WATER PARKS.

WKRP IN CINCINNATI Best remembered for its classic episode in which the station dropped live turkeys from a helicopter as a Thanksgiving promotion, *WKRP* enjoyed a decent run from 1978 through 1982. Men watched, in part, to participate in an updated version of the famous Wilma/Betty and Ginger/Maryann debates. Namely, they ruminated over who was hotter, Hooters-waitress-like Loni Anderson or girl-next-doorer Jan Smithers (by the way, the scar on Smithers' chin was the result of a teenage car crash). Women could ogle

< 307 >

Tim Reid as Venus Flytrap, pre-*Head of the Class* Howard Hesseman as Johnny Fever, and lead Gary Sandy, who came out of nowhere and then quickly returned there (post-*WKRP* career highlight: a starring role in the horror flick *Troll*). Series creator Hugh Wilson went on to direct the first installment of the *Police Academy* movie series, while three members of the supporting cast, Richard Sanders (reporter Les Nessman), Gordon Jump (station boss Arthur Carlson), and Frank Bonner (Herb Tarlek, he of the embarrassing suits) took a page from the *AfterMASH* handbook and returned in 1991's *New WKRP in Cincinnati*. See also HOOTERS and POLICE ACADEMY MOVIES.

WONDERBRA, THE An engineering feat likened to the eighth architectural wonder of the world (especially if you were a B cup with aspirations), this suspension bridge for bosoms not only lifted and supported the bustline, it also gave good cleavage. Created in 1964 by Canadian designer Louise Poirier, it accomplished this by using 54 separate design elements, including a three-part cup, underwires, a precision-angled back, rigid straps, and removable pads called "cookies." Though Poirier created it for a Canadian lingerie company, a European firm gained the manufacturing rights and marketed it for decades. Then in 1994 the Sara Lee Corporation acquired the rack-enhancing design. Within five months it became another of the dessert maker's sweet successes. When the Wonderbra Push-Up Plunge Bra first appeared in U.S. stores, it sold at the rate of one every 15 seconds, inflating to first year sales of approximately $120 million.

These days the Wonderbra comes in "Three Degrees of Wonder"—a triad of designs ranging from the 1st Degree (slightly lined), to the 2nd Degree (a padded or "add-a-size" model), and the 3rd Degree (a complete push-up bra). Though this cleavage-enhancing creation remains wildly popular, the shame its wearers feel isn't all that different from the days when they stuffed their training bras with Kleenex. Because no matter how perfect the illusion, the truth will come out (in the most literal sense) as soon as your date gets to first base. And once you wear a Wonderbra, it's all you can *ever* wear, lest you risk noticeable cup-jumping (going from a shapely C down to an abysmal B) from one day to the next, in front of coworkers, friends, and neighbors. See also FREDERICK'S OF HOLLYWOOD and VICTORIA'S SECRET CATALOGS.

WONDER BREAD This monument to America's culinary naiveté began life in 1921 as a 1.5-pound loaf produced

< 308 >

by the Taggart Baking Company of Indianapolis. It was named Wonder Bread after the wonder that company vice president Elmer Cline allegedly felt as he watched a balloon race (hence the balloons on every wrapper).

Of course, from day one it was the antithesis of quality bread, with a wimpy, barely there crust, the consistency of cotton candy, and the flavor of, well, there really isn't any flavor. None of which stopped it from becoming a huge hit. Each loaf came in a wrapper (a big plus for hygiene-conscious buyers) and was chock full of vitamins. Today the Interstate Bakeries Corporation turns out the gummy loaves at 63 bakeries nationwide and is also responsible for the Dolly Madison and Hostess snack lines. See also TWINKIES.

WONDERFUL WORLD OF DISNEY, THE Want to watch a subpar Disney live-action flick, an old Disney movie, or a shameless feature-length commercial for a Disney theme park? If it's Sunday night and nothing else is on TV (and if you're 10 years old and this is the last thing you get to do before going to bed), then of course the answer is yes. Or at least it was if said Sunday night occurred during one of this show's 35 seasons on the tube. This impressive number makes *The Wonderful World of Disney* the longest-running program in prime time television history—even though not all those years were consecutive and the show went through more name changes than Elizabeth Taylor. See also DISNEY FILMS FEATURING DEAN JONES AND/OR KURT RUSSELL and WALT DISNEY WORLD.

WORD SEARCH PUZZLES Why do people play Word Search (a.k.a. Word Find) puzzles? Probably for the same reason they wile away hours on tic-tac-toe: It's easy. Requiring neither the vocabulary necessary to conquer a decent crossword puzzle nor the brain power required to wrestle a Jumble or Crypto-quiz into submission, it only asks that we find each listed word in a rectangular grid of letters. This is fun for a couple of minutes, until you realize that spending a lot of time on Word Search puzzles is analogous to never taking the training wheels off your bike. See also JUMBLE.

WORLD'S STRONGEST MAN COMPETITIONS It's not really a sport. It's more like a *Guinness Book of World Records* freak show. Yet the World's Strongest Man Competition—which, since 1977, has pitted musclemen against each other—has a certain primal appeal. Anyone who has ever made a half-hearted attempt to get in shape through the

< 309 >

magic of bench pressing can relate to the grunts and groans of a mortal man trying to lift a car, throw a log, pull a truck, or hang on in the "Hercules Hold" (with outstretched arms holding up 290-pound weights). Masochistic, maybe, but as a home viewer, isn't it reassuring to know that even the toughest person you ever met has someone who could beat the tar out of him? An added kick: Rather than the standard U.S.A. vs. Eastern bloc formula, the WSMC showcases amazing hulks from such unlikely locales as Iceland, Finland, and Sweden. See also HERCULES (MOVIES ABOUT).

WORST-DRESSED LISTS   All hail Mr. Blackwell. The failed actor *cum* failed fashion designer's annual roll call of style victims gives us 10 reasons to feel a little bit better about ourselves. We'll even forgive the Mister's sophomoric attempt at rhyming verse, as in "Cameron Diaz: Looks like she was dressed by a color-blind circus clown. When it comes to fashion, it's chaos when Cameron's back in town!" (A whole year to think about it, and that's the best he could do?) Since Blackwell wrote his first list for *American Weekly* magazine in 1960, everyone from *People* magazine to PETA has joined the playground fight, passing judgment on all the Chers and Lara Flynn Boyles of the world—to the delight of the sweatshirt-wearing masses.

< 310 >

X-Y-Z

XANADU This 1980 cinematic epic was like a Viking funeral pyre, upon which the last shreds of disco (along with Olivia Newton-John's acting career) were incinerated. The story, such as it was, revolved around a muse (Newton-John) sent to help two guys open a roller disco. Seriously. The cast includes veteran hoofer Gene Kelly, who tries to lend some dignity to the proceedings (a task roughly analogous to putting a dress on a pig). Ironically, the movie soundtrack spawned several hit songs ("Xanadu" and "Magic" among them), and in its video afterlife the film has become a cult favorite of sorts. See also NEWTON-JOHN, OLIVIA and *SGT. PEPPER'S LONELY HEARTS CLUB BAND* (THE MOVIE).

XENA: WARRIOR PRINCESS This syndicated TV smash offered lots of illicit thrills: the near nonstop fighting, the wisecracking dialogue, and, of course, the lesbian subtext between Xena and her sidekick, the blonde waif Gabrielle. All the eye candy made it possible to overlook the fact that, when it comes to historical accuracy, the typical *Xena* episode makes a Cecil B. DeMille Bible pic look like a Learning Channel documentary. Xena is supposed to live in classical Greece. Yet in her travels she encounters refugees from Troy (circa 1000 B.C.); Xerxes, king of Persia (circa 500 B.C.); and even Julius Caesar, dictator of Rome (around 50 B.C.). There was even a "Christmas" episode, which was a pretty neat trick for a program  dealing with strictly "B.C." happenings. Still, there are worse ways to kill a slow Saturday afternoon. Did we mention the lesbian subtext? See also BIBLICAL EPICS; HERCULES (MOVIES ABOUT); and LESBIANS (MOVIE SCENES FEATURING).

XXX MOVIES See MOVIES (PORNOGRAPHIC).

YANKOVIC, WEIRD AL Everyone's heard Yankovic's music, but almost no one will confess to owning one of his albums. Which isn't surprising. Possessing the work of the man who brought us such parody classics as "My Bologna" (based on the Knack's "My Sharona") and "Eat It" (a rip on Michael Jackson's "Beat It") can earn you Permanent Resident status in Nerdville. And yet, this "artist"—born Alfred Matthew Yankovic in 1959—has 20 gold and

< 311 >

platinum records to his credit, plus a decades-long career. He got his start as a regular on the *Dr. Demento Show*, broke nationally with "My Bologna," and keeps raking in the dough by offering parody compilations with names such as *Dare to Be Stupid* and *Running with Scissors*. True aficionados (and by "aficionados" we mean 30-year-old men who still live with their parents) particularly savor Yankovic's original works, including such gems as "Theme from Rocky XIII" and "Albuquerque." See also DR. DEMENTO and *MICKEY*.

YANNI The instrumental music of Greek native (and Doug Henning look-alike) Yanni Chryssomallis seems perfect for dentists' offices, planetarium shows, and little else. Yet the man's CDs, with such New Agey titles as *Port of Mystery* and *In the Mirror*, have sold millions of copies. Yanni has even taken to holding concerts at international historic landmarks, including the Acropolis in Athens (the video of which is played ad nauseum on PBS during pledge drives), India's Taj Mahal, and China's Forbidden City. Why would the Indians and the Chinese open their monuments to such desecration? Perhaps because Yanni illustrates, better than any John Tesh album or *Lord of the Dance* concert, the insipidness of Western culture. By the way, if someone happens to spot a Yanni disc in *your* collection, just tell them you play it for your dog, to keep him company while you're at work. See also HENNING, DOUG; *RIVERDANCE*; and TESH, JOHN.

YMCA See VILLAGE PEOPLE, THE.

YOO-HOO Adults will blithely chug sports drinks the color of windshield wiper fluid, but they won't touch Yoo-hoo. At least, not while anyone's looking. Something about this first-ever chocolate-flavored soft drink seems so *infantile*. Well, take all the time you need to screw up your courage, because this concoction isn't going anywhere. Created using a supersecret heating and agitation process, Yoo-hoo in properly sealed containers will never go bad. The manufacturer is so confident of this that its bottles and cans don't carry expiration dates.

"YOU LIGHT UP MY LIFE" It's sad but true. For a couple of months in 1977, the hottest name in popular music was . . . Debby Boone. The daughter of white-loafered crooner Pat Boone released a plodding, unexceptional-in-every-way ballad that, for some reason, spent 10 weeks at No. 1 on the *Billboard* charts and 21 total weeks in the Top 40. Even stranger, the tune helped Boone win a Best New Artist

< 312 >

Grammy—after which she promptly tumbled back into obscurity. Since then she's appeared sporadically in various Broadway touring productions and (perhaps inevitably) performed in Branson. The song that made her briefly famous also lives on, mostly as a perennial musical request at Midwestern wedding receptions. See also BRANSON and ONE-HIT WONDERS.

YOUNG FRANKENSTEIN See MOVIES THAT PARODY OTHER MOVIES.

ZADORA, PIA America had a good time at the expense of this very tiny, very buxom woman during her early '80s "peak," when the former kid star of *Santa Claus Conquers the Martians* became an icon for out-of-their-league mediocrities everywhere. But it wasn't her fault. Well, not all of it, anyway. Before Pia (real name: Pia Alfreda Schipani) married international financier Meshulam Riklis in the mid-'70s, she'd built a résumé that ran from the aforementioned awful flick to Broadway's *Fiddler on the Roof.*

Unfortunately (for us and her), Riklis set out to make his modestly talented trophy wife a star. She appeared in such kitsch classics as 1982's *Butterfly* (in which she seemed to spend most of her screen time unclothed); and 1983's *Lonely Lady* (an apocryphal piece about a woman who tries to make it in Hollywood but falls in with the wrong crowd).

Accusations that Riklis "bought" her the "Most Promising New Actress" award at the Golden Globes (she won over "nobody" Kathleen Turner) cemented Pia's reputation as a no-talent goofball trying to bribe her way onto the A—or, failing that, the B—list. By the late '80s she was playing occasional bit parts, including in *Hairspray* in 1988 and *Troop Beverly Hills* in 1989. These days she's doing what she never should have stopped doing: singing Broadway standards. See also GOLDEN GLOBES.

ZIGGY Imagine if Charlie Brown grew up, went bald, lost all his friends, got fat, and completely let himself go. That's Ziggy. Invented by Tom Wilson, the former creative boss at American Greetings and the licensing "genius" behind the Care Bears and Strawberry Shortcake, the decades-old cartoon character remains a multimedia phenomenon. He (we *think* it's a he) is also the sappy greeting card character of choice when the drugstore is out of Peanuts and Holly Hobbie models. A low-key, somewhat neurotic holdover from a less-cutthroat time, Ziggy spouts such truisms as "I've been on so many guilt trips, I should get bonus mileage." Remember the days when "lovable loser" wasn't an oxymoron? See also FAMILY CIRCUS, THE.

< 313 >

ZIMA Launched in the early '90s with the annoying "Zima is zomething different" campaign, this clear, malt-beverage-for-the-wine-cooler-crowd has inexplicably survived despite being labeled a "chick drink," being mocked on *Mad TV* and by stand-up comics across the country, and inspiring amateur critics to new heights of damning description. (One fellow at epinions.com described its taste as similar to that of "the saliva of an alcoholic 89-year-old man who just drank some orange juice.") What's the draw? Perhaps the boast by manufacturer Coors that one Zima packs the punch of two beers. Or perhaps the rumor that a Zima buzz won't show up on a breathalyzer. By the way, the word Zima means "winter" in Russian. In English, it might as well mean "don't let your buddies see you drinking it." See also GIRL DRINKS.

< 314 >

Guilty pleasures come from the oddest places. For instance, John "Mr. Colorado" Denver was in fact born in the UFO hotbed of Roswell, New Mexico, and Lawrence "Anna Wun, Anna Two, Anna Tree" Welk is a native not of some Bavarian village, but of North Dakota. The following list of GPs sorted by state and nation makes it easy to see what and who goes where. There are plenty of surprises (Minnesota is the homeland of cheerleading?), along with some fairly obvious linkages as well. For instance, is anyone particularly surprised that Texas was knee-deep in the development both of Slurpees and Big Mouth Billy Bass?

DOMESTIC GUILTY PLEASURES

Alabama
Mardi Gras

Alaska
Cruises

Arizona
Romy and Michelle's High School Reunion

Arkansas
Clinton, Bill
Wal-Mart

California
Allen, Irwin
Baywatch
Beverly Hillbillies, The
Beverly Hills 90210
Bob's Big Boy
Bombs (Big-budget Movies That Turn Out To Be)
Car Chases (Televised)
Celebrity Trials
"Confidential" and "Babylon" (Book Titles That Include the Words)
Dragnet
eBay
Elvira, Mistress of the Dark
Fantasy League Sports
Frederick's of Hollywood
Hollywood Squares, The
Hollywood Walk of Fame
Laser Shows
Orange Julius
Pez
Quincy, M.E.
Rice-a-Roni
Salad in a Bag
Sanford and Son
Schwarzenegger, Arnold
Sharper Image, The
Super Soakers
Water Beds
Wine Coolers
Wine in a Box

Colorado
Denver, John
Dynasty
South Park

Connecticut
Pez
Professional Wrestling

Delaware
Outlet Centers

Florida
Home Shopping Network, The

< 315 >

Hooters
Orlando
Red Lobster
Walt Disney World
Wet T-shirt Competitions

Georgia
Krofft, Sid and Marty
Macon County Line
"Night the Lights Went Out in
  Georgia, The"
Pecan Logs
Stuckey's

Hawaii
Hawaiian Shirts
Heloise
Pu Pu Platters
Michener, James

Idaho
Stunts (Insane, Televised)

Illinois
Dairy Queen
Dodge Ball
Family Matters
Fannie May Candies
Lava Lamps
Mr. T
Soul Train

Indiana
Jackson Family, The
Jiffy Pop Popcorn
Theme Parks (Not Owned by Disney)
Wonder Bread

Iowa
Bridges of Madison County, The

Kansas
Garland, Judy

Kentucky
Krispy Kreme Doughnuts
Long John Silver's
Varney, Jim

Louisiana
Mardi Gras
Rice, Anne

Maine
King, Stephen
Murder, She Wrote

Maryland
Clancy, Tom

Massachusetts
Dunkin' Donuts
Kennedy Family, The
Lifeguards
Lottery Tickets
National Lampoon

Michigan
Cadillacs
Corvettes
Muscle Cars
Paint-by-Numbers Paintings
SUVs

Minnesota
Cheerleaders

Mississippi
Presley, Elvis

Missouri
Branson
Budweiser
Hot Dogs (Stadium)

< 316 >

Monster Trucks
Precious Moments
"You Light Up My Life"

Montana
Bombs (Big-Budget Movies That
Turn Out to Be)

Nebraska
Kool-Aid

Nevada
Casinos
Clay, Andrew Dice
Diamond, Neil
Jones, Tom
Knievel, Evel
Las Vegas
Liberace
Newley, Anthony
Newton, Wayne
Presley, Elvis
Riverdance
Showgirls
Slot Machines
Stunts (Insane, Televised)
Taylor, Rip

New Hampshire
Paintball

New Jersey
Aqua Net
Atlantic City
Beauty Pageants
Casinos
Lewis, Jerry
NFL Films
Pizza, Frozen
Slot Machines
Tanning, Artificial

New Mexico
Denver, John

New York
Beauty and the Beast (The TV Show)
New York Times Book Review, The
(Reading, Instead of Actual Books)
Bowery Boys, The
Cats
Chef Boyardee
Cracker Jack
Death Wish
Demolition Derby
Dick Clark's New Year's Rockin' Eve
Dog Shows
Fame
Fisher, Amy
Frederick's of Hollywood
Fries, French
Goulet, Robert
Green Acres
Hot Dogs (Stadium)
Lillian Vernon
Macy's Thanksgiving Day Parade
Members Only Jackets
Reader's Digest
Saturday Night Fever
Sedaka, Neil
Showtime at the Apollo
Stallone, Sylvester
T.G.I. Friday's
Theme Parks (Not Owned by Disney)
Thousand Island Dressing
When Harry Met Sally . . .

North Carolina
Andy Griffith Show, The
NASCAR

< 317 >

North Dakota
Lawrence Welk Show, The

Ohio
Hickory Farms
Hustler
Roller Coasters (Enormous)
Springer, Jerry

Oklahoma
Norris, Chuck

Oregon
Harding, Tonya

Pennsylvania
American Bandstand
Cheerleaders
Fireworks, Backyard
Franklin Mint, The
Peeps
QVC
Rocky Movies

Rhode Island
Carrey, Jim

South Carolina
White, Vanna

South Dakota
Hart, Mary

Tennessee
"Confidential" and "Babylon" (Book
    Titles That Include the Words)
Elvis Impersonators
Gatlinburg
Goo Goo Clusters
Holiday Inns
Mountain Dew
Parton, Dolly

Rock City
Walking Tall

Texas
Big Mouth Billy Bass
Big Red (The Soft Drink)
Dairy Queen
Dallas
Dr. Phil
Mary Kay Cosmetics
Michener, James
Norris, Chuck
Six Flags Amusement Parks
Slurpees
Smith, Anna Nicole
Urban Cowboy

Utah
Donny and Marie

Vermont
Garcia, Cherry

Virginia
Chap Stick (Flavored)

Washington
Pictionary

Washington, D.C.
Clinton, Bill
Kennedy Family, The
Lewinsky, Monica

West Virginia
Denver, John

Wisconsin
Liberace
Wisconsin Dells

Wyoming
Barbeau, Adrienne

< 318 >

GUILTY PLEASURES FROM ABROAD

Australia
Australian Rules Football
Crocodile Hunter
Newton-John, Olivia
Thorn Birds, The

Austria
Red Bull
Schwarzenegger, Arnold
Tootsie Pops

Belgium
Foosball
Van Damme, Jean-Claude

Canada
Anderson, Pamela
Carrey, Jim
Henning, Doug
Razzles
Shatner, William
"Safety Dance, The"
Trivial Pursuit (Winning at)
Wonderbra, The

China
Kung Fu Movies

France
Bardot, Brigitte
Emmanuelle (Movies Featuring the
    Character of)
Foosball
Fries, French
Jackson, LaToya
Lacoste Shirts
Lewis, Jerry
Velour

Germany
Foosball
Hogan's Heroes
Hummel Figures

Ireland
Building Implosions

Italy
Bologna
Chef Boyardee
Lambrusco

Japan
America's Funniest Home Videos
Godzilla
Hawaiian Shirts
Iron Chef
Japanese Animation (Adult)
Karaoke
Laser Shows
Pac-Man
Precious Moments
Ramen Noodles
Speed Racer

Mexico
Nachos
Tequila

Spain
Macarena, The

Sweden
ABBA

Switzerland
Fondue

United Kingdom
Antiques Roadshow
Bee Gees, The

< 319 >

Benny Hill Show, The
Bond Films Featuring Roger Moore
Bond Girls (Suggestively Named)
British Royal Family, The
Cartland, Barbara
Collins, Jackie
Collins, Joan
Dianamania
Doctor Who
Guinness World Records
Hammer Films
Humperdinck, Engelbert
Jones, Tom
Lord of the Rings, The
Newley, Anthony
"One Night in Bangkok"
Queen of England, The
Ringo
Teletubbies
Wax Museums
Webber, Andrew Lloyd

< 320 >